OCR BUSINESS STUDIES for AS

Ian Marcousé　　**Malcolm Surridge**　　**Andrew Gillespie**

Belinda Miles　　**Naomi Birchall**　　**Marie Brewer**

Andrew Hammond　　**Nigel Watson**

Edited by Ian Marcousé

DYNAMIC LEARNING

HODDER EDUCATION
AN HACHETTE UK COMPANY

Orders: please contact Bookpoint Ltd, 130 Milton Park, Abingdon, Oxon OX14 4SB. Telephone: (44) 01235 827720. Fax: (44) 01235 400454. Lines are open from 9.00 – 5.00, Monday to Saturday, with a 24-hour message answering service. You can also order through our website www.hoddereducation.co.uk.

British Library Cataloguing in Publication Data
A catalogue record for this title is available from the British Library

ISBN: 9780340958636

First Published 2008
Impression number   10 9 8 7 6 5 4
Year   2014 2013 2012 2011 2010

Hachette UK's policy is to use papers that are natural, renewable and recyclable products and made from wood grown in sustainable forests. The logging and manufacturing processes are expected to conform to the environmental regulations of the country of origin.

Cover illustration by Oxford Designers and Illustrators
Typeset by Fakenham Photosetting Ltd, Fakenham Norfolk
Illustrations by Fakenham Photosetting; those on pages 118 and 201 by Barking Dog Art
Printed in Italy for Hodder Education, an Hachette UK Company, 338 Euston Road, London NW1 3BH

Contents

People in organisations

Operations management

Exam preparation

Acknowledgements

Contributors

Ian Marcousé is Chair of Examiners for Business Studies for a major awarding body and an experienced teacher. He is Founding Editor of *Business Review* magazine and his previous books include *The Complete A-Z Business Studies Handbook*.

Belinda Miles is an educational consultant and Fellow of the Institute of Educational Assessors. She has taught A Level Business Studies for 25 years and is a Principal Examiner for a major awarding body.

Malcolm Surridge is Chief Examiner for A Level Business Studies for a major awarding body and an experienced teacher and author.

Andrew Gillespie is Principal Examiner for A Level Business Studies for a major awarding body and an experienced teacher and author.

Naomi Birchall is an examiner for A Level Business Studies for a major examining board and an experienced teacher. She has developed a variety of resources for A Level, Applied A Level and GCSE Business Studies.

Marie Brewer is an Assistant Principal Examiner for A Level Business Studies for a major examining board and an established author and lecturer. She is also a co-author of *Business Studies for AS Revision Guide*.

Andrew Hammond is a Senior Examiner for a major examining board. He is Head of Business at Darrick Wood School and an experienced author.

Nigel Watson is Head of Business Studies and Economics at St Catherine's School and an established author.

Every effort has been made to trace and acknowledge ownership of copyright. The publishers will be glad to make suitable arrangements with any copyright holder whom it has not been possible to contact. The authors and publishers would like to thank the following for the use of photographs in this volume:

© Associated Sports Photography/Alamy, 1.1; © Andy Rain/epa/Corbis, 2.2; Courtesy of Eggxactly, 2.3; Fisher/Thatcher/Getty Images, 3.2; © Ashley Cooper/Alamy, 4.1; © Jack Sullivan/Alamy, 4.2; © Digital Nation/Photofusion, 7.1; © Tesco Photographic, 7.2; © Kay Nietfeld/dpa/Corbis, 9.1; Picture supplied by JCB, 10.1; © Rolf Haid/dpa/Corbis, 10.2; Patti the Architect, Inc/Malia Beving, 10.4; © Getty Images, 11.1; © uk retail Alan King/Alamy, 11.2; © PSL Images/Alamy, 12.3; © Motoring Picture Library/Alamy, 12.4; © Transtock Inc/Alamy, 14.1; Sakki/Rex Features, 14.2; Courtesy of FireAngel Limited, 15.5; © Mackie's of Scotland, 15.6; Courtesy of Mamas & Papas, 17.2; © Dyana/Alamy, 18.2; © David J. Green/Alamy, 20.1; Tesco/AFP/Getty Images, 21.3; Nicholas Bailey/Rex Features, 25.1; © Peter Treanor/Alamy, 26.1; © Richard Baker/Corbis, 29.1; © Cephas Picture Library/Alamy, 31.2; AP/PA Photos, 43.4; Courtesy of The Cinnamon Club, Westminster, 46.2; © Jupiter Images/Brand X/Alamy, 47.1.

The authors and publishers would like to thank the following for permission to reproduce copyright text material: Figure 6.1, page 40, Fraser, S. (2005). Finance for Small and Medium Sized Enterprises: The United Kingdom Survey of SME Finances, 2004. Warwick Business School, University of Warwick: UK Data Archive Study Number 5326.

Chart taken from a study of UK SME finances in 2004. The estimates are based on the SME population in 2002 and excludes businesses in the following sectors: Financial Services; Mining and Quarrying; Electricity; and Gas and Water Supply. The total SME population in 2002, with these exclusions, was 3.6m.

HODDER
EDUCATION
The Expert Choice

What does 'the expert choice' mean for you?

We work with more examiners and experts than any other publisher

● Because we work with more experts and examiners than any other publisher, the very latest curriculum requirements are built into this course and there is a perfect match between your course and the resources that you need to succeed. We make it easier for you to gain the skills and knowledge that you need for the best results.

● We have chosen the best team of experts – including the people that mark the exams – to give you the very best chance of success; look out for their advice throughout this book: this is content that you can trust.

Welcome to Dynamic Learning

Dynamic Learning is a simple and powerful way of integrating this text with digital resources to help you succeed, by bringing learning to life. Whatever your learning style, Dynamic Learning will help boost your understanding.

More direct contact with teachers and students than any other publisher

- We talk with more than 100 000 students every year through our student conferences, run by Philip Allan Updates. We hear at first hand what you need to make a success of your A-level studies and build what we learn into every new course. Learn more about our conferences at **www.philipallan.co.uk**

- Our new materials are trialled in classrooms as we develop them, and the feedback built into every new book or resource that we publish. You can be part of that. If you have comments that you would like to make about this book, please email us at: **feedback@hodder.co.uk**

More collaboration with Subject Associations than any other publisher

- Subject Associations sit at the heart of education. We work closely with more Associations than any other publisher. This means that our resources support the most creative teaching and learning, using the skills of the best teachers in their field to create resources for you.

More opportunities for your teachers to stay ahead than with any other publisher

- Through our Philip Allan Updates Conferences, we offer teachers access to Continuing Professional Development. Our focused and practical conferences ensure that your teachers have access to the best presenters, teaching materials and training resources. Our presenters include experienced teachers, Chief and Principal Examiners, leading educationalists, authors and consultants. This course is built on all of this expertise.

- Boost your understanding through interactive activities and quizzes available on both student and network editions.

- Network Edition gives easy access to the book's key photographs, charts and diagrams so that you can use them in your studies.

- Key business concepts are illustrated in 20 video clips with exciting young entrepreneur Fraser Doherty in the Network Edition.

You can find out more at www.dynamic-learning.co.uk

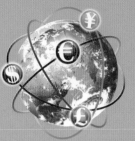

WHAT BUSINESSES DO

DEFINITION

In theory, the purpose of a business is to create wealth and prosperity, in order to enhance the lives of the population by creating employment both for its own employees and for other businesses. In practice, this is hard to achieve.

1.1 Risk

Businesses are constantly faced with conflicting information in an ever-changing market place. Objectives perceived as possible at one moment become impossible to achieve as the marketplace changes and unforeseen events occur.

Such changes can have global repercussions, such as the 2007/8 credit crunch caused by the selling of sub-prime mortgages in the USA. The effects of this action across the Atlantic may have effects on business, and in particular on the financial sector, for many years to come.

1.2 Decision making in business

Decisions about different courses of action take place every day in business. Some of these decisions will be **strategic**, such as the creation of a new product line, and will affect the long-term success of the business. Others will be **tactical** day-to-day decisions which will directly affect individuals and groups, such as the reorganisation of the workforce when a machine breaks down. All decision making in business combines the use of measurable information, such as historic evidence, future forecasts and statistics, with the knowledge, skills and experience of managers.

In recent times, decision making in business has become increasingly constrained by external forces such as legislation, changes in technology, the economy and the environment. In other words, any decision taken contains a certain amount of 'risk'. Not all events can be planned for and therefore to some extent the outcome of any decision is unsure.

Banks and financial institutions have to manage many different risks. If these risks are poorly managed, they can dent profits and attract adverse headlines in the press. But what is most feared is liquidity risk – the risk that a bank does not have enough cash to finance its lending activities.

In September 2007, Northern Rock found out the realities of a liquidity crisis with their customers queuing to withdraw their savings. This was the first 'run' on a UK bank by its depositors for more than 150 years.

Inevitably with the shortage of liquidity the cost of borrowing money – interest rates – was driven upwards. In the UK, the rate at which banks were prepared to lend to each other rose to close to 7 per cent despite the fact that Bank of England base rates were still at 5.75 per cent (normally banks lend to each other at a level very close to the prevailing level of base rates).

Source: adapted from www.open2.net/blogs/money

1.3 Opportunity cost

Decisions made by businesses not only contain risk but also mean that alternatives must be given up in order to implement the decision. Giving up the alternatives will often impact upon choices in the future. The idea of giving up other opportunities or alternatives is known as **opportunity cost**.

The idea of cost is due to the fact that all businesses face the problem of limited resources and in particular, limited money and time. For example, time spent by a manager creating a pretty website might mean too little time spent recruiting and training staff. The same issues arise with money: it can only be spent once.

Opportunity cost can best be explained with reference to football club management. In 2007 new manager Lawrie Sanchez was given a budget of £25 million to buy new players for Fulham FC. In theory, he could have spent it on Owen Hargreaves (£17 million) plus most of the left leg of Carlos Tevez. Instead he spent it on nine players, largely from lower leagues or from Premiership reserve sides. The cost of these players was £25 million. The opportunity cost was missing out on Hargreaves and part of Tevez. The £25 million could only be spent once, so it was vital to spend it wisely. The sacking of Sanchez in December 2007 implied that half of Tevez might have been a better use of the club's money.

Figure 1.1 Footballer Owen Hargreaves

1.4 Goods and services

Businesses sell both goods and services to other businesses and to the public. Goods such as confectionary (consumables), houses, cars and washing machines (durables) can be sold both in shops *to* the public but also *to* shops and businesses for their own use or for resale.

Remember: businesses do not only sell to individuals; often questions are asked about businesses who sell to business. Examples might include businesses that supply raw materials for use in manufacturing or machinery to factories (industrial goods) but they also include many of the service industries. Businesses could not survive without the support of commercial organisations such as banking, insurance, warehousing, transportation and advertising. These are known as commercial services because they support and allow business to operate. Direct services such as hairdressers also contribute to the needs of stakeholders, but are mainly targeted at the individual.

In recent times it has become increasingly accepted that a business must look to the needs of *all* its stakeholders and not just the owners and shareholders. These stakeholders include any groups that have an interest in the business:

- customers
- managers
- suppliers/creditors
- owners/shareholders
- employees
- government
- local community.

1.5 Adding value

Businesses attempt to meet the needs of stakeholders by adding value to inputs. These inputs, sometimes known as factors of production, are land, labour, capital and enterprise. Each business needs to combine these inputs in order to create products and services. Figure 1.2 shows the example of a car production plant.

'Adding value' refers to the way in which a business creates products and services to meet the needs of stakeholders in a profitable way. The cost of producing and selling the goods must be less than the revenue from

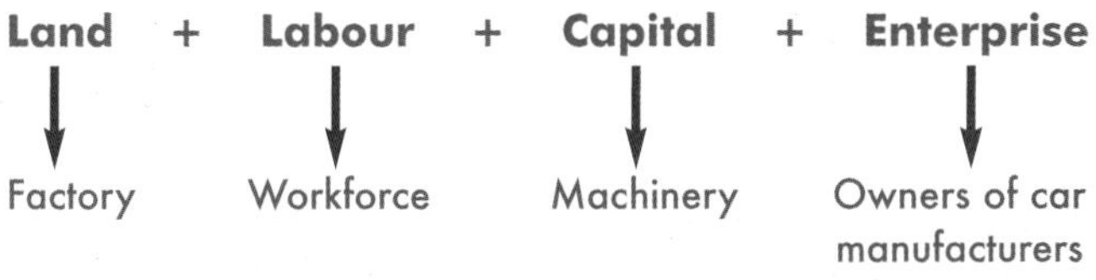

Land + Labour + Capital + Enterprise

↓	↓	↓	↓
Factory	Workforce	Machinery	Owners of car manufacturers

Figure 1.2 Inputs to a car production plant

selling them. Adding value not only includes the cost of transforming a raw material into a product but also anything that makes it seem more valuable to the consumer, who will therefore pay a higher price in comparison with the cost of creating that value. This value can be added, for example, by brand names, styles and fashion and extra features.

Although 'the bottom line', or profit, remains the driving force for many entrepreneurs, business is continually constrained by external factors which inhibit their ability to satisfy all stakeholders. Shareholders will require high profits from low costs and increased revenue. Legislation, such as health and safety and the minimum wage, increases costs and therefore conflicts with these objectives. Once again the cost of meeting the needs of one set of stakeholders may conflict with the needs of another.

Key terms

Adding value: any method by which a business adds value to inputs in order to make a profit.

Entrepreneur: someone who makes a business idea happen, either through their own effort, or by organising others to do the work.

Opportunity cost: the cost of the next best alternative foregone.

Stakeholder: any person or group of people who have a direct interest in the business.

Strategic decisions: these concern the long-term objectives and overall plans of a business, and are taken by senior management and directors.

Tactical decisions: these are short- or medium-term decisions made on a day-to-day basis, such as ordering stock and planning production schedules.

1.6 What businesses do
an evaluation

Decisions are an everyday occurrence in business, and although many strategic decisions are taken only by senior management for the long term, recent events have shown that these managers ignore market changes at their peril. Any decision carries an element of risk and results in the loss of alternative courses of action. Opportunity cost is a cost which is sometimes ignored when decisions are made quickly.

Exercises

A. Revision questions

(8 marks; 8 minutes)

1 Explain in your own words why time is an important aspect of opportunity cost. (3)

2 Give two ways of measuring the opportunity cost to you of doing this homework. (2)

3 Outline one opportunity cost to a restaurant chef/owner of opening a second restaurant. (3)

B. Revision exercises

B1 Group tasks

(45 marks; 1 hour 5 minutes)

1 Think of a strategic decision taken by business and identify any risks which the business might have to take when making the decision. (10)

2 Using a business with which you are familiar, take each stakeholder group and discuss how each might be affected by the business' need to add value to their products and services. (20)

3 It is relatively easy to see how value can be added to a product. It is much more difficult to do this with a service. Investigate how businesses such as banks and insurance companies add value to their services. (15)

B2 Data response

James Sutton had a job as a marketing manager, paying £55,000 a year. His career prospects looked very good, yet he handed in his notice to start up his own online business. He knew that it would take him away from 9–5 work and towards the dedication of 8–9. If he took on a member of staff, the wage bill would rise by £16,000.

Questions

(10 marks; 15 minutes)

1 Outline three opportunity cost issues within this short passage. (6)

2 Outline the possible impact on James of the increase in the workload. (4)

Unit 2

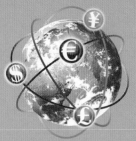

CASH FLOW AND SOURCES OF FINANCE

DEFINITION

Cash flow is the flow of money into and out of a business in a given time period. All businesses need money. Where the money comes from is known as 'sources of finance'.

2.1 The importance of cash flow management

Managing cash flow is one of the most important aspects of financial management. Without adequate availability of cash from day to day, even a company with high sales could fail. As bills become due there has to be the cash available to pay. If a company cannot pay its bills, suppliers will refuse to deliver and staff will start looking for other jobs. Cash flow problems are the most common reason for business failure. This is particularly true for new businesses. It is estimated that 70% of businesses that collapse in their first year fail because of cash flow problems.

Businesses need to continually review their current and future cash position. In order to be prepared and to understand future cash needs, businesses construct a **cash flow forecast**. This sets out the expected flows of cash into and out of the business for each month. In textbooks cash flows are normally shown for six months but they can be done for any period of time. Most firms want to look 12 months ahead, so the cash flow forecast is constantly updated.

High-grade application

A bit of a steal

In 2007, a year when Premier League clubs spent more than £500 million on transfers, Fulham were pleased to get David Healy for just over £1 million. As the highest-scoring striker in the European Nations Cup qualifiers, why would Leeds sell him for such a modest fee? Healy's 32 international goals included winning strikes against England and Spain.

Part of the reason was that Healy was desperate to leave, quite simply because he was not getting paid. By mid-July, Leeds United's players had still not been paid their June wages. Cash flow problems can quickly spread throughout a business.

2.2 Who needs to use a cash flow forecast?

All businesses can benefit from using cash flow forecasts, but they are particularly useful for business start-ups. A carefully planned cash flow forecast will help ensure that the business has enough finance to keep afloat during the early months. This is the most difficult period for a business as sales may be slow. There will be little income but bills still need to be paid.

Existing businesses also need to be aware of their cash position. In many cases there are seasonal factors that make cash hard to manage. A seaside hotel has, every year, to cope with winter months when there will almost certainly be **negative cash flow** – in other words, cash out will be higher than cash in. A cash flow forecast will help to ensure that the business plans for future cash needs and can cope if unexpected events happen. If a business is growing, cash flow forecasts can be particularly useful. They enable the business to ensure that any growth is backed by sufficient funding.

A year ago, a busy bar in Wimbledon closed down. Regulars were surprised – shocked even – that such a successful business had failed. The business *was* operating profitably, but the owners had become too excited by their success. Their investment into two new bars elsewhere in London had drained too much cash from the business, and the bank had panicked over the mounting debts. It forced the business to close. A profitable business had run out of cash.

2.3 The need for finance

Starting up

New businesses starting up need money to invest in long-term assets such as buildings and equipment. They also need cash to purchase materials, pay wages, and to pay the day-to-day bills such as water and electricity. Inexperienced entrepreneurs often underestimate the capital needed for the everyday running of the business. Generally, for every £1000 required to establish the business, another £1000 is needed for day-to-day needs.

Growing

Once the business is established there will be income from sales. If this is greater than the operating costs the business will be making a profit. This should be kept in the business and used to help the business to grow. Later on, the owners can draw money out of the business, but at this stage as much as possible should be left in. Even so, there may not be enough to allow the business to grow as fast as it would like to. It may need to find additional finance and this will probably be from external sources.

Other situations

Businesses may also need finance in other circumstances. They may have a cash flow problem caused by changes in market conditions. A major customer may refuse to pay for the goods, causing a huge gap in cash inflows. Or there may be a large order, requiring the purchase of additional raw materials. In all these cases businesses will need to find additional funding.

2.4 Internal and external sources of finance

Finance for business comes from two main sources:

1 inside the business – known as 'internal sources of finance'

2 outside the business – known as 'external sources of finance'.

Internal sources

- Existing capital can be made to stretch further. The business may be able to negotiate to pay its bills later or work at getting cash in earlier from customers; the average small firm waits 75 days to be paid (i.e. two and a half months); if that period of time could be halved, it would provide a huge boost to cash flow.

- Nothing soothes a difficult cash situation better than profit. It is also the best (and most common) way to

finance investment into a firm's future. Research shows that over 60% of business investment comes from reinvested profit.

External sources

If the business is unable to generate sufficient funds from internal sources then it may need to look to external sources. There are two sources of external capital: loan capital and **share capital**.

Loan capital

The most usual way is through borrowing from a bank. This may be in the form of a bank loan or an overdraft. A loan is usually for a set period of time. It may be short term (one or two years), medium term (three to five years) or long term (more than five years). The loan can either be repaid in instalments over time or at the end of the loan period. The bank will charge interest on the loan. This can be fixed or variable. The bank will demand **collateral** to provide security in case the loan cannot be repaid.

An overdraft is a very short-term loan. It is a facility that allows the business to be 'overdrawn'. This means that the account is allowed to go 'into the red'. The length of time that this runs for will have to be negotiated. The interest charges on overdrafts are usually much higher than on loans.

Share capital

Alternatively, if the business is a limited company it may look for additional share capital. This could come from private investors or **venture capital** funds. Venture capital providers are interested in investing in businesses with dynamic growth prospects. They are willing to take a risk on a business that may fail, or may do spectacularly well. They believe that if they make ten investments, five can flop, and four do OK as long as one does fantastically. Peter Theil, the original investor in Facebook, probably turned his $0.5 million investment into $200 million or more (i.e. made a profit of 39,900%!).

Once it has become a **public limited company (plc)**, the firm may consider floating on the stock exchange. For smaller businesses this will usually be on the Alternative Investment Market (AIM).

High-grade application

Financing growth

How do rapidly growing small firms finance their growth? By venture capital? By loans? To find an answer to this question, Hamish Stevenson from Templeton College, Oxford, looked at 100 of the fastest-growing UK firms. One of these is R Frazier, a firm that recycles computers. Its sales grew from £294,000 to £7,400,000 in just three years. In common with the majority of the firms, R Frazier's early growth was self-funded – in other words, from reinvested profits and trade credit. 'These are the real entrepreneurs,' says Stevenson. 'They grab money where they can. It is fly-by-the-seat-of-their-pants finance.' The 54 firms that used this method were doing so 'through default not by design', according to the research. In other words, they had no alternative.

Twenty-one of the firms received external finance from share capital: 15 from venture capital houses and 6 from business angels. Just ten used long-term bank debt. Having survived, even thrived, through these hectic early years, as many as 40 of the firms are looking at, or in the process of, floating their firms on the London **stock market**. This would secure the finance for the next stage of growth.

2.5 How much finance can the business obtain?

The type and amount of finance that is available will depend on several factors. These are as follows.

- *The type of business:* a sole trader will be limited to the capital the owner can put into the business plus any money he or she is able to borrow. A limited company will be able to raise share capital. In order to become a plc it will need to have share capital of £50,000+, and a track record of success. This will make borrowing easier.

- *The stage of development of the business:* a new business will find it much harder to raise finance than an established firm. As the business develops it is easier to persuade outsiders to invest in the business. It is also easier to obtain loans as the firm has assets to offer as security.

- *The state of the economy:* when the economy is booming, business confidence will be high. It will be easy to raise finance both from borrowing and from investors. It will be more difficult for businesses to find investors when interest rates are high. They will invest their money in more secure accounts such as building societies. Higher interest rates will also put up the cost of borrowing. This will make it more expensive for the business to borrow.

2.6 Advantages and disadvantages of sources of finance

Internal sources

Reinvested profit

The profit generated by the business will provide a return for the investors in the business and can be ploughed back into the business to help it to grow. The advantage of reinvested profit is that it does not have an associated cost. Unlike loans it does not have to be repaid, and there are no interest charges. The disadvantage is that it may be limited so will constrain the rate of business expansion.

Cash squeezed out of day-to-day finances

By cutting stocks, chasing up customers or delaying payments to suppliers, cash can be generated. This has the advantage of reducing the amount that needs to be borrowed. However, this is a very short-term solution and if the cash is taken from working capital for a purpose such as buying fixed assets, the firm may find itself short of day-to-day finance.

Sale of assets

An established business has assets. These can be sold to raise cash. The business loses the asset but has the use of the cash. It makes good business sense for businesses to dispose of underused assets. They can finance development without extra borrowing. If the asset is needed, it may be possible to sell it, but immediately lease it back. In this way the business has use of the money and the asset. This is known as sale and leaseback.

External sources

Bank overdrafts

This is the commonest form of borrowing for small businesses. The bank allows the firm to overdraw up to an agreed level. This has the advantages that the firm needs to borrow only when and as much as it needs. It is, however, an expensive way of borrowing, and the bank can insist on being repaid within 24 hours.

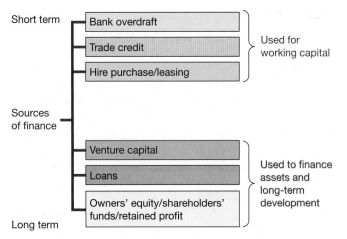

Figure 2.1 *Short- and long-term sources of finance*

Trade credit

This is the simplest form of external financing. The business obtains goods or services from another business, but does not pay for these immediately. The average credit period is two months. It is a good way of boosting day-to-day finances. A disadvantage might be that other businesses may be reluctant to trade with the business if they do not get paid in good time.

Venture capital

This is a way of getting outside investment for businesses that are unable to raise finance through the stock markets or loans. Venture capitalists invest in smaller, riskier companies. To compensate for the risks, venture capital providers usually require a substantial part of the ownership of the company. They are also likely to want to contribute to the running of the business. This dilutes the owner's control but brings in new experience and knowledge. The term 'dragon' became a well-known term for a venture capital provider thanks to the BBC TV series *Dragons' Den*.

2.7 Finance should be adequate and appropriate

Having adequate funding means ensuring the business has sufficient access to finance to meet its current and future needs. This is a major issue for new firms and for those that are expanding rapidly. When a business expands without a sufficient finance this is known as **overtrading**.

Appropriate financing means matching the type of

finance to its use. A distinction is made in company financing between short- and long-term finance (see Figure 2.1). Short-term finance is usually considered to be for less than one year; medium-term finance is for one to five years; long-term finance is for longer than five years.

Short-term finance should not be used to finance long-term projects. Using short-term finance such as overdrafts puts continual pressure on the company's cash position. An overdraft should only be used to cope with ups and downs in cash flows. By its very nature, growth is a long-term activity, so appropriate long-term finance should be sought to fund it.

High-grade application
Northern Rock

In September 2007 Northern Rock became the first British bank in 150 years to suffer a 'run on the bank', as savers feared for the bank's solvency. Northern Rock had expanded rapidly, financing its long-term growth with short-term finance; when the finance dried up, the bank collapsed. The business proved to have neither adequate nor appropriate finance. This was especially ironic given that banks are supposed to advise individuals and businesses on financial management. The crisis was averted only when the Bank of England guaranteed that no customers would lose their money.

Figure 2.2 *Queues outside Northern Rock*

Issues For Analysis

When analysing or suggesting appropriate sources of finance, ask yourself the following questions.

- *Why is the business seeking finance?* The key here is to ensure that the finance is suitable for the business in its particular circumstances. A new business will have very different needs from a growing business. Remember, the finance should be adequate and appropriate.

- *Is the business stable or risky?* If risky, the form of financing should be as safe as possible. Remember that financial institutions are unlikely to lend to risky or unproven enterprises.

- *What is the owner's attitude to sharing the business?* If the owners are reluctant to lose control of the business it is not a good idea to suggest raising finance by selling more shares. Financing growth by borrowing may be more appropriate.

Key terms

Cash flow forecast: estimating future monthly cash inflows and outflows, to find out the net cash flow.
Collateral: an asset used as security for a loan. It can be sold by a lender if the borrower fails to pay back a loan.
Negative cash flow: when cash outflows are greater than cash inflows.
Overtrading: when a firm expands without adequate and appropriate funding.
Public limited company (plc): a company with limited liability, and shares that are available to the public. Its shares can be quoted on the stock market.
Share capital: business finance that has no guarantee of repayment or of annual income, but gains a share of the control of the business and its potential profits.
Stock market: a market for buying and selling company shares. It supervises the issuing of shares by companies. It is also a second-hand market for stocks and shares.
Venture capital: high-risk capital invested in a combination of loans and shares, usually in a small, dynamic business.

2.8 Sources of finance

an evaluation

Finding finance may involve balancing conflicting interests. Internal sources of finance may be too limited to provide opportunities for business development. Obtaining external finance increases the money available, but has its downsides. Borrowing too much can be risky. Raising extra share capital dilutes the control held by existing shareholders.

Having adequate and appropriate finance at each stage in the firm's development will ensure it stays healthy. Decisions about where to obtain the finance will be a matter of considering the business objectives, the stage of development of the business and the reasons for the funding requirement.

A well-run business plans ahead for its financing needs. To run out of cash (as with Northern Rock) suggests management incompetence.

Exercises

A. Revision questions

(36 marks; 30 minutes)

1 What is meant by 'cash flow'? (2)

2 Why is it important to manage cash flow? (4)

3 Describe the problem caused to a company if a major customer refuses to pay a big bill. (3)

4 Why do banks demand collateral before they agree to provide a loan? (2)

5 Outline two ways in which businesses can raise money from internal sources. (4)

6 What information might a bank manager want when considering a loan to a business? (4)

7 Read the 'Application' report on Northern Rock. Explain the two mistakes made by the bank. (4)

8 Outline two sources of finance that can be used for long-term business development. (4)

9 Explain why a new business might find it difficult to get external funding for its development. (5)

10 Outline one advantage and one disadvantage of using an overdraft. (4)

B. Revision exercises

B1 Activity

Dragons' Den

The BBC TV series *Dragons' Den* is the *X-Factor* for entrepreneurs: a talent contest in which entrepreneurs present their ideas to a panel of super-wealthy investors. The five 'dragons' sit sternly, with piles of cash in front of them, while someone climbs the stairs into the den, then nervously makes a presentation. Fewer than one in twenty get the investment they seek. Just occasionally, though, contestants walk away with £150,000 or £200,000 of cash investment into their business.

In August 2006 James Seddon came to the den to demonstrate his invention for a better way to cook 'boiled' eggs. Instead of a pan of boiling water, *Eggxactly* works like a sandwich toaster to cook an egg for the exact time you want. A soft-boiled (runny yolk) egg might take three minutes, while a hard-boiled egg takes four. Seddon has a patent pending on his invention (i.e. he has applied for one and is waiting for it to be granted). If accepted, it will provide 20 years' protection from rivals.

Figure 2.3 The Eggxactly single cooker

Computer software expert Seddon stood up to give his sales pitch, explaining the benefits of the product, then flicked a switch on the machine to start his demonstration. Four minutes later he opened up the Eggxactly to reveal nothing. He had forgotten to put an egg in! The 'dragons' are impatient with time-wasters, so this was not much help. He then put an egg in, re-set the machine and they chatted until, four minutes later, he took out the egg, broke into it and runny egg went everywhere. It was uncooked.

Despite this incompetence, the investors were so impressed with the man (his intelligence and confidence) and the idea that two of them agreed to invest £75,000 to help Seddon get Eggxactly to market. For their money, the two investors were each to take a 20% share in the business. This could prove a bargain given that one of them, Richard Farleigh, suggested that the device could 'sell zillions'.

Questions

(25 marks; 30 minutes)

1 If your £75,000 was at stake, what research would you carry out before investing in James Seddon's Eggxactly? Explain your reasoning. (8)

2 Outline the risks being taken on by the investors of £75,000. Are they wise? (6)

3 The £75,000 investment was share capital in exchange for 40% of James Seddon's business. Discuss whether James Seddon should accept the offer or turn it down. (11)

B2 Data response

Mayday Printers

Mayday Printers specialises in last-minute printing for firms. Its major selling point is that it will turn a job around within 24 hours, provided the artwork is ready. Mayday is able to charge a premium for this service and is seldom short of work. The firm does, however, need to be extremely flexible. This means having a flexible workforce and very reliable machines. It has had to turn away several large jobs lately because of a lack of machinery, and now the managers are considering buying an additional large printer. Although they know that this will not be used at full capacity they are worried that turning away business will damage their reputation and lead to a loss of business in future. The company is in good financial health with a strong cash flow, though the cash position can be strained sometimes when there is a rush of work. To complete an order Mayday might have to pay bonus wages to staff, often before payment is received.

The finance director has come up with two proposals that he will present to the next board meeting. The first is to buy a new printer and to fund the purchase with a bank loan. The printer will cost £100,000, so he suggests taking out a loan for that amount. The loan will be at bank rate plus 8% and will be for ten years. The bank rate is currently 4%.

The alternative proposal is to rent this new machine. He has found a company that will do this. The cost of the rental, including a maintenance contract, would be £1500 per month. The marketing department expects to pick up at least five additional contracts during the first year. These should generate at least £20,000 of revenue, but, just as importantly, will protect the company's reputation and existing business.

Question

(20 marks; 30 minutes)

1 Prepare a report for the board, outlining the advantages and disadvantages of each proposal. End your report with a clear recommendation. (20)

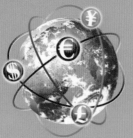

Unit 3

HUMAN RESOURCE MANAGEMENT

DEFINITION

Recruitment (and selection) is concerned with filling job vacancies that may arise within a business. The process involves a number of activities, including defining the job, attracting suitable candidates and selecting those best suited to fill it. Training is a provision of work-related education, where employees learn new skills or develop the skills they already possess.

3.1 The need for effective recruitment

Every service business relies on its staff to present the face of the organisation to the customer. It can be a gloomy, perhaps bored, face – or it can be lively and smiling. Many factors are involved in this stark difference, but it certainly helps if you recruit bright, enthusiastic staff in the first place.

In 2006, Marks & Spencer recruited over 20,000 new customer service assistants. A further 19,000 temporary staff were taken on between November and December to help meet seasonal demand. The company employs 40 people in its recruitment centre at its head office in London, and others in stores nationwide.

Despite the significant costs involved, businesses like Marks & Spencer recognise the importance of committing sufficient resources to recruitment. Ensuring that the right number and type of workers are available when they are needed is vital if company objectives are to be achieved.

3.2 The recruitment process

The recruitment process may be triggered by a number of events. For example, an existing employee may have chosen to leave their job, perhaps as a result of

High-grade application

Wanted: high-fliers

The rapid growth of low-cost airlines has forced Ryanair and easyJet to compete fiercely for the scarcest resource: qualified pilots. To attract them, this is what each airline was offering in August 2007:

Table 3.1 Packages for pilots

	easyJet	**Ryanair**
Annual salary:	£73,792	'Up to £100,000'
Days off a year	137 days	162 days
Extra remuneration	7% pension contribution	Share option scheme
Extra attraction	Share options	Home every night

Source: easyjet.com, ryanair.com

retirement or after finding employment elsewhere. At this point, it would be worth analysing the vacant job role – do all the responsibilities associated with the vacant job still need to be carried out, or are some redundant? Could the remaining duties be reorganised among existing employees? Alternatively, additional workers may need to be recruited in order to support a firm's expansion strategies, or employees with new skills may be required to help develop new products or new markets.

Once the firm has established its human resources requirements, the next step is to consider the nature of the work and workers required in order to draw up a **job description** and a **person specification**.

A job description relates directly to the nature of the position itself, rather than the person required to fill it. Typically, a job description would contain the following information:

- the title of the post
- details of the main duties and tasks involved
- the person to whom the job holder reports, and any employees for whom the job holder is responsible.

A person specification identifies the abilities, qualifications and qualities required of the job holder in order to carry out the job successfully. The main features of a person specification include:

- any educational or professional qualifications required
- necessary skills or experience

High-grade application
Recruitment at easyJet

A major growth industry of recent years has been budget airlines; easyJet, for example, needed to hire 1300 more cabin staff in 2007. The airline's 'people director', Mike Campbell, worked out this number after allowing for its 90% retention level. In other words, every year 90% of staff stay, meaning that 10% leave. easyJet needs enough new recruits to cover its 10% level of labour turnover, plus extras to allow for the 13 new routes it is opening up in 2007.

Campbell said, in June 2007: 'We need more cabin crew so we need to retain the crew we have. It meant that last year we asked cabin crew what made their jobs less enjoyable. The first thing they said was that their uniform was uncomfortable, so we let them design their own.'

- suitable personality or character (e.g. ability to work under pressure or as part of a team).

Both documents have an important influence on both recruitment and selection – not only can they be used to draw up job adverts, but also to assess the suitability of candidates' applications; they may also form the basis of any interview questions.

3.3 Internal recruitment

A business may choose to fill a vacancy internally (i.e. from the existing workforce). This could be done either by redeploying or promoting a worker from elsewhere in the business. Although **internal recruitment** can have a number of benefits, it also has a number of disadvantages and is obviously of no use when a business needs to expand its workforce in order to respond to an increase in demand.

Table 3.2 Internal recruitment: advantages and disadvantages

Advantages	Disadvantages
It is likely to be quicker and cheaper than external recruitment	Existing workers may not have the skills required, especially if the business wants to develop new products or markets
Greater variety and promotion opportunities may motivate employees	Relying on existing employees may lead to a stagnation of ideas and approaches within the business
It avoids the need (and cost) of induction training	It may create a vacancy elsewhere, postponing external recruitment rather than avoiding it
The firm will already be aware of the employee's skills and attitude to work	

3.4 Recruiting external candidates

Firms can choose from a range of methods to attract external candidates to fill a job vacancy (**external recruitment**). Such methods include the following.

- *Media advertising*: placing job adverts in newspapers or specialist magazines, on the radio, TV or by using dedicated employment websites such as www.jobstoday.co.uk.

- *Jobcentres*: government-run organisations that offer a free service to firms, and tend to focus on vacancies for skilled and semi-skilled manual and administrative jobs.

- *Commercial recruitment agencies:* such as Alfred Marks or Reed, which take on a number of human resources functions, including recruitment, on behalf of firms in return for a fee.

- *Executive search consultants:* paid to directly approach individuals – usually those in relatively senior positions (known as poaching or headhunting).

In addition, many businesses have careers pages on their own websites, which are used to advertise vacancies.

The choice of recruitment method or methods used by a business will depend on a number of factors, including:

- the cost of the recruitment method

- the size of the recruitment budget

- the location and characteristics of the likely candidates.

Table 3.3 External recruitment: advantages and disadvantages

Advantages	Disadvantages
It should result in a wider range of candidates than internal recruitment	It can be an expensive and time-consuming process, using up valuable resources
Candidates may already have the skills required to carry out the job in question, avoiding the need for (and cost of) training	It can have a demotivating effect on members of the existing workforce, who may have missed out on promotion

3.5 Selecting the best candidate

Once a number of suitable candidates have applied for the vacancy, the selection process can begin. This will involve choosing the applicant who most closely matches the criteria set out in the person specification for the job. A number of **selection techniques** exist, including the following.

- *Interviews:* still the most frequently used selection technique, interviews may consist of one interviewer or a panel. Interviews are relatively cheap to conduct and allow a wide variety of information to be

obtained by both sides, but are often susceptible to interviewer bias or prejudice and are, therefore, considered to be an unreliable indicator on their own of how well a candidate will carry out the job in question.

- *Testing and profiling:* aptitude tests measure the level of ability of a candidate (e.g. the level of IT skills), whereas psychometric profiling examines personality and attitudes (e.g. whether the candidate works well under pressure or is an effective team player). Profiling is commonly used as part of management and sales consultancy recruitment, but it is questionable as to whether recruiting a 'personality type' for a particular job is desirable – recruiting a wider range may lead to a more interesting and creative environment.

- *Assessment centres:* these allow for more in-depth assessment of a candidate's suitability by subjecting them to 'real-life' role plays and simulations, often over a number of days. Although assessment centres are considered to be an effective selection method, they can be expensive, and tend, therefore, to be reserved for filling more senior, management positions.

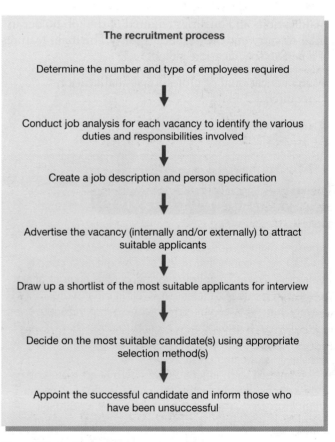

Figure 3.1 The recruitment process

Although a firm can be certain that the right person has been recruited only once he or she starts work, effective recruitment and selection will reduce the risk involved. There are a number of methods that can be used to evaluate the process, including calculating the cost and time involved in filling a vacancy, the percentage of candidates who actually accept job offers and the rate of retention of staff once employed.

High-grade application

Put off by poor recruitment procedures

Many graduates are put off taking up job opportunities with organisations as a result of poor recruitment processes, according to the results of research by Reed, one of the UK's leading recruitment firms. The survey, carried out in 2006, found that more than two-thirds of the 2500 graduates questioned had walked away from potential employers because of poor practices, including 'advertised jobs changing or no longer being available', 'lack of feedback' and 'long delays before being called for final interviews'. Over two-thirds complained that they had not been contacted at all by an organisation after submitting a job application.

Source: Adapted from 'Bad recruitment methods alienate graduates', 11 August 2006 (http://managementissues.com/2006/8/24/research/bad-recruitment-methods-alienate-granduates.asp) Management Issues

3.6 Training

The purpose of training is to help employees to develop existing skills or gain new ones. Types of training include the following.

Induction training

Induction training aims to make newly appointed workers fully productive as soon as possible by familiarising them with the key aspects of the business. Induction would typically include:

● information on important policies and procedures, such as health and safety

● a tour of the organisation and an introduction to colleagues

● details of employment (e.g. payment arrangements, holiday entitlement) and basic duties.

On-the-job training

On-the-job training is where employees are not required to leave their workplace but actually receive instruction while still carrying out their job. This means that workers can receive training while remaining productive to some extent. Common methods include mentoring, coaching and job rotation.

Off-the-job training

Off-the-job training is where employees leave their workplace in order to receive instruction. This may involve using training facilities within the firm (e.g. seminar rooms) or those provided by another organisation, such as a university, college or private training agency. Although this will inevitably involve a temporary loss of production, it should allow the trainee to concentrate fully on learning, and perhaps allow access to more experienced instructors than those available within the workplace.

Table 3.4 Training: benefits and costs

Benefits	Costs
It increases the level and range of skills available to the business, leading to improvements in productivity and quality	It can lead to a more motivated workforce by creating opportunities for development and promotion
It increases the degree of flexibility within a business, allowing it to respond quickly to changes in technology or demand	It can be expensive, both in terms of providing the training itself and also the cost of evaluating its effectiveness Production may be disrupted while training is taking place, leading to lost output
	Newly trained workers may be persuaded to leave and take up new jobs elsewhere (known as poaching), meaning that the benefits of training are enjoyed by other businesses

Labour market failure

Like any market, the labour market is made up of supply (labour services provided by those who wish to work) and demand (firms in need of workers to produce goods or provide services). An efficient labour market would require firms to provide training for their workers in order to improve their skills and knowledge. However, the danger of poaching may create a general disincentive for firms to invest in training, for fear that the short-term costs and disruption of training may not be recouped if newly trained employees are enticed to work elsewhere (**labour market failure**). In such circumstances, the government may become involved in training provision, in order to ensure the economy remains competitive.

Training and the government

The UK government uses a number of methods to support and encourage firms to train their workers, including the following.

- *Modern Apprenticeships:* structured programmes aimed at improving the level of technical skills within the workforce. Apprentices receive a combination of on-the-job training within a firm participating in the scheme and off-the-job training, usually by day-release to a local college, over a period of at least 12 months.

- *The New Deal:* aims to give unemployed people the opportunity to gain work experience and new skills to improve their employment opportunities. Candidates are screened and matched to suitable vacancies and, in some cases, financial help is provided in the form of subsidies and grants to the employer.

- *Investors In People:* promotes training by setting out a set of criteria, or 'standards', for firms to work towards. Those who do are allowed to display the Investors In People logo and are likely to enjoy a number of benefits, including improved quality, a reduction in costs and enhanced employee motivation.

High-grade application

Skills development 'in your hands'

In July 2007, the UK government launched an advertising campaign to encourage people to upgrade their skills. The three-year initiative, entitled 'Our future, it's in our hands', was designed to create a culture or desire to learn among the UK workforce. The campaign was seen as a response to the Leitch Report, published in December 2006. The report demanded a radical change in training within the UK in order to plug the skills gap and stop Britain from lagging behind its international competitors. The report claimed that 5 million adults have insufficient literacy skills and over 17 million lack basic numeracy skills. The report also claimed that one-third of employers provide no training at all for their staff.

Source: Adapted from www.bbc.co.uk/news

3.7 People in management

People management affects every aspect of the operations of a business. Clearly, workers are not machines and, despite what some managers may continue to think, treating them as such has been discredited by many theorists as an ineffective approach to managing them. Each worker is unique, with moods and motivations that may change on a daily basis, often affecting performance. This makes human resources management a complex, and at times frustrating, activity. However, like machinery, effective investment in a firm's human resources – in the form of recruitment, training, organisation and motivation – can have a dramatic impact on productivity. All businesses, regardless of size, need to manage all aspects of their human resources carefully. For instance:

- How should the workforce be structured and what job roles should be adopted?

- How should a business choose between the training and development of existing staff and the recruitment of new employees?

- What techniques can be used to improve motivation, and how might these change over time and between different groups of workers?

- How can workforce performance be measured and improved?

Perhaps one of the most difficult aspects of human resource management responsibilities is 'severance' or the ending of employment with the business. This can take different forms, voluntary or involuntary. The

Figure 3.2 Employee training

ending of employment may come about naturally through voluntary redundancy or the ending of a specific contract. However, severance is often more difficult to deal with, when it involves disciplinary procedures or redundancy. This may have long-term effects upon the parties involved and will require excellent communication skills on the part of the Human Resources Manager.

3.8 People in organisations

It is tempting to deal with people in organisations by dividing the area into separate topics – such as recruitment, training and motivation – and tackling them one by one. While this might help the initial learning process, A-grade students need to go further, making connections between individual topics in order to unlock the underlying themes. For example, a sudden decrease in labour productivity may be linked to falling motivation, which, in turn, may result from a change in policy aimed at bringing in new staff to fill a skills gap, rather than promoting existing employees.

There is plenty of scope for misunderstanding within the people section of the specification. Weaker candidates, for example, often fall into the trap of believing that managers should be working towards creating a happier workforce, confusing motivation with contentment. Stronger candidates will recognise the connection between motivation and the benefits of improved productivity, lower costs and greater profits for the firm. A-grade candidates need more than just an understanding of the people concepts – they need to be able to discuss and assess their relative significance for individual firms and the circumstances they face.

Issue 1: the link between human resources decision making and the business objectives

Regardless of whether a business is struggling to survive or to manage rapid growth, the contribution of the workforce will be crucial. The 'human' element of the business is responsible for generating new ideas, ensuring that production is carried out, and that customers and suppliers receive a service that meets or beats expectations. Employees also represent a major cost to the business and any individual performing below their potential will act as a drain on profits. Ensuring that a business has the right number of people, with the right skills, performing the right roles at the right time, is a major challenge. It is a necessary one, though, if a business is to achieve its long-term objectives.

Issue 2: the link between training and the success of a business

Improving and maintaining the quality of the workforce comes at a cost. Regular training to ensure that employees' skills remain relevant and up to date can be expensive. Any business behaviour that contributes to increased costs should surely be avoided – or should it? Assuming that training is justified and effective in improving the performance of the workforce, it may provide the business with its only way of competing successfully. Investment in training not only creates a skilled workforce but is also likely to produce a more motivated and efficient workforce. Ultimately, a firm's attitude to training will depend on its ability and willingness to accept higher short-term costs in the hope of benefits in the long term.

Issue 3: training

Staff training can begin once the firm has decided on its customer service policies and practices. Note, however, that firms will have varying levels of commitment to training for staff. Some firms may offer staff just 30 minutes' informal training in customer service. They cannot expect their policies to be implemented as effectively as the firm that sends all new staff to a training centre for a full day's training. In America, McDonald's began a programme of getting staff to work with **zero training**. This was just at the start of the period when the firm's sales and profits collapsed in the period 2002–2005. The zero training approach disappeared when new managers decided that McDonald's needed more customer training, not less. At McDonald's, and everywhere else, the cost involved in improving the level of customer service must be set against the cost of not doing so.

3.9 Factors to consider in recruitment

Recruitment can be an expensive process, and has to be considered in relation to the wider objectives of the firm. Therefore, before spending time and money hiring staff, there are a number of factors to think about.

The business should start by identifying what skills, qualities and experience are required in order to allow it to continue to operate successfully. This will require a clear understanding of the exact nature of the firm's product and the market in which it operates. A detailed analysis of the marketplace usually forms a major part of a firm's business plan.

The next step would be to pinpoint current skill strengths and weaknesses, so that gaps in expertise can be filled. For example, trying to get the books to balance without the financial skills required to do so can use up a great deal of time. This could be spent more profitably promoting products, dealing with customers and managing suppliers.

Another factor to consider is the length of time that workers are likely to be needed. For instance, additional staff may be taken on in order to respond to an increasing workload. Is this increase likely to be temporary or permanent? How many extra hours of work will be needed each week? Once a business has developed a clear understanding of its workforce needs, it will be in a position to choose from a number of employment options.

3.10 Legal responsibilities

Regardless of whether workers are employed on a full- or part-time, temporary or permanent basis, firms must be aware of the responsibilities involved in taking on additional staff. Employers have a number of obligations, including the need to provide a safe and secure environment, to treat workers fairly and avoid discrimination. All workers must be given a written statement of the terms and conditions of their contract of employment, and have a number of legal entitlements, including:

- the right to receive the **National Minimum Wage.**

  In October 2007 the rates were set at:

  Over 21 £5.52 per hour

  18–21 £4.60 per hour

  16–17 £3.40 perr hour

- minimum levels of rest breaks

- paid holidays and statutory sick pay.

Employers are required to register with HM Revenue & Customs (HMRC) and establish a payroll in order to deduct income tax and National Insurance Contributions from employees' pay.

Part-time and fixed-term employees have the same employment rights as their full-time colleagues. This means that, by law, employers must treat staff in the same way, regardless of the basis for their employment. Therefore part-time staff should receive, pro rata, the same terms and conditions, including rates of pay, holidays and access to training, promotion and redundancy. Failure to treat staff fairly could result in an employee making a complaint to an **employment tribunal**, potentially leading to the firm having to pay compensation.

High-grade application

The employer and the law

The fear of legal action from employees has discouraged nearly one-third of small firms in the UK from taking on additional staff, according to recent research. The survey, carried out in 2005 by Sage HR Advice, also confirmed that 19% of respondents had considered giving up their business as a direct result of employment legislation.

Source: Adapted from www.startups.co.uk

Issues For Analysis

Successful small businesses will make huge efforts to get their recruitment and training right, as one 'bad apple' can poison morale in a small office. When Google started, they put candidates through up to seven rounds of interviews before deciding on appointments. Yet why should the entrepreneur with the flair to think up a new business idea also be good at hiring and training staff? So it is always sensible to question whether the boss's recruitment skills are sufficient, and to marvel at any entrepreneur who has these among so many other necessary skills. Perhaps the ideal start-up was that of Innocent Drinks, with three ex-university friends having different skills, yet a shared attitude to the business.

Opportunities for analysis are likely to focus on the following areas:

- the reasons for and against a small business expanding its workforce

- the advantages and/or disadvantages to a firm of employing staff on a part-time or full-time basis

- the benefits and drawbacks of employing staff on a temporary or full-time basis

- the suitability of using consultants or contractors to a firm in given circumstances

- the advantages and/or disadvantages of a firm using internal or external recruitment to fill job vacancies

- the suitability of recruitment and/or selection methods used in a given situation

- the costs and benefits involved in training
- the relevance of a particular training programme in terms of meeting the needs of both the employer and the employee.

With so much customer service being provided by phone, call centres feature high in the customer service agenda. NatWest Bank is just one of many companies now stating clearly in its promotional literature that it uses only UK call centres. Why should it use UK call centres when the cost is far higher than for those located in India, and the staff in a UK call centre will be less qualified than their Indian counterparts? Customer service could be argued to be more qualitative than quantitative. Perceptions of customers are probably more important than the service they actually receive; the link between this area of operations management and the marketing department is strong.

Some companies, notably DIY chain B&Q, believe that some types of people are better at customer service than others. Many major retailers use students and school-leavers as a huge portion of their shop-floor staff. However, B&Q feels that students and school-leavers are naturally less polite than older members of staff. The result is that B&Q actively encourages retired and semi-retired people to apply for positions in its stores, since it believes that these staff can provide the most effective customer service.

Key terms

Employment tribunal: an informal courtroom where legal disputes between employees and employers are settled.

External recruitment: where a job vacancy is filled by appointing a candidate from outside the business.

Induction training: familiarises newly appointed workers with key aspects of their jobs and their employer, such as health and safety policies, holiday entitlement and payment arrangements. The aim is to make employees fully productive as soon as possible.

Internal recruitment: where a job vacancy is filled by appointing someone from the existing workforce.

Job description: a document that outlines the duties and responsibilities associated with a particular job role.

Labour market failure: in the context of training, this refers to the reluctance of employers to invest in training for fear that staff, once trained, will be poached by other firms attempting to avoid training costs. If sufficient firms are discouraged from training employees, overall skill levels within the workforce will fall, leading to a loss of competitiveness for the economy as a whole.

National Minimum Wage: the lowest hourly wage rate that an employer can legally pay to an employee.

Off-the-job training: where employees leave their normal place of work in order to receive instruction, either within the firm or by using an external organisation such as a college or university.

On-the-job training: where employees acquire or develop skills without leaving their usual workplace, perhaps by being guided through an activity by a more experienced member of staff.

Person specification: a document that outlines the qualifications, skills and other qualities needed to carry out a particular job successfully.

Selection techniques: the processes used by an organisation to choose the most appropriate candidate for a job, such as interviewing or testing.

Zero training: the opposite of customer service, in that it implies that staff need neither skills nor positive attitudes to work for the business.

3.11 Human resource management
an evaluation

Recruitment and training are key aspects of human resources management (HRM), and the importance of effective HR strategies in helping a firm – however large or small – to achieve its objectives cannot be overstated. 'Having the right person with the right skills in the right job at the right time' will allow a business to maintain or improve its competitiveness – having the wrong person is likely to lead to a deterioration in performance and an increase in costs. Many organisations continue to view training in particular as an avoidable expense, choosing to cut training budgets when under pressure to cut costs, or to poach employees already equipped with the necessary skills from other firms. New employees can bring a number of benefits, including fresh ideas and approaches to work. However, such an approach may fail to weigh up the possible long-term impact on the quality and motivation of the workforce, and the implications of this for productivity and competitiveness.

Taking on extra workers is one of the hardest decisions that an entrepreneur is likely to face. This is the point in the firm's development where the individual is forced to admit that s/he can't do everything. There may also be a reluctance to hand over some control to others – people who may have different opinions and challenge the way the business is run. Employing someone with strongly opposing views is likely to lead to conflict and, unless everyone is heading in the same direction, the business will not move forward. However, a successful firm requires a range of skills and experience. Refusing to bring in additional support and expertise can seriously damage the potential of the business to continue to survive and thrive.

Exercises

A. Revision questions

(56 marks; 56 minutes)

1 Outline two reasons why a business might need to recruit new employees. (4)

2 Outline two factors that would influence the method of recruitment used by a business. (4)

3 Suggest two reasons why internal recruitment may not be a suitable means of filling vacancies for a rapidly expanding business. (2)

4 Outline one advantage and one disadvantage of external recruitment. (4)

5 Examine one suitable method for recruiting applicants to the following job roles:
   (a) caretaker for a local school (3)
   (b) a temporary sales assistant for a high-street retailer over the Christmas period (3)
   (c) a marketing director for a multinational company. (3)

6 Examine one advantage and one disadvantage of using interviewing as a method of selecting candidates for a job vacancy. (4)

7 Suggest two methods that a firm could use to evaluate the effectiveness of its recruitment and selection procedure. (2)

8 Outline two reasons why a firm should provide induction training for newly recruited employees. (2)

9 State two reasons why a business might choose to recruit internally rather than externally. (2)

10 Identify three methods of recruiting staff from outside the business. (3)

11 Explain the difference between on-the-job and off-the-job training. (3)

12 State two benefits to a firm of training its workers. (2)

13 Outline three reasons why a small business may need to take on additional staff. (6)

14 Suggest two reasons why the owner of a small business might be reluctant to employ more staff. (2)

15 Explain why a business should consider any plans to expand the workforce in relation to its wider objectives. (4)

16 Briefly explain the main risks for a small business from failing to adhere to legislation regarding the employment of workers. (3)

B. Revision exercises

B1 Data response

Performance-based recruitment at O₂

Mobile phone company O_2 has developed a new approach to hiring staff, based on candidates' performance profiles rather than on skills and competency. The recruitment model, developed for the business by consultancy firm Ferguson McKenzie, involves an interview that assesses between four and six accomplishments in the candidate's career. Potential recruits also have their 'tactical' skills and behaviour compared to a 'talent assessment matrix', which rates their likelihood of success in the job role. The new recruitment model was initially piloted at O_2's call centre in Glasgow, where it was used to hire 500 new staff. It was also used to take on 20 sales advisers in four different areas of the company's UK retail operations.

O_2's UK resourcing manager, Fiona Davidson, said that the new technique allowed recruitment assessors to 'probe more and have more meaningful dialogue with candidates'. According to her, the new model provided a better assessment of applicants' motivation and work ethic, as well as guaranteeing a more consistent approach across the selection process. When the model is eventually deployed across O_2's UK retail and customer service divisions, it will fill between 2500 and 3000 job vacancies each year.

Source: 'O_2 lines on performance', 23 August 2001, *People Management* Magazine

Questions

(25 marks; 30 minutes)

1 Outline three 'tactical' skills that an employee would need to successfully carry out the role of a customer services adviser at O_2. (6)

2 Analyse two ways in which O_2 could assess the effectiveness of the new recruitment model. (8)

3 Assess the importance of effective recruitment and selection for a company like O_2. (11)

B2 Data response

Solving skills shortages at Mulberry

Mulberry is a leading manufacturer of luxury handbags and leather goods, based in the south-west of England. Its reputation depends to a great extent on maintaining a highly skilled workforce, trained to handle valuable materials and use a variety of leatherworking techniques, such as cutting and stitching. These techniques are complicated to teach, requiring lengthy training periods before workers can become productive.

With an ageing workforce and a chronic shortage of workers with the appropriate manufacturing skills across the UK textile industry generally, Mulberry was faced with a dilemma: if it recruited and trained workers in-house it would not qualify for the public funding available for employees undertaking recognised qualifications. However, the courses offered by external training providers were too general and, therefore, failed to address the company's specific training needs.

The company's solution was to set up a partnership with Bridgewater College, a further education institution with a reputation for supporting local employers. The collaboration resulted in a new two-year apprenticeship qualification, designed precisely to meet Mulberry's training needs. Apprentices spend the majority of their time at the company's industrial plant in Somerset, training 'on the job' and learning a range of techniques. The apprentices also spend half a day each week at the college, learning about the leather industry and developing skills such as teamwork and communication. The scheme allows Mulberry to control the content of the training and, because

the scheme is recognised by the relevant awarding bodies, the company receives £2500 of public funds for each apprentice trained.

Source: Skillfast UK

Questions

(25 marks; 30 minutes)

1 Briefly explain, using examples, the difference between on-the-job and off-the-job training. (4)

2 Analyse one benefit and one drawback to a company such as Mulberry of its new apprenticeship scheme. (8)

3 To what extent do you agree that the reputation, and therefore success, of UK manufacturers like Mulberry depends on maintaining a highly skilled workforce? (13)

B3 Data response

HRM and social networking

Social networking was the internet phenomenon of 2007, with over 100 million users on MySpace alone. While many businesses complain about the amount of the time wasted by staff chatting online, others are embracing the trend as an opportunity for more effective recruitment and communication. For instance, accountancy firm Ernst & Young uses Facebook as part of its recruitment strategy, by sponsoring its own page on the site, where graduates can learn more about the firm.

For smaller firms, social networking can provide a cost-effective means of accessing a large pool of potential recruits. Helen Wright, head of people at marketing agency Iris, claims that the sites are the 'perfect medium' for recruitment. Staff can pass on details of job vacancies to suitably qualified friends who can then make their details available to the firm looking to recruit. Developments in the USA suggest that, in the future, recruitment is less likely to happen on the high street and more likely to occur in a virtual world. Computer giant IBM is one of a number of employers who have participated in 'virtual job fairs'. Jobseekers are able to create their own online personas (known as avatars), speak to representatives and even attend interviews.

However, there are also a number of potential problems that could arise from using social networking as a method of recruitment. Judging a candidate on the basis of a social profile may lead to bias, either positive or negative, on behalf of the recruiter. Other firms question the ethics of using the sites to research candidates. According to Donna Miller, European director for Rent-a-Car, the practice is comparable to 'going into somebody's house and searching through their cupboards'.

Source: PM Online

Questions

(25 marks; 30 minutes)

1 Suggest two methods, other than the internet, that a business could use to recruit candidates for a job vacancy. (4)

2 Analyse the main advantages for a small business of using the internet to recruit new staff. (9)

3 To what extent do you agree with the view that, in the future, recruitment is more likely to take place via computer than by using more traditional methods? (12)

B4 Case study

Managing staff at Innocent

Top UK smoothie maker Innocent has grown rapidly since being set up in 1999. By 2006 it already employed over 100 staff, both in the UK and a number of other countries, including Eire and France. According to its website, its vision is to be the most talent-rich company in Europe. Despite its laid-back image, Innocent's recruitment and selection procedures are very demanding. Job applicants apply initially by email or post with a full CV and one-page letter. As well as explaining their reasons for applying, the letter must also outline a recently solved problem, a situation where applicants showed initiative and an issue that they are passionate about. Next, would-be employees face a set of three interviews, conducted by members of Innocent's People and Environment (P&E) team, line managers and, in the case of the final round, a company director or 'founder'. Candidates are assessed for their knowledge of the company, problem-solving skills, and their creativity and initiative. Typical challenges include acting as a

buyer in a role-play or creating a new smoothie bottle label.

The lucky few who make it through the recruitment and selection process receive a two-week induction programme to get a full picture of how Innocent works and how their role fits in. Staff development is central to Innocent's human resource management. In January, employees are set objectives outlining what they are expected to do in order to carry out their jobs successfully. In addition to weekly one-to-one meetings with managers, performance reviews take place in May and November. Staff receive detailed feedback and are given the opportunity to discuss development. In 2006, the company introduced the Innocent Academy – an in-house training school. Everyone in the company completes a two-day programme, working in small groups on ways to become more effective employees.

Source: www.innocentdrinks.co.uk

Questions

(25 marks; 30 minutes)

1 Identify two benefits to Innocent of using its own website to recruit new employees. (4)

2 Examine one advantage and one disadvantage to Innocent of using in-house training to develop its staff. (9)

3 Evaluate the effectiveness of Innocent's approach to managing the company's 'human element' in helping it to achieve its long-term objectives. (12)

C. Essay questions

(40 marks each)

1 Stamford Software Solutions, a medium-sized IT company based in the south-east of England, needs to recruit a new sales manager. Consider how the company should go about doing this.

2 According to the Leitch Report, UK employers spend an estimated £33 billion in total each year on training, yet one-third of employers provide no training at all. Evaluate the main consequences for firms that choose not to train their staff.

3 'People are the main assets of a business.' Discuss this statement in the context of a small business.

4 To what extent should new businesses be concerned about taking on staff?

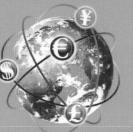

MARKET RESEARCH AND SAMPLING

DEFINITION

Market research gathers information about consumers, competitors and distributors within a firm's target market. It is a way of identifying consumers' buying habits and attitudes to current and future products. Market research data can be numerical (e.g. 'What proportion of 16–24 year olds buy the *Sun* newspaper every day?') or psychological (e.g. 'Why do they buy the *Sun*?').

4.1 Conducting market research

Where do you start? What do you need to know first? And how do you find it out?

The starting point is to discover the marketing fundamentals: how big is the market you are thinking about (market size), what is its future potential and what are the market shares of the existing companies and brands?

Market size means the value of the sales made annually by all the firms within a market. For example, in 2007 the UK yoghurt market was worth £1350 million. Market potential can be measured by the annual rate of growth. In the case of yoghurt, this has been at a rate of 4% per year, by value. This implies that, by 2010, the potential market size will be over £1550 million.

When looking at a completely new market, these statistics will not be available. So research may be needed into other indicators. For example, the producer of an innovative new fishing rod would find out the number of people who go fishing regularly.

Market shares are also of crucial importance when investigating a market, as they indicate the relative strength of the firms within the market. In 2007, 27% of the yoghurt market was held by Müller, making it the leading brand by far. A benefit it received for its strong market share was a distribution level of almost 100% – nearly every grocery store stocked Müller. If one firm dominates, it may be very difficult to break into the market.

So how can firms find out this type of information? The starting point is **secondary research**: unearthing data that already exists.

Figure 4.1 Supermarket shelves stocked with Müller yoghurt

4.2 Methods of secondary research

The internet

These days most people start by 'Googling' the topic. This can provide invaluable information, though online providers of market research information will want to charge for the service. With luck, Google will identify a relevant article that can provide useful information.

Figure 4.2 Internet search engine Google

Trade press

All the above data about the yoghurt market came from an article in the magazine *The Grocer*. Every major market is served by one or more magazines written for people who work within that trade. Spending £1.75 on an issue of *The Grocer* provides lots of statistical and other information. Many trade magazines are available for reference in bigger public libraries.

Government-produced data

The government-funded National Statistics produces valuable reports, such as the *Annual Abstract of Statistics* and *Economic Trends*. These provide data on population trends and forecasts (e.g. for someone starting a hair and beauty salon, to find how many 16–20-year-old women there will be in 2012).

Having obtained background data, further research is likely to be tailored specifically to the company's needs, such as carrying out a survey among 16–20-year-old women about their favourite haircare brands. This type of first-hand research gathers primary data.

4.3 Methods of primary research

The process of gathering information directly from people within your target market is known as **primary research** (or field research). When carried out by market research companies it is expensive, but there is much that firms can do for themselves.

For a company that is already up and running, a regular survey of customer satisfaction is an important way of measuring the quality of customer service. When investigating a new market, there are various measures that can be taken by a small firm with a limited budget. Here are some examples.

● *Retailer research:* the people closest to a market are those who serve customers directly – the retailers. They are likely to know the up-and-coming brands, the degree of brand loyalty, the importance of price and packaging – all crucial information.

● *Observation:* when starting up a service business in which location is an all-important factor, it is invaluable to measure the rate of pedestrian (and possibly traffic) flow past your potential site compared to that of rivals. A sweet shop or a dry cleaners near a busy bus stop may generate twice the sales of a rival 50 yards down the road.

For a large company, primary research will be used extensively in new product development. For example, if we consider the possibility of launching Orange Chocolate Buttons, the development stages – plus research – would probably be those shown in Table 4.2.

Table 4.1 The pros and cons of primary and secondary research

	Secondary research	**Primary research**
Pros	● often obtained without cost ● good overview of a market ● usually based on actual sales figures, or research on	large samples
● can aim ques tions	directly at your research objectives ● latest information from the marketplace ● can assess the psychology of the customer	**Cons**

Table 4.2 *Orange Chocolate Buttons launch: likely development stages*

Development stage	Primary research
1 The product idea (probably one of several)	1 Group discussions among regular chocolate buyers – some young, some old
2 Product test (testing different recipes – different sweetness, 'orangeyness', etc.)	2 A taste test on 200+ chocolate buyers (on street corners, or in a hall)
3 Brand name research (testing several different names, and perhaps logos)	3 Quantitative research using a questionnaire on a sample of 200+
4 Packaging research	4 As 3
5 Advertising research	5 Group discussions run by psychologists to discover which advertisement has the strongest effect on product image and recall
6 Total proposition test: testing the level of purchase interest, to help make sales forecasts	6 Quantitative research using a questionnaire and product samples on at least 200+ consumers

High-grade application
The Toyota MR2

When Toyota launched its MR2 sports car, sales were higher than expected. The only exception was France, where they were very poor. The Japanese Head Office asked the executives of Toyota France to look into this. Why had it been such a flop? Eventually the executives admitted that they should have carried out market research into the brand name MR2 prior to the launch. Pronounced 'Em-Er-Deux' in France, the car sounded like the French word 'merde' (crap).

4.4 Qualitative research

Qualitative research is in-depth research into the motivations behind the attitudes and buying habits of consumers. It does not produce statistics such as '52% of chocolate buyers like orange chocolate'; instead it gives clues as to *why* they like it (e.g. is it really because it's orange, or because it's different/a change?). Qualitative research is usually conducted by psychologists, who learn to interpret the way people say things as well as what they say.

Qualitative research takes two main forms, as described below.

1 *Group discussions (also known as focus groups)*: free-ranging discussions led by psychologists among groups of six to eight consumers. The group leader will have a list of topics that need discussion, but will be free to follow up any point made by a group member. Among the advantages of group discussions are: it may reveal a problem or opportunity the company had not anticipated; it reveals consumer psychology, such as the importance of image and peer pressure.

High-grade application
Researching Häagen-Dazs

Group discussions were used prior to the UK launch of Häagen-Dazs. Groups of men and women were each given a half-litre tub of Häagen-Dazs and asked questions about when, how and with whom they would like to eat it. Respondents spoke about sharing a spoon with their partner, feeding each other and 'mellowing out' in front of a video. This led to a breakthrough in food advertising: Häagen-Dazs was advertised as a sensual pleasure to be shared. Its huge success when launched has become recognised as a success for qualitative research.

2 *Depth interviews*: informal, in-depth interviews between a psychologist and a consumer. They have the same function as group discussions, but avoid the risk that group opinion will be swayed by one influential person.

Table 4.3 Typical research questions to be answered by qualitative and quantitative research

Qualitative research	Quantitative research
• Why do people *really* buy Nikes? • Who in the household *really* decides which brand of shampoo is bought? • What mood makes you feel like buying Häagen-Dazs ice cream? • When you buy your children Frosties, how do you feel?	• Which pack design do you prefer? • Have you heard of any of the following brands: Ariel, Daz, Persil…etc.? • How likely are you to buy this product regularly? • How many newspapers have you bought in the past seven days?

4.5 Quantitative research

Quantitative research asks pre-set questions on a large enough sample of people to provide statistically valid data. Questionnaires can answer factual questions such as 'How many 16–20 year olds have heard of Chanel No 5?' There are three key aspects to quantitative research:

1 sampling (i.e. ensuring that the research results are typical of the whole population, though only a sample of the population has been interviewed)

2 writing a questionnaire that is unbiased and meets the research objectives

3 assessing the validity of the results.

Sampling

The two main concerns in sampling are how to choose the right people for interview (**sampling method**) and deciding how large a number to interview (**sample size**). There are three main sampling methods.

Random sample

This involves selecting respondents to ensure that everyone in the population has an equal chance of being interviewed. This sounds easy, but is not. If an interviewer goes to a street corner one morning and asks passers-by for an interview, the resulting sample will be biased towards those who are not in work, who do not own a car and have time on their hands (the busy ones will refuse to be interviewed). As a result the sample will not be representative. So achieving a truly random sample requires careful thought.

Research companies use the following method.

● Pick names at random from the electoral register (e.g. every 50th name).

● Send an interviewer to the address given in the register.

● If the person is out, visit up to twice more before giving up (this is to maximise the chances of catching those who lead busy social lives and are therefore rarely at home).

This method is effective, but slow and expensive.

Quota sample

This is selecting interviewees in proportion to the consumer profile within your target market. Table 4.4 gives an example.

Table 4.4 Quota sampling: an example

Adult		
	Chocolate buyers	Respondent quota (sample: 200)
Men	40%	80
Women	60%	120
16–24	38%	76
25–34	21%	42
35–44	16%	32
45+	25%	50

This method allows interviewers to head for busy street corners, interviewing whoever comes along. As long as they end up achieving the correct quota, they can interview when and where they want to. As this is a relatively cheap and effective way of sampling, it is the one used most commonly by market research companies.

Stratified sample

This involves interviewing only those with a key characteristic required for the sample. For example, the producers of Olay might decide only to interview women aged 30–45, the potential buyers of the future. Within this stratum/section of the population, individuals could be found at random (hence *stratified random* sample) or by setting quotas based on factors such as social class and region.

Sample size

Having decided which sampling method should be used, the next consideration is how many interviews should be conducted: 10, 100, 1000? The most high-profile surveys conducted in Britain are opinion polls (e.g. asking people how they will vote in a general election). These quota samples of between 1000 and 1500 respondents are considered large enough to reflect the opinions of an electorate of 45 million. How is this possible?

Of course, if you interviewed only ten people, the chances are slim that the views of this sample will match those of the whole population. Of these ten, seven may say they would definitely buy Orange Chocolate Buttons. If you asked another ten, however, only three may say the same. A sample of ten is so small that chance variations make the results meaningless. In other words, a researcher can have no statistical confidence in the findings from a sample of ten.

A sample of 100 is far more meaningful. It is not enough to feel confident about marginal decisions (e.g. 53% like the red pack design, 47% like the blue one), but is quite enough if the result is clear-cut (e.g. 65% like the name 'Spark'; 35% prefer 'Valencia'). Many major product launches have proceeded following research on as low a sample as 100.

With a sample of 1000 a high level of confidence is possible. Even small differences would be statistically significant with such a large sample. So why doesn't everyone use samples of 1000? The answer is money. Hiring a market research agency to undertake a survey on 100 people would cost approximately £10,000. A sample of 1000 people would cost three times that amount – good value if you can afford it, but not everyone can. As shown in the earlier example of launching Orange Chocolate Buttons, a company might require six surveys before launching a new product. So the spending on research alone might reach £180,000 if samples of 1000 were used.

Writing a questionnaire

Quantitative research is expensive and its results may influence major decisions such as whether to launch a new product. So a mistake in writing the questionnaire may prove very costly. For instance, the wording may influence respondents to sound more positive about a new product than they really feel. What are the key features of a good questionnaire?

● Clearly defined research objectives. What exactly do you need to find out?

● Ensure that questions do not point towards a particular answer.

● Ensure that the meaning of each question is clear, perhaps by testing (piloting) questions before putting them into fieldwork.

● Mainly use closed questions (i.e. ones with a limited number of pre-set answers that the respondent must tick); only in this way can you ensure quantifiable results.

● It is useful, though, to include a few open questions, to allow respondents to write a sentence or two, providing more depth of understanding.

● Ensure that the questionnaire finishes by asking for full demographic and usership details (i.e. the respondent's sex, age, occupation – and therefore social class – and buying habits). This allows more detailed analysis of sub-groups within the sample.

4.6 Other important considerations in primary research

Response rate

If a company sends out 2000 questionnaires and only 200 people send back a response, the following questions must be asked: 'Are those who respond typical of those who do not respond? Or is there a **bias** built into the findings as a consequence of the low response rate?'

Face-to-face versus self-completion

In the past, most surveys were conducted by interviewers who asked the questions face-to-face. This had drawbacks such as cost and the risk of bias (a bubbly young interviewer may generate more positive responses). Clear benefits, however, included a high response rate and the assurance that the interviewer could help to explain an unclear question. Today, self-completion questionnaires are increasingly common.

4.7 Market research today

Market research is increasingly influenced by technology. Instead of standing on windy street corners, interviewers are more likely to be sitting in a telephone booth in an office. There are also more and more internet opinion polls, in which a pop-up questionnaire appears on the screen. For instance, someone looking at the Amazon.com shopping site might be asked to answer questions about book buying.

An even stronger trend is towards database-driven research. Instead of finding the right people by trial and error, client firms supply research companies with database information on current or ex-customers. Retailers such as Tesco and Sainsbury's have millions of customer names on their databases, gained from customers' membership of loyalty card schemes such as Tesco's Clubcard. Shoppers are grouped into categories such as regular/irregular shoppers, petrol buyers, disposable nappy buyers, and so on. If Tesco wants to survey customer satisfaction with its baby products section, it knows exactly who should be contacted.

The future of market research is clearly bound up in technology. The basics will remain crucial, however: the avoidance of bias in the wording of questions, large enough sample sizes to provide valid data, and intelligent analysis of the research findings.

Issues For Analysis

When developing an argument in answer to an exam question, market research offers the following main lines of analysis:

● the key role of market research in market orientation (i.e. basing decisions upon the consumer's, rather than the producer's, needs or opinions)

● the need for a questioning approach to data – when presented with a research finding one needs to know: was the sample size large enough, who paid for the research; businesspeople learn to ask questions about every 'fact' shown by research

● the importance of market knowledge – large, established firms have a huge advantage over newer, smaller firms because of their knowledge of consumer attitudes and behaviour, built up from years of market research surveys

4.8 Market research and sampling
an evaluation

In large firms, it is rare for any significant marketing decision to be made without market research. Even an apparently minor change to a pack design will be carried out only after testing in research. Is this overkill? Surely marketing executives are employed to make judgements, not merely do what surveys tell them?

The first issue here is the strong desire to make business decisions as scientifically as possible. In other words, to act on evidence, not on feelings. Quantitative research, especially, fits in with the desire to act on science not hunch. Yet this can be criticised, such as by John Scully, former head of Apple Computers, who once said 'No great marketing decision has ever been made on the basis of quantitative data.' He was pointing out that true innovations, such as Apple's iPod, were the product of creativity and hunch, not science.

The second issue concerns management culture. In some firms, mistakes lead to inquests, blame and even dismissal. This makes managers keen to find a let-out. When the new product flops, the manager can point an accusing finger at the positive research results: 'It wasn't my fault. We need a new research agency.' In other firms, mistakes are seen as an inevitable part of learning. For every Sinclair C5 (unresearched flop) there may be an iPod (unresearched moneyspinner). In firms with a positive, risk-taking approach to business, qualitative insights are likely to be preferred to quantitative data.

Key terms

Backdata: keeping records of the results from past research to provide a comparison with the latest results.

Bias: a factor that causes research findings to be unrepresentative of the whole population (e.g. bubbly interviewers or misleading survey questions).

Primary research: finding out information first-hand (e.g. Coca-Cola designing a questionnaire to obtain information from people who regularly buy diet products).

Secondary research: finding out information that has already been gathered (e.g. the government's estimates of the number of 14–16 year olds in Wales).

Sample size: the number of people interviewed; this should be large enough to give confidence that the findings are representative of the whole population.

Sampling method: the approach chosen to select the right people to be part of the research sample (e.g. random, quota or stratified).

Exercises

A. Revision questions

(35 marks; 35 minutes)

1 State three ways in which a cosmetics firm could use market research. (3)

2 Outline three reasons why market research information may prove inaccurate. (6)

3 Distinguish between primary and secondary research. (3)

4 What advantages are there in using secondary research rather than primary? (3)

5 Which is the most commonly used sampling method? Why may it be the most commonly used? (4)

6 State three key factors to take into account when writing a questionnaire. (3)

7 Explain two aspects of marketing in which consumer psychology is important. (4)

8 Outline the pros and cons of using a large sample size. (4)

9 Identify three possible sources of bias in primary market research. (3)

10 Why may street interviewing become less common in the future? (2)

B. Revision exercises

B1 Market research assignment

Hampton is a medium-sized producer of health foods. Its new company strategy is to break into the £400 million market for breakfast cereals. It has thought up three new product ideas that it wishes to test in research before further development takes place. These are as follows.

1 *Cracker:* an extra-crunchy mix of oats and almonds.

2 *Fizzz:* crunchy oats that fizz in milk.

3 *St James:* a luxury mix of oats, cashews and pecan nuts.

The research objectives are to identify the most popular of the three, in terms of product trial *and* regular usage; to identify price expectations for each; to find what people like and dislike about each idea and each brand name; and to be able to analyse the findings in relation to consumers' demographic profile and current usage patterns.

Questions

(30 marks; 30 minutes)

1 Write a questionnaire based upon the above details, bearing in mind the advice given in Section 5.5. (12)

2 Explain which sampling method you would use and why. (6)

3 Interview six to eight people using your questionnaire, then write a 200-word commentary on its strengths and weaknesses. (12)

B2 Data response

Each year more than £1000 million is spent on pet food in the UK. All the growth within the market has been for luxury pet foods and healthier products. Seeing these trends, in early 2008 Town & Country Petfoods launched 'HiLife Just Desserts', a range of pudding treats for dogs. They contain Omega-3 but no added sugar and therefore have no more than 100 calories per tin.

Sales began well, especially of the Apple & Cranberry version. Now sales have flattened out at around £1 million a year and the company thinks it is time to launch some new flavours. Three weeks ago it commissioned some primary research that was carried out using an online survey linked to pet care websites. The sample size was 150.

The main findings were as follows:

1 Have you ever bought your dog a pet food pudding?

EVER BOUGHT:	Never	Just once	Yes in past, but no longer	Yes, still do
	61%	13%	12%	14%

2 Which of these flavours might you buy for your dog?

MIGHT TRY:

	Never	Might try	Might buy monthly	Might buy once a week
Muesli yoghurt	61%	19%	15%	5%
Rhubarb crumble	43%	33%	22%	2%
Apples and custard	52%	34%	12%	2%

The marketing director is a bit disappointed that none of the new product ideas has done brilliantly, but happy that there's one clear winner. She plans a short qualitative research exercise among existing HiLife customers, and hopes to launch two new flavours in time for the annual Crufts' Dog Show in three months' time.

Questions

(20 marks; 30 minutes)

1 Outline whether the sample size of 150 was appropriate in this case. (4)

2 Examine the marketing director's conclusion that 'none of the new product ideas has done brilliantly, but happy that there's one clear winner'. (7)

3a Explain one method of qualitative research that could be used in this case. (3)

3b Analyse two ways in which qualitative research might help the marketing director. (6)

C. Essay questions

(40 marks each)

1 'Market research is like an insurance policy. You pay a premium to reduce your marketing risks.' To what extent do you believe this statement to be true?

2 After ten years of rising sales, demand for Shredded Wheat has been slipping. Discuss how the marketing manager might make use of market research to analyse why this has happened and help decide the strategy needed to return Shredded Wheat to sales growth.

3 Steve Jobs, boss of Apple, once said that he ignored market research in the early stages of the iPod. He believes that research is useful in relation to existing products, but does not work with innovative new products.

(a) Why may this be?

(b) How could research be used to best effect for assessing new innovations?

Unit 5

THE SIZE AND SCALE OF BUSINESS

DEFINITION

Businesses are diverse in size, purpose and structure. The size of a business can be measured in many ways, such as profit, revenue, number of employees or geographical area.

5.1 Transforming inputs into outputs

Within every economy there are three sectors: primary, secondary and tertiary.

1 **Primary sector:** growing, fishing, farming, extracting or mining raw materials, such as wheat, cocoa, copper or gold. In less developed economies, such as Sierra Leone or Malaysia, primary industries remain crucial. In Britain they represent fewer than 2% of the jobs available. Nevertheless everything we eat or wear starts with raw materials from the primary sector – some from this country, plus many that are imported from overseas.

2 **Secondary sector:** turning raw materials into finished, processed, probably packaged products. This sector includes all manufacturing, engineering, construction and the oil industry. Traditionally it is where value is added in the process of turning sheets of steel into cars, bundles of wheat into Weetabix or small pieces of plastic and metal into iPods.

3 **Tertiary sector:** the service sector, dominated by wholesaling and retailing, plus financial services, tourism and all the business services you can see in every high street or in the *Yellow Pages*.

The importance of this distinction can be seen below. The primary producer receives only 5p for what is sold in a British supermarket for £1.75. The big winner in this case is the 'roaster' – the manufacturer, such as Nestlé, which turns raw coffee into the branded product Nescafé (see Table 5.2). The journey from producer to Starbucks is even more stark, with the beans in a £2 latte yielding no more than 1p to the Kenyan farmer.

Table 5.1 The differences between primary, secondary and tertiary producers

Primary	Secondary	Tertiary
Rely largely on big buyers, such as manufacturers or big supermarket chains; may find that buyers force them to keep prices low	No direct contact with customers, so brand names are crucial for image and repeat purchase	Direct contact with customers, so well-motivated, well-trained staff are crucial for image and customer loyalty
Hard to make their products seem different from others, e.g. a kilo of wheat = anyone else's kilo of wheat	Can make products seem very different from those of rivals, e.g. the design and manufacturing quality in a BMW compared to a Ford	Making a service stand out can be done by clever planning or by effective marketing (e.g. 'This is not just food, it's M&S Food')
Location is rarely of importance, though the issue of **food miles** may start to make consumers prefer local suppliers	Factory location can be anywhere in the world, as long as the transport links are good and the right staff skills are available	Most service businesses have direct customer contact (e.g. plumber, retailer, café, pub) so location must be close to where customers live

Table 5.2 The value chain for a jar of coffee

Producer sells for	5p
World coffee price	35p
Roaster (e.g. Nestlé)	£1.20
Tesco store price	£1.75

Source: Adapted from *Observer*, 25 February 2007

In exams, it is important to highlight the differences between primary, secondary and tertiary producers (see Table 5.1).

5.2 The size and scale of a business

There is no optimum or best size for a business. Businesses can be organised and run by one person at the corner of a street or by many owners in every corner of the world.

Most businesses are started on a small scale by entrepreneurs to exploit an idea, through necessity due to redundancy or simply to realise a dream.

In order to understand how businesses operate and why, it is necessary to understand how business size can be measured and why growth may or may not be an objective of a business.

The size of a business can be measured in various ways, including measurement by turnover, number of employees or profit.

Turnover

Turnover measures the value of sales revenue over a period of time, usually a year. Businesses can be classified as small if turnover is less than £1.4 million, medium if it is between £1.4 million and £5.75 million, and large if it is over £5.75 million.

Number of employees

A popular method for measuring the size of a business is by number of employees. This can be measured and compared both within the business and with other businesses. However, this can be misleading, because many of the largest businesses are very capital intensive and/or use extensive technology rather than a large labour force. This means that they could be classified as large in terms of turnover but medium or small in terms of the number of employees. Businesses with fewer than 50 employees are classified as small, those with between 50 and 250 employees as medium, and those with over 250 as large.

Profit

Profit is not a particularly accurate measure of the size of a business, because it can be affected by so many different variables year on year. Small businesses can make very large profits and large businesses very large losses.

5.3 Economies and diseconomies of scale

Why might a business want to grow? One reason is that, as a business grows, it is able to achieve economies of scale. Scale refers to size – in this case large scale. Economies mean savings or lower average costs. Therefore **economies of scale** refer to the fact that, in most cases, larger businesses can lower their average costs as the scale of their operation increases. Businesses can grow in two ways.

1 **Internal growth:** through expansion of products and markets at home and abroad. Many large retailers, such as Tesco and Vodafone, have achieved this type of internal growth. However, it does take a long time!

2 **External growth:** through merger, acquisition and takeover. In recent years this has become a popular method of growth with businesses sharing expertise, markets and innovations. Two of the most successful mergers have been Cadbury/Schweppes and Rowntree/Nestlé. Mobile phone companies are now realising the advantages of merging, as can be seen from the article reproduced below.

T-Mobile UK and 3 UK, two British mobile phone operators, recently said they would combine their 3G networks in an effort to save each of them £1 billion over the next decade. Vodafone and Orange, two other British mobile phone companies, have been talking since February [2007] about making a similar deal.

Think of it as McDonald's and Burger King getting together to share the cost of the trucks that deliver meat, potatoes and tomatoes to their outlets. While unthinkable in most industries, including fast food, this sort of collaboration is under way between mobile phone companies and is likely to accelerate.

Source: *International Herald Tribune*, December 2007

Economies of scale can be achieved in a variety of ways. *Internally*, through:

- technical economies – for example, the capital costs and running costs of factories do not rise in proportion to their size; large-scale plants can use specialist and indivisible equipment (e.g. photocopiers) more efficiently than a small business

- managerial economies – large firms can employ specialist managers to increase efficiency and lower average costs

- financial economies – larger businesses have a greater variety of financial sources to choose from, very often gaining from better deals in terms of lower interest rates

- purchasing/marketing economies – large firms gain from discounted prices on bulk buying; a large firm does not increase its costs proportionately when its administration costs rise, such as those related to advertising and distribution.

- risk bearing economies – large firms can diversify into a number of product areas to spread the risk of failure. they can also invest more time and money in terms of research and development to reduce this risk.

And, *externally*, through the reductions in cost, which a business might enjoy as it grows. This is more likely to be the case in areas where a particular industry is concentrated – for example, the City of London (financial services), the Thames Valley (ICT, communications, computers), Sheffield (steel/cutlery industry), Birmingham (car industry). In such instances:

- a skilled labour force will be created in certain areas, therefore reducing training costs

- specialist services, such as banking, insurance, waste disposal, distribution and component manufacturers, will develop in the area to lower costs of transportation and communication.

Diseconomies of scale

The reduction in average costs does not continue regardless of how big a firm becomes. As with many large organisations, and even countries, big is not always easy to control or to organise. There is a point at which this control and organisation breaks down and average costs begin to rise. Such rises in long-term average costs are known as **diseconomies of scale**. These diseconomies take many forms, such as poor quality control, increased absenteeism, poor delivery, poor customer service, and increased congestion and pollution, and can ultimately limit the growth of many businesses.

Key terms

Diseconomies of scale: the increase in long run average costs as a business expands beyond its ability to control and manage itself.
Economies of scale: the reduction in average costs as a result of savings brought about by an increase in the scale of production.
Primary sector: companies and people working to extract raw materials from the earth or sea (e.g. fishing, farming and mining).
Secondary sector: businesses that transform raw materials into finished goods, e.g. car manufacturing or food processing.
Tertiary sector: companies and people who provide services, either to the public (e.g. retailing or dry cleaning) or to businesses (e.g. accountancy, solicitors).

Exercises

A. Revision questions

(38 marks; 40 minutes)

1 Analyse why both small and large businesses can operate successfully within the same environment. (8)

2 Explain why the tertiary sector is an important part of the production process. (6)

3 How important is it that a business has the objective of growth? Give reasons for your answers. (12)

4 Using an example, explain the meaning of the term 'diseconomy of scale'. (4)

5 The computer games industry is dominated by a few large businesses, such as Microsoft, Sony and Nintendo. Analyse the economies of scale they might enjoy. (8)

B. Revision exercises

B1 Data response

In 2002 a cooperative agreement between coffee farmers in 250 Ugandan villages broke down. It had taken years to put together, but disagreements made it collapse. The prize for a successful cooperative was to produce organic coffee beans grown to Fairtrade standards for partners such as Café Direct. This would ensure getting significantly higher prices for the raw coffee beans and also much better credit terms (being paid quickly to help with cash flow).

Over the next two years countless hours of work were put into forming a new cooperative. In early 2004 the new 'Gumutindo' coffee cooperative was Fairtrade certified. Over 3000 farmers are now part of Gumutindo. They receive a guaranteed price of $1.26 per pound of coffee beans, whereas the world price has been under $0.80 for the last six years. The extra (and stable) income should help the farmers, of whom only 25% have running water, and 79% live in mud huts with iron sheet roofing. In future, the Fairtrade organisation will support the cooperative in starting up its own production plant to convert the raw coffee into packs of coffee ready for sale.

Source: www.fairtrade.org.uk

Questions

(20 marks; 25 minutes)

1 Is the work of the Ugandan villagers in the primary, secondary or tertiary sector? (1)

2 What would be the opportunity cost of the farmers who put 'countless hours of work into forming a new cooperative'? (3)

3 Outline one risk for the farmers and one risk for the Fairtrade organisation in forming a new cooperative with high guaranteed prices for the coffee beans. (6)

4a Into which of the three sectors will the Gumutindo cooperative move if it starts its own production plant? (1)

4b Discuss whether producing coffee ready for sale would definitely increase the income levels of the 3000 members of the cooperative. (9)

BUSINESS OWNERSHIP

Unit 6

DEFINITION

The legal structure of a business is crucial in determining how serious the financial impact is on the owners, if things go wrong. It also has an impact on the taxation levels to be paid by the business and its owners.

6.1 Businesses with unlimited liability

Unlimited liability means that the finances of the business are treated as inseparable from the finances of the business owner(s). So if the business loses £1 million, the people owed money (the **creditors**) can get the courts to force the individual owners to pay up. If that means selling their houses, cars etc., so be it. If the owner(s) cannot pay, they can be made personally **bankrupt**. Two types of business organisation have unlimited liability: sole traders and partnerships.

Sole traders

A **sole trader** is an individual who owns and operates his or her own business. Although there may be one or two employees, this person makes the final decisions about the running of the business. A sole trader is the only one who benefits financially from success, but must face the burden of any failure. In the eyes of the law the individual and the business are the same. This means that the owner has unlimited liability for any debts that result from running the firm. If a sole trader cannot pay his/her bills, the courts can allow personal assets to be seized by creditors in order to meet outstanding debts. For example, the family home or car may be sold. If insufficient funds can be raised in this way the person will be declared bankrupt.

Despite the financial dangers involved, the sole trader is the most common form of legal structure adopted by UK businesses. In some areas of the economy this kind of business dominates, particularly where little finance is required to set up and run the business and customers demand a personal service. Examples include trades such as builders and plumbers, and many independent shopkeepers.

There are no formal rules to follow when establishing a sole trader, or administrative costs to pay. Complete confidentiality can be maintained because accounts are not published. As a result many business start-ups adopt this structure.

The main disadvantages facing a sole trader are the limited sources of finance available, long hours of work involved (including the difficulty of taking a holiday) and concern with respect to running the business during periods of ill health.

Partnerships

Partnerships exist when two or more people start a business without forming a company. Like a sole trader, the individuals have unlimited liability for any debts run up by the business. Because people are working together but are unlimitedly liable for any debts, it is vital that the partners trust each other. As a result this legal structure is often found in the professions, such as medicine and law. If the partners fail to draw up a formal document, the 1890 Partnership Act sets out a series of rules that govern issues such as the distribution of profits.

The main difference between a sole trader and a partnership is the number of owners. The key advantages and disadvantages in forming a partnership are outlined below.

Advantages

- *Additional skills*: a new partner may have abilities that the sole trader does not possess. These can help to strengthen the business, perhaps allowing new products or services to be offered, or improving the quality of existing provision.

● *More capital*: a number of people together can inject more finance into the business than one person alone. This, plus the extra skills, makes expansion easier.

● *Shared strain*: the new partner will help to share the worry of running the business, as well as taking on a share of the workload. This should help to reduce stress and allow holidays to be taken.

Disadvantages

● *Sharing profit*: the financial benefits derived from running the business will have to be divided up between the partners according to the partnership agreement made on formation. This can easily lead to disagreements about 'fair' distribution of workload and profits.

● *Loss of control*: multiple ownership means that no individual can force an action on the business; decision making must be shared.

● *Unlimited liability*: it is one thing to be unlimitedly liable for your own mistakes (a sole trader), but far more worrying, surely, to have unlimited liability for the mistakes of your partners. This problem hit many investors in the Lloyds insurance market in the 1990s. Certain partnerships (called syndicates) lost millions of pounds from huge insurance claims. Some investors lost their life savings.

High-grade application

Yan Wu and Taurean Carter began an informal partnership selling jewellery. She bought and he sold. From small beginnings they built up a £120,000 a year business by year 3. Then they decided to open their first shop, and took the opportunity to go from 50/50 partners to 50%-50% shareholders. They had decided that they wanted the protection of limited liability status.

6.2 Businesses with limited liability

Limited liability means that the legal duty to pay debts run up by a business stays with the business itself, not its owner/shareholders. If a company has £1 million of debts that it lacks the cash to repay, the courts can force the business to sell all its assets (cars, computers, etc.). If there is still not enough money, the company is closed down, but the owner/shareholders have no personal liability for the remaining debts.

To gain the benefits of limited liability, the business must go through a legal process to become a company. The process of **incorporation** creates a separate legal identity for the organisation. In the eyes of the law the owners of the business and the company itself are now two different things. The business can take legal action against others and have legal action taken against it. Each owner is protected by limited liability, and their investment in the business is represented by the size of their shareholding. Limited liability sounds unfairly weighted towards the shareholders, but it encourages individuals to put forward capital because the financial risk is limited to the amount they invest.

In order to gain separate legal status a company must be registered with the **Registrar of Companies**. The following two key documents must be completed.

1 The Memorandum of Association, which governs the relationship between the company and the outside world. This includes the company name, the object of the company (often recorded simply as 'as the owners see fit'), limitation of liability and the size of the authorised share capital.

2 The Articles of Association, which outline the internal management of the company. This includes the rights of shareholders, the role of directors and frequency of shareholder meetings.

The key advantages and disadvantages that result from forming a limited company are as follows.

Advantages

● Shareholders experience the benefits of limited liability, including the confidence to expand.

● A limited company is able to gain access to a wider range of borrowing opportunities than a sole trader or partnership. This makes funding the growth of the business potentially easier.

Disadvantages

● Limited companies must make financial information available publicly at Companies House. Small firms are not required to make full disclosure of their company accounts, but they have to reveal more than would be the case for a sole trader or partnership.

● Limited companies have to follow more, and more expensive, rules than unlimited liability businesses (e.g. audited accounts and holding an annual general meeting of shareholders); these things add several thousand pounds to annual overhead costs.

In 2003, Duncan Goose quit his job and founded One Water. He wanted to finance water projects in Africa from profits made selling bottled water in Britain. The particular water project was 'Playpumps': children's roundabouts plumbed in to freshly dug water wells. As the kids play, each rotation of the roundabout brings up a litre of fresh, clean water.

Duncan thought of forming a charity, but soon realised that the regulations governing charities force them to be inefficient. So, for £125 he founded a limited company, Global Ethics Ltd. This enabled him to set the rules – for instance, that the shareholders receive no dividends and the directors receive no fees. But, of course, it ensured that he and other volunteers who put time into One Water are protected should something go wrong and big debts build up.

6.3 Private limited companies

A small business can be started up as a sole trader, a partnership or as a private limited company. For a private limited company, the start-up capital will often be £100, which can be wholly owned by the entrepreneur, or other people can be brought in as investors. The shares of a private limited company can not be bought and sold without the agreement of the other directors. This means the company can not be listed on the stock market. As a result it is possible to maintain close control over the way the business is run. This form of business is often run by a family or small group of friends. It may be very profit focused or, like Global Ethics Ltd, have wholly different objectives than maximising profit.

A legal requirement for private companies is that they must state 'Ltd' after the company name. This warns those dealing with the business that the firm is relatively small and has limited liability. Remember, limited liability protects shareholders from business debts, so there is a risk that 'cowboy' businesspeople might start a company, run it into the ground, then walk away from its debts. Therefore the cheques of a Ltd company are not as secure as ones from an unlimited liability business. This is why many petrol stations have notices saying 'No company cheques allowed.'

6.4 Public limited companies

When a private limited company expands to the point of having share capital of more than £50,000, it can convert to a public limited company. This means it can be floated on the stock market, which allows any member of the general public to buy shares. This increases the company's access to share capital, which enables it to expand considerably. The term 'plc' will appear after the company name (e.g. Marks & Spencer plc, Tesco plc).

The principal differences between private and public limited companies are:

- a public company can raise capital from the general public, while a private limited company is prohibited from doing so

- the minimum capital requirement of a public company is £50,000. There is no minimum for a private limited company

- public companies must publish far more detailed accounts than private limited companies.

Almost every large business is a plc. Yet the process of converting from a private to a public company can be difficult. Usually, successful small firms grow steadily,

Table 6.1 When should a business start up as a sole trader and when as a private limited company?

Sole trader	Private limited company
When the entrepreneur has no intention of expanding, e.g. just wants to run one restaurant in Warwick	When the entrepreneur has ambitions to expand quickly and therefore needs it to be easier to raise extra finance
When there is no need for substantial bank borrowing, i.e. start-up costs are low	When large borrowings mean significant chances of large losses if things go wrong
When the business will be small enough to mean that one person can make all the big decisions	When the business may require others to make decisions, e.g. when the entrepreneur is on holiday or unwell

perhaps at a rate of 10 or 15% a year. Even that pace of growth causes problems, but good managers can cope. The problem of floating onto the stock market is that it provides a sudden, huge injection of cash. This sounds great, but it forces the firm to try to grow more quickly, otherwise the new shareholders will say 'What are you doing with our cash?' (see the 'High-grade application' on Sports Direct).

High-grade application

Sports Direct

On 28 February 2007, Mike Ashley made over £900 million when he floated Sports Direct onto the London stock market. Ashley had owned 100% of Sports Direct, and sold 43% of his shares at 300p a share. Within a few months City analysts were troubled by the way Ashley seemed too keen to spend his money. He bought 3% of the shares in Adidas, then made a takeover bid for Newcastle United. He also seemed desperate to spend the money raised by Sports Direct, as it went on a shopping spree including Blacks Leisure, Field & Trek and the Everlast boxing equipment company. With so much going on, it seemed that no one was paying enough attention to the company's trading position. Revenues and profits dropped back and, within six months of the float, the shares had halved in value.

Other problems with public limited companies

- When a firm becomes a plc, it becomes hard to hold on to any objective other than profit. This is because City analysts and business journalists criticise heavily any business that is not making more money this year than last. This pressure may have been the underlying problem that led BP to underspend on safety measures in America, leading to the deaths of 15 of its workers at a refinery in Texas in 2005.

- The extent to which any one individual, or group, can maintain control of an organisation is severely limited by the sale of its shares on the stock exchange. For example, a family may find its influence on a business diminished when a listing is obtained. In turn, this means that publicly quoted companies are always vulnerable to a takeover bid. In 2007 the Sainsbury family, with just a 25% stake in the family business, nearly lost the family grocer to a multi-billion-pound takeover bid.

- Shareholders are the owners of public limited companies, but they do not make decisions on a day-to-day basis. Many have little detailed knowledge of the firm's operations; nor can they know the directors who, theoretically, they vote on to and off the board. In fact, it is usually the chairman and chief executive who run the show. They have control, though the shareholders supposedly have the power. This situation is known as the 'divorce of ownership and control', and it may lead the directors to pursue the interests of their own careers and bank balances rather than the best interests of the business and its staff.

- A separate problem that may be caused by the divorce of ownership and control is 'short-termism'. In private companies, where shareholders and directors are usually family members, the desire is to build a successful business to hand over to the next generation. This is how the great retail firms such as Sainsbury's and Marks & Spencer built themselves up. In plcs, the lack of concern about the long-term future of the shareholders may lead directors to focus too much on the short term. Much research has shown that British managements are more likely than others to focus upon short-term issues, possibly to the neglect of long-term investment in research and development (R&D) or staff training.

6.5 Other forms of business organisation

Franchises

Franchises exist so that large businesses can cooperate with sole proprietors. This has become a very popular type of business ownership in recent years because it takes away some of the risk associated with running a business.

A franchise consists of the franchiser, which is usually a large plc such as McDonalds, and a franchisee who sets up the business using the brand name. In return for the name, marketing, training and product, the franchisee pays the franchiser an initial fee and continuing royalty payments. These royalty payments are a percentage payment made for the use of the franchiser's product and property.

Like all forms of business ownership this has advantages and disadvantages for both the franchiser and the franchisee.

The franchisee obviously gains increased likelihood of success from the established name and product, and from the continuing support of the franchiser. They may also find it easier to raise money. However there are royalties to be paid, less independence than a sole trader and the risk that the franchise may not be renewed.

The franchiser is able to expand without investing large amounts of capital and this often results in large injections of cash into the business. The disadvantage is the loss of some control over how the brand is being sold, which could impact on the image of the company.

Cooperatives

These can be worker-owned, such as John Lewis/ Waitrose, or customer owned, such as the retail Coop. Cooperatives have the potential to offer a more united cause for the workforce than the profit of shareholders. Workers at John Lewis can enjoy annual bonuses of 20% of their salary as their share of the company's profits. The Coop has been less successful, though its focus on ethical trading has made it more relevant to today's shoppers.

Not-for-profit organisations
Mutual businesses

Mutual businesses, including many building societies and mutual life assurance businesses, have no shareholders and no owners. They exist solely for the best interests of their members (i.e. customers). In the 1980s and 1990s traditional mutual societies such as Abbey National and the Halifax turned into private companies. Nationwide now says it is 'proud to be different', as it is still a true building society (i.e. it has no shareholders pressuring for profits).

Charities

Many important organisations have charitable status; these include pressure groups such as Greenpeace and Friends of the Earth. They also include conventional charities such as Oxfam and Save The Children Fund. Charitable status ensures that those who fund the charity are not liable for any debts. It also provides significant tax benefits.

Issues For Analysis

When analysing which type of organisation is the most suitable for a business, consider the following factors.

- The financial risks involved: manufacturing businesses require heavy investment in plant and equipment before anything is available for sale. Therefore a great deal of capital is put at risk. This

suggests limited liability is essential. Some service businesses such as tax advisers or dry cleaners require relatively little capital outlay. If the owner intends to finance the start-up without any borrowings, there is no need to seek limited liability.

- The image you wish to portray: although cautious businesses may refuse company cheques, most people think 'M. Staton Ltd' sounds more established and professional than 'Mervin Staton'. In the same vein, a small software production company called TIB Ltd changed its name to TIB plc. It rightly thought that this sounds bigger and more impressive. What's in a name? Ask Coca-Cola …

- An organisation considering a move to public company status and a stock market listing has far bigger issues to consider. It must weigh the benefits to be gained, particularly in terms of raising additional finance, against the costs incurred and the loss of control. Many business questions can be analysed fruitfully by considering the short versus the long term. Private (family) versus public (stock market investor) ownership is a classic case in point.

6.6 Business ownership
an evaluation

Business organisation is a dry, technical subject. It does contain some important business themes, however; three are particularly valuable sources of evaluative comment.

1 The existence of limited liability has had huge effects on business. Some have been unarguably beneficial. How could firms become really big if the owners felt threatened by equally big debts? Limited liability helps firms take reasonable business risks; it also, however, gives scope for dubious business practices. Start a firm, live a great lifestyle, then go into liquidation leaving the customers/ creditors out of pocket. Then start again. All too often this is the story told by programmes such as the BBC's *Watchdog*. Companies Acts try to make this harder to do, but it still happens. Such unethical behaviour is why government intervention to protect the consumer can always be justified.

2 Bill Gates and Richard Branson are worth billions of dollars (at the time of writing!). How can such wealth be justified for people who do not save lives (doctors) or help build them (teachers)? The answer lies in the risks involved in business. For every Richard Branson there are hundreds

of thousands of small entrepreneurs who sunk their life savings into a business and saw those savings sink. Sadly, there are thousands every year who end up personally bankrupt. In other words, in a business world in which risk is ever present, rewards for success should be accepted.

3 Short-termism is a curse for effective business decision making. There is no proof that a stock exchange listing leads to short-termism, only the suspicion that in many cases it does. Of course, massive companies, such as Unilever, Nestlé and Shell, are likely to be above the pressures for short-term performance. In many other cases, though, it seems that British company directors focus too much on the short-term share price. Could this be because their huge bonuses depend on how the share price is? Worries about shareholder pressures or takeover bids may distract managers from building a long-term business in the way that companies such as BMW and Toyota have done.

Key terms

Bankrupt: when an individual is unable to meet personal liabilities, some or all of which can be as a consequence of business activities.

Creditors: those owed money by a business (e.g. suppliers and bankers).

Incorporation: establishing a business as a separate legal entity from its owners, and therefore giving the owners limited liability.

Limited liability: owners are not liable for the debts of the business; they can lose no more than the sum they invested.

Registrar of Companies: the government department that can allow firms to become incorporated; located at Companies House, where Articles of Association, Memorandums of Association and the annual accounts of limited companies are available for public scrutiny.

Sole trader: a one-person business with unlimited liability.

Unlimited liability: owners are liable for any debts incurred by the business, even if this requires them to sell all their assets and possessions and become personally bankrupt.

Exercises

A. Revision questions

(25 marks; 25 minutes)

1 Explain two differences between a sole trader and a partnership. (4)

2 In your own words, try to explain the importance of establishing a separate legal entity to separate the business from the individual owner. (4)

3 You can start a business today. All you have to do is tell the Inland Revenue (the taxman). Outline two risks of starting in this way. (4)

4 Briefly discuss whether each of the following businesses should start as a sole trader, a partnership or a private limited company:

(a) a clothes shop started by Claire Wells with £40,000 of her own money plus £10,000 from the bank; it is located close to her home in Wrexham (3)

(b) a builders started by Jim Barton and Lee Clark, who plan to become the number one for loft extensions in Sheffield; they've each invested £15,000 and are borrowing £30,000 from the bank. (3)

5 Explain the possible risks to a growing business of making the jump from a private limited company to 'going public', then floating its shares on the stock market. (5)

6 In what way may the type of business organisation affect the image of the business? (2)

B. Revision exercises

B1 Data response

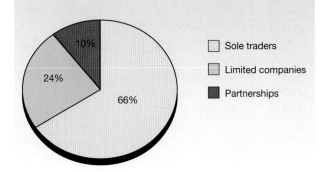

Figure 6.1 UK business organisations (total = 3,600,000)
Source: Fraser, S. (2005). *Finance for Small and Medium Sized Enterprises: The United Kingdom Survey of SME Finances, 2004.*

Questions

(20 marks; 20 minutes)

1a Calculate the number of sole traders in the UK; then calculate the number of limited companies. (3)

1b Explain two possible reasons why there are so many more sole traders than companies. (6)

2 What proportion of British businesses operate with unlimited liability? (1)

3 Dr Fraser's research also shows that one in five businesses is principally owned by a woman, and that 93% are owned by white and 7% by non-white ethnicity.

a Examine two possible reasons why women are so much less likely to own a business than men. (6)

b The % figures for non-white business ownership are slightly below the number of non-whites in the population (between 8 and 9%). Outline two reasons that might explain this. (4)

B2 Data response

In April 2007 Bernice Armstrong opened Devoted 2 Vintage in Hemel Hempstead, just north of London. She believed there was a gap locally for an independent shop buying and selling vintage clothes. Her own love of vintage clothes made her keen to start, and gave her insight both into sources of supply and distinguishing desirable clothes from ones that should go to charity shops.

In 2007 celebrity magazines were full of swirly 1960s clothes, so Bernice made every effort to focus on 1960s originals, for example by Mary Quant, inventor of the mini skirt. Her price range was from £10–£100, making the clothes affordable for all. By late summer 2007 Bernice was focusing her efforts on developing an online vintage clothing store.

To follow up this story, go to www.devoted2vintage.co.uk

Questions

(20 marks; 25 minutes)

1a The name of the business is Devoted 2 Vintage. Does that suggest it's a sole trader or a private limited company? (1)

1b Bearing in mind your answer to 1a, outline two factors Bernice should remember about the legal structure of the business she is running. (6)

2 As Bernice expands the business to develop online, should she consider changing the legal structure of the business? If so, why and how? (6)

3 Discuss how well Bernice has done so far in setting up her first business. (7)

B3 Data response

Polar plc is a refrigeration business based in the south-west of England. It maintains and sells refrigeration units to large supermarkets and storage facilities all over the country. The board of directors would like to expand their operations into the growing economies of India and China. This would require them either to build or buy factories and storage facilities in these areas or to franchise out the operations to local manufacturers. This expansion will cost about £10 million to put into effect. The board is hoping that they will get the support of their shareholders at the next AGM.

Questions

(30 marks; 40 minutes)

1 Explain the role of the board of directors in a public limited company. (4)

2 Analyse two ways in which Polar plc might finance the proposed expansion. (6)

3 Explain two disadvantages for Polar plc of franchising their operations abroad. (6)

4 Polar plc has many stakeholders. Which stakeholders would be most affected by the decision to expand? Give reasons for your answer. (12)

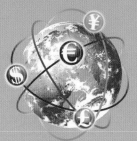

CORPORATE OBJECTIVES AND STAKEHOLDERS

7.1 Objectives and stakeholders

At the heart of every organisation is a set of goals or objectives. They provide it with direction and a sense of purpose. The business will also have a number of **stakeholders**; these are managers, employees, customers, suppliers/ creditors, owners/shareholders, government and the local community – in fact, all those who have an interest in the business. In theory, the stakeholders will be motivated and unified by these common aims and objectives. In reality, often the stakeholders have different objectives and conflict can sometimes arise.

In the **public sector**, the state runs a variety of activities and enterprises, such as trust hospitals and schools. The objectives of this sector are primarily to provide a high-quality but cost-effective service, and any profit made is used to improve the quality of the service or to reduce taxation. However, this does not mean that stakeholders are any the less interested in the achievement of the objectives, as many of them are regularly affected by the success or failure of these organisations.

The objectives of a new business will differ from those of more established organisations, and may well emphasise survival as the main objective in the first years. In later years, however, this objective, although still important, might be superseded by the desire to expand or achieve higher levels of profit. In all cases, the objectives of a business will depend on its legal status, size, the products/services it offers and its organisational culture. Business success comes when directors, managers and workers share a common vision for the firm's future.

7.2 Mission statements

It is unlikely that any business will have only one objective. When a business is formed it will have broad aims, which might be expressed in its **mission statement**. For example:

> Gap Inc. is a brand-builder. We create emotional connections with customers around the world through inspiring product design, unique store experiences and compelling marketing.

For many stakeholders, the first reaction when reading this would be: 'What?!' Mission statements such as this are often criticised as public relations tools of no real use to a business. Would stakeholders actually remember it and would it affect what they do?

What it might do is to set standards against which the activities of the business can be judged. A 'unique store experience' is one measure against which the customer can judge the firm. This encourages the business to be **accountable** to the customer. It could be measured by:

- short queues at checkouts
- width of aisles
- accessibility of products for older or disabled people
- level of knowledge from assistants
- range of products.

Would a manager define 'a unique customer experience' in the same way? Would a shareholder be interested? Would the government care?

Tesco has taken this idea and incorporated it into its overall strategy, identifying that customers are a very important stakeholder group and should be treated as such.

Figure 7.1 Its accessibility for the disabled is a standard by which a business may be judged by customers

High-grade application

Tesco

'Customers have told us they want: clear aisles, to be able to get what they want at a good price, no queues, and great staff. We call this our Every Little Helps Shopping Trip for customers, and use it every day to ensure we are always working hard to make Tesco a better place to shop, at home and abroad.'

7.3 Implementing objectives

Unlike mission statements, objectives need to be specific in terms of quantitative value, the area of business (department) and the time period involved. This idea of measurement is often referred to as SMART:

- **S**pecific — What do they want to achieve?

- **M**easurable — Has it been achieved based on performance criteria?

- **A**greed — All those stakeholders responsible understand and agree the objectives

- **R**elevant — to the organisation

  and

- **R**ealistic — or capable of being achieved

- **T**ime-bound — Final date for completion is timetabled

A business needs to consider where it is, where it wants to be, how it is progressing and what it needs to do. When considering this, the board of directors will decide upon **corporate objectives** – for example, market growth, profitability and increased dividends paid to shareholders.

From this starting point the board or senior managers set the **strategic objectives**. These are then applied at corporate or divisional level, and seen as medium- to long-term targets. In the case above the strategic objectives might relate to market share, sales revenue, cost-cutting and productivity. For example:

Strategic objectives: To increase sales revenue by 8% next year

To reduce operating costs by 5% over the next 3 years

To increase productivity by 25% in the next 5 years

Senior and middle managers then draw up **tactical objectives**, which are short-term departmental performance targets. These might include raising output by 6% in the next six months. At this stage it is important that any objective set is realistic and achievable. Consultation and proper research are paramount if the objective is to be achieved in a realistic time scale.

This process of setting objectives is often referred to as the **hierarchy of objectives**. Each firm's objectives will be unique, and will often depend upon the relative power of the stakeholders. Problems arise when different stakeholders want different things (see Table 7.1).

Conflict between stakeholders is perhaps inevitable, and often due to a breakdown in communication between the interested parties. Some of the conflict in recent years has been caused by changes in society, global movement of labour, outsourcing of production, outsourcing of customer service, loss of pensions, high fuel prices, increased use of technology, waste management, and so on. It is in no one's interests that these conflicts exist if a business is to thrive.

7.4 Accountability

However, no business can stand still. The world changes and priorities change. Businesses and governments come under pressure to change the way they produce and sell their goods and services. They have become *accountable* for their actions. For example, in the last 30 years, more and more businesses have realised that **social**

Table 7.1 Potential areas of conflict between different stakeholders

Stakeholder	Needs	Example of conflict
Manager	Salary, status, independence, responsibility	With employees over targets With customers over prices, service, quality
Employee	Good wage, security, prospects	With managers over hours, wages With shareholders over cost, profit and dividend payments
Customer	Low prices, good quality, good service	With employees/managers over prices etc.
Government	Profits, exports, employment	With business over legislation, e.g. minimum wage
Community	Jobs, no pollution, sponsorship	Levels of traffic, noise, demise of high street
Suppliers/creditors	Prompt payment, regular orders	With managers over payment and terms
Shareholders	High dividends, increased share value	With board and managers over high costs, low profits

responsibility should form part of their strategic objectives. For example:

Energy efficiency in Thailand

Tesco is committed to reducing our energy consumption and use of greenhouse gases.

In Thailand, Tesco Lotus has spent £3.1 million on energy conservation at 49 stores, which has resulted in energy savings of approximately £2 million. At our new flagship 'green' store in Bangkok, solar panels the area of three football pitches cover more than half of the roof. These provide 12.5% of the store's energy consumption and save 400 tonnes of carbon dioxide. It is the largest rooftop solar energy system in the region. Even the benches at the front of the store are made of photo-voltaic panels. Tesco Lotus is evaluating the success of this scheme and hopes to introduce similar measures in new stores.

With some aspects of these changes the business has a choice; in others, changes in objectives are forced upon firms through legislation such as the minimum wage, health and safety, fuel emissions and noise pollution.

Any move towards social responsibility, whether by choice or not, will in most cases result in increased costs

Figure 7.2 Tesco Lotus's flagship 'green' store in Bangkok

for the firm. Large businesses in the developed world can to some extent afford to bear these increased costs if they choose to do so, and if it does not create too much conflict with other stakeholders. In less affluent countries, such as China and India, companies often have different priorities when setting objectives. They feel that, for now, growth in sales and profits are more important than the environment.

7.5 Corporate objectives and stakeholders
an evaluation

This chapter identifies how businesses deal with an ever-changing environment. In the past 150 years, the impact of invention and innovation has transformed the market, which has become truly global. Therefore when questions are asked about the objectives of business and what businesses do, the whole picture must be assessed. No single part of business or the environment in which it operates can be ignored, if any past, present or future action is to be evaluated effectively.

Businesses sell products and services both to individuals and to other businesses. Every business must attempt to meet the needs of some, if not all, of its stakeholders. It attempts to do this by adding value to its products and services by transforming inputs into outputs, and by enhancing the end product through marketing techniques.

Key terms

Accountable: the idea that a business and its owners are responsible and answerable to the stakeholders for their activities.

Corporate objectives: long/medium-term objectives that reflect the overall aims of the business.

Hierarchy of objectives: a model of how the different objectives relate to each in a hierarchical manner.

Mission statement: a statement that expresses the goals of the business and the image that the organisation stands for.

Public sector: in this sector organisations are owned and run on behalf of the public by central or local government.

Social responsibility: the responsibility of an organisation to maximise positive impact on society and minimise negative impact on society.

Stakeholders: people or groups who have an interest in the success of the business.

Strategic objectives: long/medium-term objectives that enable the business to achieve the corporate objectives.

Tactical objectives: medium/short-term objectives that enable the business to achieve the strategic objectives.

Exercises

A. Revision questions

(30 marks; 30 minutes)

1 What is meant by a stakeholder? (2)

2 Distinguish between the 'shareholder' and 'stakeholder' concepts. (3)

3 Some people believe that an increasing number of firms are now trying to meet their social responsibilities. Explain why this might be the case. (3)

4 Outline two responsibilities a firm may have to each of the following stakeholders:
   (a) Its employees (4)
   (b) Its customers (4)
   (c) The local community (4)

5 Some managers reject the idea of stakeholding. They believe a company's duty is purely to its shareholders. Examine one point in favour and one point against this opinion. (6)

6 What factors are likely to determine whether or not a firm accepts its responsibilities to a particular stakeholder group? (4)

B. Revision exercises

B1 Data response

Shareholders versus stakeholders

In a recent poll, 72 per cent of UK business leaders said shareholders were served best if the company concentrated on customers, suppliers and other stakeholders. Only 17 per cent thought focusing on shareholders was the only way to succeed. This represents a marked change from five years ago, when the stakeholding idea was widely ignored.

However, not everyone agrees with the stakeholder view. According to two UK writers, Shiv Mathur and Alfred Kenyon, '[The stakeholder view] mistakes the essential nature of a business. A business is not a moral agent at all. It is an investment project ... Its raison d'etre is financial.'

Others believe the stakeholder and shareholder views do not necessarily conflict with each other. For example, the US consultant James Knight writes:

'Managing a company for value requires delivering maximum return to the investors while balancing the interests of the other important constituents, including customers and employees. Companies that consistently deliver value for investors have learned this lesson.'

Source: adapted from *The Financial Times*

Questions

(30 marks; 35 minutes)

1 Distinguish between shareholders and stakeholders. (4)

2 Analyse the possible reasons for the growth in popularity of the stakeholder view in recent years. (8)

3 Examine the factors which might influence whether a firm adopts the stakeholder or shareholder approach. (8)

4 Discuss the view that the interests of shareholders and stakeholders necessarily conflict. (10)

B2 Case study

BP: shareholder or stakeholder approach?

'Our business is run on the principles of strong corporate governance, a clear system of delegating accountability and a set of values and policies that guide our behaviour.'

Source: BP's website

On 23 March 2005, a huge explosion at BP's Texas oil refinery killed 15 people and injured more than 180. Most of those were its own staff. The refinery, America's third biggest, had suffered safety problems before. In 2004, 2 workers died when scalded by super-heated water that escaped from a high-pressure pipe.

In Texas, the local media were outraged by 'yet

another' safety scandal involving BP. However, BP's reputation in Britain was largely unaffected. It remained a media darling for its constant references to global warming, sustainability and social responsibility. Journalists were used to praising BP for its ethical standards. Its website used – and uses – lots of green colours to communicate its message: BP is a socially responsible, ethical company.

In 2006, more bad headlines came from another part of America. In January, BP was fined $1.42 million for safety violations at its Prudhoe Bay oilfield in Alaska. Two months later, a hole in an oil pipeline leaked more than 1.2 million litres of oil, creating an environmental 'catastrophe'. BP had failed to maintain the pipeline properly.

In November 2006, an official US report made it clear that BP managers had known of 'significant safety problems' at the Texas refinery long before the deadly explosion. The US Chemical Safety Board (CSB) found numerous internal BP reports setting out maintenance backlogs and poor, ageing equipment. Late in October 2006, the CSB Chairwoman blamed the explosion on 'ageing infrastructure, overzealous cost-cutting, inadequate design and risk blindness'.

She went on to say that 'BP implemented a 25 per cent cut in fixed costs from 1998 to 2000, that adversely impacted maintenance expenditures at the refinery'. The report stated

that 'BP's global management [i.e. the British head office] was aware of problems with maintenance spending and infrastructure well before March 2005'. Yet they did nothing about it. The Chairwoman delivered the final critique:

'Every successful corporation must contain its costs. But at an ageing facility like Texas City, it is not responsible to cut budgets related to safety and maintenance without thoroughly examining the impact on the risk of a catastrophic accident.'

BP confirmed that its own internal investigation had findings 'generally consistent with those of the CSB'.

Questions

(30 marks; 40 minutes)

1 Explain two possible reasons why BP went wrong in its attitude to human and environmental safety in its US operations. (6)

2 Given the evidence in the case study, comment briefly on the statement at the top of the box, taken from BP's website. (4)

3 Discuss whether BP was taking a 'shareholder' or 'stakeholder' approach to its decision making during the period covered by the text. (10)

4 Is it time for stronger government controls on business activities? (10)

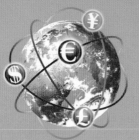

Unit 8

THE MARKETPLACE

8.1 Types of market

Local vs national

Most new small firms know and care little about the size of the national market. If you have just bought an ice cream van that you intend to operate in Chichester, it doesn't matter whether the size of the UK market for ice cream is £500 million or £600 million a year. Your concern is the level of demand and the level of competition locally. And you will probably be delighted if you achieve annual sales of £0.1 million (£100,000).

In the case of the market for ice cream in Chichester there are several things to consider.

- How do locals buy ice cream at the moment? (Multipacks from supermarkets? Individual cones from ice cream stalls or vans?)

- How many tourists come to the city? Do they come all year round? What type of ice cream do they buy? Where do they buy it?

- How much competition is there, what do competitors offer and charge at the moment? Are there gaps in the market that you can move into?

Other firms are focused more on the national market. For example, Klein Caporn is a small food company that started in 2005. It produces high-quality, high-priced ready-to-eat meals. It started by targeting small grocers, but soon found that the sales volumes were too low to cover its costs. A sales breakthrough in Waitrose supermarkets was followed in 2007 by acceptance by Sainsbury's. This enables the company to deliver to just two warehouses, cutting the business costs dramatically; then Waitrose and Sainsbury's distribute to their local shops. So Klein Caporn has a national presence even

though sales remain well below 1% of the market for ready meals.

To deal on the national level, Klein Caporn has to deal professionally with the supermarket buyers, and produce eye-catching packaging that can compete effectively with that of national and multinational competitors.

Physical and electronic (virtual)

All markets used to be physical. The London Stock Exchange was a place where buyers met sellers and face-to-face agreements took place. Similarly, auctions were physical, with bidders having to catch the eye of the auctioneer.

Today an increasing number of markets are electronic. The stock market exists only on computer screens, and the likes of eBay are transforming auction and other markets worldwide.

From a business point of view the key factors about electronic markets (e.g. for finding hotel rooms or flights) are that:

- they are fiercely price competitive, so the companies supplying services have huge pressure to keep their costs as low as possible

- they do not rely on physical location (e.g. a business can easily be run from a bedroom, such as selling PS1 computer games)

- the market is easy and quite cheap to enter, so new competitors can arrive at any time

- they provide a 'long tail' of competitive, profitable small businesses, able to carve their own little niche in markets; this is very difficult to achieve in the high street, where rents are so high that only big firms can afford them.

8.2 Factors determining demand

Demand is the desire of consumers to buy a product or service, when backed by the ability to pay. It is also known as 'effective demand' (i.e. only when the customer has the money is demand effective). Several factors determine the demand for a specific product/service.

Price

This affects demand in three ways.

1 You may want an £80,000 Mercedes convertible, but you cannot afford it (i.e. the price puts it beyond your income level); the higher the price, the more people there are who cannot afford to buy.

2 The higher the price, the less good value the item will seem compared with other ways of spending the money (e.g. a Chelsea home ticket costing £48 is the equivalent of going to the cinema six to eight times, so is it worth it?); the higher the price of an item, the more there will be people who say 'It's not worth it.'

3 It should be remembered that the price tag put on an item gives a message about its 'value' (i.e. a ring priced at 99p will inevitably be seen as 'cheap', whether or not it is value for money), so although lower prices should boost sales, firms must beware of ruining their image for quality.

Incomes

The British economy grows at about 2.5% a year. This means that average income levels double every 30 years. Broadly, when your kids are about 16–18 years old, you are likely to be twice as well off as your parents are today. Economic growth means we all get richer over time (and lazier, and fatter, and spend more time in traffic jams).

The demand for most products and services grows as the economy grows. Goods like cars and cinema tickets are **normal goods**, for which demand rises broadly in line with incomes. In some cases it grows even faster (e.g. if the economy grows by 3% in a year, the amount spent on foreign holidays can easily rise by 6%). This type of product is known as a **luxury good**.

Still other goods behave differently, with sales falling when people are better off. These products are known as **inferior goods**. In their case, rising incomes mean falling sales. For example, the richer we get, the more Tropicana fruit juice we buy and the less Tesco orange squash. As orange squash is an inferior good, a couple of years of economic struggle (and perhaps more people out of work) would mean sales would increase as people switch from expensive Tropicana to cheap squash.

Actions of competitors

Demand for British Airways' Heathrow–New York flights does not only depend on their price and the incomes of consumers. It also depends on the actions of BA's rivals. If Virgin Atlantic is running a brilliant advertising campaign, demand for BA flights might fall as customers switch to Virgin. Or if American Airlines pushes its prices up, people might switch to BA.

The firm's own marketing activities

Following the same logic, if British Airways is running a new advertising campaign, perhaps based on improved customer service, it may enjoy increased sales. In effect its sales will rise if it can persuade customers to switch from Virgin and American Airlines to BA. One firm's sales increase usually means reduced sales elsewhere.

Seasonal factors

Most firms experience significant variations in sales through the year. Some markets boom in the summer and slump in the winter, such as ice cream, soft drinks, lager and seaside hotels. Others boom at Christmas, such as sales of perfume, liqueurs, greetings cards and toys. Other products that have less obvious reasons for seasonal variations in demand include cars, cat food, carpets, furniture, TVs and newspapers. The variation is caused by patterns of customer behaviour; nothing can be done about that. A well-run business makes sure it understands and can predict seasonal variations in demand, and then has a plan for coping.

8.3 Factors determining supply

Supply is the quantity of a product/service producers are prepared to sell at a particular price. In a dynamic and ever changing marketplace, the interaction of demand and supply is key to the success of an economy. This is particularly true in a free enterprise economy where the interaction of buyers and sellers determines the success of the market. Like demand, several factors determine the supply of products/services. These include:

- changes in the cost of inputs
- changes in technology
- changes in taxes or subsidies.

Price

In general terms, as price increases the quantity the supplier is prepared to supply increases. This is because, when the price is low, producers will be unable to make a profit, so the supply is limited. At high prices many small, large and even inefficient producers can enter the market and make a profit, therefore supply is large. Obviously it is logical to assume that firms will make more of a product/service if they can get a good price for it.

Cost of inputs

A key factor in supply is the cost of the materials (e.g. ingredients) used in the production process. The higher the costs, the harder it will be to make a profit, unless it is possible to pass on the higher costs to customers by increasing prices. In February 2008, shares in Premier Foods fell from 120p to 85p when the company said that its Hovis brand was struggling to pass on the huge price increase in wheat.

Changes in taxes or subsidies

If the government decides to increase a tax such as national insurance, firms may choose to reduce their supplies. This is because higher taxes on employees make it less profitable to supply.

8.4 Interaction of demand and supply

In theory the quantity buyers wish to buy and the quantity the suppliers are prepared to offer will determine the **equilibrium price**. In reality this is rarely the case. Many internal/external factors act upon both consumers and producers to set prices at levels other than those of the equilibrium price.

Some of these factors are:

- minimum price legislation – minimum wage

- EU policies – Common Agricultural Policy (CAP).

When a price is set *above* the equilibrium price more will be supplied at that price and demand will fall. This will result in **excess supply**. An example of this situation is the CAP. The **European Union (EU)** buys surplus food at intervention prices and stores it for future release in times of shortage. These high prices encourage producers to produce more of these products knowing that they will be bought. This results in excess supply, and butter mountains, beef mountains and wine lakes have been created as a consequence.

If a price is set *below* the equilibrium price then less will be supplied and demand will rise. This will lead to **excess demand**. In the long term a free market that is unregulated will attempt to push the price towards the equilibrium. Sometimes, increased competition will force prices down, or the use of cheap labour and payment in cash can avoid the problem of regulations such as the minimum wage.

Most markets, however, are regulated to some extent and therefore surpluses and shortages may continue in the long term.

The article reproduced below illustrates how two different products can be linked in terms of the interaction of demand and supply.

Leading dairy companies claim that milk supplies are already 10 per cent down because persistent rainfall has forced farmers to keep cattle indoors, which reduces milk yield. July production figures are to be published shortly, and it is possible that the decline may be more marked.

Industry experts believe that prices to farmers must rise from 20p to at least 25p a litre and that with global pressure on food such as wheat, chicken and meat, and shortages of vegetables caused by floods, supermarkets will be forced to put up prices.

Traditionally, retail chains have absorbed extra costs of staple items such as milk and bread and sell them as loss-leaders. They may do so again but insiders believe the era of cheap food in Britain is coming to an end and that they will have to pass on increases to customers in the autumn.

Source: *Times Online*, July 2007

In reality most markets do not self-regulate. In most cases there is a degree of regulation put in place to protect the buyer and the seller. In a free market, the market should ensure that the consumer obtains the products they want at the lowest possible price. In this case anyone can enter the market and products are generally undifferentiated. However, in the modern world there is interference in the market from governments and organisations such as the EU, which restrict this level of competition and, at the other end of the scale, rein back the monopolistic tendencies of large business.

There is a great deal of competition and businesses have to fight for their place in the market. Profit is the driving force behind this. It is the reward for risk taking, it encourages efficiency and it provides the resources for expansion and growth.

8.5 The marketplace

an evaluation

When England flopped out of the European Championships in November 2007, the shares in Sports Direct plc fell by 20%. Not only was its retail business going to suffer from a collapse in sales of England shirts, but the company also had a 29.9% share stake in Umbro, England's kit-maker. Share buyers reasoned that a slump in the market for England shirts would shrink the size of the market for sports leisurewear. Well-run businesses try to make sure that they can benefit from opportunities, but avoid being too badly hit by slumps. They understand their market – from customers through to competitors.

Key terms

Equilibrium price: the price at which producers are prepared to supply and consumers are prepared to buy.

European Union (EU): a union of countries in Europe with close economic, social and political ties.

Excess demand: where prices are set at a low level and consumers are prepared to buy more than suppliers are prepared to supply.

Excess supply: where prices are set at a high level and producers are prepared to supply more than consumers are prepared to buy.

Inferior goods: products that people turn to when they are hard up, and turn away from when they are better off (e.g. Tesco Value Baked Beans instead of Heinz).

Luxury goods: Products that people buy much more of when they feel better off (e.g. jewellery, sports cars and holidays at posh hotels).

Normal goods: Products or services (e.g. travel and fast food) for which sales change broadly in line with the economy (i.e. economy grows 3%, sales rise 3%).

Supply: the quantity of a product that a producer is prepared to sell at a particular price.

Exercises

A. Revision questions

(24 marks; 45 minutes)

1 Outline three features of the market for fast food near to where you live. (6)

2 Section 8.2 lists five factors determining the demand for a product: price, incomes, actions of competitors, marketing activities and seasonality. Identify which two of these would most heavily affect sales of:
  (a) strawberries
  (b) easyJet tickets to Barcelona
  (c) tickets to see Newcastle United
  (d) DFS furniture. (8)

3 Analyse the effect of minimum wage legislation on the demand and supply for labour, taking account of the long-term effects on:
  • wages
  • costs
  • prices
  • demand for products
  • employment. (10)

B. Revision exercises

B1 Data response

Prices to rise as 'era of cheap food is over'

The price of a loaf of bread is likely to rise 5p as a result of spiralling wheat prices, a leading firm of agricultural accountants has said. The price of milk, poultry and pork is also expected to rise as a result of an increase in the cost of livestock feed, according to Deloitte.

Wheat and maize prices are now at the highest level in more than a decade. Arable farmers are now making £130 a ton for their wheat, up from £80 last year, and the trend in prices is up.

Mark Hill, food and agriculture partner at the firm, warned that rising demand for wheat and maize was bound to result in increases in the price of staple foods for British consumers.

Mr Hill said the era of cheap subsidised food, which had lasted since the war, was over. He added, 'I think we are going to see sustained price inflation – a general upward trend for staple foods such as grains, milk and meat. The reason is a very finely balance between supply and consumption. The International Grains Council is predicting wheat production this year at 623 million tons and consumption at 622 million tons.'

He said that an increasing trend of turning wheat and corn into alternative fuels, had come at a time when grain stocks had been run down. Grain supplies were already under pressure as a result of bad weather which reduced harvests and pushed up prices last year.

Over 20 per cent of the maize crop in the United States is now used for the production of ethanol. The knock-on effect on the price of wheat, an alternative in processed food, suggested the wheat price was 'only headed one way', said Mr Hill.

European farmers have asked the European Commission to allow them to grow crops on the 8 per cent of land currently taken out of production as 'set-aside' next year. But Mr Hill said that even if this was approved it was unlikely to make a large difference as most of the land currently taken out of production was of the lowest quality. And although the EU has nearly ten million acres of land which could be returned to farm production, much of it is in environmental schemes, he added.

In the longer term, predicted growth in the world population from the current six billion to nine billion by 2050, plus growing consumer affluence in China and India, could double global grain consumption within the next 40 years, say Deloitte.

Source: Charles Clover, The Daily Telegraph, 17 April 2008

Questions

(20 marks; 25 minutes)

1 Using the information in the article, explain two reasons why there has been an increase in the price of wheat. (4)

2 Using your knowledge of the determinants of demand and supply, explain why the increase in the price of wheat affects the prices of other products. (6)

3 To what extent do environmental considerations impact on the future of wheat supplies? (10)

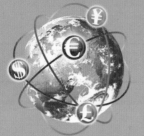

Unit 9 · MARKET STRUCTURES

DEFINITION

Markets in different countries operate differently and include monopolies, oligopolies, small and large businesses. Competitiveness measures a firm's ability to compete (i.e. compares its consumer offer to the offers made by its rivals).

9.1 Introduction: what is a competitive market?

In the past, markets were physical places where buyers and sellers met in person to exchange goods. Street markets are still like that. Today, some buyers and sellers never meet each other, a good example being eBay.

Some markets are more competitive than others. In general, a competitive market could be described as one where there is intense rivalry between producers of a similar good or service. The number of firms operating within a market influences the intensity of competition; the more firms there are, the greater the level of competition. However, the respective size of the firms operating in the market should also be taken into account. A market consisting of 50 firms may not be particularly competitive, if, for instance, one of the firms holds a 60% market share and the 40% is shared between the other 49. Similarly, a market composed of just four firms could be quite competitive because the firms operating within this market are of a fairly similar size.

Consumers enjoy competitive markets. However, the reverse is true for the firms that operate in these markets. In competitive markets, prices and profit margins tend to be squeezed. As a result, firms operating in competitive markets try hard to minimise competition, perhaps by creating a unique selling point (**USP**) or using **predatory pricing**.

It could be argued that marketing is vital no matter what the level of competition is within the market. Firms that fail to produce goods and services that satisfy the needs of the consumers that make up their target market will find it hard to succeed in the long term. Ultimately, consumers will not choose to waste their hard-earned cash on products that fail to meet their needs.

9.2 The degree of competition within a market

One dominant business

Some markets are dominated by one large business. Economists use the word '**monopoly**' to describe a market where there is a single supplier, and therefore no competition. In practice pure textbook monopolies rarely exist; even Microsoft does not have a 100% share of the office software market (though it does have a 90% share).

Monopolies are bad for consumers. They restrict choice, and tend to drive prices upwards. For that reason most governments regulate against monopolies and near monopolies that exploit consumers by abusing their dominant market position. The UK government's definition of a monopoly is somewhat looser. According to the Competition Commission, a monopoly is a firm that has a market share of 25% and above.

Deciding whether or not a firm has a monopoly is a far from straightforward task. First of all, the market itself has to be accurately defined – for example, Camelot has been granted a monopoly to run the National Lottery; however, it could be argued that Camelot does not have a dominant market position because there are other forms of gambling, such as horse racing and the football pools, available to consumers in the UK. Second, national market share figures should not be used in isolation because some firms enjoy local monopolies. In 2007 the Competition Commission accused Tesco of abusing its market position in towns such as Inverness and Slough by occupying sites previously occupied by its rivals. In both towns, consumers had to travel more than 15 minutes by car to reach another supermarket chain.

Firms implement their marketing strategy through the marketing mix. In markets dominated by a single large business, firms do not need to spend heavily on promotion because consumers are, to a degree, captive. Prices can be pushed upwards and the product element of the marketing mix should be focused on creating innovations that make it harder for new entrants to break in to the market. Apple spends millions of dollars on research and development in order to produce cutting-edge products such as the iPod Touch (see Figure 9.1). Apple is still the market leader in MP3s with a 60%-plus share of the massive US market. To ensure that Apple maintains its dominant market position new product launches are patented to prevent me-too imitations from being launched by the competition.

Figure 9.1 Apple's cutting-edge iPod Touch

Competition among a few giants

The UK supermarket industry is a good example of a market that is dominated by a handful of very large companies. Economists call markets like this **oligopolistic**. The rivalry that exists within such markets can be intense. Firms know that any gains in market share will be at the expense of their rivals. The actions taken by one firm affect the profits made by the other firms that compete within the same market.

In markets made up of a few giants, firms tend to focus on **non-price competition** when designing the marketing mix. Firms in these markets tend to be reluctant to compete by cutting price. They fear that the other firms in the industry will respond by cutting their prices too, creating a costly price war where no firm wins.

The fiercely competitive market

Fiercely competitive markets tend to be fragmented, made up of hundreds of relatively small firms, each of which competes actively against the others. In some of these markets competition is amplified by the fact that firms sell near identical products, called commodities. Commodities are products such as flour, sugar or blank DVDs that are hard to differentiate. Rivalry in commodity markets tends to be intense. In markets such as this firms have to manage their production costs very carefully because the retail price is the most important factor in determining whether the firm's product sells or not. If a firm cannot cut its costs it will not be able to cut its prices without cutting into profit margins. Without price cuts market share is likely to be lost.

In fiercely competitive markets firms will try, where possible, to create product differentiation. For example, the restaurant market in Croydon, Surrey, is extremely competitive. There are over 70 outlets within a two-mile radius of the town centre. To survive without having to compete solely on price, firms in markets like this must find new innovations regularly because points of differentiation are quickly copied.

Very little competition			Extremely competitive
Monopoly	Oligopoly	Competition between many firms	Competition between commodity products

Figure 9.2 Scale of market competition

9.3 Determinants of competitiveness

The key to competitiveness is customer satisfaction. If consumers are satisfied with quality and value for money, the firm concerned should be competitive. Competitive firms find it easier to hold on to, or even gain, market share. Competitiveness is a function of internal factors that are within the firm's control, and external factors, which are not.

Efficiency

Ryanair is a highly efficient company that manages its costs very effectively. The company's business model focuses on cost minimisation, by:

- avoiding airports that have high take-off and landing charges; instead, Ryanair prefers flying from secondary airports, some of which actually pay it for using them

- operating only one type of aircraft – the Boeing 737; staff employed to pilot or service Ryanair's aircraft need only be trained on one plane, minimising staff training and stock holding costs (for plane components)

- cutting out free food, drinks and newspapers; passengers that wish to consume these items have to pay for them; charging for food and drink has converted a cost into an important source of revenue.

Cost-efficient businesses such as Ryanair can charge lower prices than their less efficient rivals, yet make the same or more profit per unit supplied. In highly competitive commodity markets, such as low-cost air travel, price cutting is a highly effective way of gaining market share.

Design

Some firms are highly competitive because they sell products that have been differentiated by their design. In countries such as the UK, where wage rates are relatively high, manufacturers cannot compete on price alone. Production costs are too high compared with rivals in countries where wage rates are lower. By using design as a USP, British manufacturers can compete on quality rather than price, making them less vulnerable to competition from China and India. Good-looking design can add value to a product. For example, the BMW Mini relies upon its retro 1960s styling to command its price premium within the small car market.

Brand image

In many markets brand image is crucial. The results of blind tests indicate that, in many cases, consumers are unable to tell the difference between supermarket own-label products and premium-priced brands. Clever branding and advertising may be the only thing ensuring that Stella Artois carries on outselling Tesco's Premium Lager.

External factors

Competitiveness is also partially determined by external factors that are beyond the firm's control. The going wage rate in a country is an excellent example of an external factor that is beyond any single firm's control.

High wages tend to drive up costs, making a firm less competitive. On average, factory workers in the USA get paid somewhere in the region of $15–$30 per hour. In China the corresponding figure is less than $1 per hour. Firms try to improve their competitiveness by making internal changes to help compensate for factors, such as labour costs, that are beyond their control. European car manufacturers such as VW and Mercedes have decided to close down some of their European factories and reopen them in low-cost countries such as China in an attempt to improve their competitiveness.

9.4 Methods of improving competitiveness

Training

Some firms aim to improve their efficiency by increasing the amount they spend on staff training. Well-trained staff create the following competitive advantages.

- *Lower costs:* training tends to increase the productivity of labour because trained staff can work faster and make fewer mistakes; if output per worker increases, unit labour costs will tend to fall.

- *Improved product quality:* trained staff know what they are doing, improving the build quality of the finished product, which could give the firm concerned a competitive advantage in the market.

- *Better customer service:* effective training can dramatically improve customer service; for example, in some supermarkets untrained staff are still sent straight to the checkouts to learn how to use the till on the job; this can lead to queues and irritated customers.

Management

The quality of management has an important impact on the competitiveness of a business. For many years newspapers blamed British workers for the decline of UK car producers such as Rover. Yet, today, the Nissan plant in Sunderland is the most productive car factory in Europe. This implies that British management methods were at fault, as the Nissan plant's workforce is British. Improving the quality of management within an organisation is notoriously difficult, requiring a change in an organisation's culture.

Modernisation and investment

Some firms try to improve their competitiveness by purchasing new machinery and technology designed to improve efficiency. For example, a car manufacturer could drive down unit costs by replacing labour with the latest CAM (computer-aided manufacturing) technology. It is hoped that the new machinery will boost efficiency by driving up productivity, while at the same time reducing the firm's wage bill.

Issues For Analysis

● Every firm is different, and so is every market. It is always essential to think hard about the structure of the market, as this can affect every aspect of management within individual firms. Facing the same opportunity (e.g. for robot window-cleaners), a small firm may react very differently from a large one.

● It is then necessary to remember the huge difference between what firms do and what is right. Many firms try to improve their competitiveness by cost-cutting, such as the attempt by McDonald's to operate a 'zero training' policy. From a marketing point of view that was a poor idea as it would inevitably affect customer service.

9.5 Marketing and competitiveness
an evaluation

Competitiveness is a much wider issue than marketing. It is affected by the quality of the design and build of the products, and by the enthusiasm of the staff. These are clearly operations and personnel issues. Nevertheless marketing is at the heart of competitiveness for many firms. Mars knows how to produce Galaxy chocolate, so the key to the firm's success next year is how well the brand can be marketed. The managers must understand the customers, and then have the wisdom and the creativity to find a way to make the product stand out.

Key terms

Monopolistic competition: occurs when the firms competing within a marketplace have sufficient product differentiation to achieve a degree of monopoly power. This usually results from the development of brand names strong enough to prevent competition being purely on the basis of price.

Monopoly: when one seller controls more than 25 per cent of the market. Monopolies are price makers.

Non-price competition: rivalry based on factors other than price (e.g. advertising, sales promotions or 'new improved' products).

Oligopolistic: a market in which a few large companies have a dominant share (e.g. the UK chocolate market with a 70% share divided between Cadbury, Nestlé and Mars).

Predatory pricing: when a large company sets prices low with the deliberate intention of driving a weaker rival out of business.

USP: a point of genuine difference that makes one product stand out from the crowd (e.g. the Toyota Prius 'hybrid synergy drive').

Exercises

A. Revision questions

(35 marks; 35 minutes)

1 What is a competitive market? (2)

2 Explain how the marketing mix of Virgin Trains might be affected by a decision by government to allow other train operating companies to compete on Virgin's routes. (4)

3 Describe the main features of an oligopolistic market. (3)

4a What is a price war and . . . (3)

4b why are they rare? (3)

5 Explain why product differentiation becomes more important as competition within a market increases. (3)

6 Identify four factors that could be used to identify whether or not a business is competitive. (4)

7 How might the size of an organisation affect its efficiency? (3)

8 Why might a firm that is struggling to be competitive increase its training budget? (3)

9 Explain how the quality of management can impact upon an organisation's efficiency. (4)

10 Apart from market research, how might a firm achieve its goal of attempting to get closer to the consumer? (3)

B. Revision exercises

B1 Data response

At the beginning of the 1960s Indian food was a niche market business: there were just 500 Indian restaurants in the whole of the UK. As the table below illustrates, in the two decades that followed, the UK Indian restaurant market grew at a spectacular rate. In more recent times the market has continued to grow, however the rate of growth has declined. Today, the Indian restaurant market is firmly established. The industry is one of Britain's largest, employing over 60,000 people.

Number of Indian restaurants in UK

Year	No. of restaurants	Market growth rate (%)
1960	500	–
1970	1200	140
1980	3000	150
1990	5100	70
2000	7940	56
2004	8750	10

The Indian restaurant market is extremely decentralised. The market is made up of thousands of small, independent operators. In most British high streets there are several Indian restaurants that compete aggressively against one another. Indian food is very popular: over 23 million portions of Indian food are sold in restaurants each year. In the 1960s and 1970s, the growing affluence and cosmopolitan nature of the British public boosted takings at most Indian restaurants. Indian restauranteurs began to make serious money from the industry. Most owners chose to use some of the profit made to upgrade their facilities. Gradually the Indian restaurant scene became more sophisticated (e.g. luxurious-looking tables, chairs and tablecloths, piped Indian music, air conditioning, dinner-jacketed waiters and flock wallpaper). Some 30 years ago Indian restaurants tended to look the same. Most had fairly similar menus too. As a result Indian restaurants were forced into competing against each other on price. Unfortunately, intense price competition led to falling profit margins. Indian restauranteurs began to realise the importance of product differentiation as a competitive weapon. The first real attempt to create differentiation occurred in the early 1960s when a handful of forward-looking Indian

9.6 Workbook

restaurants, such as the Gaylord in Mortimer Street, London, imported tandoors. A tandoor is a special type of oven made from clay that gives the food cooked inside it a distinctive taste. Restaurants using tandoor ovens found that they could charge slightly higher prices without emptying their restaurants. Today, Indian restaurants use a variety of tactics to compete including those listed below.

- *Décor and design:* in recent times several now famous London-based Indian restaurants, such as the Cinnamon Club, opened in 2001 at a cost of £2.6 million in the Old Westminster Library, ditched the old-style traditional Indian restaurant décor (including the flock wallpaper!) in favour of a more upmarket-looking modern minimalistic interior design style. This change inspired many other Indian restaurants up and down the land to upgrade their fixtures and fittings in the hope that they too could charge Cinnamon Club-style premium prices (e.g. smoked rack of lamb with Rajasthani corn sauce and pilau rice for £22.00).

- *Exotic-sounding premium-priced menu items:* for example, Seabass Kaylilan prepared with fenugreek and tamarind.

Other restaurants have adopted a different approach. For example, the Khyber in Croydon has tried to win customers by emphasising its authenticity. The restaurant's website informs the reader that the Khyber won the Carlton TV London Indian Restaurant award in 1997 and that 'Our success is based on more traditional recipes.' The slogan 'It's just how mum would cook it back home' also features prominently on its internet menu. It also offers:

- balti cooking, including the super-sized big-as-your-table Nan breads!

- a prestigious imported German lager on draught, or a selection of fine wines

- flying in celebrated curry chefs from the Indian subcontinent for a limited period to cook up special food for a Curry Festival – the equivalent of a nightclub flying in a celebrity DJ.

Questions

(35 marks; 40 minutes)

1 Using the table, explain what has happened to the degree of competition within the UK Indian restaurant market over the last 50 years. (6)

2 Giving your reasons, discuss whether the Indian restaurant market in the UK is an example of a fiercely competitive market. (6)

3a Explain how efficiency might affect the competitiveness of an Indian restaurant. (4)

3b How might an Indian restaurant set about improving its efficiency? (4)

4 Identify and explain three internal factors that might affect the competitiveness of an Indian restaurant. (6)

5 Product differentiation is essential if an Indian restaurant is to survive in the long run. Discuss. (9)

Figure 9.3 The Cinnamon Club's bar and food

B2 Case study

Tesco's £9 toaster.

The prices of consumer electronics, such as toasters, satellite TV set-top boxes and MP3 players, have tumbled in recent years. Supermarket chains such as Tesco now sell DVD players that previously cost hundreds of pounds for under £10. So, why have the prices of these goods fallen? In part, the price falls reflect the falling price of the components that go into consumer electronics. Low prices also reflect the fact that there is now more competition in the market. In the past, consumers typically bought items such as TVs and computers from specialist retailers such as Currys. Today, the situation is somewhat different: in addition to these specialist retailers, consumers can now buy electrical goods over the internet and from supermarkets. Some industry analysts also believe that some of the supermarket chains are using set-top boxes and DVD players as loss leaders.

In today's ultra-competitive environment, manufacturers of consumer electronics face intense pressure from retailers to cut costs so that retail prices can be cut without any loss of profit margin. To cut prices without compromising product quality, manufacturers such as the Dutch giant Philips have transferred production from the Netherlands to low-cost locations such as China.

Questions

(35 marks; 40 minutes)

1 Describe three characteristics of a highly competitive market. (6)

2 Why has the market for consumer electronics become more competitive? (4)

3 Explain three factors that would affect the competitiveness of a manufacturer of consumer electronics. (6)

4 What is a loss leader and why do supermarkets use this tactic? (4)

5 How might the degree of competition impact upon the marketing mix used by a Chinese manufacturer of own-label toasters? (5)

6 In today's increasingly competitive market for consumer electronics, firms must constantly cut costs and prices if they are to survive. Discuss. (10)

TECHNOLOGICAL CHANGE

10.1 Introduction

Information technology (IT) applications in business are various and rapidly changing. Often, though, the changes are to processing speed and business jargon – the essential tasks remain the same. In recent years, the most important business IT innovation has been the emergence of the internet. This will be covered relatively briefly, because the pace of change means that magazine articles will provide a more up-to-date understanding of the internet's business potential than is possible here.

Key applications of technology are:

- automated stock control systems
- computer-aided design (CAD)
- robotics
- information technology, including electronic data interchange (EDI) and the internet
- database management (the software behind efficient delivery systems such as Tesco Home Delivery).

10.2 Automated stock control systems

Modern stock control systems are based on laser scanning of bar-coded information. This ensures the computer knows the exact quantity of each product/ size/colour that has come into the stockroom. In retail outlets, a laser scanning till is then used to record

Table 10.1 An example of aged stock analysis

Garment	Received (days ago)	Number received	In stock today
Green *Fabrice* dress, size 8	285	2	1
Blue *Channelle* dress, size 14	241	1	1
Red *Channelle* dress, size 8	241	2	2
Red *Grigio* jacket, size 10	235	4	3
Black *Grigio* dress, size 8	205	3	2
Black *Fabrice* dress, size 12	192	2	1
Blue *Florentine* suit, size 8	179	1	1

exactly what has been sold. This allows the store's computer to keep up-to-date records of current stocks of every item. This data can enable a buyer to decide how much extra to order, or an electronic link with the supplier can re-order automatically (see the section on EDI, below).

All this information will be held in the form of a database. This makes it easy for the firm to carry out an aged stock analysis: the computer provides a printout showing the stock in order of age. Table 10.1 shows a list of stock in a clothes shop, with the oldest first. It enables the manager to make informed decisions about what to do now and in the future. In this case:

- big price reductions seem to be called for on the first five items – they have been around too long

- there should be fewer orders in future for size 8 dresses.

10.3 Design technology

Computer-aided design (CAD) has been around for more than 20 years, but is now affordable and hugely powerful. Before CAD, product designers, engineers and architects drew their designs by hand. A CAD system works digitally, allowing designs to be saved, changed and reworked without starting from scratch. Even better, CAD can show a 3D version of a drawing and rotate to show the back and sides.

For multinationals such as Sony, a product designed in Tokyo can be sent electronically to Sony offices in

High-grade application

JCB

In August 2006 the British firm JCB gained worldwide publicity for breaking the diesel vehicle land speed record in the JCB Dieselmax. It reached speeds of 328 miles an hour, more than 100 miles an hour faster than the previous record. JCB gave praise publicly for the contribution made by a sophisticated CAD system made by UGS. It enabled the JCB team to take early design ideas right through to rigorous virtual safety testing of 3D models. The same software then helped in building real models and gave the technical details for the manufacture of the real vehicle. JCB praised the 'integrity and accuracy of the (CAD) data [which] was something we relied on heavily throughout the development phases'.

Source: Adapted from 'World record breaking JCB Diesal max owes succes to UGS NX CAD' 23 August 2006, www.mcsolutions.co.uk

America and Europe, for local designers to tweak the work to make it better suited to local tastes. And when work is behind schedule, designers in Tokyo can pass a design on to London at the end of the Japanese working day, then the design is sent on to America. The time differences mean that 24-hour working can be kept up.

Figure 10.1 The record-breaking JCB Dieselmax

The benefits of CAD systems to successful design are that:

- the data generated by a CAD system can be linked to computer-aided manufacturing (CAM) to provide integrated, highly accurate production

Figure 10.2 Guggenheim Museum, Bilbao, designed by Frank Gehry

- they are hugely beneficial for businesses that are constantly required to provide designs that are unique, yet based on common principles (e.g. designing a new bridge, car or office block)

- CAD improves the productivity of designers and also helps them to be more ambitious; the extraordinary buildings of Frank Gehry could not have been produced without CAD (because only computers could calculate whether the unusual structure would fall down in a high wind). See Figure 10.2.

10.4 Robotics

Industrial robots are fundamental to the car industry worldwide, and are becoming increasingly important in the production of electrical goods such as TVs and computers. Nevertheless, it remains a bit of a surprise that robots have not become a more powerful force in industry. Thirty years ago, people assumed that few workers would be left in factories – the robots were coming. In Britain today there are fewer than 50 robots per 10,000 workers. Even in Japan (with more than 40% of the world's robots) the figure is only 350 robots per 10,000 manufacturing workers.

The surprise is the greater when you look at the graph in Figure 10.3. Robot prices have fallen since 1990 by about 50%, yet their quality, efficiency and speed have risen. So robots are now a bit of a bargain!

Industrial robots have important advantages over human labour. They are programmed to do the same thing over and over again, so repetitive tasks can be completed

with 100% consistency. This can be vital – for example, in the production of components for aircraft engines, or in the production of heart pacemakers. Robots are also likely to prove cheaper than people, as long as the business is able to use them effectively (e.g. for 20 hours a day).

Yet robots are clearly not a magic solution, or else they would have taken over. They are inflexible, so they cannot easily switch jobs in the way that people can; and they have rarely proved as reliable as they perhaps should be.

High-grade application

Toshiba robots

Three Toshiba robots are used at a pet food factory in Bremen, northern Germany. The company has made substantial investment in factory automation in order to improve productivity. Toshiba Machine robots now package birdseed sticks at a rate of 90 per minute. Where once there were seven people working on the application across three shifts, now three Toshiba Machine TH350 robots achieve the same results. The people have been redeployed across the plant.

The robots are part of a production line that manufactures birdseed sticks that are like a fat-based lollypop, embedded with nuts and seeds. The sticks are fed down three conveyors, each with a ceiling-mounted robot at its end. As this happens, the boxes are fed down another conveyor. A robot gripper then picks up the seed sticks and transfers them into boxes on a moving conveyor. Ceiling-mounted SCARA robots make the best use of the available work area.

10.5 Communication with customers

There are two main ways firms communicate electronically with their customers. The first is a website – for example, easyJet receives over 95% of its bookings in this way. The second is through careful database management. A database is a store of information that can be rearranged and sorted in numerous ways. For example, if you had a database of all your friends, classmates and work colleagues, you might like to:

- sort them by birthday, so that you never missed the chance of a party invitation

- sort them by activity, so that you could rustle up a football or hockey team when needed

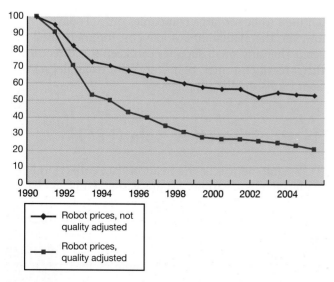

Figure 10.3 Price index of industrial robots, 1990–2005
Source: Adapted from 'Antomated Valve Fitting' 23 August 2007
http://tmrobotics.co.uk

- sort them by location, to give you a mailing list for organising a school reunion.

For businesses, the ability to store information on thousands, perhaps millions, of customers is invaluable. In order to maximise the speed and flexibility of a database, every type of information needs to be held in a different 'field'. Field 1 may be the surname, field 3 the address, field 7 the age, and so on. This enables the data to be sorted, or picked out, in different ways. If you have a new product aiming at the over-40s, those aged 40 and over can be picked out and a mailing list produced in seconds.

To obtain this data, businesses use various approaches:

- asking customers to fill in their name and address when purchasing goods

- recording the information on product warranty cards

- supplying 'loyalty' cards, such as Tesco's Clubcard

- buying databases from companies that specialise in gathering data.

If building a database, firms are legally required to register it with the Data Protection Registrar. The Data Protection Act 1984 gives people the right to see their personal file – for example, one held by a bank on a customer's creditworthiness.

Marketing and database management

Mailing lists have existed for decades. American Express, *Reader's Digest* and many others have built their business through well-targeted direct mail (sometimes referred to as 'junk mail'). They achieved this through the use of large, expensive mainframe computers. Nowadays even the smallest firm can afford a computer and some database software. Customers can be sorted into regular, light and occasional users, and be sent an appropriate mailshot. Each letter can be personalised (e.g. 'Dear Miss Hendrick...') and is therefore better suited to building a relationship with the customer. Alternatively, telephone sales staff can make direct contact to check on customer satisfaction and inquire whether any extra services are required.

The pursuit of an up-to-date, detailed database has reached its high point with supermarket loyalty cards. A Tesco Clubcard application form requires the customer to state details such as address, number of children, job and income. These details can be related to their lifestyle by recording what they buy and how much they spend. If Tesco then wants to promote wine costing more than £8 per bottle, it can invite to an in-store

tasting all those who have spent over £6 on a bottle of wine over the past six months. Having an accurate database minimises the waste, and therefore the cost, of such mailings. This makes them a more attractive proposition when compared to other advertising media.

These are all ways in which technology can cut costs, reduce waste, improve customer service quality and increase productivity.

10.6 Communication with suppliers

Electronic data interchange (EDI)

EDI is a permanent link between computers on different sites, enabling specified types of data to be exchanged. By establishing an EDI link, firms can ensure that the latest information is available instantly to other branches of their business, or even to other businesses. For example, Heinz's link with Tesco enables it to see how sales of soups are going this week. If chicken soup sales have pushed ahead 20% (perhaps because they were featured on a TV programme), production increases can be planned even before the Tesco head office phones through with a large order. This makes a just-in-time operation far more feasible.

Of course, Tesco does not want Heinz to have access to all its computer files, so the EDI link covers only specified data. Heinz might allow Tesco access to its stock levels and production plans in exchange for Tesco's daily sales data. This cooperation can help ensure that shelves are rarely empty.

EDI used to be for large companies only. Today, however, the availability of low-cost internet-based EDI means that any small supplier can keep this direct link with a retail customer. Sainsbury's, for example, set up JSnet for its smaller suppliers.

Electronic point of sale (EPOS)

EPOS equipment is at the heart of data collection by retailers. Laser scanning systems gather data from bar codes, which allow the computer to record exactly what has been bought and at what price. This forms the basis of the stock control system and also the recording of sales revenues. As with other aspects of IT, rapid falls in the cost of EPOS systems make them increasingly affordable for small shops.

Issues For Analysis

Information technology provides a series of tools that can be used to help businesses operate more effectively. This raises many issues for analysis, a couple of which are discussed below.

- Will electronic shopping mean shops are on the way out? The answer is probably no. But internet shopping will put new competitive pressures on high streets and shopping centres. If this book could be ordered in minutes on the internet and arrive in three days' time, would it make sense to go and look for it in a bookshop where it might not be in stock? Retailers are going to have to think very hard about whether they are offering the level of personal service that makes a visit worthwhile.

- Most managers and staff accept that new technology is necessary for businesses to keep up with their competitors. Yes, there are often problems when the time comes to update technology. Staff may worry that suggested 'improvements' are excuses for making people redundant. Managers need to be sensitive to people's fears, and win them over by honesty and openness.

10.7 Technological change
an evaluation

Years ago the managers at Guinness thought change management was a technical question. When a change was needed, such as a new distribution system, they hired consultants, whose main focus was to establish effective information and communications technology (ICT) links. Time after time they were disappointed by the results.

Improvements began only when they realised that the key variable was not the technology but the people. Not only were results better if staff were consulted fully, but also the new systems were successful only if staff applied them with enthusiasm and confidence.

Technology is only a set of tools. It can form the basis of a major competitive advantage, as with easyJet's 1995 initiative with internet bookings. More often, though, the successful application of IT relies on good understanding of customer and staff needs and wants. This suggests that good management of information technology is no different from good management generally.

Figure 10.4 Complex design files are effortlessly portable on iPhone's high-res widescreen display

Exercises

A. Revision questions

(35 marks; 35 minutes)

1 A database could be used by an aircraft manufacturer such as Boeing to record the supplier and batch number of every part used on every aircraft. How might this information be used? (3)

2 State two benefits of good database management in achieving efficient stock control. (2)

3 Read the High-grade application on JCB Dieselmax. Identify two benefits of 'virtual safety testing'. (2)

4 Look at Figure 10.3. Explain one possible implication for:
   (a) a UK factory owner feeling under pressure from competition from China (3)
   (b) a UK worker, with few qualifications or skills, thinking of taking a job in a factory. (3)

5 Explain one benefit and one drawback of computer-aided manufacture (CAM). (4)

6 From your reading of the whole unit, outline three ways in which technology can lead to improved quality. (6)

7 How significant might internet retailing become for each of the following types of business:
   (a) a music shop specialising in 1960s classic pop and rock (2)
   (b) a builders' merchant (selling bricks, cement, etc.) (2)
   (c) a mail-order clothing firm? (2)

8 From your reading of the whole unit, explain two ways in which technology can reduce waste within a business. (6)

B. Revision exercises

B1 Data response

Robots

Recently TM Robotics (Europe) Ltd worked with a major UK manufacturer to fit three Toshiba robots as part of an automated system to increase its output of valves.

The managers had to consider: the cost of the robots; the cost of installation and maintenance; the training required for key staff to manage the operation. All of this has to be weighed up against the cost of a manual alternative. One must also bear in mind potential downtime if the automated system is replacing an existing manual one.

The key factors in the success of the automation process were accuracy and flexibility. Accuracy was provided by the $+/-0.02$ mm repeatability of the Toshiba robot, and flexibility allowed the system to cope with 240 different product variants, all consisting of at least five component pieces.

One of the key factors in the installation process was ensuring a quick changeover period between different product variants, in order to minimise downtime. This is where a manual process can be advantageous – the worker simply finishing a batch of one product type and collecting the components for another, with no long changeover period required. Careful design ensured that the average changeover time was just 15 minutes, giving an impressive operating efficiency of 90%.

The total cycle time for the three robots to assemble the fitting is just 7.8 seconds, 4.2 seconds faster then the manual method. Furthermore, the automation has the obvious advantage of constant running. It doesn't slow down when it's tired, it doesn't take coffee breaks and never takes long lunches. Faster production time and constant output mean that the robot quickly pays for itself.

Source: adapted from www.tmrobotics.co.uk

Questions

(30 marks; 35 minutes)

1a Explain in your own words the meaning of 'downtime'. (3)

1b Why may firms be keen to minimise downtime? (4)

2 Examine the importance to this 'major UK manufacturer' of the accuracy and flexibility of these three robots. (6)

3a Calculate the % increase in production speed now that the robots are producing rather than people. (3)

3b Analyse two ways in which the manufacturer can benefit from the extra speed. (6)

4 Using the information in the case and your own knowledge, discuss two ways in which human workers may be more valuable than robots. (8)

B2 Data response

An architect and her iPhone

Patti the Architect, a small architectural firm based in Florida, is turning Apple's iPhone into a productivity-boosting mobile resource for construction-site communications.

With the Apple iPhone, architect Patricia 'Patti' Stough and her staff can now easily access their full library of design and construction documents on the move. The firm designs all its projects in CAD on high-performance Mac hardware, making the files effortlessly portable and displayable on iPhone's high-res widescreen display.

This mobility enables the firm to more easily communicate design intentions to customers on the site, as well as consult more effectively with builders, subcontractors and regulatory inspectors. And even if they had forgotten a document, they can easily retrieve it wirelessly via iPhone's Wi-Fi.

With a slight tap or pinch of their fingers, users can easily zoom in and out of drawings and 3D high-resolution photos on iPhone, drilling down to the finest of details or panning out for a big picture view via iPhone's revolutionary touchscreen interface. 'The days of hauling scrolls of paper drawings to job sites only to discover I

forgot a critical document are over,' says Stough. 'I can now carry even the largest, most complex and detailed CAD models in the palm of my hand. The ability to bring 3D digital drawings on site is a huge advantage, enabling me to better communicate and coordinate with everyone involved in the project.'

Patti the Architect is an award-winning architectural firm that specialises in beachfront townhouses, hotels, churches, schools, offices, retail additions and commercial interior renovations. Stough says that the huge productivity gains of designing in and working with 3D virtual building models are further enhanced through the mobility of iPhone.

Source: adapted from www.architosh.com, 14 August 2007

Questions

(25 marks; 30 minutes)

1 Outline three benefits of the CAD system to this architectural business. (6)

2 Explain how the iPhone-linked CAD has reduced time wastage for the business. (4)

3 Examine Patti Stough's suggestion that having CAD on the iPhone leads to 'huge productivity gains'. (6)

4 To what extent is the portable CAD system likely to improve Patti's customer service? (9)

C. Essay questions

(40 marks each)

1 Information technology is reducing the need to meet people face to face. Discuss the implications of this for running a successful business.

2 If industrial robots get cheap enough, they may replace almost all unskilled factory workers in the future. Discuss the benefits and costs of this to society.

3 'Internet retailing will mean the death of the high street.' Discuss.

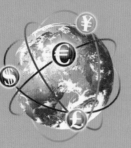

11 Unit

SOCIAL, CULTURAL, MORAL AND ETHICAL INFLUENCES

DEFINITION

A business cannot operate in a vacuum. From a local to a global level, firms must continually assess the market and monitor the changes that are taking place in it.

11.1 Social, cultural, moral and ethical change

In some cases, market changes are quantifiable, such as changes in demography or in the lifestyles of the population (social and cultural). Much of the information for these factors can be taken from government statistics. This helps businesses to identify how their markets are changing and adjust their overall strategy to match these changes.

For example, the UK population is ageing, people are living longer and this group has some of the highest levels of disposable income. How have businesses changed their products, services and marketing to attract older age groups?

Nintendo has launched *Brain Training* to target older people and to move away from its image of targeting only game players. Tourist companies have expanded into extreme activity holidays for this age group. Society changes all the time and businesses must change with it if they are to survive.

> **Task**
> How have the following businesses changed their image in order to meet the changing needs of society?
> • Tesco
> • Marks & Spencer
> • Vodafone

Figure 11.1 Nintendo has launched Brain Training *to target an ageing UK population*

11.2 The responsibilities of business

In other cases changes in the market are less tangible. These changes are slow moving and are based upon a set of beliefs, values and expectations (moral and ethical) rather than quantifiable evidence. A business uses these values and beliefs to form a culture within which it will operate. (A business's '**ethics**' encompass a set of morals and beliefs that it may lay down for its employees.) The problem that businesses have to face is huge: decisions have to be made to satisfy a number of stakeholders.

For example, in 2008 the government asked the major supermarkets to stop cutting prices on alcoholic drinks. It argued that cheap drinks encouraged 'binge drinking'. The supermarket bosses all said that they agreed, yet the price-cutting continued. The opportunity for extra sales and profit was too good to miss.

There is only one social responsibility of business – to use its resources and engage in activities designed to increase profits so long as it stays within the rules of the game, engages in open and free competition, without deception or fraud.

(Milton Friedman)

This is known as the *shareholder view*, and concerns itself only with the business's responsibility towards its shareholders and investors.

But the mood of the world has changed and business in general accepts that it has a corporate, legal and moral responsibility to all its stakeholders.

Tomorrow's company will ... be well informed when it is confronted with the need to trade off the differing expectations of customers, suppliers, employees, investors and the community in which it operates.

(Royal Society of Arts, 1994)

This is known as the *stakeholder view*.

There is clearly a conflict between these two views. If the stakeholder view is adopted then shareholders' profits might be reduced due to increased costs, reduced sales and charitable donations. It is this assessment of costs against benefits that provides businesses with a dilemma. Those that take an ethical stance, such as the Cooperative Bank and the Body Shop, may incur losses in the short term and alienate shareholders.

The Institute of Business Ethics identifies the following as the most important issues for businesses to consider today:

Supply chain management is becoming an increasingly important issue for companies, as consumers learn more about the potential environmental and social impact of the products they purchase. Other recent concerns include customer data protection, work–home balance and the responsible treatment of suppliers. As well as being asked to identify and address their wider impacts on society, companies have been under pressure to consider 'product responsibility': for example, regarding fast food companies and the nutritional value of their products, and alcohol companies regarding 'binge drinking' by young people.

(Institute of Business Ethics)

Most businesses have identified that they are accountable to all their stakeholders and there is much more transparency than there ever has been. However, in reality it is still the case that those with the most influence will tip the balance in their favour. In spite of the communication and media revolution, many businesses, especially those that operate on a global scale, manage to avoid scrutiny by the outside world.

> ### Key terms
>
> **Ethics:** set of morals and beliefs that a company may lay down for its employees. These values often form the culture and objectives of the business.
> **Business ethics:** the interface between decision making and morals.

Figure 11.2 The Body Shop has adopted the stakeholder view of business responsibility

Exercises

A. Revision questions

(30 marks; 30 minutes)

1 Outline two possible reasons why Maltesers are still selling successfully, over 75 years after the brand was created. (4)

2 As the UK's Polish population grew, Sainsbury's launched a range of Polish foods, before the other major supermarket chains did so. How might Sainsbury's have benefited from being the first supermarket to provide fully for Polish shoppers in Britain? (5)

3 In February 2008, Cadbury's announced a range of Easter eggs that would not have any outer packaging, just be sold in a foil wrapper.
   (a) Outline one advantage and one disadvantage of this. (4)
   (b) Do you think this approach will be successful for Cadbury's? Explain your reasoning. (4)

4 Choose two of the following examples and explain whether you believe these businesses are pursuing a profitable marketing approach or a good social purpose. (8)
   (a) HSBC bank running a 'January sale', based on linking its products to environmental improvements
   (b) B&Q deciding in January 2008 to stop selling outdoor patio heaters.
   (c) Coca-Cola sponsoring the London marathon.

5 Should shoppers see it as their personal responsibility to think about how a shop is able to sell a new suit for £25 or a chicken for £1.99? (5)

B. Revision exercises

B1 Data response

More than 3,000 products now bear the Fairtrade logo, and supermarkets including Tesco, Sainsbury's and Marks & Spencer are falling over each other to prove their Fairtrade credentials. Fairtrade sales reached £290.6m in the UK in 2006 and were expected to reach at least £348m last year [2007].

The wave of interest from major consumer brands is not driven by a sudden burst of altruism but by increasing demand from shoppers, who want to believe that they and the brands they buy are 'doing the right thing'. Recent research from the Cooperative Group shows that 80 per cent of shoppers are prepared to pay a little more to be reassured about the ethics of a product. Meanwhile, six in ten are prepared to boycott products that don't meet their ethical expectations.

Dan Welch, of *Ethical Consumer* magazine, says the Fairtrade brand holds significant power in the retail market.

'It is an incredibly important brand, more than any other ethical labelling scheme,' he says. 'It has brought quite complex ideas about supply chains and conditions for workers in the third world into mainstream consciousness.'

Mark Varney, Fairtrade's business development manager, says Fairtrade has effectively become shorthand for 'ethical' for many consumers and that carrying the label reaps dividends for brands.

Source: Sarah Butler, SocietyGuardian.co.uk

Questions

(27 marks; 35 minutes)

1a Calculate the percentage increase in expected sales between 2006 and 2007. (3)

1b Explain **two** reasons why this increase might have taken place. (4)

2 Using examples from the data, analyse to what extent ethical issues should influence business objectives. (8)

3 Apart from ethical issues, evaluate the impact of one other external influence on businesses in the retail sector. (12)

B2 Data response

Leading food and drink companies have joined forces to help the environment by cutting back their use of water, it was announced yesterday. The pledge by 21 companies including Cadbury Schweppes, Premier Foods, Tate & Lyle and Nestlé UK is part of an initiative by the industry's trade body, the Food and Drink Federation (FDF), to cut carbon dioxide emissions, packaging and waste, and improve energy efficiency. If other firms followed suit, the initiative could save 140m litres of water per day, with a combined saving of about £60m per year on water bills. Food and drink manufacturers account for 10% of industrial water usage, and the aim is to slash this by 20% by 2020.

The companies that have signed up to the voluntary agreement insisted there would be no compromise on the use of water in health and safety areas. Cadbury was prosecuted and fined £1m last year after unclean pipes were found to be at the heart of a national salmonella outbreak which gave 42 people food poisoning and put three of them in hospital.

Graham Neale, general manager of signatory GSK Nutritional Healthcare, said: 'As makers of household drinks Ribena, Lucozade and Horlicks, we intend to keep sustainability at the centre of our renewal and growth. We know this makes good business sense – but we also know that it is the right and necessary way to do things.' Fiona Dawson, managing director of Mars Snackfood UK, said: 'At Mars we view water as a precious resource and have been working hard to reduce our usage. We used 40% less in 2007 than we did in 2006.'

Source: www.guardian.co.uk/environment , 29 January 2008

Questions

(20 marks; 25 minutes)

1 Explain why it is important that many of the businesses in the food industry adopt this water-saving objective. (5)

2 Explain why this water-saving objective might be described as a S.M.A.R.T. objective. (5)

3 To what extent would the following stakeholders benefit from this objective?
- Customers
- Shareholders
- Government
- Community (10)

B3 Data response

Green, healthy and fair

The Sustainable Development Commission (SDC) reported in February 2008 that supermarkets were not doing enough to control their impact on the environment and public health. The food chain (including fertilisers, transport and waste) contributes one-fifth of the UK's greenhouse gas emissions, and is the biggest way in which the average household contributed to climate change.

The report also said that by 2010, a quarter of UK adults will be obese, and that supermarkets contributed to this problem by promoting unhealthy lifestyles. For example, advertisements and special offers for high-calorie foods far outnumbered those for healthy options.

The SDC argued that government needed to work with businesses to address these issues. The website www.businessgreen.com (18 February 2008) reported on reactions to the report from businesses:

The British Retail Consortium (BRC) has hit back at suggestions supermarkets are not doing enough to limit their environmental impact, insisting that the UK's largest retailers are already investing heavily in improving their green credentials. ... A spokesman for the BRC said that the supermarkets were already working to meet many of the recommendations made by the report. 'In essence the Sustainable Development Commission is calling for more collaboration with government to allow supermarkets to use their influence to good effect,' he said. 'Supermarkets are already doing that both with government and through their own environmental initiatives.' However, he insisted that the report's suggestion that multi-buy promotions increased waste levels and that supermarkets were not doing enough to tackle transport emissions were wide of the mark.

Questions

(24 marks; 30 minutes)

1a) Outline briefly what is meant by the phrase 'greenhouse gas emissions'. (3)

1b) To what extent are they the responsibility of supermarkets such as Tesco? (6)

2 What evidence is provided in the article in support of the view that stores are to blame for 'promoting unhealthy lifestyles'? (5)

3 A supermarket might respond to the Sustainable Development Commission's report by pointing out that all it is trying to do is provide choice and an efficient service to its customers. Discuss whether this is a justified response to the report. (12)

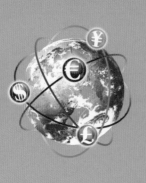

MARKETING OBJECTIVES, ANALYSIS AND PLANS

DEFINITION

Effective marketing achieves the firm's sales and profit targets by convincing customers to buy the firm's products again and again.

12.1 What is effective marketing?

The term 'marketing' is widely misunderstood by people who have not studied business and management. Many people think that 'marketing' is just another interchangeable term for selling, advertising and other forms of promotion (e.g. sponsorship). Some people even think that marketing is about persuading consumers to buy or use a product they do not want. So, if marketing isn't just about designing glitzy advertising, or aggressive high-pressure 'selling', what is it?

Marketing is the business function that aims to identify, influence and then satisfy consumer wants profitably. Effective marketing starts with identifying an opportunity, just as Nintendo did with its Wii console. Instead of assuming that all consoles had to target players of shoot-em-up games, Nintendo identified other opportunities among girls (*Nintendogs*) and older people (*Brain Trainer*).

In many small businesses the owner will come into regular contact with customers. This allows the owner to hear first-hand the needs and wants of the target market. In large businesses, formal market research is undertaken because head office managers cannot feel sure that they know what customers think and want. Once consumer wants have been identified, products and services will need to be designed to match consumer preferences. Finally, a launch marketing mix must be decided. This involves decisions such as setting price, choosing an appropriate distribution channel and setting a promotional strategy.

12.2 Why is effective marketing important?

Consumers tend to be quite rational. They will seek out fairly priced products that satisfy their needs. In a competitive market firms stand or fall according to their ability to satisfy the needs of the consumer. Generally, firms that fail will lack customer loyalty and be punished automatically by the market. These firms will lose market share and profit. Firms with products and services that offer genuine consumer benefits will attract revenue and profit.

Consumer tastes do not tend to stay the same for very long. Therefore, a key aspect of effective marketing is the ability to respond, quickly, to any change in consumer tastes. Firms that fail to adapt their business model, at a time when consumer tastes are changing, are normally forced out of business. In recent years retail chains such as KwikSave, Unwins and the Gadget Shop have collapsed.

High-grade application

Fopp

In June 2007 the music retailer Fopp announced that it was closing down all 105 of its UK stores. The management of Fopp had failed to react fast enough to a change in consumer preferences for buying music. In the last five years there has been a growing trend towards purchasing music via internet downloads. Fopp tried to respond by lowering its prices. Unfortunately for Fopp, this tactic failed to generate the revenues required by the company to break even, proving that low prices alone cannot save a business from closure, especially if consumers no longer wish to purchase the product that the business concerned sells.

Figure 12.1 The Fopp logo

12.3 The characteristics of effective marketing

Identifying the target market

When a business creates a new market (as Richard Branson is attempting currently with space tourism) it can aim its product at everyone who can afford the product. Some time later competitors will arrive, and usually focus on one segment of the market. In space tourism, perhaps some firms will focus on thrill-seekers, while others target wealthy, older travellers seeking a super-safe, luxury version of the same thrill.

To succeed at marketing you need to know and understand the customers within your target market: what do they *really* want from your product? The satisfaction of using/having the product, or the satisfaction of showing it off to friends? What are their interests and lifestyle?

Having a clear idea of the age, sex, personality and lifestyle of the target market enables the business to do the following things.

● *Focus market research by interviewing only those who make up the target market:* this should make the findings far more reliable. If the target market is clearly defined, the firm's market research budget can be spent with greater effect. Quota sampling could be used instead of a wide random sample; only those that meet the specific criteria for the target market will be interviewed, saving the firm time and money.

● *Focus advertising spending on the people most likely to buy the product:* one national TV commercial can cost £500,000; it will reach millions of people, but how many are really in the target market? Men do not need to know that 'Maybe it's Maybelline'. A product targeting young women would be advertised

far more cost-effectively in magazines such as *More* or *Look*.

Segment markets

Most markets are not made up of identikit consumers who all want exactly the same product. In practice, consumer preferences can vary greatly. Firms that market their products effectively in this situation produce a range of products, each targeted at specific market segments.

A good example of a company that has used market segmentation to great effect is British Sky Broadcasting (BSkyB); in 2007 the company made a pre-tax profit of close to £800 million.

Before Sky joined the market, the choice of what to watch on TV was limited. The BBC, ITV and Channel 4 tried in vain to produce a range of programmes in an attempt 'to be all things to all men'. Today Sky offers subscribers a choice of over 800 different channels. Among the target segments are kids, sports fans (men), ethnic minorities and fans of different music types – e.g. MTV Base and Performance (classical music). The output of each channel is carefully matched to a particular consumer interest or hobby. Many of these channels attract additional charges, which has helped BSkyB to increase its monthly income (see Figure 12.2).

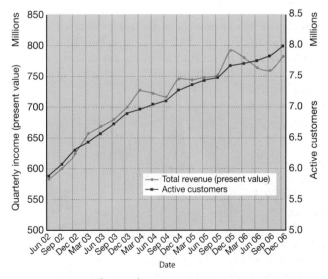

Figure 12.2 BSkyB subscription income

Customer-orientated marketing

Effective marketing is usually based around an approach that is customer-orientated rather than product-orientated. In a customer-orientated (also known as market-orientated) business managers take into account the needs of the consumer before making any decision.

They put the customer at the heart of the decision-making process.

Some firms still use a production-orientated approach to marketing. Product orientation (also known as production orientation) leads managers to focus on what the firm does best; internal efficiency comes before consumer preferences. The product-orientated approach to marketing may lead the business towards the following approaches.

● *The hard sell:* employing a large salesforce to go out and convince consumers that they should buy your product. Individualised sales targets, low basic salaries and high rates of commission ensure that sales staff will be 'motivated' to hit their targets, ensuring that the firm sells the products that it has already produced.

● *Cutting costs and prices:* if a production-orientated firm's products are not selling very well, managers tend to respond to this crisis by cutting costs. If costs can be cut, retail prices can also be cut without any loss of profit margin.

On the other hand, there are some weaknesses in customer orientation. The death of Rover Cars (once one of the world's biggest car producers) was partly due to this. Rover management seemed convinced that customers could be attracted by marketing gimmicks such as 'special edition' cars or cars with angular steering wheels. A greater focus on the quality and reliability of the product would have been far more effective. The ideal approach is that of a firm such as BMW, which is hugely proud of its products, but always makes sure that it understands what its customers really want from them.

Figure 12.3 The clothing retailer Gap

High-grade application
Gap

The American clothes retailer, Gap, has suffered from falling sales and market share because it has failed to keep up to date with changes in fashion. Gap built its reputation around selling 'preppy' clothes.

Consumer tastes have moved on, but Gap has not. In 2007 the company announced a 19% increase in quarterly profits, created by cost-cutting measures. However, at the same time, sales fell by 5%. In the long term, price cuts made possible by lower costs will not help the company. Gap operates within a highly competitive market. To survive, Gap will probably have to abandon its 'preppy' clothes and instead switch to a more market-orientated approach. Market research needs to be given a bigger role. Focus groups could be carried out to identify popular contemporary style and fashion. New lines of clothing can then be designed that will have a better chance of appealing to Gap's target market.

A coherent brand image

Firms that market their products successfully use the marketing mix in an integrated manner to create a coherent and attractive brand image that appeals to the target market. Marketing success depends upon getting all four marketing mix decisions right. A good product that is properly priced and promoted will still fail if distribution is poor. Firms use the marketing mix to create an attractive and coherent brand image for each of the products that they sell. Creating the right brand image is important. If the brand image created by the marketing mix appeals to the target market there should be an increased chance that the product will succeed.

The most important thing to remember is that all four elements of the mix must be coordinated. If the marketing mix is not coordinated mixed product messages will be sent out to the target market. This could create confusion, leading to disappointing sales. The key, then, is to think through the brand image that you want to create *before* making any other decisions on your product, how you might want to price it, promote it and distribute it.

Marketing and business objectives

The marketing function is only one part of the whole operation of a business. It cannot and should not be mutually exclusive from other areas. In most businesses the objectives of the marketing department will be driven by target sales and profit which are, in most cases, objectives shared by the whole business.

Continued awareness and communication with the market is essential if businesses are to maintain their place in the market, and this benefits the whole firm. Therefore the objectives of marketing are closely related to those of the whole business since growth in sales will allow a business to gain market share and achieve the levels of profit required to grow, reinvest and survive.

It must however be remembered that profit can only be achieved if the costs involved in achieving sales are not too high. If this is the case the money available to invest in marketing may be limited and a conflict may arise with the rest of the business. Conflict can also arise in terms of what image the business wishes to build in the market. Environmental, legal and economic considerations may require the business to adopt a strategy that conflicts with the aims of marketing. Once again the marketing budget may be squeezed by the extra costs needed by other areas of the business.

Many Japanese firms do not have a marketing department. Firms that adopt this approach believe that every employee has a part to play in marketing their business. Marketing should not be the preserve of a specialised marketing department – it is everyone's responsibility. To be successful the management has to create the right culture. Every member of staff must see their role as to better serve the needs and wants of the consumer.

12.4 How is customer service delivered?

Face to face

The most immediate, most powerful situation in which customer service is seen is in direct, face-to-face dealings with customers. Retailers must focus clearly on how shop staff interact with their customers. This is a situation with which you are likely to be highly familiar, perhaps from both sides. Here, the face of the employee is the face of the company to the customer.

Telephone

Much of customer service activity now happens in call centres. From finding out the price of a train from Leeds to Plymouth, to making an insurance claim following a car crash, the telephone is a key factor in customer service. Call centres are thought to be cost efficient,

partly because they can be located in Birmingham, Belfast or Bangalore. It is highly questionable, though, as to whether they deliver 'customer service'. Most customers want to talk to an individual, not someone who is reading a script.

High-grade application

Customer service at home

Companies looking for a less controversial alternative to basing call centres in Asia may have found an answer in a concept known as home-shoring. An alternative to 'off-shoring' where customer service is provided from a call centre in another country, 'home-shoring' bases customer service assistants in their own homes. Research evidence seems to suggest that this boosts productivity and increases the level of service provided. The *Guardian* reports that all 1000 reservations staff at US airline JetBlue work at home. The customer complaint level is, amazingly, just one per 300,000 passengers, while staff turnover is just 3.5%, way below that experienced in a traditional call centre.

Source: Adapted from *Guardian*, 15 October 2005

Internet

Many online booking systems have eliminated direct human contact from customer service. Behind the scenes, though, the attitudes within the business remain all-important. You may book a bargain flight online, ticking the box for same-day delivery of the tickets. If the business fails to deliver the tickets on time, you are not going on holiday. Will the tickets arrive? Only if the faceless staff do their jobs on time. As customers, we have to trust that an online service will soon fail if it cannot meet its promises.

12.5 Market size and trends

Market size is the measurement of all the sales by all the companies within a marketplace. It can be measured in two ways: by volume and by value. Volume measures the quantity of goods purchased – perhaps in tons, in packs or in units. Market size by value is the amount spent by customers on the volume sold. So the difference between volume and value is the price paid per unit.

Take, for example, the figures for the UK take-home fruit juice market shown in Table 12.1.

Market size matters because it is the basis for calculating market share (i.e. the proportion of the total market

Table 12.1 UK take-home fruit juice market

2007 market by value	£987 million
2007 market by volume	936 million litres
Average price per serving	105.4 pence (£987/936)

Source: *The Grocer*, 5 May 2007

held by one company or brand). This, in turn, is essential for evaluating the success or failure of a firm's marketing activities. Market size is also the reference point for calculating trends. Is the market size growing or declining? A growth market is far more likely to provide opportunities for new products to be launched or new distribution initiatives to be successful.

Recent figures and forecasts for the car market in China help show the importance of market trends. Ten years ago the UK car market was four times bigger than China's. In 2006 China accelerated past Britain. And look at the forecasts for the coming years in Table 12.2.

By 2020 China will be the world's biggest car market. Clearly these figures show that success in China will be far more important to car firms than success in Britain.

12.6 Market share

Market share is the proportion of the total market held by one company or product. It can be measured by volume, but is more often looked at by value. Market share is taken by most firms as the key test of the success

Table 12.2 Sales of automobiles (actual and forecast)

Year	China	Britain
2005	2,400,000	2,450,000
2006	2,800,000	2,350,000
2007	3,800,000	2,450,000
2010 (forecast)	6,500,000	2,500,000
2020 (forecast)	20,000,000	2,600,000

Source: Forecasts by industry experts

of the year's marketing activities. Total sales are affected by factors such as economic growth, but market share only measures a firm's ability to win or lose against its competitors. As shown in Table 12.3, rising market share can also lead to the producer's ideal of market leadership or market dominance. Magnum has market leadership among ice cream brands. Walkers has market dominance among crisps and snacks. The position of Pampers is stronger still, with its only rival (Huggies) far behind.

There are many advantages to a business in having the top-selling brand (the brand leader). Obviously, sales are higher than anyone else's, but also:

● the brand leader gets the highest distribution level, often without needing to make much effort to achieve it; even a tiny corner shop stocks Whiskas as well as a Happy Shopper own-label cat food; success breeds success

Table 12.3 Brands with the highest UK market share

Leading brand in its market	Sales of leading brand	Market size (by value)	Market share	Share of nearest competitor
Walkers Crisps*	£417 million	£1900 million	21.9%	7.6%
Cadbury's Dairy Milk	£370 million	£2928 million	12.6%	6.2%
Pampers	£256 million	£419 million	61.1%	18.7%
Actimel	£103 million	£250 million	41.2%	14.4%
Magnum Ice Cream	£71 million	£399 million	17.8%	8.0%

*Not including Sensations, Potato Heads or other Walkers brands
Source: *The Grocer*, 15 December 2007, quoting from IRI Infoscan

- brand leaders are able to offer lower discount terms to retailers than the number two or three brands in a market; this means higher revenues and profit margins per unit sold

- the strength of a brand-leading name such Walls Magnum makes it much easier to obtain distribution and consumer trial for new products based on that brand name.

12.7 Market segmentation

Most markets can be subdivided in several different ways. If you go to WHSmith and look at the magazine racks, you will see the process in action. There are magazines for men and (many more) for women. Within the women's section there are kids' magazines, teen mags, young adult mags, middle-aged mags and some for the elderly. Then there are magazines that target different interests and hobbies, from football to computer consoles to gardening.

Market segmentation is the acknowledgement by companies that customers are not all the same. 'The market' can be broken down into smaller sections in which customers share common characteristics – from the same age group to a shared love of Manchester United. Successful segmentation can increase customer satisfaction (if you love shopping and celebs, how wonderful that *Look* magazine is for you!) and provide scope for increasing company profits. After all, customers may be willing to pay a higher price for a magazine focused purely on the subjects they love, instead of buying a general magazine in which most of the articles stay unread.

The keys to successful market segmentation are as follows.

- Research into the different types of customer within a marketplace (e.g. different age groups, gender, region, personality types).

- See if they have common tastes/habits (e.g. younger readers may be more focused on fashion and celebrities than older ones).

- Devise a product designed not for the whole market, but for a particular segment; this might achieve only a 1% market share, but if the total market is big enough, that might be highly profitable.

Issues For Analysis

- The key to analysis is precision. Terms such as inferior goods and normal goods have to be understood so well that you spot where they are relevant and are able to use them to develop your answer. Every student would recognise that a Mercedes sports car is a luxury product. Few could continue by saying that its sales will therefore grow especially fast when times are good, but may slump when the economy is struggling.

- To analyse the market that a business is operating in, make sure to consider the market size, trends and share, the degree of segmentation, the factors determining demand, and the type of market (e.g. local versus national). This is a powerful combination of concepts that should provide a lot of scope for analytic answers.

- Weak exam answers present marketing as a set of simple tools: the 4Ps. In fact, effective marketing is remarkably difficult, even for the biggest and best companies. An October 2007 survey by *The Grocer* magazine placed Coca-Cola as Britain's most valuable brand. Yet Coca-Cola has been responsible for some dreadful new product flops in this country recently, including Dasani water, Coke Blak (coffee-flavoured Coke!) and Vanilla Coke. Good exam answers acknowledge that marketing is difficult because it is based on judgements about the future: future competition, future consumer tastes and future consumer attitudes.

- Achieving success depends on devising a genuinely new type of product that meets an actual consumer need or desire. Apple's iPhone did exactly that, as did Innocent Drinks when they made smoothies an everyday drink for wealthy young adults.

12.8 Marketing objectives, analysis and plans
an evaluation

To judge the likely effectiveness of a firm's marketing plans requires a full understanding of the market. Therefore, just as the marketing manager must research into the market, so you must take care to study the evidence available within the case material. An exam question based on Cadbury might lead to very different answers to the same question based on Mars or Nestlé – even though they all make chocolate. Good judgement comes from good application to the market and to the company.

Exercises

A. Revision questions

(74 marks; 1 hour 20 minutes)

1 In your own words, explain the meaning of the term 'marketing'? (3)

2 Explain why some firms choose not to carry out market research. (3)

3 Why do you think most firms decide to review their marketing strategy at fairly regular intervals? (3)

4 What is meant by the phrase 'target market'? (2)

5 Outline two reasons why it is important for firms to be able to identify their target market. (4)

6a Distinguish between a production-orientated and a market-orientated approach to marketing. (3)

6b Outline whether a production-orientated or market-orientated approach would be better for *one* of the following companies:
(a) Manchester United FC
(b) easyJet
(c) Topshop. (4)

7 Explain how market segmentation has helped companies such as BSkyB to improve their profitability. (4)

8 What are the marketing advantages of not having a specialised marketing department? (4)

9 Explain how the use of a mystery shopper can help to maintain standards of customer service. (4)

10 Briefly explain how the following businesses might benefit from providing excellent customer service:
(a) a café
(b) a manufacturer of washing machines
(c) a bank. (9)

11 Explain why a small local plumber might benefit from offering better customer service than all her local rivals. (4)

12 Explain two benefits that an electricity supplier such as npower might find as a result of gaining a customer service quality standard such as the Charter Mark. (6)

13 Explain in your own words the difference between market size by volume and market size by value. (2)

14a Toyota's share of the UK car market is about 6%. If it continues with that share, how many UK car sales would that amount to in 2020; and how many would there be in China in 2020, assuming the same market share? (4)

14b Outline two ways Toyota might respond to that sales difference. (4)

15 Why might a shoe shop focusing on 'Little Feet' be able to charge higher prices per pair than a general shoe shop? (2)

16 Explain in your own words how the market for shoes could be segmented. (3)

17 Look at Table 12.3. Discuss which business should be happier with its market position: Walkers or Pampers. (6)

B. Revision exercises

B1 Discussion point

The role of chance/luck

Effective marketing usually comes about as a result of careful planning and market-orientated decision making. However, in some cases, firms stumble across a successful marketing strategy by chance. Morgan cars is a conservatively run private business. The production methods used by the company have hardly changed at all in 40 years. Cars are still made largely by hand. Morgan's best-selling cars are based on designs that have not been changed for decades. In most industries this approach would be a recipe for disaster. Fortunately for Morgan, the cars continue to sell well within a tiny niche comprised of customers that want to purchase a hand-built British sports car, built in the Brooklands tradition. Morgan has not deliberately engineered its niche market position, it has just happened accidentally – it has just been fortunate.

Questions

1 From your reading of the text, is it really true that all Morgan's success is down to luck?

2 What marketing problems might the business face if it attempts to expand?

B2 Case study

Wimbledon Quality Cars

Wimbledon Quality Cars (WQC) sells second-hand cars. The business was set up five years ago when the economy was still booming. The owner of the business, Roger Raymond, believes that most businesses over-complicate their marketing. According to Roger, 'marketing is just a set of tools to sell more products, in my case, cars'. The marketing mix of WQC could be summarised as follows.

● *Price:* according to Roger, the bulk of second-hand car buyers are interested in only one thing – low prices. Most of the cars sold by WQC are sold for less than £2000 – an important psychological pricing point.

● *Promotion:* Roger spends £300 per week advertising his cars in the south London press. He also employs two salesmen, Andy and John, who are paid a basic wage of £200 per week and a flat rate commission of £250 per car sold.

● *Product:* Roger believes that the bulk of his customers are not fussy about the make or model of car that they buy. 'Most of my punters want a cheap runaround. The majority of them don't know a good car from a death trap. In our market quality always comes second to a low price.' Roger buys most of his cars from car auctions.

● *Place:* WQC has an old, run-down car showroom, just opposite Wimbledon dog track.

Last year WQC enjoyed its most profitable year yet: sales were up 40% on the previous year. Unfortunately, events took a dramatic turn for the worse last month. To Roger's horror WQC was the subject of a TV documentary investigating

sharp practice in the second-hand car market. The programme alleged that WQC sold cars that were not roadworthy. The implication was that Roger was happy to put the profits of WQC before his customers' safety. Ex-customers of WQC claimed that they had been tricked into buying poor-quality cars by WQC salesmen who failed to disclose faults with the cars.

Questions

(30 marks; 35 minutes)

1 According to Roger, 'Marketing is just a set of tools to sell more products.' Explain the possible drawbacks of this approach. (7)

2 How would you describe WQC's marketing philosophy? Is it production orientated or is it market orientated? (7)

3 Using the example of WQC, explain why an unethical approach towards marketing can often yield profitable results in the short-term. (8)

4 Outline two internal and two external factors that might affect the effectiveness of WQC's marketing? (8)

Figure 12.4 Car production at Morgan

B3 Data response

The chiropractor

Brian Lima runs a hugely successful chain of chiropractors. A chiropractor is a specialist in spinal manipulation, who can relieve all sorts of physical complaints by working on the spine. Brian has always prided himself on operating to the very finest standards, not only in terms of the skills of his professional chiropractors, but also in terms of the level of customer service offered within each practice. Waiting rooms are decorated to the very highest standards, and equipped with all manner of calming and soothing accessories, including spacious and well-stocked fish tanks, along with soothing mood music. Receptionists are recruited very carefully to ensure that they are able to offer the levels of service his customers expect, while training for all staff focuses on meeting customers' expectations. A meticulously collated customer database allows his firm to provide relevant information to all customers and previous customers, who are also regularly contacted to conduct a customer satisfaction survey twice each year, while all staff are proud of having achieved the ISO quality standard for customer complaint handling – although a minuscule complaint level means that there is plenty of time to deal with any problems that do arise.

Questions

(20 marks; 25 minutes)

1a Briefly explain how Brian's business seeks to identify customer expectations. (2)

1b Explain two features of Brian's business that you consider may be vital elements of good customer service for medical practitioners. (4)

2 Explain how Brian's business attempts to monitor and improve customer service levels within the business. (6)

3 Analyse two possible benefits to Brian of providing the highest levels of customer service. (8)

B4 Data response

In late August 2007 entertainment retailer ChoicesUK called in the receivers. It was unable to continue trading after losing money consistently during 2007. As many as 1700 jobs were threatened at ChoicesUK's 200 branches.

This came on top of the collapse of Fopp music retailers earlier in the year. At the same time, industry giant HMV suffered a halving of its profits. The reason was the same – the collapse in the total market for CDs and DVDs, compounded by a switch to buying online or downloading. The UK CD market, for example, fell by 10% in the first half of 2007.

Questions

(15 marks; 15 minutes)

1 Outline two reasons why a whole market may shrink in size, as happened to CD sales in the first half of 2007. (4)

2 ChoicesUK collapsed as the market declined. Explain two ways in which it might have set about boosting its market share (to combat the decline in the market as a whole). (6)

3 In the past, more than half the annual sales of ChoicesUK have taken place in the three months before Christmas. Should the directors have kept the business going a few months more? (5)

B5 Data response

Lidl and Aldi: winning grocery wars

Discount grocers are the big winners in 2007, TNS Worldpanel figures show. The grocery market grew by 4% year-on-year in the 12 weeks to 16 July 2007. Tesco, Sainsbury's and Asda all grew slightly faster than the total market, while Somerfield sales actually fell by 6%. Lidl and Aldi bucked the trend, with sales growth of 13% and 11% respectively. Iceland also performed well, growing by 12%. Perhaps these three low-cost grocers benefited from the collapse of Kwik-Save.

The changes leave Tesco as the market leader with 31.5% (unchanged on 2006), while Asda's share grew from 16.6% to 16.7% and Sainsbury's from 16% to 16.2%. Morrisons

12.9 Workbook

suffered a fall in market share, from 11.3% to 11.1%. A decline of 0.2% may seem trivial, but as the value of the UK grocery market is £128.2 billion a year, 0.2% market share represents sales of £256.4 million!

Questions

(30 marks; 35 minutes)

1a What was the grocery market size and market growth in 2007? (2)

1b Identify three possible reasons why sales at Somerfield fell in 2007. (3)

2a Show the workings to calculate that a 0.2% share of the UK grocery market equals £256.4 million. (3)

2b Use the figures and the bar chart to work out the value of the UK 2007 sales of Lidl. (2)

2c Examine two *possible* reasons why Lidl enjoyed the biggest sales growth within the grocery market in 2007. (6)

3a Outline two ways in which Tesco may benefit from being the grocery market leader. (4)

3b Ten years ago, Sainsbury's was the UK grocery market leader. Discuss whether it could return to that position within the next ten years. (10)

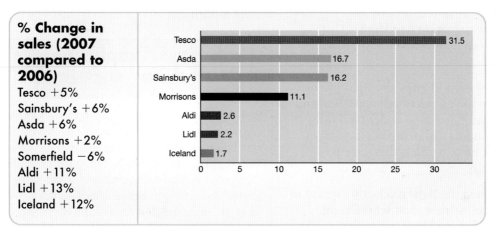

% Change in sales (2007 compared to 2006)

Tesco +5%
Sainsbury's +6%
Asda +6%
Morrisons +2%
Somerfield −6%
Aldi +11%
Lidl +13%
Iceland +12%

	% change in sales
Tesco	31.5
Asda	16.7
Sainsbury's	16.2
Morrisons	11.1
Aldi	2.6
Lidl	2.2
Iceland	1.7

Figure 12.5 UK grocery market share 2007
Source: TNS Worldpanel and Nielsen, quoted in *The Grocer*, 28 July 2007

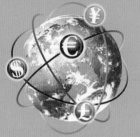

13 Unit

MARKETING STRATEGY

DEFINITION

The marketing mix is the balance between the four main elements needed to carry out the marketing strategy. It consists of the '4Ps': product, price, promotion and place. Marketing strategy is dynamic and continually changing. Alongside the overall aims of the business, the marketing mix can never stand still.

13.1 Components of the marketing mix

When working out how to market a product successfully, there are four main variables to consider (the **marketing mix**).

1 *Product:* the business must identify the right product (or service) to make the product both appealing and distinctive; to do this, it needs to understand fully both its customers and its competitors. No product will have long-term success unless this stage is completed successfully.

2 *Price:* having identified the right product to appeal to its target market, the business must set the right price. The 'right' price for a Versace handbag might be £1,200 – it is a great mistake to think that low prices or special discounts are the path to business success.

3 *Promotion:* marketing managers must identify the right way to create the right image for the product and present it to the right target audience. This might be achieved best by national TV advertising, but specific markets can be reached at far lower cost by more careful targeting (e.g. advertising lawnmowers in magazines such as *Amateur Gardening*). 'Promotion' includes both media advertising (TV, press, cinema, radio) and other forms of promotion (e.g. special offers, public relations, direct mail and online).

4 *Place:* for products, 'place' is how to get your product to the place where customers can be persuaded to buy; this might be through a vending machine or on a Tesco shelf, or positioned just by the till at a newsagent (the prime position for purchases bought on impulse); for service businesses, place may be

online, or in the location of a retail outlet (e.g. Tesco Direct and Tesco stores).

The units that follow this one deal with each of these factors in turn.

High-grade application

Both McVitie's Jaffa Cakes and Burton's Jammie Dodgers are well-known biscuit brands, but the former is distributed in 90% of retail outlets, whereas the latter is in only 64%. Clearly this restricts sales of Jammie Dodgers, because few customers would make a special journey to find them. Both companies have a similar view of the right outlets for their products (e.g. supermarkets, corner shops, garages, canteens and cafés), so why may Burton's be losing out to McVitie's in this particular race? Possible reasons include:

● Jaffa Cakes have higher consumer demand, therefore retail outlets are more willing to stock the product
● Jammie Dodgers may have more direct competitors; high product differentiation may make Jaffa Cakes more of a 'must stock' line
● if Jaffa Cakes have more advertising support, retailers know customers will ask for the product by name while the advertising campaign is running
● McVitie's has a much larger market share, therefore the company is in a stronger position to cross-sell (i.e. persuade a shopkeeper to buy a range of McVitie's brands).

13.2 How is the marketing mix used?

The marketing mix can be used by a new business to develop ideas about how and where to market a product or service. A very small business start-up may look no further than leaflets to be handed out or posted in neighbouring front doors. In a larger business, a senior manager is likely to set a maximum budget, then the individual marketing managers will look at each of the ingredients in the mix. They then decide what marketing actions need to be taken under each of the '4P' headings. If marketing activity is to be effective, each ingredient needs to be considered.

For each market situation managers are trying to set the ideal combination of the ingredients based on a balance between cost and effectiveness. The ingredients need to work with each other. A good product poorly priced may fail. If the product is not available following an advertising campaign the expenditure is wasted. A successful mix is the one that succeeds in putting the strategy into practice (Figure 13.1).

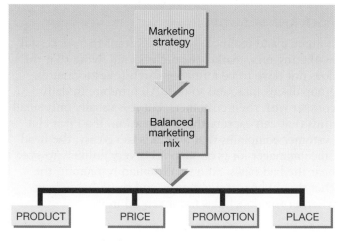

Figure 13.1 A balanced marketing mix

For each market situation there will be a different mix

The focus of the marketing mix will vary according to the market in which the firm is operating. Careful market research should reveal the attitudes and tastes of the target market. An important issue will be whether the goods are:

- regular purchases
- impulse purchases
- emergency purchases.

Impulse purchases (such as chocolate brands) are interesting because they require strong branding, great distribution and display, and eye-catching packaging. In other words, the mix focuses on place and promotion. Price is much less important and the quality of the product may not be hugely important.

Table 13.1 Different types of purchasing and the marketing mix

Type of purchasing	Most important elements of the mix
Regular purchases	Product, promotion and price
Impulse purchases	Place and promotion (including packaging)
Emergency purchases	Place and product

Within each market there may be many different segments

The differences in customers and buying habits result in many 'markets within markets'; these are known as market segments. Each segment will require its own marketing mix. The fashion industry is an example. At one end, cheap, cheerful with mass availability is the key; at the other end exclusivity, quality workmanship and a famous brand name are important.

The ingredients are not equally important

In most cases the product is the vital ingredient. No amount of marketing effort will make a poor product succeed. When selling to other businesses, reliability and quality will probably be far more important than brand image. However, a good product without good support may also fail. The balance will vary. In a price-sensitive market, pricing will be important. This is seen in the petrol market. If one company reduces its price the others follow rapidly.

13.3 Influences on the marketing mix

Finance

Every marketing director is attempting to achieve the best mix of marketing factors to enable the marketing strategy to be a success. S/he must decide how big a budget is needed to market the product successfully, and then how to divide the budget between the 4Ps. If £1 million is available, should it all be put into a TV advertising campaign, or should half the budget be kept for offering special discounts to retailers who stock the product for the first time?

If the budget is big enough, the company will be able to do all the things it wants. Yet even Cadbury, with a £12 million **marketing budget** for its Dairy Milk brand, cannot do everything. This is not surprising, given that a single week of strong TV advertising nationally would cost more than £1 million.

If the budget is very tight, the business may have to be clever about setting the right marketing mix. Small, upmarket food producer Klein Caporn started in 2005 with a strategy based on advertising in classy magazines, and distribution through small, independent food shops. After 12 months it became clear that this would never be profitable because of the costs of delivery to lots of small shops. So bosses Paddy Klein and Ed Caporn changed approach, cutting their price level and targeting the main supermarkets. Waitrose provided

High-grade application

A 2007/08 YouTube sensation in America is Will It Blend. It features a geeky-looking Chief Executive of a small US producer of food blenders. Although any other advertiser would show fruit being blended, Tom Dickson shows the machine's power to blend anything. Word had already spread about his clips blending an American football, a long-handled paddle and a set of golf balls. Then came his biggest hit: blending a brand new iPhone. This received 2 million hits (and rising). People go to the site for the fun of seeing the demonstration, but go away convinced that this is quite some machine. Dickson's company, Blendtec, claims a 650% increase in its online sales as a result of its YouTube campaign. The cost has been close to zero, as Dickson produces the clips himself, then just uploads them.

distribution in its London stores and then, in 2007, the company made a breakthrough into Sainsbury's outlets nationally. They also changed their promotional strategy, hiring a public relations company to get them features in the press instead of spending on advertising. The new approach is working well.

Technology

As shown above in the YouTube example, clever firms need to keep up with modern customers. Years ago, a peak-time advertisement on ITV could reach 33% of the population. Now it would reach only 15%, and less than 10% of the key market of 15–24 year olds. Fewer and fewer families sit together through a night's television: grannies are on Google, while the 15–24 year olds may be in their bedroom on Facebook, playing *Halo 3* or swapping digital files with WiFi-connected friends.* Tesco showed the sharpness of its management in going into online sales and delivery in the 1990s. It left rivals such as Morrisons and Asda trailing. Long-term success in marketing requires that firms keep up with changes in technology.

Market research

If finance and technology are important to a successful marketing mix, market research is vital. Note that this does not have to be formal research (questionnaires, group discussions, and so on). All firms are in daily contact with their customers, but it is usually only small firms that can capture this information. If a Pizza Hut customer complains that a pizza is too greasy, the head office manager for pizza supplies is very unlikely to ever hear the bad news. At a small Italian restaurant, the chef should hear straight away and think hard about whether the dough has too much oil in it.

Medium-sized and large firms need primary research to keep the senior managers in touch with the customers they rarely see. Small firms should constantly be listening to what customers say – in praise or in criticism. There is no better form of market research, because getting the product right is the key to all marketing success.

* By definition this sentence will be out of date by the time you read it.

13.4 Where does the marketing mix fit into marketing planning?

In **marketing planning**, the marketing mix should follow on from the **marketing strategy**. Managers need an excellent understanding of the market if they are to mix the ingredients effectively.

● Statistical analysis should highlight trends. Investigation will reveal the reasons for them.

● Market research should provide:
 – an understanding of the product's place in the market, the market segments and target customers
 – customers' views on the product
 – reasons for the success or failure of the product
 – an understanding of competitive activity.

● The marketing strategy should follow from this analysis. The marketing mix will put the strategy into practice (see Figure 13.2).

Figure 13.2 Where do the 4Ps fit into marketing planning?

Issues For Analysis

When answering questions on the marketing mix consideration should be given to the following points.

● How well the mix is matched to the strategy; only if every aspect of the mix is coordinated and focused will it be effective.

● The relative importance of the ingredients in the marketing mix. Although the product is likely to be the most important element of the mix, every case is different. Taste tests show Coca-Cola to be no better than Pepsi; yet Coke outsells its rival by up to 20 times – in nearly every country in the world.

● How each of the mix ingredients can be used to achieve effective marketing. The mix elements must be tailored to each case. One product may require (and afford) national television advertising. In another case, small-scale local advertising might be supported by below-the-line activity to increase distribution. There is never a single answer to a question about the marketing mix. The best approach depends on the product, its competitive situation, the objectives and the marketing budget.

13.5 Designing an effective marketing mix

an evaluation

The concept of the marketing mix has remained unchanged since it was first introduced in the 1950s. It has proved to be a useful marketing tool. However many believe that there are strong arguments for adding a fifth ingredient – people. Many also feel that it should not be presented as a list of equally important parts but that the mix should be seen with the product at the core, supported by the other ingredients.

With the growing importance of customer service and of good sales staff, it is legitimate to extend the marketing mix to include people. A customer who feels the salesperson is rude or lacks knowledge will go elsewhere. The type of people employed, and their attitude, can be used to build the company's image. Disney employees have to be smart, without facial hair, and be 'upbeat'. Particularly in service businesses, people matter. Good exam answers do not simply repeat a theory, they show a willingness to criticise it. It is worth remembering that not everyone agrees that the mix should have only 4Ps.

Although the 4Ps are presented as a list there is no doubt that in almost every case the product is the most important ingredient. A successful marketing mix should be matched to the marketing strategy. And that strategy is rooted in how well the product is matched to the segment of the market being targeted.

Key terms

Marketing budget: the sum of money provided for marketing a product/service during a period of time (usually a year).

Marketing mix: the elements involved in putting a marketing strategy into practice; these are product, price, promotion and place.

Marketing planning: producing a schedule of marketing activities based on decisions about the marketing mix. This will show when, what and how much will be spent on a product's advertising, promotions and distribution over the coming year.

Marketing strategy: the medium- to long-term plan for meeting the firm's marketing objectives.

Exercises

A. Revision questions

(30 marks; 30 minutes)

1 Briefly outline each of the four ingredients of the marketing mix. (8)

2 Pick the marketing mix factor (the 'P') you think is of most importance in marketing any *two* of the following brands. Give a brief explanation of why you chose that factor.
   (a) The *Sun* newspaper
   (b) The iPod
   (c) Cadbury's Creme Eggs
   (d) A top-of-the-range BMW (6)

3 Outline how the marketing mix for Mars bars may affect their level of impulse sales in a small corner shop. (4)

4 What is meant by a market segment? (3)

5 Explain why new products are so important to businesses. (3)

6 List three different ways of promoting a product. (3)

7 Explain why it might be difficult for a new, small firm to get distribution in a supermarket chain such as Sainsbury's. (3)

B. Revision exercises

B1 Case study

The battle for customers

A leading UK supermarket chain is considering expanding into India. It sees this as a relatively untapped market. The home market is saturated, and price wars and loyalty cards have reduced profit margins. In the UK the supermarkets have been blamed for the disappearance of the corner shop. In India the situation is very different. A recent survey by an Indian market research firm concluded that small grocery shops will continue to dominate the food retailing market for the foreseeable future. Several firms, which have been lured to India by its rapid economic growth and over 1 billion mouths to feed, have not been successful in their attempts to establish supermarkets in India's largest cities. Neither of the two main contenders have managed to break even since opening in the early 1990s. They are continuing to expand and hoping that, eventually, economies of scale will permit lower prices and hopefully improve their standing and their profitability.

These new supermarkets have faced several problems.

● The local stores do not stock as many brands as the supermarkets, but they will stock an item if a customer wants it. If they do not have what the customer wants they will get it.

● The local stores offer a free delivery service and allow customers credit.

● The supermarkets cannot match the cost base of the local store. The poor infrastructure makes operational costs (such as transport and delivery) very expensive.

● Government laws limiting urban development mean that property prices are high. The smaller stores have often been in the family for generations, and so the initial cost of the site has long since been forgotten.

To try to gain customers, one of the supermarket chains has introduced promotions such as coupons, and has advertised in local newspapers. Another has teamed up with local manufacturers. It obtains staples such as lentils and rice locally. These are then packaged and branded by local manufacturers. This has helped to lower prices for customers and improve margins. A recent entrant into the market is trying to stay ahead of the competition. It has invested in air-conditioning and additional telephone lines to ensure that customers do not have to wait when they call.

The UK chain has looked at the existing market in India and feels it can succeed. However, the managers know they will do this only after a struggle to change customer attitudes.

Questions

(30 marks; 35 minutes)

1 What is meant by 'the home market is saturated'? (2)

2 What are the marketing implications for a business in a saturated market? (6)

3 Why might expansion allow economies of scale? (4)

4 What problems might a British retailer have in marketing its service in India? (6)

5 Using the marketing mix, analyse the existing market and evaluate the UK firm's chances of success. (12)

14 Unit

MARKETING MIX: PRODUCT

DEFINITION

A product is a good or service that is bought and sold within a market. Products are developed so that they satisfy a specific consumer need or want that has been targeted by the business.

14.1 What's in a product: actual and psychological benefits

Successful products are normally bought by consumers for more than one reason. Products such as Coca-Cola and Stella Artois deliver both physical and psychological consumer benefits. Both products taste good, delivering a fairly obvious physical benefit for the consumer. In addition, both brands also offer consumers psychological benefits: both products have brand images that consumers want to buy into.

High-grade application

Alfa Romeo

Highly successful products deliver both physical and psychological benefits that are valued by consumers.

Alfa Romeo is an Italian-based producer of distinctively designed sports cars. Alfa has a very strong brand image that it communicates clearly to the middle-aged men that make up the bulk of its target market. The psychological benefits of owning an Alfa include: beautiful, distinctive design; the company's motor sports heritage; and the fact that the car is Italian.

In the 1980s and 1990s Alfa Romeo performed badly in quality and reliability surveys compared to other car manufacturers. However, despite these weaknesses the company managed to sell enough cars to survive. During this period the product sold on an emotional basis to a hard-core group of Alfa enthusiasts. They loved the company's designs and the brand's cult status. The consumers that made up this niche market were prepared to overlook the product's physical deficiencies.

Figure 14.1 An Alfa Romeo sports car

The key to having a good product is achieving consumer satisfaction. A restaurant can improve the quality of its product in many ways. The most obvious method would be to improve the quality of food sold. Purchasing new superior tables and chairs could also improve the 'product'. However, the restaurant's product could also be improved by providing waiting staff with better training so that customer service improves. For service-sector businesses, such as hotels, a major element of the 'product' is the staff. Motivating employees so that they provide high standards of customer care is vital in terms of producing a high-quality product.

14.2 Influences on the development of new products

Technology

Technological advances can provide firms with opportunities to produce new products that offer consumers new benefits. According to 'Moore's law' computer speed and capacity doubles every two years.

Advances in computer technology have enabled firms to develop new and improved mobile phones and laptop computers that offer consumers new features. These new features enable the firm that was first to the market with these new products to steal market share away from its rivals.

Rapid technological advances in computing have major implications for computer and mobile phone producers. Product life cycles are very short in both markets. As a consequence, component suppliers face tremendous timescale pressures to launch new components before they become technologically obsolete. Even a delay of just a month could be the difference between a successful new product and a failed launch.

High-grade application
Mercedes-Benz technology at your service

Sleeping at the wheel is one of the major causes of road fatalities. To combat this problem Mercedes-Benz is trying to develop the technology necessary to detect driver fatigue. Teams of engineers, computer scientists and psychologists at Mercedes are working on the idea of installing an infra-red camera directed at the driver's eye. If eye-blink frequency drops below a critical level, indicating the onset of sleep, an audible alarm will sound inside the car to re-awaken the driver.

Competitors' actions

Firms operating in competitive markets may try to emulate a successful new product produced by one of their rivals by launching their own 'me-too' version of the successful new product. A me-too is a new brand that is largely an imitation of an existing product. Me-toos normally sell at a price discount compared to the original product.

The entrepreneurial skills of managers and owners

Most firms use market research findings to help them identify profitable new gaps in the market. Once these gaps in the market have been found, firms will then try to design new products that possess the characteristics required by the target market. Entrepreneurs need to be good at spotting gaps in the market; they also need to develop systems within their business that enable it to react first to changes in market trends.

Entrepreneurial managers can launch their new products quickly enough to benefit from 'first-mover advantage'.

Firms that can launch their new products before their rivals have the opportunity to charge premium prices until competition arrives. In most markets **brand loyalty** tends to be established at a very early stage. Businesses run by managers with weaker entrepreneurial skills, which launched their new products late will probably find it very difficult to gain a foothold in the market.

High-grade application
Zara's fast fashion revolution

Zara is one of Europe's fastest-growing fashion retailers. The company has based its success on fast fashion. The aim of this strategy is to launch new lines of cheap clothing that replicate exclusive designs, shown just a week earlier at major fashion shows. To make this strategy possible, the founder of Zara, Amancio Ortega, used lean production techniques first developed by the car maker Toyota to reduce new product development times.

14.3 Product differentiation and USPs

Product differentiation is the degree to which consumers perceive that your brand is different from its competitors. A highly differentiated product is one that is viewed as having unique features, such as Marmite or the iPhone. A highly differentiated product may have substitutes. However, if differentiation is strong enough, consumers won't even bother looking at these other brands when making their purchasing decisions. The substitutes available are *not acceptable* to the consumer. A product's point of differentiation is often described as a **unique selling point** (USP).

Creating product differentiation

Product differentiation can be created in two ways.

1 Actual differentiation that creates genuine product advantages that benefit the consumer in some way. Actual product differentiation can be created by:
   – a unique design that is aesthetically pleasing to the eye (e.g. Scandinavian furniture from IKEA)
   – a unique product function (e.g. a mobile phone with a new feature)
   – a unique taste (e.g. Dr Pepper)
   – ergonomic factors (e.g. a product that is easier to use than its rivals)
   – superior performance (e.g. a Dyson vacuum cleaner).

2 Imagined differentiation. This type of differentiation involves creating differences that exist only in the mind of the consumer. A product can be differentiated by psychological factors despite the fact that the product is not physically different from a similar product produced by the competition. Imaginary product differentiation can be created via persuasive advertising, celebrity endorsements and sponsorship. When a product is consumed it is not just the product itself that is consumed – buyers also enjoy 'consuming' the brand's image too. Many people are prepared to pay a price premium for a product that has a brand image that appeals to them.

Issues For Analysis

When developing an argument in answer to an exam question, product differentiation offers the following main lines of analysis.

● Firms operating in competitive markets need to sell products that have strong USPs if they are to hold on to market share.

● Product differentiation reduces consumer price sensitivity. The brand loyalty created by the differentiation means that prices can be increased without having to worry about a substantial fall in sales volume. Total revenue should rise when prices are increased because highly differentiated products tend to be price inelastic.

● Product differentiation boosts value-added because it makes premium prices possible.

14.4 Product
an evaluation

Product differentiation is rarely permanent. Changes in consumer tastes and technological advances can make a product's point of differentiation ineffective. Can the idea be easily copied? Is there patent protection?

Which is more effective, imagined differentiation or actual differentiation? It could be argued that imagined differentiation, created by persuasive advertising, might be more long-lasting than actual differentiation because it might be harder for a me-too to replicate a brand's distinctive personality. Magners' original differentiation was relatively weak. Competitors quickly realised that they could also package their premium ciders in pint bottles, promoting the brand to be drunk over ice. If Magners is to hold on to its market share it must identify a new USP.

Globalisation has increased the availability of products to consumers. As a result firms now face increased competitive pressure. In order to survive, firms must continually develop new, ever more powerful USPs for their products. Will small firms with modest research and development resources be able to compete against their larger rivals?

Key terms

Brand loyalty: the desire by customers to stick with one brand; perhaps to always buy that brand (e.g. always buying Galaxy instead of Cadbury's).
First-mover advantage: the benefits of being the first business into a new market sector (as Coca-Cola once was – in 1886!).
Unique selling point: one feature that makes a product different from all its rivals (e.g. Bounty – the only mass-market chocolate bar featuring coconut).

Exercises

A. Revision questions

(40 marks; 40 minutes)

1 Outline two reasons that might explain the success of products such as Coca-Cola and Stella Artois. (4)

2 Analyse how training might be used to improve the quality of the product produced by a service-sector business such as a supermarket. (3)

3 Explain how technological advances can influence the direction of new product development. (3)

4 What is first-mover advantage? State two benefits firms receive if they can achieve first-mover advantage. (4)

5 What is a me-too product and why do some firms choose to launch them? (4)

6 Explain the meaning of the term product differentiation, using your own example. (4)

7 Outline two ways in which a clothes shop might differentiate itself from its competitors. (6)

8 Explain two benefits a firm can gain from selling a differentiated product. (4)

9 Why is it particularly helpful to have a product that is differentiated by a USP? (4)

10 Outline two examples of USPs in current products or services you buy. (4)

B. Revision exercises

B1 Data response

San Paulo is a highly successful Brazilian company that runs over 2000 coffee bars across South America. The idea for the business came ten years ago when the founder of the business, Roberto Carlos, visited Italy for a family holiday. During his holiday Carlos was impressed by the décor and ambience of the traditionally styled Italian coffee shops that he visited.

On his return to Brazil, Carlos decided to set up his own Italian-styled coffee bar. To ensure authenticity and a strong unique selling point, Carlos imported all the fixtures and fittings for his café from Italy. The business was an overnight success. At the time nothing like it existed in his home town of Campo Grande, and the business quickly expanded by opening up new franchised outlets in other cities across Brazil and Argentina. Over time, trading conditions have become tougher as new competitors have entered the market. Most of these competitors have sought to replicate San Paulo's original unique selling point: classic Italian interior design. Today, San Paulo is still the market leader; a significant percentage of customers see San Paulo as being the original coffee bar of its type. However, in an attempt to grow market share Carlos recently took the decision to reduce San Paulo's price premium.

The company now has plans to enter the UK market. The first bar will be set up in Croydon. The management of San Paulo believe that they will have to charge their UK consumers substantially more than their South American customers to overcome higher European wages and rents. The UK coffee bar market is extremely competitive. Will San Paulo be able to survive against companies such as Costa, Caffè Nero and Starbucks?

Questions

(25 marks; 30 minutes)

1a Define the term 'unique selling point'. (2)

1b Identify the original unique selling point that made San Paulo a successful business in South America. (2)

2 Using the data in the case as a starting point, discuss whether constant innovation is required to maintain product differentiation. (12)

3 You have been hired to manage the new bar in Croydon. Despite your concerns about the strength of the competition locally, your English boss wants you to charge high prices. Outline three ways that could be used to create the high product differentiation required for your coffee bar. (9)

B2 Data response

Absolut vodka

Absolut vodka was developed by the Swedish state-owned monopoly provider of strong alcohol, Systembolaget, in the late 1970s. The government's goal was to create a premium-priced product that would sell well in America. Blind product tests showed that consumers were not able to tell the difference between one brand of vodka and another. The challenge, then, was to create a consumer preference for Absolut vodka where there was no real difference.

To create the product differentiation required, the advertising agency appointed to market Absolut had to create a unique image for the brand that would appeal to consumers. The first step was to create a distinctive award-winning bottle that reflected the brand's Scandinavian origins. The second step was more controversial. A brand heritage for Absolut was required to convince American consumers that the brand was authentic. Advertisements claimed that the brand was over 400 years old. Unfortunately, this was not true: Absolut was first sold in Sweden in 1879 and, for many years, the brand had been withdrawn and was unavailable for sale. Production of Absolut only restarted in 1979, just before the brand's relaunch. Less controversially, differentiation was also built up by the decision to use world-famous artists such as Andy Warhol to promote the brand. In America the company also sponsored arts and cultural events to enhance the image of the brand. The strategy worked. Today, Absolut holds over 30% of the American vodka market.

Figure 14.2 *Effective branding has helped Absolut to gain 30% of the American vodka market*

Questions

(30 marks; 35 minutes)

1 What is a premium-priced product? (2)

2 Explain why product differentiation can create premium prices. (6)

3 Outline two factors that might influence the direction of new product development in the alcoholic drinks industry. (6)

4 Analyse two ways in which product differentiation was created for the Absolut brand. (6)

5 Discuss the ethics of the marketing of Absolut vodka. (10)

PRODUCT LIFE CYCLE AND PORTFOLIO ANALYSIS

The product life cycle is the theory that all products follow a similar pattern over time, of development, introduction, growth, maturity and decline.

15.1 What is the product life cycle?

The product life cycle shows the sales of a product over time. When a new product is first launched sales will usually be slow. This is because the product is not yet known or proven in the market. Retailers may be reluctant to stock the product because it means giving up valuable shelf space to products that may or may not sell. This involves a high risk. Customers may also be hesitant – many may want to wait until someone else has tried it before they purchase it themselves.

If the product does succeed, then its sales will grow and it enters the growth phase of the product life cycle. However, at some point sales are likely to stabilise; this is known as the maturity phase. This slowing down of the growth of sales might be because competitors have introduced similar products or because the market has now become saturated. Once most households have bought a dishwasher, for example, sales are likely to be relatively slow. This is because new purchases will mainly involve people who are updating their machine, rather than new buyers.

At some point sales are likely to decline. This may be because new technology means the product has become outdated. An example is the way CD sales have fallen due to the rise of downloading. A decline in sales may also be because competitors have launched a more successful model or you have improved your own product – for example, the PlayStation 3 (PS3) replacing the PS2.

The five key stages of a product's life cycle are known as: development, introduction, growth, maturity and decline. These can be illustrated on a product life cycle diagram. The typical stages in a product's life are shown in Figure 15.1.

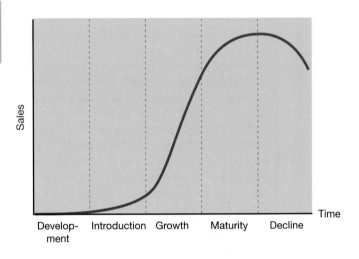

Figure 15.1 The product life cycle

Do remember that many products never make it as far as being launched. Many would-be entrepreneurs have what they think are great ideas. Unfortunately, it turns out they are not financially viable or they cannot find a way of successfully getting them to market. Just think how many ideas are rejected each series on the BBC TV show *Dragons' Den*, because the investors do not think demand is going to be high enough.

Even well-established firms will find that many of their new ideas do not prove commercially viable. Cadbury's rejects 20 new product ideas for every one that reaches the market. Apple's iPod may have been a great success but its internet software Cyberdog lasted about a year, and its first phone – launched with Motorola in 2005 and called the ROKR – was a flop. Thousands of products are taken out of production each year because they fail to hit their initial sales targets and have not reached the growth stage of the life cycle.

Table 15.1 *Examples of how the marketing mix may vary at different stages of the product life cycle*

	Development	**Introduction**	**Growth**	**Maturity**	**Decline**
Sales	Zero	Low	Increasing	Growth is slowing	Falling
Costs per unit	High; there is investment in product development but only a few prototypes and test products being produced	High, because sales are relatively low but launch costs are high and overheads are being spread over a few units	Falling as overheads are spread over more units	Falling as sales are still growing	Still likely to be low as development costs have been covered and reduced promotional costs are needed to raise awareness
Product	Prototypes	Likely to be basic	May be modified given initial customer feedback; range may be increased	Depends – may focus on core products and remove ones in the range not selling well; may diversify and extend brand to new items	Focus on most profitable items
Promotion	As development is nearly finished it may be used to alert customers of the launch	Mainly to raise awareness	Building loyalty	May focus on highlighting the differences with competitors' products	
Distribution	Early discussions with retailers will help in finalising the product packaging	May be limited as distributors wait to see customers' reactions	May be increasing as more distributors willing to stock it and product is rolled out to more markets	May focus on key outlets and more profitable channels	Lower budgets to keep costs down
Price	Not needed	Depends on pricing approach, e.g. a high price if skimming is adopted (if demand is high and not sensitive to price); a low price if penetration is adopted to gain market share	Depends on demand conditions and strategy adopted; e.g. with a skimming strategy the price may now be lowered to target more segments	May have to drop to maintain competitiveness	Likely to discount to maintain sales

15.2 What use is the product life cycle?

The product life cycle model helps managers plan their marketing activities. Marketing managers will need to adjust their marketing mix at different stages of the product life cycle, as outlined below.

● In the introduction phase the promotion may focus on making customers aware that a new product exists; in the maturity phase it may focus more on highlighting the difference between your product and competitors that have arrived since.

● At the beginning of the life cycle, a technologically advanced product may be launched with a high price (think of the iPhone); over time the price may fall as newer models are being launched. By considering the requirements of each stage of the life cycle, marketing managers may adjust their marketing activities accordingly.

High-grade application
Energy-efficient light bulbs

The lighting industry is now working on a third generation of energy-efficient light bulbs, designed to last a lifetime. Already in use outdoors and in some shops and galleries, these light-emitting diodes (LEDs) have bulbs with a lifespan of up to 100 years. Since October 2006 the front of Buckingham Palace has been lit up with LED bulbs.

Although some energy-efficient bulbs already exist, and are growing in popularity, LEDs for the home are still at the development phase of the product life cycle. They are expected to be on sale in the next four years. A typical light bulb lasts up to one year and costs around 20 pence. The LED will cost over £4. In America, General Electric, the world's biggest bulb manufacturer, is closing seven of its 54 factories and warehouses. It is forecasting a downturn in demand for conventional bulbs as people switch to energy-efficient versions.

Managers know that the length of the phases of the life cycle cannot easily be predicted. They will vary from one product to another and this means the marketing mix will need to be altered at different times. For example, a product may be a fad and therefore the overall life of the product will be quite short. Many fashions are popular only for one season and some films are popular only for a matter of weeks. Other products

have very long life cycles. The first manufactured cigarettes went on sale in Britain in 1873. By chance, sales hit their peak (120,000 million!) exactly 100 years later. Since 1973 sales have gently declined. They now stand at 70,000 million.

It is also important to distinguish between the life cycle of a product category and the life cycle of a particular brand. Sales of wine are growing, but a brand that was once the biggest seller (Hirondelle) has virtually disappeared as wine buyers have become more sophisticated. Similarly, confectionery is a mature market but particular brands are at different stages in their life cycles: Mars bars are in maturity while Trident chewing gum is in its growth stage.

15.3 The product life cycle and capacity

When considering the future sales of the business, managers will need to link their forecasts to their plans for the firm's capacity. The capacity of an organisation is the maximum it can produce given its existing resources. If managers choose a capacity level that is relatively low this means that a sudden increase in sales (e.g. if the product enters the growth phase quickly) may mean customers have to be turned away. This happened to the Nintendo Wii in 2007/08, to the delight of rival Sony. On the other hand, if the chosen capacity level is high, if the product is not successful the business will have invested in facilities that are not required; this is inefficient and expensive. Trying to match the capacity of the business to the likely sales is a difficult challenge for managers.

High-grade application
Magners

In 2006 Magners cider was sold in England for the first time. Supported by heavy investment in promotion it was an incredible success. Sales grew 225% in one year and it was clearly in the growth phase of the product life cycle. In fact, the success of Magners prompted an interest in all kinds of cider, and total market sales grew 23% to 965 million pints in 2006. The growth of Magners led its managers to invest £135 million to increase capacity. Unfortunately, however, sales in 2007 were hit by bad weather and the entry of competitor brands.

15.4 Cash flow and the product life cycle

In the development phase before a product is launched, cash flow will be negative. The firm will be spending money on research and development, market research and production planning, but no revenue is yet being generated. Prototypes and models are being made (Dyson produced 5000 prototypes of the Dyson vacuum cleaner before launching it) but income is zero. The business may also decide to test-market the product, which again costs money.

Once the product is on sale cash should begin to come in. However, at this stage, sales are likely to be low and the firm will still be promoting the product heavily to generate awareness. Overall cash flow may continue to be negative for some time. In many cases, the cash flow will not become a positive figure until some way into the growth stage of the life cycle. It may only be at that stage that the firm reaches operational break-even. Cash flow should then continue to improve until the decline stage, when the volume of sales and the amount of cash coming in begin to fall.

It is important, therefore, for firms to manage their cash flow effectively during the life cycle, and to plan ahead. Although a product may prove successful in the long term it may also cause the firm severe cash flow problems in the short term unless its finances are properly managed. Careful budgeting is important at this stage, to avoid overspending.

High-grade application
Ocado

Ocado is an online grocer that is in partnership with the supermarket Waitrose. Ocado was established in 2001 and, within its first six years, had gained sales of £300 million a year. Even so, it was still not making a profit because of the huge costs of establishing the business. For example, Ocado invested in an enormous central warehouse where the products are stocked and packed. This is the size of seven football pitches and six storeys high. By 2007 the warehouse was still operating at 35% capacity. However, the managers of Ocado remain positive about the future of the business. They are anticipating annual growth of up to 30% and believe they will start to make a profit in the coming year.

15.5 Extension strategies

The aim of an **extension strategy** is to prevent a decline in the product's sales. There are various means by which this can be achieved, as noted below.

- By *targeting a new segment of the market:* when sales of Johnson & Johnson's baby products started to fall, the company repositioned the product and aimed it at adults. Alternatively, a new geographic market may be targeted, e.g. China.

- By *developing new uses for the product:* the basic technology in hot-air paint strippers, for example, is no different from that in a hairdryer.

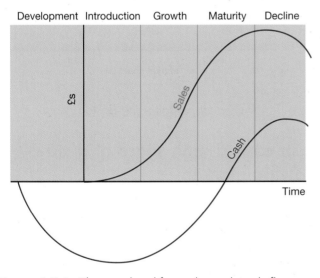

Figure 15.2 The product life cycle and cash flow

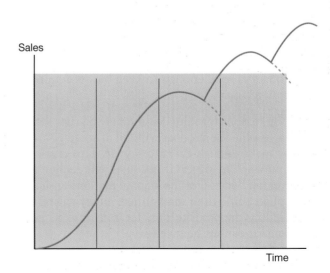

Figure 15.3 The effect of extension strategies

● *By increasing the usage of a product*: Actimel's 'challenge' was for consumers to eat one pot a day for a fortnight – a wonderful way to encourage increased consumption.

The continued success of products such as Coca-Cola and Kellogg's cornflakes is not just due to luck; it is down to sophisticated marketing techniques, which have managed to maintain sales over many years despite fierce competition. The Kellogg's logo is regularly updated, new pack sizes are often introduced, and various competitions and offers are used on a regular basis to keep sales high. The company has also tried to increase the number of students and adults eating its products. It has run advertising campaigns to encourage people to eat the product throughout the day as well as in the morning.

Given the fact that developing a product can involve high costs and that there is a high failure rate of new products, it is not surprising that if a product is successful managers will try to prolong its sales for as long as it is profitable. Who would have thought, in the 1880s, that a frothy drink would still be a huge seller more than 125 years later? Clever Coke.

15.6 Is a decline in sales inevitable?

In the standard product life cycle model it seems as if a decline in sales is inevitable. This may be true in some situations. For example, developments in technology may make some products obsolete. On the other hand, the decline in sales may be the result of poor marketing. Effective extension strategies may ensure that a product's sales are maintained. The long-term success of products and services such as Monopoly and KitKat shows that sales can be maintained over a very long period of time. Creative marketing can avoid the decline phase for a substantial period of time – but only if the product is good enough to keep buyers coming back for more.

One of the reasons for sales decline may be that some managers assume the product will fail at some point and so do not make enough effort to save it. This is known as 'determinism': managers think sales will decline and so sales do fall because of inadequate marketing support. Instead of adapting their marketing strategy to find new ways of selling the product, they let it decline because they assume it cannot be saved.

It is important to remember that a life cycle graph only shows what has happened – it is not a prediction of the future. Top marketing managers try to influence the future, not just let it happen. They try to shape the product life cycle not let it shape their success.

15.7 The product portfolio

Product **portfolio analysis** examines the existing position of a firm's products. This allows the firm to consider its existing position and plan what to do next. There are several different methods of portfolio analysis. One of the best known was developed by the Boston Consulting Group, a management consultancy; it is known as the Boston Matrix.

The Boston Matrix shows the market share of each of the firm's products and the rate of growth of the markets in which they operate. By highlighting the position of each product in terms of market share and market growth, a business can analyse its existing situation and decide what to do next and where to direct its marketing efforts. This model has four categories, as described below.

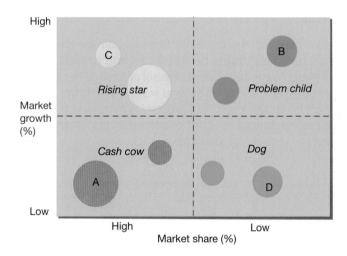

Figure 15.4 Product portfolio: the Boston Matrix

Cash cow: a high share of a slow-growing market

In Figure 15.4, product A has a high market share of a low-growth market. The size of the circle depends on the turnover of the product. This type of product is known as a **cash cow**. An example of a cash cow might be Heinz Baked Beans. The overall market for baked beans is mature and therefore slow growing. Within this market, the Heinz brand has a market share of more than 50%. This type of product generates high profits and cash for the company because sales are relatively high, while the promotional cost per unit is quite low.

Consumers are already aware of the brand, which reduces some of the need for promotion. High and stable sales keep the cost per unit relatively low. Heinz can therefore 'milk' cash from baked beans to invest in newer products such as Heinz Organic Ketchup.

Problem child: a low share of a fast-growing market

Product B, by comparison, is in a high-growth market but has a low market share. This type of product is known as a **problem child** (also called a 'question mark'). A problem child may well provide high profits in the future; the market itself is attractive because it is growing fast and the product could provide high returns if it manages to gain a greater market share. However, the success of such products is by no means certain and that is why they are like problem children – they may grow and prosper or things may go wrong. These products usually need a relatively high level of investment to promote them, get them distributed and keep them going. A new Heinz recipe might be in this position.

Rising star: a high share of a growing market

Rising stars such as product C have a high market share and are selling in a fast-growing market. These products are obviously attractive – they are doing well in a successful market. However, they may need protecting from competitors' products. Once again, the profits of the cash cows can be used to keep the sales growing. Heinz Organic Soups are in this category. They are very successful, with fast-growing sales, but still need heavy promotion to ensure their success.

Dogs: a low share of a stable or declining market

The fourth category of products are known as **dogs**. These products (like product D in Figure 15.4) have a low share of a low-growth market. They hold little appeal for a firm unless they can be revived. The product or brand will be killed off once its sales slip below the break-even point.

The purpose of product portfolio analysis

Product portfolio analysis aims to examine the existing position of the firm's products. Once this has been done

the managers can plan what to do next. Typically this will involve four strategies:

1 *building* – this involves investment in promotion and distribution to boost sales; this is often used with problem children (question marks)

2 *holding* – this involves marketing spending to maintain sales; this is used with rising star products

3 *milking* – this means taking whatever profits you can without much more new investment; this is often used with cash cow products

4 *divesting* – this involves selling off the product and is common with dogs or problem children.

The various strategies chosen will depend on the firm's portfolio of products. If most of the firm's products are cash cows, for example, it needs to be developing new products for future growth. If, however, the majority are problem children then it is in quite a high-risk situation; it needs to try to ensure some products do become stars. If it has too many dogs then it needs to be investing in product development or acquiring new brands.

Issues For Analysis

When analysing the importance of the product life cycle and portfolio model it might be useful to consider the following points.

- Portfolio analysis examines the position of all the firm's products, and helps managers decide what to do with each of them (e.g. invest more or milk them).

- The models do not in themselves tell the firm what to do; managers must interpret their findings and decide on the most effective course of action.

- Managers must avoid letting these models become self-fulfilling (e.g. deciding the product is in decline and so letting its sales fall).

- Product life cycles are generally becoming shorter due to the rapid developments in technology and the increasing levels of competition in most markets.

- As well as the life cycle for a particular product it can be useful to study the life cycle of a category of products (e.g. examining the life of Flora margarine and the life cycle for the whole margarine market).

Both the product life cycle and product portfolio analysis are marketing tools to help firms with their marketing planning. By analysing their existing situation they can identify what needs to be done with the marketing mix to fulfil their objectives. However, like all planning tools, simply being able to examine the present position does not in itself guarantee success. Firms still have to be able to select the right strategy and implement it successfully.

15.8 Product life cycle and portfolio analysis
an evaluation

The product life cycle model and portfolio analysis are important in assessing the firm's current position within the market. They make up an important step in the planning process. However, simply gathering data does not in itself guarantee success. A manager has to interpret the information effectively and then make the right decision. The models show where a business is at the moment; the difficult decisions relate to where the business will be in the future.

Product portfolio analysis is especially useful for larger businesses with many products. It helps a manager look critically at the firm's product range. Then decisions can be made on how the firm's marketing spending should be divided up between different products. By contrast, the product life cycle is of more help to a small firm with one or two products. A company called Filofax made a fortune in the 1990s marketing a paper-based 'personal organiser'. When people switched to electronic products such as the BlackBerry, Filofax wasted years (and many millions) persisting with its paper product. The business needed to acknowledge when a life cycle decline was unstoppable.

Key terms

Cash cow: a product that has a high share of a low-growth market.

Dog: a product that has a low share of a low-growth market.

Extension strategy: marketing activities used to prevent sales from declining.

Portfolio analysis: an analysis of the market position of the firm's existing products; it is used as part of the marketing planning process.

Problem child: a product that has a small share of a fast-growing market.

Rising star: a product that has a high share of a fast-growing market.

Exercises

A. Revision questions

(35 marks; 35 minutes)

1 Identify the different stages of the product life cycle. Give an example of one product or service you consider to be at each stage of the life cycle. (4)

2 Explain what is meant by an 'extension strategy'. (4)

3 Outline the likely relationship between cash flow and the different stages of the life cycle. (4)

4 How is it possible for products such as the Barbie doll to apparently defy the decline phase of the product cycle? (6)

5 What is meant by 'product portfolio analysis'? (3)

6 Distinguish between a cash cow and a rising star in the Boston Matrix. (4)

7 Explain how the Boston Matrix could be used by a business such as Cadbury. (4)

8 Firms should never take decline (or growth) for granted. Therefore they should never take success (or failure) for granted. Explain why this advice is important if firms are to make the best use of product life cycle theory. (6)

B. Revision exercises

B1 Data response

Fire Angel

Sam Tate and his partner have developed an innovative smoke detector called Fire Angel. This product is placed in a light fitting and its energy supply is automatically recharged when the light is turned on. This way the danger of your smoke detector failing to work because of flat batteries should be reduced and, because it recharges itself, customers don't need to buy new batteries. Fire Angel is now stocked in around 6000 stores.

Figure 15.5 Fire Angel smoke detector

Before launching Fire Angel Sam did lots of market research. He spoke to the Fire Brigade and the government office responsible for fire safety, to ensure that there was a need for this sort of product, and to estimate the market size and market growth. He then interviewed people in the street to see what they thought, as well as analysing competitors' products. He also examined different ways of getting the product to market and eventually decided that selling through the supermarkets was the key to achieving a high volume of sales.

The average price of smoke detectors is between £5 and £10 but Sam felt he could charge a premium price because his product does not need a battery and lasts for up to ten years, so he set the price of the Fire Angel at £20. He felt it was better to go in with a higher price than a lower one because it is more difficult to lower the price than increase it later on. It took three years to get the Fire Angel from the idea stage to the launch stage; most of this time was spent on design and testing, but it did take many months to convince some of the retailers to stock it.

Source: adapted from Business Link

Questions

(30 marks; 35 minutes)

1 What is meant by 'market growth'? (2)

2 Outline the unique selling point of the Fire Angel, and explain how this can benefit the business. (6)

3 Analyse the possible benefits to Sam of undertaking market research before launching the Fire Angel. (7)

4 Explain why Sam might have had cash flow problems in the first few years of his business. (6)

5 At the moment the Fire Angel is still in its growth phase. Discuss the ways in which the marketing mix of the Fire Angel might change as it enters the maturity phase. (9)

B2 Data response

Mackie's ice cream

Figure 15.6

Mackie's is a maker of luxury ice cream, based in Scotland.

All Mackie's ice cream is made at its farm in Aberdeenshire. Its production chain includes the wind that provides the business with renewable energy, its own crops that feed its cattle, and its own cows that produce the milk and cream for the ice cream. 'It's a real plough to plate – or cow to cone story,' says the company.

Mackie's employs 70 people and produces over 7 million litres of luxury ice cream a year.

Mackie's ice cream is well established as the brand leader in the luxury ice cream market in Scotland, has an increasing market share in England, and is being exported to Seoul (South Korea) and Norway.

The Mackie family have been farming at Westertown farm since the turn of the century, but it was only in 1986 that they started pilot trials for an ice cream. In 1993 some of the farm's facilities were converted to a modern ice cream dairy capable of producing more than 10 million litres a year. In 1996 the New Product Development Kitchen was added. In 2006 production machinery was added to raise capacity in the ice cream dairy to 6000 litres per hour. It sells through shops, restaurants and ice cream parlours.

Its luxury ice cream products include: Raspberry, Honeycomb, Strawberry and Cream, Chocolate Mint, and Absolutely Chocolate. These are available in a variety of sizes. It also produces 100%-fruit frozen smoothies, sorbets and organic ice cream.

Source: http://www.mackies.co.uk/

Questions

(30 marks; 35 minutes)

1 What is meant by the term 'market share'? (2)

2 Explain the factors that Mackie's might have considered before expanding its capacity. (5)

3 Explain how the promotion of a new Mackie's ice cream might vary at different stages in its life cycle. (5)

4 Examine the possible benefits to Mackie's of having a portfolio of products. (8)

5 Consider whether new product development is likely to be essential for success in the ice cream market. (10)

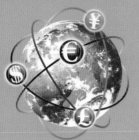

MARKETING MIX: PRICE

DEFINITION

Price is the amount paid by the customer for a good or service.

16.1 How important are decisions about price?

Price is one of the main links between the customer (demand) and the producer (supply). It gives messages to consumers about product quality and is fundamental to a firm's revenues and profit margins. As part of the marketing mix it is fundamental to most consumer buying decisions. The importance of price to the customer will depend on several factors, as discussed below.

Customer sensitivity to price

Consumers have an idea of the correct price for a product (see Figure 16.1). They balance price with other considerations. These include:

- the quality of the product – products seen as having higher quality can carry a price premium; this may be real or perceived quality

- how much they want it – all purchases are personal; customers will pay more for goods they need or want

- their income – customers buy products within their income range; consumers with more disposable income are less concerned about price; uncertainty about future income will have the same effect as lower income; if interest rates are high, hard-pressed home-buyers will be much more sensitive to price; they need to save money and so they check prices more carefully and avoid high-priced items.

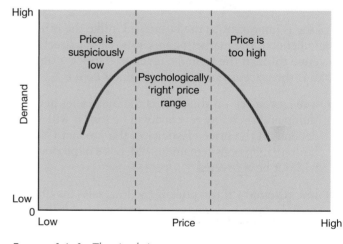

Figure 16.1 The 'right' price

Table 16.1 Price sensitivity in practice

Products, services and brands that are highly price sensitive	Products, services and brands that are not very price sensitive
No-frills air travel	Business-class air travel
Fiat and Ford cars	BMW and Mercedes cars
Children's white school shirts	Pampers disposable nappies
Monday-night cinema tickets	Saturday-night cinema tickets

The level of competitive activity

The fiercer the competition in a market, the more important price becomes. Customers have more choice, so they take more care to buy the best-value item, whereas a business with a strong **monopoly** position is able to charge higher prices.

The availability of the product

If the product is readily available consumers are more price conscious. They know they can go elsewhere and find the same product – perhaps cheaper. Scarcity removes some of the barriers to price. This is why perfume companies such as Chanel try to keep their products out of supermarkets and stores like Superdrug – they want to avoid shops price-cutting brands such as Chanel No 5.

16.2 Price determines business revenue

Pricing is important to the business. Unlike the other ingredients in the marketing mix it is related directly to revenue through the formula: revenue = price × units sold. If the price is not right the business could:

● lose customers – if the price is too high, sales may slump and therefore revenue will be lost; it will depend on the **price elasticity** of the product (see Unit 19); if goods remain unsold, costs of production will not be recovered

● lose revenue – if the price is too low, sales may be high, but not high enough to compensate for the low revenue per unit.

Pricing involves a balance between being competitive and being profitable.

16.3 How do businesses decide what price to charge?

At certain times during a product's life cycle pricing is especially important. Incorrect pricing when the product is launched could cause the product to fail. At other stages in the product's life, pricing may be used to revive interest in the brand.

There are two basic pricing decisions: pricing a new product and managing prices throughout the product life. Both decisions require a good understanding of the market – consumers and competitors.

Pricing decisions require an understanding of costs. These costs must include purchasing, manufacturing, distribution, administration and marketing. Cost information should be available from the company's management accounting systems.

The lowest price a firm can consider charging is set by costs. Except as a temporary promotional tactic (a loss leader), businesses must charge more for the product than the variable cost. This ensures that every product sold contributes towards the fixed costs of the business.

The market determines the highest price that can be charged. The price that is charged will need to take account of the company objectives. The right price will be the one that achieves the objectives.

There are several ways that businesses obtain market information:

● market research can provide consumer reactions to possible price changes

● competitive research tells the company about other products and prices

● analysis of sales patterns shows how the market reacts to price and economic changes

● sales staff can report on customer reactions to prices.

When making changes to product prices the business needs to understand the relationship between price changes and demand. Demand for some products is more sensitive to price changes than for others. Price

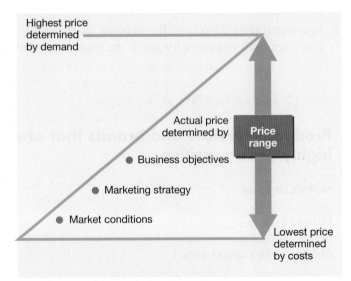

Figure 16.2 Determining the price

elasticity of demand measures how sensitive demand is to price changes. If demand for a product is sensitive to price changes an increase in price could cut total revenue.

16.4 Pricing strategies

A pricing strategy is a company's plan for setting its prices over the medium to long term. In other words it is *not* about deals such as 'This week's special: 40% off!' Short-term offers are known as tactics. Medium- to long-term plans are called strategies.

Pricing strategies for new products

For new products, firms must choose between two main pricing strategies:

1 skimming, i.e. pricing high

2 penetration, i.e. pricing low to achieve high sales volume.

Skimming is used when the product is innovative. As the product is new there will be no competition. The price can therefore be set at a high level. Customers interested in the new product will pay this high price. The business recovers some of the development costs, making sure that enthusiasts who *really* want the product pay the high price they expect to pay. For

example, the first DVD players came onto the UK market at a price of around £1000. Firms use the initial sales period to assess the market reaction. If sales become stagnant the price can be lowered to attract customers who were unwilling to pay the initial price. The price can also be lowered if competitors enter the market.

Penetration pricing is used when launching a product into a market where there are similar products. The price is set lower to gain market share. Once the product is established the price can be increased. It is hoped that high levels of initial sales will recover development costs and lead to lower average costs as the business benefits from bulk-buying benefits.

Pricing strategies for existing products.

For existing products the key is to be clear about where your brand stands in the market. Pricing strategy on the latest Mercedes sports car will be based on the confidence of the company in the strength of its brand name. Mercedes will not worry what Ford or Mazda charge for a sports car, nor even the prices of its BMW or Lexus rivals. The Merc will be a 'price leader': where it sets prices, others will follow. Weaker brands, such as Chrysler or Fiat, are the followers. They are 'price takers' (i.e. they have to take the lead set by the strong brands, usually pricing their own products at a lower level).

Table 16.2 Advantages and disadvantages of price skimming and price penetration

	Price skimming	**Price penetration**
Advantages	High prices for a new item such as the iPhone help establish the product as a must-have item **Early adopters** of a product usually want exclusivity and are willing to pay high prices, so skimming makes sense for them and for the supplier Innovation can be expensive, so it makes sense to charge high prices to recover the investment cost	Low-priced new products may attract high sales volumes, which make it very hard for a competitor to break into the market High sales volumes help to cut production costs per unit, as the producer can buy in bulk and therefore get purchasing costs down Achieving high sales volumes ensures that shops will provide high distribution levels and good in-store displays
Disadvantages	Some customers may be put off totally by 'rip-off pricing' at the start of a product's life When the firm decides to cut its prices its image may suffer Buyers who bought early (at high prices) may be annoyed that prices fell soon afterwards	Pricing low may affect the brand image, making the product appear 'cheap' It may be hard to gain distribution in more upmarket retail outlets, due to mass-market pricing Pricing on the basis of value for money can cause customers (and therefore competitors) to be very **price sensitive**

Price leader

This is where the price is set above the market level. This is possible when the company has strong brands or there is little effective competition. In Britain the accepted price of chewing gum is set by Wrigley's, which has a 90% market share. Other brands have little choice but to charge at or below the level set by Wrigley's.

Price taker

This is when the price is set at the market level or at a discount to the market. This happens in highly competitive markets or in markets where one brand dominates. When Branston Baked Beans were launched in 2006, they were priced at 41p, compared to the 44p charged by the price leader, Heinz.

Choosing a pricing strategy

The choice of pricing strategy will depend on the competitive environment. Figure 40.3 shows how the choice of pricing strategy will vary according to the level of competition.

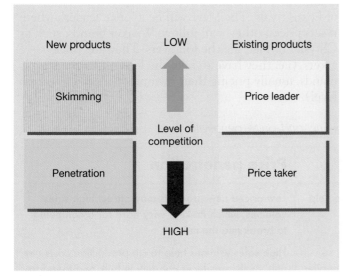

Figure 16.3 Factors affecting choice of pricing strategy

16.5 Pricing tactics

Whichever strategy has been selected, there are tactics that should also be considered. They can be part of normal pricing or used as one element in the firm's promotional tactics. They include the following.

- *Loss leaders:* prices are set deliberately low – so low that the firm may make a loss on every unit sold. The idea is to encourage customers to buy other products or **complementary goods** that generate profit. Supermarkets commonly use this approach. At Christmas they may attract custom by selling tree lights for 49p – confident that shoppers will end up with a full trolley of other goods. Children's sticker albums may also be offered very cheaply – but the packs of stickers to go inside are often expensive.

- *Psychological pricing:* prices are set at a level that seems lower to the customer. Without thinking about it, customers see a price of £9.99 as quite significantly lower than £10.50. The loss of 51p per item is more than made up for by higher sales.

- *Special offer pricing:* for example, buy one get one free; or offers made for a short period or to clear stocks.

Issues For Analysis

When answering a question on pricing it is important to understand the following points.

- *The relationship between price and demand:* in other words, a change in price will almost always affect the demand for a product.

- *The role of pricing as one part of the overall marketing mix:* the price should match the image suggested by the product design, advertising, branding and distribution outlets; an expensive-looking perfume displayed in Harrods would have its image undermined if it were priced at £9.99.

- *The influence of price upon profitability:* many products have profit margins of only 20%; therefore a 10% price cut will halve profit per unit. It would take a huge increase in demand to compensate.

- *The factors influencing pricing:* for example, cost, customer psychology and competitors.

16.6 Price
an evaluation

Economists think of price as a neutral factor within a marketplace. Its impact upon demand can be measured, predicted and captured in the concept of price elasticity (see Unit 19). Many businesses would disagree – especially those selling consumer goods and services. The reason is that consumer psychology can be heavily influenced by price. A '3p off' flash makes people reach for the Mars bars, but if they are half price people wonder whether they are old stock or have suffered in the sun – they are *too* cheap.

When deciding on the price of a brand new product, marketing managers have many options. Pricing high might generate too few sales to keep retailers happy to stock the product. Yet pricing too low carries even more dangers. Large companies know there are no safe livings to be made selling cheap jeans, cheap cosmetics or cheap perfumes.

If there is a key to successful pricing, it is to keep it in line with the overall marketing strategy. When Häagen-Dazs launched in the UK at prices more than double those of its competitors, many predicted failure. In fact the pricing was in line with the image of adult, luxury indulgence and Häagen-Dazs soon outsold all other premium ice creams. The worst pricing approach would be to develop an attractively packaged, well-made product and then sell it at a discount to the leading brands. In research, people would welcome it, but deep down they would not trust the product quality. Because psychology is so important to successful pricing, many firms use qualitative research, rather than quantitative, to obtain the necessary psychological insights.

Key terms

Complementary goods: products bought in conjunction with each other, such as bacon and eggs, or Gillette shavers and Gillette razors.

Early adopters: consumers with the wealth and the personality to want to be the first to get a new gadget or piece of equipment; they may be the first to wear new fashion clothes, and the first to get the new (and expensive) computer game.

Monopoly: a market dominated by one supplier.

Price elasticity: a measurement of the extent to which a product's demand changes when its price is changed.

Price sensitive: when customer demand for a product reacts sharply to a price change (i.e. the product is highly price elastic).

Exercises

A. Revision questions

(35 marks; 35 minutes)

1 Explain why price 'is fundamental to a firm's revenues'. (3)

2 Look at Figure 16.1. Outline two factors that would affect the 'psychologically right price range' for a new Nokia phone. (4)

3 Explain how the actions of Nike might affect the footwear prices set by Adidas. (3)

4 Look at Table 16.1 on the price sensitivity of products, brands and services. Think of two more examples of highly price sensitive and two examples of not-very-price-sensitive products, services or brands. (4)

5 Explain the difference between pricing strategy and pricing tactics. (3)

6 For each of the following, decide whether the pricing strategy should be skimming or penetration. Briefly explain your reasoning.
   (a) Richard Branson's Virgin group launches the world's first space tourism service (you are launched in a rocket, spend time weightless in space, watch the world go round, then come back to earth). (4)
   (b) Kellogg's launches a new range of sliced breads for families in a hurry. (4)
   (c) The first Google phone is launched (called G-Fone) with free, instant WiFi access to Google. (4)

7 Is a cash cow likely to be a price maker or a price taker? Explain your reasoning. (3)

8 Identify three circumstances in which a business might decide to use special offer pricing. (3)

B. Revision exercises

B1 Data response

On 24 September 2007, Tesco Pricecheck provided the following information on the prices of shampoo brands. Study the table opposite then answer the questions that follow.

Questions

(25 marks; 30 minutes)

1 Briefly explain why it might be fair to describe Elvive Anti-Dandruff shampoo as a price-taker. (3)

2 Neutrogena shampoo is priced at nearly 100 times the level of supermarket budget shampoos (per ml). Explain why customers might be willing to pay such a high price. (6)

3 Examine the position of the long-established brand Pantene Pro-V within the UK market for shampoo. What pricing strategy does it seem to be using and why might it be able to use this approach? (7)

4 Discuss whether dogs should have 'better' shampoo than kids. (9)

Product description	Tesco price	Sainsbury's price	Asda price
Neutrogena Shampoo 250 ml	£6.15	£6.15	£6.15
Pantene Pro-V Express 250 ml	£2.98	£2.97	£2.97
Head & Shoulders 250 ml	£2.39	£1.89	N.A.
Elvive Anti-Dandruff 250 ml	£1.96	£1.96	£1.97
Herbal Essences 250 ml	£1.99	£1.99	N.A.
Own-label Kids' Shampoo 250 ml	£0.38	£0.59	£0.38
Own-label Budget Shampoo 1000 ml	£0.28	£0.28	£0.28
Bob Martin Dog Shampoo 300 ml	£3.35	£3.35	£3.35

N.A. = Not available; Own-label means the supermarket's own brand.

B2 Data response

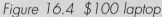

Figure 16.4 $100 laptop

The $100 laptop

Computer enthusiasts in the developed world will soon be able to get their hands on the so-called '$100 laptop'

The organisation behind the project has launched the 'give one, get one' scheme, which will allow US residents to purchase two laptops for $399 (£198). One laptop will be sent to the buyer while a child in the developing world will receive the second machine. The G1G1 scheme, as it is known, will offer the laptops for just two weeks, starting on 12 November.

Price hike

The XO laptop has been developed to be used by children and is as low cost, durable and simple to use as possible. It packs several

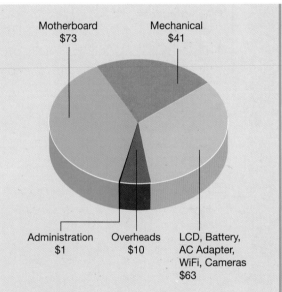

Figure 16.5 Breakdown of costs

innovations, including a sunlight readable display so that it can be used outside. It has no moving parts, can be powered by solar, foot-pump or pull-string powered chargers, and is housed in a waterproof case.

The machine's price has recently increased from $176 (£88) to $188 (£93), although the eventual aim is to sell the machines for $100 (£50).

Governments can buy the green and white machines in lots of 250,000. In July, hardware suppliers were given the green light to ramp-up production of all the components needed to build the low-cost machines. The decision suggested that the organisation had met or surpassed the three million orders it needed to make production viable. The names of the governments that have purchased the first lots of machines have not been released.

Early adopter

The first countries to receive the donated laptops will be Cambodia, Afghanistan, Rwanda and Haiti. Other least developed countries (LDCs), as defined by the UN, will be able to bid to join the scheme. The laptops will go on sale for two weeks through the xogiving.org website. They will only be available for two weeks to ensure OLPC can meet demand and so that machines are not diverted away from countries that have already placed orders.

Source: Adapted from bbc.co.uk

Questions

(30 marks; 35 minutes)

1 Describe the objectives behind the pricing of the XO laptop. (4)

2a Compare the 'breakdown of costs' pie chart in Figure 16.5 to the text to work out the recent profit per unit made on selling the XO laptop. (3)

2b Given that level of profit, how could the company hope 'to sell the machines for $100'? (4)

3a Explain what is meant by an 'early adopter'? (3)

3b Why may early adopters be important to a business? (4)

4 Some people see the XO laptop as a brave, charitable idea; others see it purely as a clever form of penetration pricing strategy. To what extent can you agree with either view? (12)

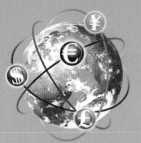

Unit 17

MARKETING MIX: PROMOTION

DEFINITION

Promotion is the part of the marketing mix that focuses on persuading people to buy the product or service.

> I know that half the money I spend on advertising is wasted, but I can never find out which half. (*Lord Leverhulme, British industrialist*)
>
> Source: Stuart Crainer (1997) *The Ultimate Book of Business Quotations*, Capstone Publishing

17.1 What is promotion?

Promotion is a general term that covers all the marketing activity that focuses on letting customers know about a product and persuading them to buy that product. It is not just about advertising. The different elements of promotion can be grouped into two broad categories: those that stimulate short-term sales and those that build sales for the long term.

17.2 Types of promotion for building long-term sales

These include branding, persuasive advertising and public relations.

Branding

One of the best forms of promotion is branding. Branding is the process of creating a distinctive and lasting identity in the minds of consumers. Establishing a brand can take considerable time and marketing effort, but once a product brand is established it becomes its own means of promotion. The brand name is recognised and this makes it more likely that the customer will buy the product for the first time. If the experience is satisfactory the customer is very likely to continue to choose the brand. Once established, branding has many advantages, such as:

- it enables the business to reduce the amount spent on promotion

- customers are more likely to purchase the product again (repeat purchases)

- it is easier to persuade retailers to put the products in their stores

- other products can be promoted using the same brand name.

Table 17.1 Examples of persuasive advertising

Company	Slogan	Meaning
Tesco	'Every little helps'	We understand your needs and we try to help (we're not just a great big, greedy business)
L'Oréal	'Because you're worth it'	Go on, spoil yourself; you can afford that bit extra, so buy our products, not our competitors'
Innocent Drinks	'Nothing, but nothing, but fruit'	Our products are pure (whereas others are not)

Persuasive advertising

Persuasive advertising is designed to create a distinctive image. A good example is BMW, which has spent decades persuading us that it produces not a car but a 'Driving Machine'. Advertising of this kind has also helped create clear consumer images for firms such as Tesco and L'Oréal (see Table 17.1).

High-grade application

Activia

In 2007 a £12 million marketing campaign saw Activia yoghurt's share of 'Active Health' yoghurts rise to 75%. The brand's sales grew by 440% in the period 2002–2007. Danone spent most of the marketing budget on TV advertising, assuring women that Activia would fight 'that bloated feeling'. The huge marketing push made it impossible for competitors to keep up. The once powerful Benecol brand saw its market share fall from 5.8% in 2006 to just 3.2% in 2007, while Müller Vitality slipped from 19.2% to 16.0%. Somehow, the Activia message hit home. There may not really be that many women worried about feeling bloated, but Danone persuaded them that Activia would be better for you than ordinary yoghurt.

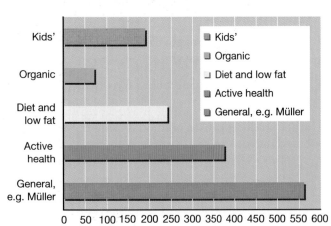

Figure 17.1 Sectors in the £1440m yoghurt market, 2007

Public relations

This is the attempt to affect consumers' image of a product without spending on media advertising. It includes making contacts with journalists to try to get favourable mentions or articles about your product. It would also include activities such as sponsorship of sport or the arts. The London Olympic Games in 2012 has Lloyds TSB as one of its main sponsors. This allows the business to advertise and use its logo alongside the Olympic logo.

These include those described below.

Sales promotions

These range from on-pack competitions to in-store offers such as buy one get one free (BOGOF). These can be very effective at boosting sales, but there are risks involved, such as: customers may stock up at (in effect) half price, then not need to buy more items in the weeks following the offer; special offers may undermine the brand image (what would it say to consumers if Apple started offering 'buy one iPhone get one free'?). These risks are worthwhile only if the promotion succeeds in attracting brand new customers, who come for the offer and then stay loyal after the offer has ended (which is asking a lot).

Direct selling

Potential customers are approached directly. At one time this would be done by door-to-door salesmen. Nowadays the main mechanism for direct selling is telesales. Both approaches are expensive, because one-to-one selling implies high labour costs. A TV advertisement sounds expensive at, perhaps, £100,000. But that money would buy you an audience of 5 million people. Therefore the cost per person is £100,000/5m = £0.02 (i.e. 2p). Just think how much more expensive it would be to pay someone to travel to you and spend time selling a product to you personally (2 hours @ £8 an hour + £4 travel costs = £20, and that's the absolute minimum). Therefore direct selling is affordable only if there are huge financial rewards to the seller (e.g. selling financial products or double glazing).

Merchandising

This requires staff to visit shops to ensure that a brand's display looks eye-catching and tidy. Merchandisers may set up 'dump bin' displays at the end of shopping aisles, perhaps featuring a newly launched product. The shop will charge rent for the space, but the extra sales can more than make up for this. Merchandisers may also offer shoppers free product samples, to encourage them to make their first trial purchase.

17.4 The promotional mix

Few businesses would use just one method of promotion. A snack bar might do no more than hand out leaflets, but most firms will have a mixture of activities. This is known as the **promotional mix**. An example would be Innocent Drinks, whose promotional mix has been successful enough to build the company's sales from £0.5 million to over £100 million in less than ten years. Its mix includes:

- TV advertising (to build brand awareness)

- newspaper advertising to target high-income young adults (who do not watch much TV)

- an annual 'Fruitstock' free concert, to build loyalty among existing customers

- continually working on its website, so that regular customers return to find out the latest new product ideas or recipes.

The mix of promotional activities chosen by a company will depend on the following factors.

- *The size of the market:* if the market is large the business will primarily use advertising through the mass media. If the market is very small this method will be too expensive and inefficient. Direct marketing or selling will probably be the best focus.

- *The type of product:* a consumer product will require different promotion to an industrial product. The market for industrial products can be huge, e.g. more than £1000 million is spent per year on large lorries. The number of potential buyers is, of course, very limited, so direct selling would be more effective than T.V. advertising.

- *The cost:* a small or new business is unlikely to be able to spend large amounts of money on promotion. This means that some forms of promotion, such as TV advertising, are out of the cost range of the business. The business will need to find cheaper alternatives, such as local advertising and direct marketing or selling.

Getting the promotional mix right will require the business to understand the nature of its product, its customers and its competitors. Good **market research** will provide the essential information to make the right decisions about the promotional mix.

High-grade application
Mamas & Papas

Mamas & Papas receives significant sales and footfall lift with new fashion maternity campaign

Mamas & Papas, the designer nursery brand, witnessed the biggest ever fashion sales in the first week of its new autumn/winter 2007 fashion campaign. Maternity fashion sales saw a 43% uplift compared to the same trading period in 2006.

The new face of Mamas & Papas, Emma Bunton, gave the brand a positive halo effect for the collection, encouraging shoppers to discover what the retail trade press has named 'the best kept secret on the UK high street'.

The company's marketing campaign not only focused on parents through the parenting press, but also targeted a broader audience. The promotional mix included a comprehensive public relations strategy, national mainstream advertising in *Vogue* and *Red* magazines, plus direct marketing and store events to encourage brand awareness.

Source: http://www.mamasandpapas.co.uk/news/news_14.php

Figure 17.2 Mamas & Papas's nursery wear

17.5 Promotional activity needs to fit in with marketing strategy

The type of promotion used and the level of promotional activity will vary not only from company to company and product to product but also in terms of the

Table 17.2 Marketing strategies and types of promotion

Marketing strategy	Promotion needs to:
Launching a new product	• be informative • reach the target customers
Differentiating the product	• identify the special features of the product • persuade customers that it is different/better than rival products
Extending the life of an existing product	• reinforce the reasons for customers choosing it • highlight any new features • attract new customers
Increasing market share	• attract new customers • reinforce buying in existing customers
Building brand identity	• increase awareness of the company/product name • create customer recognition and loyalty

marketing strategy being followed. Different forms of promotion will achieve different purposes. Much will depend on what the business is trying to achieve (Table 17.2).

The correct promotional mix will be achieved only if the business has clear marketing objectives. Once the objectives and strategy are determined it is much easier for the business to develop an effective promotional campaign.

17.6 Promotion and market research

In order to develop the best promotional campaign it is important that market research is carried out so that the business has the necessary knowledge about the product and the market. The more information the business has about its customers and its competitors the easier it will be to develop an effective promotional campaign.

● If the business knows who is likely to buy the product it can determine its target audience and specifically target that group with its promotional activity.

● If the business understands why customers are choosing a rival product it can specifically design promotional material that addresses these issues.

● If the business understands what makes its product attractive to customers it can use this knowledge to reinforce the promotional message.

Market knowledge is always important if promotional

activity is to be effective. However, it is vital for a new business. If the business is unable to target the right **market segment** or to persuade customers to buy the product, then the promotional expenditure will be wasted. Ultimately no sales means no business.

17.7 Promotion needs to be effective

Being effective means striking a balance between coverage, cost and results. TV advertising is expensive but has huge coverage. However, if the target customers are a small segment of the population the coverage may be wasted. There is no point in advertising table tennis equipment on TV at peak viewing times – it is more effective to use a specialist magazine for table tennis players; if players belong to clubs they could also be targeted by direct mail.

The business needs to constantly monitor promotional activity to see if it is having the desired effect. A prime-time TV advert may reach a huge audience but is ineffective if it does not increase sales.

There are many ways that businesses can monitor the effect of any promotional campaign. The most obvious is to see if there is any increase in sales. Other ways include using market research to see if the campaign has affected public perception of the product.

Table 17.3 Advantages and disadvantages of various promotion methods

	Advantages	**Disadvantages**
Advertising (e.g. on TV)	Reaches a large audience Increases prestige of the product/company Can be targeted to viewing groups	Very expensive Can be too broad-based to reach target customers
Direct selling	With good research enables the customer to be targeted directly	Can get a reputation as a nuisance caller Unless properly researched can be difficult to target
Direct marketing	With good research can be cost-effective	Wide coverage often produces only small response
Merchandising	Good product displays can increase the rate of impulse purchase, and can build brand awareness	Expensive as it relies on personal calling by sales staff
Sales promotions (such as buy one get one free)	Increases sales immediately and, possibly, dramatically	Customers may have bought anyway
Public relations (PR)	Gets the company name seen	Hard to measure effectiveness

17.8 How important is promotion?

Promotion is vital for a new business. How else will customers know that it exists and what its products are? Existing businesses may need to spend less on promotion.

The importance of promotion will depend on the following factors.

- *The competitiveness of the market:* where no alternatives are available the consumer will have less choice; there will be less need to persuade the customer to buy.

- *Availability:* if the product is in short supply there will be little need to promote it; where several products are competing for customer approval in crowded markets promotion becomes very important.

- *How easily the product can be differentiated in the market:* if the differences are obvious to the customer there may be less need for promotion.

- *The stage of the product life cycle:* a new product will usually need promotional support; promotion will tell customers that the product is available; it will persuade them to try the new product; if the product has been altered, promotion will tell customers of the changes.

In **industrial markets** where one business is selling to another, there may be less need for promotion. This is particularly true where a business is supplying products to the customer's specification and has established a long-term relationship with the buyer.

Issues For Analysis

● Promotion is about telling the customer about the product and persuading the customer to make a purchase. It is therefore vital when answering a question on promotion to consider the business, its product and the market. Analysis should consider the different promotional methods that are available but should concentrate on those that are suitable for the particular business. There is no point suggesting that a new small business should look at advertising on TV or consider promoting a major sporting event.

● The single best form of analysis, though, is to consider promotion in relation to the timescale of the firm's objectives. If it wants to build a brand for the long term, it can do damage by using short-term tactics such as price promotions. Carefully targeted advertising designed to build the 'right' image is the key – 'right' being the image that best suits the customers being targeted. Over-60s may respond very well to secure, warm images, whereas the 16–25 age group may want images based on fun and celebrity.

17.9 Promotion

an evaluation

Promotion is generally considered to be a good thing for businesses to do. But is it? How do they know if it is money well spent? It is very hard to measure the effect of promotion. If the business is using a mix of promotional methods it is very difficult to separate the effect of one from the other.

It is 100 years since Lord Leverhume made the famous statement quoted at the start of this chapter. Amazingly, the statement is still true today.

> **Key terms**
>
> **Industrial markets:** where businesses sell to other businesses (not directly to the public)
> **Market research:** gathering information about customers and competitors
> **Market segment:** a smaller part of a larger market
> **Promotional mix:** the combination of promotional methods used by a business in marketing its products.

Exercises

A. Revision questions

(35 marks; 35 minutes)

1 Why is promotion an important element of the marketing mix? (4)

2 Outline one advantage and one disadvantage of TV advertising. (4)

3 What is meant by the promotional mix? (2)

4 Explain what form of promotion you think would work best for marketing:
 (a) a new football game for the PS3 (3)
 (b) a small, family-focused seaside hotel (3)
 (c) organic cosmetics for women. (3)

5 Why is it important for businesses to monitor the effect of their promotional activity? (4)

6 What is meant by the phrase 'promotion needs to be effective'? (3)

7 Explain why promotion is essential for new businesses. (4)

8 Discuss whether Pepsi-Cola would be wise to sponsor the *X-Factor* TV programme. (5)

B. Revision exercises

B1 Data response

Green & Black's second bite

In 2005 organic chocolate-maker Green & Black's launched two varieties of biscuit. In 2007 it withdrew the products after accepting that they had flopped. Due into Asda in January 2008 is the replacement product line-up, including two new biscuits and two cereal bars. The cereal bars will come in packs of three, priced at £2.49. They feature unusual combinations such as Almond, Cherry and Apricot. The intention is to catch the key trends towards indulgence, organic and health. The company also intends to launch seasonal biscuit varieties in selected supermarkets.

Green & Black's is targeting sales of £7 million for the first year. To achieve this, the 2008 marketing campaign will include merchandising and product sampling in-store. The sampling will be to encourage product trial, with the company hoping that the quality of the product ensures high levels of repeat purchase.

Source: *The Grocer*, 20 October 2007

Questions

(30 marks; 35 minutes)

1 Outline two possible explanations of why the 2005 biscuit launches failed. (6)

2 Explain how the sales of the new biscuit varieties could be helped by a programme of in-store merchandising. (5)

3 Discuss whether 'sampling in-store' is likely to be a sufficiently powerful form of promotion for the new biscuit range. (12)

4 Outline the other aspects of the marketing mix being used by Green & Black's. (7)

B2 Data response

Getting your furniture noticed

Simon Heaton and Lyndon Jeremiah were bored with teaching and decided to set up their own business. Heaton & Jeremiah now employs ten staff but the business struggled before the pair hit upon a unique marketing ploy. Heaton and Jeremiah wanted to combine their backgrounds: furniture design and software development. They investigated the household market but found it saturated. Then they hit upon the idea of corporate logos inlaid in office furniture.

The pair tried a variety of marketing approaches, including product cards, adverts in retail magazines, the *Yellow Pages* and designer handbooks, but they were not reaching their target market. While the marketing generated interest, it tended to be members of the public 'phoning up for a bedside table worth £20,' said Jeremiah.

They decided to take a more proactive

approach. They made up a hitlist of the big companies in their area – such as Jaguar and British Airways – and started to work out how they could reach them. The approach had to be daring. The annual round of multinational companies exhibiting at Birmingham's National Exhibition Centre gave them an idea. They managed to get hold of a copy of the exhibition schedule and produced tables for ten exhibitors. The tables were smuggled in at the start of the day. 'The show started at 9 am and we were receiving calls from companies at 8.45 am to say thanks' says Jeremiah. Heaton and Jeremiah extended their 'knocking on doors technique' to companies not at the exhibition, making tables to leave in reception areas. 'We were showing them a product they didn't know they wanted until they got it,' said Lyndon.

It was a big, but calculated, risk. They drew up a prototype budget and with their hitlist focused only on companies that could provide them with big contracts. The product was sold through persistence. 'We had such a unique product that unless we got in people's faces it didn't really work,' said Lyndon. They now have a full order book and work is booked for two months in advance. The business now survives on word of mouth – the best form of marketing!

Source: © Startups MMVII (http://www.startups.co.uk/6678842910880448540/heaton-and-jeremiah.html)

Questions

(46 marks; 60 minutes)

1a What is a corporate logo? (2)

1b Why do companies have logos? (4)

2 What is meant by 'target market'? (4)

3 The initial promotional efforts did not reach the target market. Explain why this might have happened. (8)

4a Explain how promoting a unique product might differ from promoting a mass-market product. (4)

4b Discuss the advantages and disadvantages of two forms of promotion for a unique product such as Heaton & Jeremiah's. (12)

5 Discuss why word of mouth might be the best form of advertising for a new business. (12)

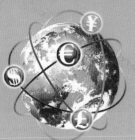 # MARKETING MIX: PLACE

18.1 Introduction

The word 'place' can be unhelpful, because it suggests that manufacturers can place their products where they like (e.g. at the entrance of a Tesco store). The real world is not like that. Obtaining distribution at Tesco stores is a dream for most small producers – and a very hard dream to turn into reality. For new firms in particular, place is the toughest of the 4Ps.

Persuading retailers to stock a product is never easy. For the retailer, the key issues are opportunity cost and risk. As shelf space is limited, stocking a particular chocolate bar probably means scrapping another. Which one? What revenue will be lost? Will one or two customers be upset? ('What! No Coffee Walnut Whips any more?') The other consideration is risk. A new, low-cal chocolate bar endorsed by a supermodel may be a slimmer's delight, but high initial sales may then flop, leaving the shopkeeper with boxes of slow-moving stock.

18.2 Choosing appropriate distributors

When a new business wants to launch its first product, a key question to consider is the distribution channel – in other words, how the product passes from producer to consumer. Sold directly, as with pick-your-own strawberries? Or via a wholesaler, then a retailer, as with newspapers bought from your local shop? This decision will affect every aspect of the business in the future, but especially its profit.

In 2008 entrepreneur James Seddon will launch his Eggxactly egg cooker in the UK. Since his appearance on the BBC TV series *Dragons' Den*, retailers such as John Lewis have made clear their interest in stocking the product at launch. But James has decided to start by selling purely from his own website. His reasoning is that this will transform his cash flow position. Instead of getting 50,000 machines produced in China (with the cash to be paid in advance) he could get them made in England in response to orders. This way, the customer cash is received before he has to pay out to get the machines made. This would solve another problem: instead of having to guess how many red and how many blue ones to make, he would respond to customer orders.

Manufacturers must decide on the right outlets for their own product. If Chanel chooses to launch a new perfume, 'Keira', backed by Keira Knightley, priced at £49.99 a bottle, controlling distribution would be vital. The company will want it sold in a smart location where elegant sales staff can persuade customers of its wonderful scent and gorgeous packaging. If Superdrug or Woolworths want to stock the brand Chanel will try hard to find reasons to say no.

Yet the control is often not in the hands of the producer, but of the retailer. If you came up with a wonderful idea for a brand new ice cream, how would you get distribution for it? The freezers in corner shops are usually owned by Walls and Mars, so they frown upon independent products being stocked in 'their' space. Offering a third freezer free would be hugely expensive, leading to impossibly high costs per unit, especially if you had only one product line to sell. Furthermore, shopkeepers would lack the floor space to be willing to accept your 'free' gift. To the retailer, every foot of shop floor space has an actual cost (the rental value) and an opportunity cost (the cost of missing out on the profits that could be generated by selling other goods). In effect, then, your brand new ice cream is likely to stay on the drawing board, because obtaining distribution will be too large a **barrier to entry** to this market.

18.3 Distribution channels

There are three main channels of distribution. (See Figure 18.1 below).

1 *Traditional:* small producers find it hard to achieve distribution in big chains such as B&Q or Sainsbury's, so they usually sell to wholesalers who, in turn, sell to small independent shops. The profit mark-up applied by the 'middleman' adds to the final retail price, but there is no way that a small producer can afford to deliver individually to lots of small shops.

2 *Modern:* Tesco, B&Q and WHSmith do not buy from a wholesaler. They buy direct from producers and then organise their own distribution to their outlets. Their huge selling power gives them huge buying power. Therefore they are able to negotiate the highest discounts from the producers.

3 *Direct (i.e. the producer selling directly to the consumer):* manufacturers can do this through mail order or – far more likely today – through a website. This ensures that the producer keeps 100% of the product's selling price.

Often a manufacturer receives only half the shop selling price of an item, after the retailer and the wholesaler have taken their cut. So the benefit of the direct distribution channel is that the producer's higher profits can finance more spending on advertising or on new product development.

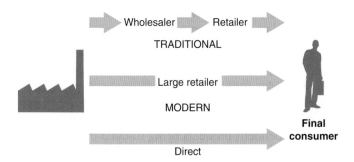

Figure 18.1 Channels of distribution

In the first half of 2007, Tesco Online enjoyed a 29% rise in its sales revenue. This compared with a 12% rise for Tesco stores. This repeats a growth pattern typical within the company in the last few years. Interestingly, Online is more profitable for Tesco than its normal shops. The figures in Table 42.1 show that Tesco Online gives higher net profit margins than the traditional business. No wonder Tesco has extended its internet business by launching Tesco Direct, which will deliver Tesco clothes and other non-food items direct to the consumer's door.

Table 18.1 Tesco stores vs Tesco Online, 26 weeks to 26 August 2007

	Tesco plc	**Tesco.com**
Sales	£22700m	£554m
Operating (net) profit	£1090m	£33.8m
Net profit margin	4.8%	6.1%

Source: Tesco plc, 2007 interim report and accounts

18.4 How does a small firm obtain good distribution?

To obtain distribution for the first time, a small firm producing organic biscuits would have to take the following steps.

● Announce, display and hand out free samples of the product at a trade exhibition, and/or use direct mail to send advertising messages and product samples to trade buyers. (But does it have a good mailing list? McVitie's will know every key decision maker in the grocery retail trade.)

● Advertise in the trade press (e.g. *The Grocer* magazine). The advertisement will show the attractiveness of the packaging and will emphasise the market gap that has been identified, the generous trade profit margins available, the heavy consumer advertising support and the package of point-of-sale

(POS) display materials that are being provided to increase the level of **impulse purchasing** within the store.

● Identify and agree distribution and sales targets for each area of the country, and type of outlet. A major company such as McVitie's is likely to be confident of achieving distribution targets as high as 80%. A new small firm may find it very difficult to gain distribution at 15% of stores. Having set distribution targets, it should send sales representatives to visit each of the main wholesale and retail buyers. A possible way to break into major multiples is to agree on an exclusive arrangement (e.g. that the new product will be stocked only at Tesco for its first six months). This gives the retailer the possibility of a worthwhile benefit: Tesco scores a minor triumph in its competitive battle against Sainsbury's and the others.

Issues For Analysis

For exam purposes there are two key factors to consider about 'place'.

● A successful business must find where customers want to buy the product, then get it stocked at that place. If the product is ready-to-eat popcorn, the place must be the cinema; if it's unpopped corn, the place must be in the grocery store. Naive businesspeople try to get their product stocked everywhere, without thinking about the high costs of delivery, advertising materials and ongoing customer service. Today's customers value convenience highly, so the right product must be available in the right place at the right time. Clever firms look for appropriate outlets, not simply as many as possible.

● Anyone can have a brilliant new idea; anyone can decide on the price and the name of this new product – but getting shops to take a chance on a newcomer is more of a problem. Many new small manufacturers have been defeated by the costs, the slowness and the difficulty of obtaining product distribution. Therefore 'place' (sometimes called 'the silent P') is a critical part of the marketing mix.

18.5 Place
an evaluation

Place is of particular importance in Business Studies because it can represent a major barrier to entry, especially for new small firms. The practical constraint on the amount of shop floor space makes it hard for new products to gain acceptance, unless they are genuinely innovative. Therefore existing producers of branded goods can get quite complacent, with little serious threat from new competition.

Famously, in the nineteenth century Ralph Waldo Emerson said that 'If a man can make a better mousetrap, though he builds his house in the woods the world will make a beaten path to his door.' In other words, if the product is good enough, customers will come and find you. In a modern competitive world, though, the vast majority of products are not *that* exciting or different from others. So it is crucial to provide customers with convenient access to your products and/or shelf space in an eye-catching location. Getting products into the right place should not be taken for granted.

> **Key terms**
>
> **Barrier to entry:** factors that make it hard for new firms to break into an existing market (e.g. strong brand loyalty to the current market leaders).
>
> **Impulse purchasing:** buying in unplanned way (e.g. going to a shop to buy a paper, but coming out with a Mars bar and a Diet Coke).

Exercises

A. Revision questions

(30 marks; 30 minutes)

1 Outline the meaning of the term 'place'. (2)

2 Explain in your own words why it may be that 'place is the toughest of the 4Ps'. (4)

3 Outline what you think are appropriate distribution channels for:
(a) a new magazine aimed at 12–15-year-old boys (3)
(b) a new adventure holiday company focusing on wealthy 19–32 year olds. (3)

4 Retailers such as WHSmith charge manufacturers a rent on prime store space such as the shelving near to the cash tills.
(a) How might a firm work out whether it is worthwhile to pay the extra? (4)
(b) Why might new small firms find it hard to pay rents such as these? (4)

5 Explain in your own words what is meant by the phrase 'a better mousetrap'. (4)

6 Outline three reasons for the success of direct distribution over the internet in recent years. (6)

B. Revision exercises

B1 Data response

Getting distribution right

Secondary data can be hugely helpful to new companies looking for distribution of their first products. A company launching the first 'Kitten Milk' product has to decide where to focus its efforts. Where does cat food sell? Is it in pet shops, in corner shops or in supermarkets? Desk research company BMRB reports that, whereas 65% of dog owners shop for pet food at supermarkets, 81% of cat owners do the same. A different source (TNS, 52 weeks ending 12 August 2007) puts the cat food market size at £829 million. TNS also shows that the market is rising in value by around 2.5% a year.

Further secondary data (reported in *The Grocer*, 19 May 2007) shows that pet food shoppers spend only 80% of the amount they intend to when they go to a shop. This is because poor distribution stops them finding what they want. And 50% of shoppers will not return to the same store after being let down twice by poor availability.

Questions

(20 marks; 25 minutes)

1 State the meaning of the term 'market size'. (2)

2a The Year 1 sales target for Kitten Milk is £5 million. What share of the total market for cat food would that represent? (3)

2b Explain why it might be hard to persuade retailers to stock a product with that level of market share. (6)

3 The marketing manager for Kitten Milk is planning to focus distribution efforts on getting the brand placed in pet shops. Discuss whether this seems wise. (9)

B2 Data response

An arm's length from desire

From its origins in America in 1886, Coca-Cola has been a marketing phenomenon. It was the world's first truly global brand; it virtually invented the red, jolly Christmas Santa, and its bottle design (1919) was the first great piece of packaging design.

Yet a 1950 *Time* magazine article quoted another piece of marketing genius: 'Always within an arm's length of desire.' The marketing experts at Atlanta (home of Coca-Cola) realised nearly 60 years ago that sales of Coca-Cola were limited mainly by availability. Especially on a hot day, a cold Coke would be desired by almost anyone who had it an arm's length away. This led the company to develop a distribution strategy based on maximum availability, maximum in-store visibility and therefore maximum impulse purchase.

From then on, Coca-Cola targeted four main types of distribution:

1 in supermarkets and grocers

2 in any kiosk in a location based on entertainment (e.g. a bowling alley or a cinema)

3 in any canteen, bar or restaurant

4 in a vending machine near you; automatic vending proved one of the most valuable ways of building the market until worries about healthy eating saw them banned in schools in 2005 and 2006; a vending machine is the ultimate barrier to entry, i.e. it makes it very hard for newcomers to break into the market.

Overall, though, the Coca-Cola approach to distribution set out in 1950 what most companies still try to do today.

Questions

(25 marks; 30 minutes)

1 Explain how a vending machine can be a 'barrier to entry' to new competitors. (5)

2 Explain what the text means by the difference between 'maximum availability' and 'maximum visibility'. (5)

3 Explain why 'an arm's length from desire' might be less important for a business that does not rely upon impulse purchase. (7)

4 From all that you know about today's Coke, Diet Coke and Coke Zero, discuss whether Coca-Cola's distribution strategy was at the core of the firm's marketing success. (8)

Figure 18.2 Vending machines are one of Coca-Cola's main methods of distribution

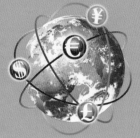

ELASTICITY AND DECISION-MAKING

DEFINITION

Price elasticity measures the extent to which demand for a product changes when its price is changed. Income elasticity measures the extent to which demand for a product changes when its price is changed.

19.1 Introduction

When a company increases the price of a product, it expects to lose some sales. Some customers will switch to a rival supplier; others may decide they do not want (or cannot afford) the product at all. Economists use the term 'the law of demand' to suggest that, almost invariably:

Price up $\longrightarrow$ Demand down

Price down $\longrightarrow$ Demand up

Price elasticity looks beyond the law of demand to ask the more subtle questions 'When the price goes up, by how much do sales fall?', 'Do they collapse or do they fall only slightly?'

Elasticity measures the extent to which price changes affect demand.

19.2 Price elasticity of demand

In the short term, the most important factor affecting demand is price. When the price of the *Guardian* newspaper increased from 70p to 80p in 2007 sales fell by 8%, whereas a 30p increase in the price of the *Financial Times* newspaper in the same year cut sales by just 1.5%. Readers of the *Guardian* proved much more price sensitive than readers of the *Financial Times*. Therefore the owners of the *Financial Times* could feel delighted with their pricing decision. Selling 1.5% fewer papers but receiving 30% more for each one sold meant that revenue rose by more than a quarter.

The crucial question is *how much* will demand change when the price is changed? This question can be answered by calculating the price elasticity of demand. Price elasticity is not about whether demand changes when price changes, it is about the degree of change. Consequently, price elasticity is a unit of measurement rather than being a thing in itself.

A price cut will not cause price elasticity to fall; instead the price elasticity figure explains the effect the price cut is likely to have on demand. Will demand rise by 1%, 5% or 25% following the price cut? The answer can be known only by referring to the product's price elasticity of demand. Price elasticity measures the *responsiveness* of demand to a change in price.

Some products are far more price sensitive than others. Following a 5% increase in price the demand for some products may fall greatly, say by more than 20%. The demand for another type of product may fall by less than 1%.

Price elasticity can be calculated using the formula shown below:

$$\text{Price elasticity} = \frac{\%\ \text{change in quantity demanded}}{\%\ \text{change in price}}$$

Price elasticity measures the percentage effect on demand of each 1% change in price. So if a 10% increase in price led demand to fall by 20%, the price elasticity would be 2. Strictly speaking, price elasticities are always negative, because price up pushes demand down, and price down pushes demand up. For example:

$$\frac{-20\%}{+10\%} = -2$$

The figure of -2 indicates that, for every 1% change in price, demand is likely to change by 2%. All price elasticities are negative. This is because there is a negative **correlation** between price and quantity demanded. In the short term, a price cut will always boost sales and a price rise will always cut sales.

19.3 Determinants of price elasticity

Why do some products, services or brands have low price elasticity and some high elasticity? Why is the price elasticity of Branston Baked Beans higher than that of Heinz Baked Beans? Or the price elasticity of the *Financial Times* as low as 0.05 while the elasticity of *Look* magazine is as high as 2.0 (i.e. 40 times higher)?

The main determinants of price elasticity are as follows.

● *The degree of product differentiation:* that is, the extent to which customers view the product as being distinctive compared with rivals. *Look* may be an excellent magazine, but it is offering the same mix of fashion, shopping and celebs as many other magazines aimed at young women. So if the cover price is increased, it is easy for readers to switch to an alternative, whereas readers of the *Financial Times* have nowhere else to go. Therefore the higher the product differentiation the lower the price elasticity.

● *The availability of substitutes:* customers may see Tango and Fanta as very similar orange drinks. In a supermarket they might buy the cheaper of the two. At a cinema, though, only Fanta may be available. At a train station vending machine, almost certainly Fanta will be the only orange drink. This is because it is a Coca-Cola brand and the distribution strength of Coke places Fanta where Tango never goes. When Fanta is on its own, its price elasticity is much lower; therefore the brand owner (Coke) can push the price up without losing too many customers.

● *Branding and brand loyalty:* products with low price elasticity are those that consumers buy without thinking about the price tag. Some reach for Coca-Cola without checking its price compared to that of Pepsi, or buy a Harley-Davidson motorcycle even though a Honda superbike may be £4000 cheaper. Strong brand names with strong brand images create customers who buy out of loyalty. Note that some strong brands create very little loyalty, such as BP; when buying petrol, drivers buy the cheapest they can, therefore the price elasticity of retail petrol brands such as BP is very high.

19.4 The significance of price elasticity

Being able to estimate a product's price elasticity is a hugely valuable aid to marketing decision making. When Wigan FC was promoted to the Premiership, its managers assumed that the attractions of Arsenal, Manchester United and the rest would make it easy to push up the price of match tickets. In fact ticket sales proved much worse than expected, forcing the club to cut its prices halfway through the 2006/2007 season. A firm that knows its price elasticity can make better decisions than one that is in ignorance.

Data on a product's price elasticity can be used for two purposes, as outlined below.

Sales forecasting

A firm considering a price rise will want to know the effect the price change is likely to have on demand. Producing a sales forecast will make possible accurate production, personnel and purchasing decisions. For example, when Sony cut the price of its PS2 by 25%, from £200 to £150, sales rose by 20%. The price elasticity of the PS2 proved to be:

$$\frac{-20\%}{+25\%} = -0.8$$

Sony could then use that knowledge to predict the likely impact of future price changes. Another price cut of 10% could lead to a sales increase of 8% ($-10\% \times -0.8 = +8\%$). This is valuable information to know. Before implementing the price cut the company could make sure to produce an extra 8% more stock to cope with the extra orders.

Pricing strategy

There are many external factors that determine a product's demand, and therefore its profitability. For example, a soft drinks manufacturer can do nothing about a wet, cold summer that hammers sales and profits. However, the price the firm decides to charge *is* within its control, and it can be a crucial factor in determining demand and profitability. Price elasticity information can be used in conjunction with internal cost data to forecast the implications of a price change on revenue.

Example

A second-hand car dealer currently sells 60 cars each year. Currently he charges his customers £2500 per car. This means the business has a revenue of:

Total revenue = £2500 × 60 = £150,000

From past experience the salesman believes the price elasticity of his cars is approximately 0.75. The dealer is thinking about increasing his prices to £3000 per car, an increase of 20%. Using the price elasticity information a quick calculation would reveal the impact on revenue:

Percentage change in demand   = +20% × −0.75
   = −15%

A 15% fall in demand on the existing sales volume of 60 cars per year will produce a fall in demand of nine cars per year. So demand will fall to 51 cars per year after the price increase. On the basis of these figures the new revenue would be:

Total revenue   = new price × new sales volume
   = £3 000 × 51 cars
   = £153 000

So, even though the price rise cuts sales to 51 cars, the revenue actually increases. Obviously, in this case, the car dealer should change his pricing strategy. However, this is all based on two assumptions:

1   that the price elasticity of the cars actually proves to be −0.75

2   other factors that could also affect demand remain unchanged following the price increase.

19.5 Classifying price elasticity

Price-elastic products

A **price-elastic product** is one with a price elasticity of more than 1. This means that the percentage change in demand is greater than the percentage change in price that created it. For example, if a firm increased prices by 5% and as a result demand fell by 15%, price elasticity would be:

$$\frac{-15\%}{+5\%} \times 100 = -3$$

For instance, for every 1% change in price, there will be a 3% change in demand. The higher the price elasticity figure, the more price elastic the product. Cutting price on a price-elastic product will boost total revenue. This is because the extra revenue gained from the increased sales volume more than offsets the revenue lost from the

price cut. On the other hand, a price increase on a price-elastic product will lead to a fall in total revenue.

It is important to note that price cutting can damage brand image. Customers often associate high prices with high quality. In addition, a price-cutting decision is usually difficult to reverse due to consumer resistance to price increases. Finally, the actions of the competition must also be taken into account. If your price cut prompts a price war the much needed gains in sales volume might not arise.

Price-inelastic products

Price-inelastic products have price elasticities below 1. This means the percentage change in demand is less than the percentage change in price. In other words, price changes have hardly any effect on demand – perhaps because consumers feel they *must* have the product or brand in question: the stunning dress, the trendiest designer label or – less interestingly – gas for central heating. Customers feel they must have it, either because it really is a necessity, or because it is fashionable. Firms with price-inelastic products will be tempted to push the prices up. A price increase will boost revenue because the price rise creates a relatively small fall in sales volume. This means the majority of customers will continue to purchase the brand but at a higher, revenue-boosting price.

19.6 Problems measuring price elasticity

What is the price elasticity of KitKat? Naturally, owners Nestlé would like to know, so that the right pricing decisions can be made. Therefore the company will do all it can to work out the price elasticity figure for this £100 million-plus brand. But how? All a firm can do is to work out what the price elasticity has been in the past, because it can only be calculated using past data. For example, if demand fell by 8% on the last occasion the price of KitKat was pushed up by 10%, the calculation is that the price elasticity was −0.8 (−8%/+10%).

Yet if that was a year ago, will the same be true today? Competition today may be a bit fiercer, making the price elasticity a bit higher. And today's consumer may be that much more sensitive about eating fatty foods, making a price rise a reason to stop buying KitKats altogether.

The price elasticity of a brand is a complex combination of its fashionability, the number of direct competitors it faces and the loyalty of its existing customers. All these things can change over time, causing the elasticity to go up or down. It is also possible that elasticity changes over a product's life cycle. It may be highly price elastic at the start, when people are suspicious of a new product. In its growth phase it may become trendy, making it less sensitive to price. In its decline phase people may keep buying the product only if the price is attractive, making it price elastic again.

In conclusion, it is unwise to talk about a product's price elasticity as if it is a fact. Firms make decisions using their assumptions or estimates about the price elasticity of their products. These assumptions are usually based on data that may now be out of date.

19.7 Strategies to reduce price elasticity

All businesses prefer to sell price-inelastic products. Charging more for a price-inelastic product guarantees an increase in short-term profit. If a firm has price-elastic products it will always feel vulnerable, as a rise in costs may be impossible to pass on to customers. And if a firm is tempted to cut the price of a price-elastic product, sales will probably rise so sharply that competitors will be forced to respond. A **price war** may result.

It is important to realise that the price elasticity of a brand is not set in stone. Price elasticity is not an **external constraint**. The most important influence on a brand's price elasticity is substitutability. If consumers have other brands available that they think deliver the same benefits, price elasticity will be high. So, to make a brand price inelastic, the firm has to find ways of reducing the number of substitutes available (or acceptable). How can this be done?

Increasing product differentiation

Product differentiation is the degree to which consumers perceive that a product is different (and preferably better) than its rivals. Some products are truly different from others, such as Britain's only business newspaper, the *Financial Times*. Others are successfully differentiated by image, such as Versace Jeans or the iPhone. The purchasers of highly differentiated products like Versace Jeans often remain brand loyal despite price rises. The reason for this low price elasticity is that wearing Versace Jeans makes a statement about the wearer, even if the cloth itself is no different from that used by Levi's or Wrangler.

Predatory pricing

Predatory pricing is a deliberate attempt to force a competitor out of a market by charging a low, loss-making price. Once the competitor has been forced out of the market, the consumer has one less source of supply. The reduction in the number of substitutes available to the customer allows the predator to raise prices successfully. If there are no cheaper substitutes available the customer is forced to pay the higher prices or go without. The same effect can be achieved by takeover bids (e.g. the purchase by Morrisons of Safeway food stores).

Issues For Analysis

In examinations, elasticity of demand is a key discriminator between good and weak candidates. Really weak candidates never bring the concept into their answers at all. Better candidates apply it, but imprecisely. Top-grade students see where it is relevant and show a clear understanding of the concept and its implications. Here are two ways to use price elasticity for business analysis.

● Whenever answering any question about pricing, elasticity is a vital factor. Even if a firm faces severe cost increases, a price rise will be very risky if its products have a high price elasticity. Pricing decisions must always start with careful consideration of price elasticity.

● People naturally assume that marketing (especially advertising) is always about trying to increase sales. In fact, most firms are far more interested in their image; a glance at any commercial break will confirm this. Companies focus upon their image because that is the way to differentiate themselves from others. That, in turn, is the way to reduce price elasticity and therefore give the company stronger control over its pricing.

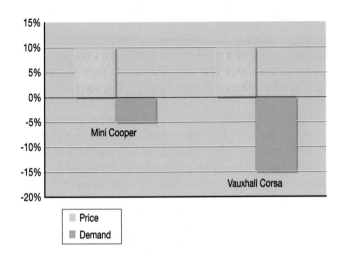

Figure 19.1 The impact on sales of a 10% price rise in two models of car

19.8 Income elasticity of demand

Elasticity can be used as a tool to look at many other aspects of influences on demand – for example, advertising, fashion and the price of other goods. Demand responds to a change in any one of the determinants, and each can be measured using elasticity as a tool. Apart from price, probably the most important determinant of demand is the *level of income*. In general terms, and for most goods, an increase in income will lead to an increase in demand. The demand for *luxury goods* such as foreign holidays or large cars will increase sharply as incomes rise; the demand for basic goods, such as bread and potatoes, may decrease as income increases and people buy more meat and fish. This will lead to negative **income elasticity of demand**. These goods are known as *inferior goods*.

The formula for calculating income elasticity of demand is:

$$\frac{\% \text{ change in quantity demanded}}{\% \text{ change in income}}$$

When analysing the effects of income elasticity it is important to consider the type of product in question, the time period and the type of market being targeted. Above all else, it is important to remember that a luxury product that enjoys sales in a boom period will probably suffer badly if the economy slips towards recession. *Necessity* products, such as toothpaste, on the other hand, are affected very little by changing incomes – their income elasticity is close to zero.

19.9 Elasticity and decision-making

an evaluation

For examiners, elasticity is a convenient concept. It is hard to understand, but very easy to write exam questions on! But how useful is it in the real world? Would the average marketing director know the price elasticities of his or her products?

In many cases the answer is no. Examiners and textbooks exaggerate the precision that is possible with such a concept. Figure 19.1 shows the impact on sales of a 10% price rise in two models of car. The Mini Cooper's price elasticity is – 0.5 while the Corsa is – 1.5. But just because those figures were true in the past, will they still be in the future. Price elasticities change over time, as competition changes and consumer tastes change.

Even though elasticities can vary over time, certain features tend to remain constant. Strong brands such as Apple and Coca-Cola have relatively low price elasticity. This gives them the power over market pricing that ensures strong profitability year after year. For less established firms, these brands are the role models: everyone wants to be the Coca-Cola of their own market or market niche.

Key terms

Correlation: the relationship between one variable and another.
External constraint: something outside the firm's control that can prevent it achieving its objectives.
Income elasticity of demand: the responsiveness of demand to a change in income.
Predatory pricing: pricing low with the deliberate intention of driving a competitor out of business.
Price-elastic product: a product that is highly price sensitive, so price elasticity is above 1.
Price-inelastic product: a product that is not very price sensitive, so price elasticity is below 1.
Price war: when two or more companies battle for market share by slashing prices, perhaps selling at or below cost.

Exercises

A. Revision questions

(40 marks; 40 minutes)

1a If a product's sales have fallen by 21% following a price rise from £2 to £2.07, what is its price elasticity? (4)

1b Is the product price elastic or price inelastic? (1)

2 Outline two ways in which Nestlé might try to reduce the price elasticity of its Aero chocolate bars. (4)

3 A firm selling 20,000 units at £8 is considering a 4% price increase. It believes its price elasticity is −0.5.
   (a) What will be the effect upon revenue? (5)
   (b) Give two reasons why the revenue may prove to be different from the firm's expectations. (2)

4 Explain three ways a firm could make use of information about the price elasticity of its brands. (6)

5 Identify three external factors that could increase the price elasticity of a brand of chocolate. (3)

6 A firm has a sales target of 60,000 units per month. Current sales are 50,000 per month at a price of £1.50. If its products have a price elasticity of −2, what price should the firm charge to meet the target sales volume? (4)

7 Why is price elasticity always negative? (2)

8 Explain why the manager of a product with a price elasticity of −2 may be reluctant to cut the price? (4)

9 When recession hit, a 3% fall in consumers' real incomes caused sales of brand X to rise from 40,000 to 44,800.
   (a) Calculate the income elasticity of brand X. (4)
   (b) Suggest what type of product it is. (1)

B. Revision exercises

B1 Data response

A firm selling Manchester United pillow cases for £10 currently generates an annual turnover of £500,000. Variable costs average at £4 per unit and total annual fixed costs are £100,000. The marketing director is just about to impose a price increase of 10%.

Questions

(20 marks; 25 minutes)

1 Given that the price elasticity of the product is believed to be −0.4, calculate:
   (a) the old and the new sales volume (3)
   (b) the new revenue (3)
   (c) the expected change in profit following the price increase. (6)

2 If the firm started producing mass-market white pillow cases, would their price elasticity be higher or lower than the Manchester United ones? Why is that? (8)

B2 Data response

The iPhone

The date 9 November 2007 was going to be an important one for Apple geeks. It saw the UK launch of the iPhone. Already a sensation in the States, with sales of more than one million units, it was the most eagerly awaited product launch in years. The appeal was simple: the best-looking phone ever, with the easiest user interface.

But what price should Apple charge for the phone, and how should it distribute it? To help keep competition down, it struck a deal to make O_2 – Britain's largest mobile operator – its exclusive British network for the handset. Apple knew from the outset that it could not take UK sales for granted. Nokia and Sony Ericsson are both bigger brands here than in the USA, so competition would be fiercer. Even more important, perhaps, would be the missing power:

by late 2007 more than 20% of UK phones were on the powerful 3G connection, making internet access fast and easy. The iPod was a more backward 2.5G.

A marketing analyst was quoted in the *Financial Times* as saying: 'On November 8th there will be iGeeks waiting outside the Apple store on Regent Street [London] with their sleeping bags and cups of coffee. . . There will be a big surge of interest in the beginning but, after that, there will be some difficulty in sustaining demand in the face of some very credible competition.

Apple decided to price the iPhone at £269. On top of this, users would have to sign up to an 18-month contract with a minimum payment of £35 a month, making the whole commitment a whopping £899. This compared with a 3G Sony Walkman phone priced at £120 or a Samsung Slimline 3G, available for nothing as a contract upgrade.

Source: various, including the *Financial Times*, 19 September 2007

Questions

(20 marks; 25 minutes)

1 Explain the likely logic behind Apple's decision to sign an exclusive deal with the O_2 network. (6)

2 Use your understanding of price elasticity to discuss whether or not Apple was right to price the iPhone in this way. (14)

B3 Data response

Income increases by 10% and the demand for bread per capita falls from 50 loaves to 45 loaves a year.

Source: Federation of Bakers, 2005

Questions

(10 marks; 10 minutes)

1 Calculate the income elasticity demand for bread.

2 Using your answer to question 1, how important is it for bakers to take account of the result?

B4 Data response

No scrooges in Knightsbridge

With average earnings rising by 4.2% in 2006 and an inflation rate of 2.2%, real earnings are about 2% higher than in 2005. Coming on the back of more than ten years of economic growth, this has led to some boom times for the luxury market. The upmarket jewellery retailer Boodles has reported sales 28% higher than in 2005, and a 'pleasing' level of demand for its £100,000 diamond necklace. Harrods boss Mohamed Al Fayed has just paid himself a £72 million dividend and reported 'strong trading'. Sales at the Knightsbridge store are set to hit £561 million in 2006 compared with £510 million in 2005.

Of course, not everyone's Christmas looks great. On 13 October 2006 Farepak was put into **administration**. Farepak had run a Christmas savings club since 1969. It was a way for low-earning families to cope with the cost of Christmas without running up debts. More than 4.5 million adults earn less than £6.50 an hour in Britain, making it tough to live week to week, let alone save. Farepak offered a responsible way to provide Christmas food, drink and presents for the family.

Farepak's collapse came at the worst possible time for its 120,000 customers. They had saved for most of the year, but not yet received a penny in return. For the same reasons, this was the best time of year for the company's bankers and other **creditors**. About £40 million of savings were lost in the collapse of Farepak – most of this will go to bankers HBOS (Halifax & Bank of Scotland) and to those owed money by Farepak's parent company EHR (European Home Retail).

EHR itself went into administration in August 2006. According to its bankers HBOS, EHR's practice was to 'collect customer receipts from all the subsidiary companies and use them as working capital to fund the ongoing business of the group'. So the savings of some of the poorest families in Britain were being used as if they were bank overdrafts. Worse still, EHR used this capital in highly risky ways. In 2000 the firm bought DMG, a book and toy retailer, for £30 million; after years of losses, it sold it for £4 million in 2004. Although Sir Clive Thompson, EHR's chairman, pointed the finger at HBOS for allowing Farepak to collapse, most commentators realised that Thompson himself was hugely at fault.

Out of the frying pan ...

But what of the savers, what are they to do? A compensation fund for them will result in payments of less than 10% of the sum they put in. As one single mother said to the BBC's *Working Lunch* programme: 'Not only have I lost the £240 I put in, now I have to find the money to get the food I thought I had.'

A 'solution' to this problem was soon on offer. On 2 December 2006 the *Financial Times* reported that 'Farepak victims borrow at 365%'. The doorstep lender Provident Personal Credit was reported to be targeting Farepak victims with leaflets with Christmas trees and mocked-up £500 cheques. The literature makes it clear that the typical **APR** is 177%, but this rises to 365% for those who want to repay the debt within 30 weeks. It is clear from the literature that the company is confident that customers will not understand – or be put off by – APR figures such as 177%. (To see this, go to Provident's website www.cash—loan.co.uk.)

When you see how high the interest charges are for unsecured loans to those on low incomes, it is easy to see why people signed up for a scheme such as Farepak's. Tragic, then, that people showing a responsible attitude to saving should have been let down so badly in the Farepak collapse. Christmas has always been a tough time for the less well off.

Sources include: *Financial Times*, 2 December 2006; *The Economist*, 16 November 2006, and the websites www.unfairpak.co.uk and www.statistics.gov.uk

Glossary

Administration: when decision-making powers are taken away from the directors of a failing company and placed with accountants who will oversee the closure or the sale of the business.

APR: annualised percentage rate – i.e. the interest charges on a loan, calculated over a 12-month period (when the government interest rate is 5%, a figure of 177% is incredibly, greedily, high).

Creditors: those owed money by a business (e.g. banks, suppliers, unpaid staff).

Questions

(35 marks; 45 minutes)

1a Calculate the income elasticity of demand for:

(i) Boodles (4)

(ii) Harrods (4)

1b Explain two reasons that might explain the differences between the income elasticities of these retailers. (4)

2 Farepak's cash was being used as working capital for the whole EHR group.

(a) What is meant by 'working capital'? (2)

(b) Explain why working capital should not be used to make risky long-term decisions such as buying a new business. (4)

3 At an APR of 177% per year, someone taking out a £500 Provident loan would end up repaying many thousands of pounds. Presumably they would never fall into the trap again. Examine the implications for a company such as Provident of constantly needing new customers, because so few become loyal to the brand. (8)

4 Social pressures such as 'having a happy Christmas' provide companies with the opportunity to push parents to spend more than they should. Discuss whether the managers of Provident Personal Credit are right to place Farepak savers at the heart of their pre-Christmas target market. (9)

BUDGETS AND DECISION-MAKING

A budget is a target for costs or revenue that a firm or department must aim to achieve over a given period of time.

20.1 Introduction

Budgeting is the process of setting targets, covering all aspects of costs and revenues. It is a method for turning a firm's strategy into reality. Nothing can be done in business without money; budgets tell individual managers how much they can spend to achieve their objectives. For instance, a football manager might be given a transfer expenditure budget of £20 million to buy players. With the budget in place, the transfer dealing can get under way.

A budgeting system shows how much can be spent, and gives managers a way to check whether they are on track. Most firms use a system of budgetary control as a means of supervision. The process is as follows:

1 Make a judgement of the likely sales revenues for the coming year.

2 Set a cost ceiling that allows for an acceptable level of profit.

3 This budget for the whole company's costs is then broken down by division, department or by cost centre.

4 The budget may then be broken down further so that each manager has a budget and therefore some spending power.

In a business start-up, the budget should provide enough spending power to finance vital needs such as building work, decoration, recruiting and paying staff, and marketing. If a manager overspends in one area, s/he knows that it is essential to cut back elsewhere. A good manager gets the best possible value from the budgeted sum.

There are two main reasons that budgets are used when managing a business:

1 as a means of delegating spending power

2 as a method of monitoring business performance.

20.2 What is budgeting for?

● To ensure that no department or individual spends more than the company expects, thereby preventing unpleasant surprises.

● To provide a yardstick against which a manager's success or failure can be measured (and rewarded). For example, a store manager may have to meet a monthly sales budget of £25,000 at a maximum operating cost of £18,000. As long as the budget holder believes this target is possible, the attempt to achieve it will be motivating. The company can then provide bonuses for achieving or beating the profit target.

● To enable spending power to be delegated to local managers who are in a better position to know how best to use the firm's money. This should improve and speed up the decision-making process – and help motivate the local budget holders. Management expert Peter Drucker refers to 'management by self-control'. He regards this as the ideal approach. Managers should have clear targets, clear budgets and the power to decide how to achieve them. Then they will try everything they can to succeed.

● Budgeting can motivate the staff in a department. If budget figures are used as a clear basis for assessing their performance it becomes clear to staff what they must achieve in order to be considered successful.

20.3 Types of budget

Income budget

The **income budget** sets a minimum target for the desired revenue level to be achieved over a period of time. If a manager knows, halfway through the year, that sales figures have not been strong enough to achieve the target, s/he might decide to run a price promotion or a 'buy one get one free' (BOGOF) offer.

When buying a new car it is clever to wait for the last day of the month, as showroom managers are often trying desperately to achieve their monthly sales target: their incentive may be a salary bonus or a monthly prize such as a trip to the Caribbean for the month's top-performing sales manager; your incentive is a cheaper car!

Expenditure budget

The **expenditure budget** sets a maximum target for costs – for example, the manager of the Derby McDonald's may have a staff budget of £2100 for the month of November. Spending beyond an expenditure budget occasionally will be tolerated, but a manager who persistently overspends is likely to get a stern talking-to. An intelligent boss will also question expenditure underspending (e.g. not spending the budget for safety training) as this may cause major problems later on.

High-grade application

The BP disaster

On 23 March 2005 a huge explosion at BP's Texas oil refinery killed 15 people and injured more than 180; most were its own staff. The refinery, America's third biggest, had suffered safety problems before. In 2004 two workers died when scalded by super-heated water that escaped from a high-pressure pipe and, in a separate incident, BP was fined $63,000 for safety breaches at the plant.

After an inquiry, the chairwoman of the US Chemical Safety Board (CSB) reported that 'BP implemented a 25% cut on fixed costs from 1998 to 2000 that adversely impacted maintenance expenditures at the refinery'. The report stated that 'BP's global management' (i.e. British Head Office) 'was aware of problems with maintenance spending and infrastructure well before March 2005', yet they did nothing about it. The chairwoman delivered the final critique thus:

Every successful corporation must contain its costs. But at an ageing facility like Texas City, it is not responsible to cut budgets related to safety and maintenance without thoroughly examining the impact on the risk of a catastrophic accident.

BP confirmed that its own internal investigation had findings 'generally consistent with those of the CSB'.

Source: adapted from Topical Cases, January 2007 (www.a-zbusinesstraining.com)

Profit budget

The **profit budget** is a function of the previous two budgets. The higher the income budget and the lower the expenditure, the higher the profit. Senior managers should look with care at how a profit budget has been met or beaten. For example, the profit achievement may have been a result of cost-cutting that threatens health and safety. Of course, managers are supposed to meet their profit targets, but there is more to running a business successfully than simply getting the numbers right.

20.4 Setting budgets

Setting budgets is not an easy job. How do you decide exactly what level of sales are likely next year, especially for new businesses with no previous trading to rely on? Furthermore, how can you plan for costs if the cost of your raw materials tends to fluctuate? Most firms treat last year's budget figures as the main determinant of this year's budget. Minor adjustments will be made for inflation and other foreseeable changes. Given the firm's past experience, budget-setting should be quite quick and quite accurate.

For start-ups, setting budgets will be a much tougher job. The entrepreneur will need to rely on:

- a 'guesstimate' of likely sales in the early months of the start-up

- the entrepreneur's expertise and experience, which will be better if the entrepreneur has worked in the industry before

- the entrepreneur's instinct, based on market understanding

- a significant level of market research.

An alternative approach is zero budgeting. This sets each department's budget at zero and demands that budget holders, in setting their budget, justify every pound they ask for. This helps to avoid the common phenomenon of budgets creeping upwards each year.

The best criteria for setting budgets are:

- to relate the budget directly to the business objective; if a company wants to increase sales and market share, the best method might be to increase the advertising budget and thereby boost demand

- to involve as many people as possible in the process; people will be more committed to reaching the targets if they have had a say in how the budget was set.

Table 20.1 Example of a budget statement

	January	**February**	**March**
Income	25000	28000	30000
Variable costs	10000	12000	13000
Fixed costs	10000	10000	11000
Total cost	20000	22000	24000
Profit	5000	6000	6000

Simple budget statements

A simple example of a budget statement might look like that shown in Table 20.1.

Income − Total cost = Profit

Variable cost + Fixed cost = Total cost

This information is only of value if it proves possible for a manager to believe that these figures are achievable. Only then will s/he be motivated to try to turn the budgets into reality.

20.5 Problems in setting budgets

The main problem is that individual managers want as much spending power as possible (a high budget). This will help them do their job successfully and more enjoyably (e.g. a big expense account). The bosses, though, want to keep costs as low as possible among junior managers (i.e. to set low budgets). A senior Cadbury's manager might feel sure that an advertising budget of £2 million will be enough for Creme Eggs this year. Yet the brand manager for Creme Eggs may have a convincing argument for why £3.5 million is needed. (And no one knows the 'right' figure.)

The main problems in setting budgets occur when:

● a new firm or new manager lacks experience in knowing what things really cost

● a senior manager is too arrogant to listen to his/her staff, and just sets a budget without discussion (successful budgets should be agreed, not set)

● the type of business makes it hard to set budgets in a meaningful way (meaning that managers struggle to take them seriously); see the high-grade application box.

High-grade application
Chessington World of Adventures

In April 2007 Chessington World of Adventures opened for its summer season. The newly appointed merchandise manager (in charge of all non-food sales) was given his sales budget for the year, which had been set 6% higher than for 2006. He thought it was quite ambitious, but a sunny April brought in the crowds so the sales target started to look reasonable. The period May–August, though, saw some of the wettest months on record, washing his budget targets away. As a wet day at Chessington can cut crowds by 75%, there was nothing he could do. Do budgets have a purpose in a business such as this?

Figure 20.1 Cadbury's Creme Egg

20.6 Budgets as a means of delegating spending power

Once a business grows beyond a simple one-person operation, there will be times that the boss is not around to authorise spending money – even small amounts like ordering a little extra stock or paying the window cleaner. To make sure the business can run smoothly, the boss needs to find a way to give staff the power to make spending decisions themselves. However, the boss will want to ensure that these decisions are not going to bankrupt the firm. Budgets can be used to allow employees to decide what money to spend within the limits specified by the budget. If an entrepreneur who has successfully opened a beauty salon wants to open a second branch, s/he will need to appoint a manager of the second branch. The entrepreneur can then agree budget targets for the income and expenditure of the second branch, knowing that the manager will be working hard to hit the budget targets.

The budgets for costs should help to avoid any unexpected financial surprises – since the manager would be expected to discuss any budget overspend with the entrepreneur before they are incurred. The manager can run the shop on a day-to-day basis, spending whatever money needs to be spent without checking with the boss all the time, yet the boss will be happy that the costs of the second branch are being controlled within the limits set by the budget.

This principle applies to huge multinational companies as well as businesses that have just started growing. In a huge firm, there will be many more budget holders and many more separate budgets, however the concept is the same, as shown in the simple example in Figure 20.2.

20.7 Budgets as a method of monitoring business performance

With budgets in place for each department, the management has **criteria** against which success can be measured. Budget holders will try to exceed revenue budgets or stay under cost targets. The implication, of course, is that budgeted figures will be compared with what actually happens to make a judgement on performance. It is this process of comparison that allows budgets to be used as a method of monitoring business performance.

Budgetary variances

Variance is the amount by which the actual result differs from the budgeted figure. It is usually measured each month, by comparing the actual outcome with the budgeted one. It is important to note that variances are

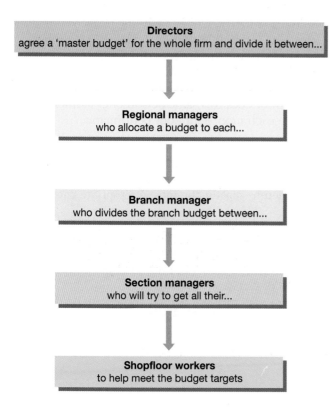

Figure 20.2 Budget holders

High-grade application
A wiser dragon

Rachel Elnough was one of the original dragons on the BBC TV series *Dragons' Den*. As founder of the gift company Red Letter Days, she was making a £1 million profit on a turnover of £10 million at the height of the firm's success. Once she stepped back from day-to-day control of the company, however, things started to go wrong. The major lesson she reports is that although budgets had been set, there was a lack of monitoring of those budgets and therefore problems in reaching targets became clear to her only once the firm was in too much trouble to save.

Table 20.2 Adverse or favourable variance?

Variable	Budget	Actual	Variance	
Sales of X	150	160	10	Favourable
Sales of Y	150	145	5	Adverse
Material costs	100	90	10	Favourable
Labour costs	100	105	5	Adverse

referred to as adverse or favourable – not positive or negative. A **favourable variance** is one that leads to higher than expected profit (revenue up or costs down). An **adverse variance** is one that reduces profit, such as costs being higher than the budgeted level. Table 20.2 shows when variances are adverse or favourable.

The value of regular variance statements is that they provide an early warning. If a product's sales are slipping below budget, managers can respond by increasing marketing support or by cutting back on production plans. In an ideal world, slippage could be noted in March, a new strategy put into place by May and a recovery in sales achieved by September. Clearly, no firm wishes to wait until the end-of-year profit and loss account to find out that things went badly. An early warning can lead to an early solution.

Management by exception

In a large company, with many separate cost centres, senior managers will have hundreds of budget statements to review each month. In order to avoid information overload, most budgeting systems work on the basis of management by exception. Senior managers will concern themselves only with departmental budgets that show large variances (probably adverse). In large companies management authority is usually **delegated** down through the organisation. Senior managers get involved only with problem areas or areas of great success.

Issues For Analysis

- Especially relevant to a small business owner will be deciding whether designing and implementing a budgeting system will cost more in terms of time and money than it might save. In other words, s/he must decide on the opportunity costs involved. In the often chaotic world of a small business start-up, it is easy to see how time spent talking to customers and suppliers would be more valuable. It is harder to appreciate how time spent in front of a computer spreadsheet estimating revenues and costs will help to enhance profit and the chances of survival.

- Variances are the key to analysing budgets. Once a variance between budgeted and actual figures has been identified, the analysis can begin. The important step is to ask why that variance occurred. Does the person responsible know the reason? Is it a one-off, or does this same person offer a different excuse each month for poor performance?

- Variance analysis is a means of identifying symptoms. It is down to the user of the variance figures to make a diagnosis as to the exact nature of any problem, and then to suggest the most appropriate cure.

- Although budgets and variances sound very focused upon numbers, they are rooted in everyday actions by people. Sales budgets will be achieved only if the salesforce is enthusiastic and well managed. Production costs will be kept down only if wastage is low and commitment is high. When analysing budgetary problems, therefore, managers soon find themselves looking at the quality of management in departments such as marketing and production.

20.8 Budgets

an evaluation

The sophistication of budgeting systems is usually directly linked to the size of a business. Huge multinationals have incredibly complex budgeting systems. For a small business start-up, any budgeting system is likely to be far more simplistic. Most will rely on a rough breakdown of how the start-up budget is to be divided between the competing demands. There is, however, no doubt that budgeting provides a more effective system of controlling a business's finances than no system at all.

Budgets are a management tool. The way in which they are used can tell you a lot about a firm's culture. Firms with a culture of bossy management will tend to use a tightly controlled budgetary system. Managers will have budgets imposed upon them and variances will be watched closely by supervisors. Organisations with a more open culture will use budgeting as an aid to discussion and empowerment.

Whatever the culture, if a manager is to be held accountable for meeting a budget, s/he must be given influence over setting it, and control over reaching it. Although budgets are set for future time periods, analysis of actual against budgeted performance can take place only after the event. This is true of all financial monitoring and leads to doubts as to its effectiveness as a planning tool. Other measures may be far more reliable in predicting future performance – market research indicating growing levels of customer complaints, for instance, may well be more useful in predicting future performance.

From an even broader perspective, it could be argued that budgets and other financial measures are unhelpful in some circumstances. Perhaps firms should look at their objectives before deciding on the most useful measure of performance. Financial measures are fine for firms attempting to maximise their profits, but sales figures will be more relevant for firms pursuing an objective of growth, while customer complaint levels will be particularly relevant to firms aiming for excellence in their levels of service.

Key terms

Adverse variance: a difference between budgeted and actual figures that is damaging to the firm's profit (e.g. costs up or revenue down).
Criteria: yardsticks against which success (or the lack of it) can be measured.
Delegated: passing authority down the hierarchy.
Expenditure budget: setting a maximum figure on what a department or manager can spend over a period of time; this is to control costs.
Favourable variance: a difference between budgeted and actual figures that boosts a firm's profit (e.g. revenue up or costs down).
Income budget: setting a minimum figure for the revenue to be generated by a product, a department or a manager.
Profit budget: setting a minimum figure for the profit to be achieved over a period of time.

Exercises

Budget statement for questions A7 and A8

	January	February	March	April
Income	4200	4500	4000	
Variable costs	1800		2000	1800
Fixed costs	1200	1600		1600
Total costs		3600	4100	
Profit				600

A. Revision questions

(67 marks; 70 minutes)

1 Explain the meaning of the term 'budgeting'. (2)

2 List three advantages that a budgeting system brings to a company. (3)

3 Why is it valuable to have a yardstick against which performance can be measured? (3)

4 What are the advantages of a zero-based budgeting system? (3)

5 Briefly explain how most companies actually set next year's budgets. (3)

6 Why should budget holders have a say in the setting of their budgets? (4)

7 Complete the budget statement at the top of the page by filling in the gaps: (8)

8 Amend the budget statement completed in question 7 to show the income levels needed to generate a profit of £1000 per month, assuming there is no change in costs. (4)

9 What are the two main advantages that using a budgeting system brings to a company? (2)

10 Why is it valuable to have a yardstick against which performance can be measured? (3)

11 How might a firm respond to an increasingly adverse variance in labour costs? (4)

12 Explain what is meant by a 'favourable cost variance'. (2)

13 Why is management by exception a useful time-saving measure for management? (4)

14 Explain two drawbacks of budgeting. (4)

15 Briefly explain why a shop with a favourable income variance might expect some cost variances to be adverse. (4)

16 Look at the table below, then answer the questions that follow.

(a) Calculate the budgeted and actual profit figures for both months (4)
(b) Identify the following:
  (i) a month with a favourable revenue variance
  (ii) a month with an adverse fixed cost variance
  (iii) a month with an adverse variable cost variance
  (iv) a month with a favourable fixed cost variance
  (v) a month with an adverse total cost variance
  (vi) a month with an adverse revenue variance
  (vii) a month with a favourable total cost variance
  (viii) a month with an adverse variable cost variance
  (ix) a month with an adverse profit variance
  (x) a month with a favourable profit variance. (10)

Table for question A16

	May		June	
	Budgeted	Actual	Budgeted	Actual
Revenue	3500	3200	4000	4200
Variable costs	1000	900	1200	1500
Fixed costs	1200	1200	1300	1100
Total costs	2200	2100	2500	2600
Profit				

B. Revision exercises

B1 Data response

The partnership began in the Atlantic Ocean. Kurt and Brian were both windsurfing fanatics and got to know each other one winter in the Canary Isles. Looking for a way to fund ever more expensive winter watersports trips, they pooled their savings to buy the lease on a flooded former gravel pit back in the UK. The location, just outside London, gave them access to a large market of affluent watersports enthusiasts. KB Wetsports could provide this market with their fix of windsurfing, dinghy sailing or kayaking. In addition to the fees for use of the lake and tuition fees for beginners, a shop would also feature at the centre, selling specialist watersport supplies that were hard to find inland. Both Kurt and Brian had studied management at university and knew that budgeting would be important. They could use it to control expenses and to motivate their small team of staff. They drew up the budget statement below.

Questions

(30 marks; 30 minutes)

1 Complete the budget statement on the opposite page by filling in the gaps. (4)

2 Adjust the budget to show the effect of a 50% increase in shop sales in the third quarter and a 25% increase in wages in quarter 4. (4)

3 Explain why a budgeting system might help KB Wetsports to:
   (a) control expenses (6)
   (b) motivate staff (6)

4 To what extent is budget-setting a crucial element of a successful small business start-up such as KB Wetsports? (10)

Budget statement for Exercise B1

	Jan–Mar	Apr–Jun	Jul–Sep	Oct–Dec
Shop sales	200	3000	5000	2000
Lake fees	0	22000	25000	2800
Stock	2500	1000	2500	1000
Wages	1000	5000	5000	1000
Overheads	1000	4000	6000	4000
Profit				

B2 Data response

Cutting work trip hotel costs

According to new research, UK organisations are overspending by £1.3 billion every year on unnecessarily extravagant business trips. Nearly half of all organisations fail to produce an official business travel policy. Therefore many employees admit to booking what they want and 88% claim not to be influenced by cost.

Stephen Alambritis, chief spokesman of the Federation of Small Businesses, comments: 'Business owners understand the importance of face-to-face meetings and consider personal contact with customers an essential part of generating new sales. But well-run firms control the cost of business travel, setting budgets for both transport and accommodation. Controlling costs across the business underpins future growth and success.'

The findings were alarming – UK businesses simply don't maintain financial control over employee business trips.

The wastage facts

- Nearly half (48%) of all organisations never set a business trip budget. This figure rises to 59% when relating to small to medium businesses.

- Over 40% of employees make their own individual business trip arrangements and claim that they can spend what they like on trips.

- An overwhelming 88% say they aren't influenced by cost.

- Almost a third (30%) of 18–29 year olds exploit business trips as perks.

- Only 12% of employees believe their organisations are interested in cost-cutting.

This clear lack of control has left employees free to squander up to £1.3 billion of their employer's money every year.

Source: Adapted from "Cutting work trip hotel costs", www.workingbalance.co.uk

Questions

(20 marks; 25 minutes)

1 Identify and explain three pieces of evidence from the text that demonstrate the problems for firms that operate without a budget. (9)

2 Explain how a small business might benefit from setting expenditure budgets for its business travel. (5)

3 Outline two problems a business might have in setting a travel budget. (6)

B3 Data analysis

Questions

(20 marks; 20 minutes)

1 What are the five numbers missing from the variance analysis below? (5)

2 Examine one financial strength and two weaknesses in this data, from the company's viewpoint. (9)

3 How might a manager set about improving the accuracy of a sales budget? (6)

	January			February		
	B	A	V	B	A	V
Sales revenue	140*	150	10	180	175	?
Materials	70	80	(10)	90	95	?
Other direct costs	30	35	(5)	40	40	0
Overheads	20	20	0	25	22	?
Profit	20	15	(5)	?	18	?

*All figures in £000s

B4 Data response

Budget data for Clinton & Collins Ltd (£000s)

	January		February		March		April	
	B	A	B	A	B	A	B	A
Sales revenue	160	144	180	156	208	168	240	188
Materials	40	38	48	44	52	48	58	54
Labour	52	48	60	54	66	62	72	68
Overheads	76	76	76	78	76	80	76	80
Profit	(8)	(18)	(4)	(20)	14	(22)	34	(14)

Questions

(25 marks; 25 minutes)

1 Use the data above to explain why February's profits were worse than expected. (5)

2 Why might Clinton & Collins Ltd have chosen to set monthly budgets? (5)

3 Explain how the firm might have set these budgets. (4)

4 The directors of Clinton & Collins Ltd knew that the recession was causing problems for the firm but were unsure as to whether things were improving or worsening. To what extent does the data suggest an improvement? (11)

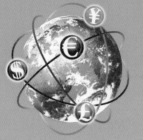

21 CASH FLOW FORECASTING

DEFINITION

Cash flow is the flow of money into and out of a business in a given time period. Cash flow forecasting is estimating the flow of cash in the future.

21.1 Preparing a cash flow forecast

To prepare a cash flow forecast businesses need to estimate all the money coming into and out of the business, month by month. These flows of money are then set onto a grid showing the cash movements in each month.

Cash in

In this example (Table 21.1) the business is a new start-up. The business will receive an injection of capital of £30,000. This will be received in March. The business will start production in April and will receive cash only when sales start in May. Cash inflows are expected to increase each month until reaching a maximum of £15,000 in August.

It is important that the income from sales is shown when the cash is received not when the sale is made.

Outflow (see Table 21.2)

In March the firm will buy machinery for £23,000.

Materials will cost £6000 each month. The first delivery in April must be paid for on delivery. After that the supplier will give the firm two months' credit so the next payments do not need to be made until July. Rent for the building costs £2000 per month, but the owner requires two months' rent in advance. Wages are estimated to be £2000 per month and there are other expenses of £1000 per month.

When these figures have been entered into the grid the total expenditure can be calculated.

The cash flow forecast can now be completed by calculating the following.

● *Monthly balance:* this is cash inflow for the month minus cash outflow. It shows each month if there is a positive or a negative movement of cash. In this case inflow is greater than outflow, except in April. When outflow is greater than inflow the monthly balance will be negative. This is shown in brackets to indicate that it is a minus figure.

● *Opening and closing balance:* this is like a bank statement. It shows what cash the business has at the beginning of the month (opening balance) and what the cash position is at the end of the month (closing balance). The closing balance is the opening balance plus the monthly balance (e.g. for August, the month starts with £1000 in the bank, another £4000 flows

Table 21.1 Cash inflow example

Month (cash inflow, £s)	March	April	May	June	July	August
Capital	30000					
Sales			7000	10000	13000	15000
Total inflow	**30000**	**0**	**7000**	**10000**	**13000**	**15000**

Table 21.2 Cash outflow example

Month (cash outflow, £s)	March	April	May	June	July	August
Equipment	23000					
Materials	0	6000			6000	6000
Rent	4000	2000	2000	2000	2000	2000
Wages		2000	2000	2000	2000	2000
Other expenses		1000	1000	1000	1000	1000
Total outflow	**27000**	**11000**	**5000**	**5000**	**11000**	**11000**

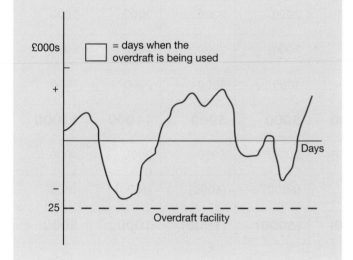

Figure 21.1 Daily cash balances for a firm with a £25,000 overdraft

in during the month, so the month closes with a bank balance of £5000).

The closing balance shows the business its expected net cash position each month.

The completed cash flow forecast will be as shown in Table 21.3.

This shows that there is a negative cash balance for the months of April, May and June. Only in July does the business start having a positive cash flow. As there is no such thing as negative money this cash flow forecast shows the business that it must take action if it is to avoid problems in the early months. The easiest remedy for a cash flow problem such as this is a bank **overdraft**.

21.4 Benefits of cash flow forecasts

A cash flow forecast will enable a business to do the following things.

- Anticipate the timing and amounts of any cash shortages: in the example above, the business can see from the cash flow forecast whether it has sufficient cash. In fact this business does not have enough cash for three months (April, May and June). There is no such thing as negative money so the business will not be able to make some of its payments. It will not be able to pay wages or the rent. This would mean that, although the business looks cash rich in the longer term – by July it has a positive cash flow – it might not survive.

- Arrange financial cover for any anticipated shortages of cash: having information about when the business will have a cash shortage means that the business can take measures to ensure that it has cash available. In the example above, the business needs to find additional finance for the three months when it has a cash shortage.

- Review the timings and amounts of receipts and payments.

- Obtain loans (if the problems are long term) or overdrafts (if the problems are short term).

If a firm wants to take out a loan, the bank will always request a cash flow forecast. Banks do this in order to ensure that the business:

- has enough cash to enable it to survive

Table 21.3 Cash flow forecast for Visible Engineering Ltd

Month (£s)	March	April	May	June	July	August
Cash inflow						
Capital	30000					
Sales			7000	10000	13000	15000
Total inflow	**30000**	**0**	**7000**	**10000**	**13000**	**15000**
Outflow						
Equipment	23000					
Materials	0	6000			6000	6000
Rent	4000	2000	2000	2000	2000	2000
Wages		2000	2000	2000	2000	2000
Other expenses		1000	1000	1000	1000	1000
Total outflow	**27000**	**11000**	**5000**	**5000**	**11000**	**11000**
Monthly balance	3000	(11000)	2000	5000	2000	4000
Opening balance	0	3000	(8000)	(6000)	(1000)	1000
Closing balance	**3000**	**(8000)**	**(6000)**	**(1000)**	**1000**	**5000**

High-grade application

Kwik Save

Fresh evidence of the cash crisis facing discount grocery chain Kwik Save emerged this weekend – only days after it announced the closure of 79 stores. *The Sunday Times* disclosed last week that dairy group Arla had stopped supplying Kwik Save with milk because of 'payment problems'. And now British Bakeries – part of Premier Foods, with brands such as Hovis and Mothers Pride – has halted bread deliveries to Kwik Save.

Premier said it could not comment on commercial agreements. But reliable sources confirmed that British Bakeries has stopped supplying Kwik Save. As with Arla, 'payment problems' were alleged to be the reason.

Some Kwik Save stores have not received any cigarettes for months. And there is said to have been disruption to the chain's supplies of chilled and frozen goods.

Kwik Save approached Costcutter last month, hoping to secure access to a number of brands for which it had been impossible to negotiate terms with manufacturers. But Costcutter said it would not start supplying unless it could secure payment upfront.

Restructuring experts at accountancy firm KPMG have been called in to see if there is a way that Kwik Save can be saved from closure. The retailer closed 79 of its 226 stores last Tuesday. It is estimated that 800 people lost their jobs.

Source: *Sunday Times*, 3 June 2007

- is able to pay the interest on the loan

- will be able to repay the loan

- is aware of the need for cash flow management.

How reliable are cash flow forecasts?

In order to prepare a cash flow forecast, businesses need to make assumptions about the future – although they may be able to make some use of actual figures, such as the monthly rent agreed with the landlord.

When looking at cash flow forecasts it is useful for the firm to be aware that the figures are estimates and to build in some safety margins. Companies should ask themselves what would happen if:

- sales are lower than expected

- the customer does not pay up on time

- prices of materials are higher than expected.

Using spreadsheets enables companies to look at some of these possibilities. With the use of spreadsheets it is possible to adjust both the timings and amounts. This enables a business to evaluate the most likely and the worst-case situations. The business also needs to be aware that the figures are based on current assumptions about the market and the economic climate. If changes

> **Example**
> Treasured Memories produces commemorative pottery. The company was approached by a London store to supply a limited edition of 1000 plates for the Queen's 60th wedding anniversary on 20 November 2007. The plates will sell to the store for £35 each. The cost of materials is £9 per plate and labour costs are £8 each. Additional variable costs will be £3 per plate.
>
> The store wanted to have the plates available for sale from January 2007. The store would pay for the goods in March 2007. The plates would take four months to produce, so production needed to start in September 2006. Production would be evenly spread over four months. They would get one month's credit for the materials. The order seemed too good to refuse, but the finance manager was worried. He produced the cash flow forecast shown in Table 13.4.

are detected look at how these will affect the cash flow position.

The cash flow forecast shows that the order could cause serious cash flow problems. The company decided to accept the order, but needed to ensure that it had sufficient cash to finance production until March. The management did this by negotiating an overdraft facility of up to £20,000. It also negotiated to pay its material

Table 21.4 Treasured Memories cash flow forecast

Month (£s)	Sept	Oct	Nov	Dec	Jan	Feb	March
Cash in							35000
Cash out							
Wages	2000	2000	2000	2000			
Materials		2250	2250	2250	2250		
Other costs	750	750	750	750			
Total cash outflow	2750	5000	5000	5000	2250		
Opening balance	0	(2750)	(7750)	(12750)	(17750)	(20000)	(20000)
Closing balance	(2750)	(7750)	(12750)	(17750)	(20000)	(20000)	15000

suppliers after two months rather than one month. Finally, it negotiated to receive payment from the store in February 2007. This reduced the cost of the overdraft by reducing the time that the company had to use the overdraft facility.

21.5 Managing the day-to-day finances

Even when the high set-up costs have been completed, new businesses can be shocked by the amount of capital needed to run the business day by day. To operate, the business needs money to buy stock, to pay wages and the day-to-day bills such as electricity and telephone bills. If the bills cannot be paid on time there are serious consequences. In the worst situation the business may fail.

The cash cycle

Managing the day-to-day finances is a continuous process. When a business starts up it takes time to generate income. Money to pay for stock and the running costs will need to be found from the initial capital invested in the business. As the business cycle gets going, income from customers will be available to pay for expenditure. The firm needs to ensure that there is always enough cash to meet daily requirements. If the business is expanding, extra care needs to be taken (see Figure 21.2).

Each business will have its own distinct cycle. Businesses may also suffer unexpected shocks and need the cash to be able to cope with these.

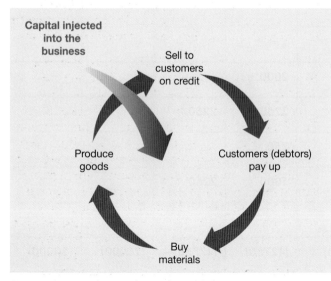

Figure 21.2 The cash cycle

Problems caused by insufficient cash flow

- *With suppliers:* a firm with too little cash will struggle to pay its bills on time. It may resort to delaying payments. Unpaid suppliers may refuse credit for a future order.

- *Banks are quick to sense a cash flow crisis* – and equally quick to reduce the bank's risk by calling in any overdrafts. As they can insist on being repaid within 24 hours, the speed of repayment can put firms in terrible difficulties.

- *Opportunities may be missed:* the business may not be able to buy supplies in bulk. This removes the advantage of lower prices. Even more importantly, it may have to refuse a large order because it cannot finance the extra cash requirement.

In the longer term, shortage of cash means insufficient funds are available for development. The business will not be able to grow as rapidly as rivals. This may make it hard for it to stay competitive.

21.6 Managing cash flow

Good management of cash flow starts with good forecasting. Cash flow forecasts will help to predict any cash shortfalls. This will enable the business to take steps to avoid any cash flow problems. It is helpful to have a generous overdraft limit, which can be drawn upon when needed. This can act as a safety net for the business. Good cash flow management also involves improving the cash position at all times. This can be done by speeding up the cash inflows into the business, and delaying or reducing cash outflows.

Improving cash flow into the business

The business can improve the flow of cash into the business in several ways, as outlined below.

- *Getting goods to the market in the shortest possible time:* the sooner goods reach the customer the sooner payment is received. Production and distribution should be as efficient as possible.

- *Getting paid as quickly as possible:* the ideal arrangement is to get paid cash on delivery. Most business, though, works on credit. Even worse, it's interest-free credit, so the customer has little incentive to pay up quickly. Early payment should be encouraged by offering incentives such as discounts for early payment.

High-grade application

Late payment woes

Surveys repeatedly show that late payment is the number one concern for small businesses. One in four small firms say this is their biggest problem. A 2007 survey showed that almost three-quarters of smaller businesses say that late payments (**bad debts**) severely affect cash flow and pose a 'considerable threat' to the viability of the firm. They are right to be worried. It is estimated that 10,000 small firms collapse each year because customers fail to pay their bills.

The government recognised the problem and tried to help by introducing legislation (the Late Payment of Commercial Debts Act 1998). This law makes it easier for firms to claim interest on late payments and to recover up to £100 of the costs of chasing the debt.

Since its introduction in 2002 some firms feel that it has helped, but problems remain with large businesses. Experian (which provides retail data) reported that, in 2006, average payment across all UK industries was 62 days, but larger companies usually take 76 days to pay. Small firms often have little or no negotiating power with large firms. Some are worried that large firms will use the new law against smaller ones, thus making it even harder for them to survive.

- *Controlling debtors*: confusingly this is known as credit control. If customers do not pay on time this will obviously mean that the cash does not come into the business when expected. Businesses can reduce the likelihood of non- or late payment by ensuring the debtor is creditworthy before granting credit (by getting a bank reference).

- *Factoring*: it may be possible to speed up payments by **factoring** money owed to the business. The company is able to receive 80% of the amount due within 24 hours of an invoice being presented. The factor then collects the money from the customer when the **credit period** is over, and pays the seller the remaining 20% less the factoring fees. These depend on the length of time before the payment is due, the credit rating of the creditor and current rates of interest. The fees are usually no more than 5% of the total value of the sale.

Reducing cash outflows from the business.

The other way of improving cash flow is to manage the outflow of cash from the business. This can be done in the ways described below.

- *Obtaining maximum possible credit for purchases*: delaying payment of bills will keep cash in the business for longer.

- *Controlling costs*: this can be done by keeping administrative and production costs to a minimum. Efficient production reduces costs. Savings may be possible by upgrading machinery to replace labour. This will benefit the firm's profit as well as its cash flow.

- *Keeping stocks of raw materials to a minimum*: good stock management, such as a just-in-time system, means that the business is not paying for stocks before it needs them for production. Controlling stock losses means that less is spent on replacements for lost or damaged stock.

Keeping cash in the business

Cash flow can also be improved by keeping cash in the business. Minimising short-term spending on new equipment keeps cash in the business. Things that the business can do include the following.

- *Lease rather than buy equipment*: this increases expenses but conserves capital.

- *Renting rather than buying buildings*: this also allows capital to remain in the business.

- *Postponing expenditure*: for example, on new company cars.

Finding additional funding to cover cash shortages

If the business is unable to keep a healthy cash flow by internal management it may need to look outside to cover cash shortages. This can be done by the following means.

- *Using an overdraft*: an overdraft is arranged with a bank. It allows the business to overdraw up to an agreed limit negotiated in advance. Overdrafts usually incur interest rates as high as 6% over base rate. However, an overdraft ensures the firm borrows money only on the days it really needs it. It is a very flexible form of borrowing. This makes it suitable for small or short-term shortages of cash. Although it should only be used to fund short-term problems, a recent study of firms in Bristol found that 70% of small firms had a permanent overdraft. A risky aspect of an overdraft is that the bank can withdraw the facility at any time and demand instant repayment. So when a firm needs it most, such as in a recession, it may not be available.

- *Taking out a short-term loan:* this incurs a lower rate of interest than an overdraft. Although less flexible than an overdraft, short-term loans offer more security and may have fixed interest charges (whereas on an overdraft they are variable).

- *Sale and leaseback of assets:* if a business has fixed assets it may be possible to negotiate a **sale and leaseback** arrangement. This will release capital and give an immediate inflow of cash. The equipment will be paid for through a leasing arrangement. This will be a regular and ongoing cost that must be budgeted for.

Figure 21.3 A Tesco Fresh & Easy shop in America

High-grade application

Tesco's sale and leaseback

In March 2007 Tesco raised £570 million from a sale and leaseback on 21 of its biggest shops. The 20-year deal will help provide the finance for Tesco's ambitious plans to open 400 more overseas stores in the coming year. These include its Fresh & Easy shops in America, plus Tesco outlets in China and Russia. Tesco said the deal would 'release funding for future growth'. Tesco has property worth more than £20 billion, so why not use it to finance its expansion?

Table 21.5 Ways to improve cash flow

Measure	Result	Drawbacks
Discounting prices	Increases sales Reduces stock Generates cash	May undermine pricing structure May leave low stocks for future activity
Reduce purchases	Cuts down expenditure	May leave business without means to continue
Negotiate more credit	Allows time to pay	May tarnish credit reputation
Delay payment of bill	Retains cash	Will tarnish credit reputation
Credit control – chase debtors	Gets payments in and sooner	May upset customers
Negotiate additional finance	Provides cash	Interest payments add to expenditure Has to be repaid
Factor debts	Generates cash A proportion of the income is guaranteed	Reduces income from sales Costs can be high
Selling assets	Releases cash	Assets are no longer available
Sale and leaseback	Releases cash Asset is still available	Increases costs – lease has to be paid Company no longer owns asset

Issues For Analysis

When answering a question on cash flow management and forecasting, it is important to understand that the figures are only the starting point for analysis and decision making. Consideration needs to be given to the following aspects.

- The validity of the figures – who constructed the forecast? Are the figures reliable and unbiased?

- What the figures show (i.e. a careful analysis of the position month by month).

- The need to take full account of the circumstances of the business. If sales are to a foreign country, payment may not be certain and, even if it arrives, changes in currency values may make cash inflows worth fewer pounds than forecast.

- The differences between cash flow and profitability.

- Especially for small firms, cash flow is the equivalent of blood circulating round the body. If the cash dries up, the firm dies. When looking at how the firm can improve its cash flow, consideration must be given to the type of firm and its market situation. There is no point suggesting that the firm should demand cash payment if it is supplying large businesses in a highly competitive market.

- Consideration could also be given to how much cash the business needs. It would be nice if there were a perfect, 'right' level of cash, but there is not. Tesco has operated successfully for decades with an apparently very tight cash position.

- When looking at solutions to cash flow problems it is important to consider what is causing the problem and how long the problem might go on for. There is a lot of difference between a problem caused by poor payment and one that is caused by poor sales.

21.7 Cash flow forecasting
an evaluation

Managing cash flow is very important for every business. Too much cash is wasteful – too little can be disastrous. Businesses need to consider their cash requirements right from the outset. Most new businesses underestimate their operating cash needs. New firms often allow only £20 of day-to-day capital for every £100 of spending on long-term assets. Accountants usually advise a ratio of £50:£50.

Improving cash flow will often uncover problems elsewhere in the business. Perhaps the reason there is poor stock control is that the person in charge is demotivated. In this respect managing cash flow is an integrated activity involving each aspect of the company. Efficient production keeps costs to a minimum and turns raw inputs into finished goods in the shortest possible time. Effective management of stock can have considerable impact on cash needs. Effective marketing ensures that the goods are sold and that demand is correctly estimated. This avoids wasted production. Cash then flows in from sales.

A business with plenty of cash flowing in and out is a healthy business.

There is no doubt that cash flow management is a vital ingredient in the success of any small business. For a new business, cash flow forecasting helps to answer key questions:

- Is the venture viable?

- How much capital is needed?

- Which are the most dangerous months?

For an existing business the cash flow forecast identifies the amount and timing of any cash flow problems in the future. It is also useful for evaluating new orders or ventures.

Nevertheless, completing a cash flow forecast does not guarantee survival. Consideration needs to be given to its usefulness and limitations. It must be remembered that cash flow forecasts are based on estimates. These estimates are not just amounts but also timings. The firm must be aware that actual figures can differ wildly from estimates – especially for a new, inexperienced firm. When preparing cash flow forecasts, managers need to ask themselves 'What if?' A huge mistake is to only look at one forecast. Far better to look at **best case** and **worst case** possibilities. Spreadsheets allow for easy manipulation of data, making it easy to see the impact of single and multiple changes to the forecast figures. This should help to reduce the risks. However, it does not guarantee results. Having completed a cash flow forecast and taken the necessary steps to ensure financing also does not guarantee success. The firm needs to be continually aware of the economic and market climate and its current cash position.

Key terms

Bad debts: Payments that are long overdue and cannot be expected to be received.

Best case: an optimistic estimate of the best possible outcome (e.g. if sales prove much higher than expected).

Credit period: the length of time allowed for payment.

Factoring: obtaining part-payment from a factoring company of the amount owed. The factoring company will then collect the debt and pass over the balance of the payment.

Overdraft: short-term borrowing from a bank; the business borrows only as much as it needs to cover its daily cash shortfall.

Sale and leaseback: a contract that, at the same time, sells the freehold to a piece of property and buys back the leasehold.

Worst case: a pessimistic estimate, assuming the worst possible outcome (e.g. sales are very disappointing).

Exercises

A. Revision questions

(64 marks; 64 minutes)

1 What is meant by 'cash flow'? (2)

2 What is a cash flow forecast? (3)

3 Explain two limitations of cash flow forecasts. (4)

4 Give two reasons why a bank manager might want to see a cash flow forecast before giving a loan to a new business. (2)

5 How might a firm benefit from delaying its cash outflows? (3)

6 What problems might a firm face if its cash flow forecast proved unreliable? (3)

7 How might a firm benefit from constructing its cash flow forecasts on a computer spreadsheet? (4)

8 Why is it especially hard for a first-time entrepreneur to produce an accurate cash flow forecast? (3)

9 Why is cash flow an especially important topic for small firms rather than large ones? (4)

10 Outline the probable cash cycle for a small sandwich shop. (4)

11 Explain why 'good management of cash flow starts with good forecasting'. (3)

12 Outline two problems that might arise if a firm is operating with very poor cash flow. (4)

13 Why might a business be unable to get a loan or overdraft if it has cash flow difficulties? (4)

14 What impact does the length of the business process have on cash flow? (4)

15 Getting money in from customers is a vital part of cash flow management. Outline two things a firm can do to ensure that cash is collected efficiently. (4)

16 How might a small producer of shelf fittings benefit from factoring? (4)

17 Outline three ways in which a business can improve its cash flow situation. (6)

18 What internal factors could affect a firm's cash flow? (3)

Cash flow table for exercise B1 (all figures in £000s)

	Jan	Feb	Mar	Apr	May	June
Cash at start						
Cash in						
Cash out						
Net cash flow						
Opening balance						
Closing balance						

B. Revision exercises

B1 Cash flow

(20 marks; 20 minutes)

A business is to be started up on 1 January next year with £40,000 of share capital. It will be opening a designer clothes shop. During January it plans to spend £45,000 on start-up costs (buying a lease, buying equipment, decorating, etc.). On 1 February it will open its doors and gain sales over the next five months of: £12,000, £16,000, £20,000, £25,000 and £24,000 respectively. Each month it must pay £10,000 in fixed overheads (salaries, heat, light, telephone, etc.) and its variable costs will amount to half the revenue.

Complete the cash flow table below to find out:

1 the company's forecast cash position at the end of June (18)

2 the maximum level of overdraft the owners will need to negotiate with the bank before starting up. (2)

B2 Data response

Merlin Construction has planning permission to convert an old office block into four flats. The directors managed to borrow £130,000 from the bank in January. They used £100,000 to buy the building that month. The work will start in January and take nine months to complete. The plan is to build and sell the two upstairs flats in June and then complete the ground-floor flats. These will be sold in September. The flats should sell for £60,000 each. Materials are estimated to cost about £10,000 a month with one month's credit. Wages and salaries will be £4000 a month. Interest charges will be £1000 a month. Other expenses will be £1000 a month.

Questions

(30 marks; 30 minutes)

1 Construct a cash flow forecast for the business for January to September. (10)

2 Outline two significant features of this cash flow forecast. (6)

3 Discuss two possible courses of action. (8)

4 Examine two ways in which the cash flow forecast might be unreliable. (6)

Cash flow forecast for D&S Jewellers (B3)

Month (£s)	September	October	November	December	January	February
Cash inflow						
From cash sales	12000	16000	20000	80000	6000	5000
From credit sales	5000	6000	10000	14000	50000	2000
Total cash in	**17000**	**22000**	a	b	c	d
Cash outflow						
Security costs	3000	3000	3000	4000	3000	3000
Buying jewellery stocks	10000	25000	55000	5000	0	2000
Rent	9000	0	0	9000	0	0
Wages	8000	8000	8000	8000	8000	8000
Other expenses	1000	1000	1000	1000	1000	1000
Total outflow	31000	37000	67000	27000	12000	14000
Monthly balance	(14000)	e	f	g	h	i
Opening balance	8000	j	k	l	m	n
Closing balance	o	p	q	r	s	t

B3 Data response

Danielle and Sujagan chose to open a jewellery shop because she loves the products and he knows how to get them: cheaply from India. They opened their first shop in May and in the period until August managed to break even. That was fine because they knew that jewellery shops make 50% of the year's takings in the run-up to Christmas. So both were confident that the first year was going well. Despite help from an uncle who has been in the jewellery business for 35 years, Sujagan has not quite finished this cash flow forecast for the next six months.

Questions

(25 marks; 25 minutes)

1 Explain two problems Sujagan may have had in drawing up this cash flow forecast for D&S Jewellers. (6)

2 Complete the job for Sujagan by working out the missing figures a–t. (10)

3 What would you recommend that Danielle and Sujagan do about this forecast? Explain the reasons behind your answer. (9)

B4 Data response

Credit crunch 'hits small firms'

Small UK firms are struggling in the face of the credit crisis to secure the loans they need to expand or even survive, a business group has warned. Those who could get loans now faced paying interest rates in excess of 10%, according to the Federation of Small Businesses (FSB). 'The issue is that the banks are being more choosy over who they lend money to until they ride out the storm,' said FSB spokesman Matthew Knowles. 'There's a bit of a "Computer Says No" mentality. Banks often see small businesses as

more of a risk – and because they aren't able to tick all the boxes which the banks set out, they struggle to borrow.'

The FSB said that some of its members were borrowing at between 10% and 11% – more than two percentage points above the rates they had previously been able to get. It added that there was a broader concern that small businesses would not be able to afford to expand. 'This is a big worry,' Mr Knowles said. 'A large majority of start-ups are not going on to employ one or two people, which is what we need to see to bring about a reduction in unemployment.'

The credit crunch has followed woes in the US sub-prime mortgage sector, which specialises in loans to people with poor credit histories or on low incomes. Rising interest rates have led to record levels of loan defaults and home repossessions – and that has sparked fears about which lenders might be exposed to the bad debts.

Questions

(30 marks; 30 minutes)

1 What is meant by the term 'credit crunch'? (2)

2 Why are banks less willing to lend to small businesses? (6)

3 What is the rate of interest that small businesses are likely to be paying? (2)

4 On a £10,000 loan with an interest rate of 12%, how much will the interest charges be for the first year of the loan? (4)

5 Why will a lack of available credit stop small businesses from expanding? (8)

6 Explain how a lack of easy credit for larger firms may affect smaller businesses. (8)

B5 Case study

Hatta Lighting

Hatta Lighting plc makes component parts for the car industry. It started out making bulbs but now also supplies a range of electrical and electronic components. The company started as a family-run business, but expansion has meant that five years ago it became a public limited company. During the last two years its performance has been mediocre and dividends paid to shareholders have been falling. The share price has also fallen. One of the largest shareholders has decided that change was necessary and has managed to exert enough pressure to replace the established chairman. The new chairman has a strong financial background but has been involved in the retailing industry for many years. He has asked the management team to produce some information. The team has come up with the following.

After examining these figures the new chairman is very concerned about the cash flow situation of the company. Several large debts totalling £500,000 are due to be paid shortly. The firm does not have sufficient cash available to pay these. He sees this as being the most urgent issue facing the company and has arranged an urgent meeting of all the managers. He has asked each of the three department heads (marketing, finance and production) to come up with ideas to solve the problem.

Questions

(35 marks; 40 minutes)

1 What might be the reasons for the increase in the stock of finished goods and materials? (6)

2 Consider what suggestions the production director might make. Explain your reasoning. (7)

3 The finance director sees slow payment as his major problem. Examine the ways in which the firm might tackle this problem. (6)

4 Outline the contribution the marketing department might make to help improve the cash flow situation. (6)

5 Apart from tackling the issue of slow payment, consider what other short-term measures the firm might take to overcome the immediate cash crisis. (10)

C. Essay questions

(40 marks each)

1 Managing cash flow is vital for the future of any business. Discuss.

2 In periods of economic downturn it is even more important for a business to control cash flow. Do you agree with this statement?

3 To what extent do you agree with the following statement? 'Managing cash flow is not just the business of the finance department, it is the responsibility of everyone in the business.'

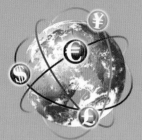

22 Unit

COSTING

DEFINITION

Revenue is the value of total sales made by a business within a period (usually one year). Costs are the expenses incurred by a firm in producing and selling its products; this is likely to include expenditure on wages and raw materials. Profit is the difference that arises when a firm's sales revenue exceeds its total costs.

22.1 Business revenue

The revenue, or income, received by a firm as a result of trading activities is a critical factor in its success. When starting up, businesses may expect relatively low revenues for several reasons:

- their product is not well known
- they are unlikely to be able to produce large quantities of output
- it is difficult to charge a high price for a product that is not established on the market.

Entrepreneurs start their financial planning by assessing the income, or revenue, they are likely to receive during the coming financial year. Businesses calculate their revenue through use of the following formula:

Sales revenue = volume of goods sold × average selling price

You can see that there are two key elements that comprise sales revenue: the quantity of goods that are sold and the prices at which they are sold. A firm seeking to increase its revenue can plan to sell more or aim to sell at a higher price. Some firms may maintain high prices even though this policy depresses sales. Such companies, often selling fashion and high-technology products, believe that this approach results in higher revenue and, ultimately, higher profits.

To sustain high revenues from relatively few sales, a business has to be confident that consumers will be willing to pay a high price for the product, and that direct competition will not appear – at least in the short term. This is possible only if the start-up business has a product or service that is really special and different – unique even. An additional advantage of a low-output strategy is that it keeps down the cost of producing the goods or services; this is important in the early stages of running an enterprise.

High-grade application
Weather hits company's revenue

The Traditional Pasty and Pie Company is a 'trailer retailer', selling its products at shows and events around the UK. The company's pies and pasties are made from fresh ingredients and then frozen. The frozen products are then cooked on the day for customers, and sold along with organic coffee.

The poor weather experienced in the summer of 2007 hit this company hard. Sales at events in the sporting and social calendar, such as Cowes Week, Goodwood and the Grand National, were down.

The co-owner of the company, Robin West, explains that for the first three days of a show you are trying to cover your costs: 'When you get to the last day, you go into profit mode. There are times when you won't manage it. It is as simple as that.' Racecourses charge retailers such as the Traditional Pasty and Pie Company a flat fee of between £1000 and £2000 for a small pitch during a prestigious meeting, while some music festivals ask five times that amount. If sales are down, these fixed costs can overwhelm revenues received.

Source: adapted from *BBC News*, 3 September 2007
(http://news.bbc.co.uk/1/hi/business/6958134.stm)

The other way to boost revenue is to charge a low price in an attempt to sell as many products as possible. In some markets this may lead to high revenues and profits. Firms following this approach are likely to be operating in markets where the goods are fairly similar and consumers do not exhibit strong preferences for any brand. This is true of the market for young holidaymakers in Ibiza or Benidorm. Price competition is fierce as businesses seek to maximise their sales and revenue (see Figure 22.1).

Some businesses adopt a revenue-orientated approach for different reasons. If the company experiences circumstances where few of its costs vary with the level of its output, then it will seek to maximise revenue. Because its costs are not sensitive to the level of its sales, maximising sales will result in maximum profits. This is the position for the operators of both theme parks and football clubs. Whereas making and selling a Mercedes creates revenue but also a lot of costs, the theme park's costs are largely **fixed costs**. Attracting extra customers on a day adds few costs. Similarly Fulham FC has the same costs whether its stadium is full or half empty. So when playing a less attractive team, prices for children are set at just £5.

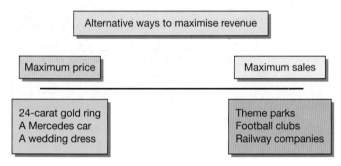

Figure 22.1 Alternative ways to maximise revenue

The new venture

Paul Merrills has achieved his lifetime ambition of opening a restaurant specialising in French cuisine in south London. Paul is a highly regarded and experienced restaurateur and wants to create a unique atmosphere in his new venture. How would you advise him to maximise his revenue in these circumstances?

You will have realised from the analysis so far that price, cost and volume are all important elements of a firm's planning and success. Each of these factors affects the others, and all of them together determine the profitability of a business.

If a business cannot control its costs then it will be unable to sell its products at a low price. In turn, this will mean a low sales volume. This will mean that overhead costs, such as the rent of a factory, will be spread over a low output, causing further pressure on costs of production.

It is to the costs of production that we now turn our attention.

22.2 The costs of production

Costs are a critical element of the information necessary to manage a business successfully. Managers need to be aware of the costs of all aspects of their business for a number of reasons.

● They need to know the cost of production to assess whether it is profitable to supply the market at the current price.

● They need to know actual costs to allow comparisons with their forecasted (or budgeted) costs of production. This will allow them to make judgements concerning the cost-efficiency of various parts of the business.

Fixed and variable costs

This is an important classification of the costs encountered by businesses. This classification has a number of uses. For example, it is the basis of calculating break-even, which is covered in a later unit.

Fixed costs

Fixed costs are any costs that do not vary directly with the level of output. These costs are linked to time rather than to level of business activity. Fixed costs exist even if a business is not producing any goods or services. An example of a fixed cost is rent, which can be calculated monthly or annually, but will not vary whether the office or factory is used intensively to produce goods or services or is hardly utilised at all.

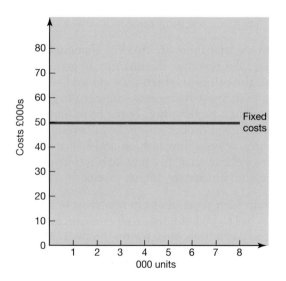

Figure 22.2 Fixed costs of £50,000

If a manufacturer can double output from within the same factory, the amount of rent will not alter – thus it is a fixed cost. In the same way, a seaside hotel has mortgage and salary costs during the winter, even though it may have very few guests. Given that fixed costs are inevitable, it is vital that managers work hard at bringing in customers, in order to keep the fixed costs covered.

In Figure 22.2, you can see that the firm faces fixed costs of £50,000 irrespective of the level of output. How much would the fixed costs per unit of production be if production were (a) 1000 units a year and (b) 8000 units a year? What might be the implications of this distinction for the managers of the business?

Other examples of fixed costs include the uniform business rate, management salaries, interest charges and depreciation.

In the long term, fixed costs can alter. The manufacturer referred to earlier may decide to increase output significantly; this may require renting additional factory space and negotiating loans for additional capital equipment. Thus rent will rise as may interest payments. We can see that, in the long term, fixed costs may alter, but that in the short term they are – as their name suggests – fixed!

Variable costs

Variable costs are those costs that vary directly with the level of output. They represent payments made for the use of inputs such as **piece-rate labour**, fuel and raw materials. If our manufacturer doubled output then these costs would double. A doubling of the sales of Innocent Strawberry Smoothies would require twice the purchasing of strawberries and bananas. There would also be extra costs for the packaging, the wage bill and the energy required to fuel the production line.

The graph in Figure 22.3 shows a firm with variable costs of £8 per unit of production. This means that variable costs rise steadily with, and proportionately to, the level of output. Thus a 10% rise in output will increase **total variable costs** by the same percentage.

However, it is not always the case that variable costs rise in proportion to output. Many small businesses discover that, as they expand, variable costs do not rise as quickly as output. A key reason for this is that, as the business becomes larger, it is able to negotiate better prices with suppliers. Its suppliers are likely to agree to sell at lower unit prices when the business places larger orders.

High-grade application
An unusual way to pay costs

Sellaband is a music website created by Johan Vosmeijer, Pim Betist and Dagmar Heijmans in August 2006 to assist bands in paying the costs of recording a professional album. It is located in Amsterdam, in the Netherlands, and was set up with the intention of helping amateur groups establish themselves.

Artists have to produce a profile of themselves, including three tracks for fans to hear. If the fans are sufficiently impressed they will buy 'parts' for $10 and become 'believers'. Any band that is able to sell 5000 parts raises $50,000 to pay for their own producer, studio and equipment to record and promote their album. In return for their investment, 'believers' are given a limited-edition copy of the album, a share of advertising revenue from the free download section of the site and revenue from the sales of the CD.

By summer 2007 over $700,000 had been invested into Sellaband and four bands had received $50,000, allowing them to pay the costs of recording an album. It remains to be seen whether this proves to be a good investment for their 'believers'.

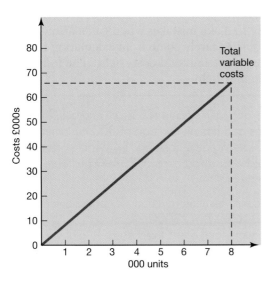

Figure 22.3 Variable costs of £8 per unit

Table 22.1 Some costs are easy to classify, some are hard

Variable costs	Fixed costs	Hard to classify
Raw materials	Rent	Delivery costs
Packaging	Heating and lighting	Electricity
Piece-rate labour	Salaries	Machine maintenance costs
Commission % on sales	Interest charges	Energy

Total costs

When added together, fixed and variable costs give the **total costs** for a business. This is, of course, a very important element in the calculation of the profits earned by a business.

The relationship between fixed, variable and total costs is straightforward to calculate but has some important implications for a business. If a business has relatively high fixed costs as a proportion of total costs, then it is likely to seek to maximise its sales to ensure that the fixed costs are spread across as many units of output as possible. In this way the impact of high fixed costs is lessened. For small businesses, it is often variable costs that are high – for example, high food costs at a restaurant. This may make them push their prices up to a level that makes customers reluctant to use them regularly. This can be the start of a slippery slope downwards for the business.

Direct and indirect costs

Costs can also be classified as direct, that is those that are directly affected by the level of production or sales. Raw materials are direct costs. These costs are often stated in terms of unit cost, as the amount used varies with every unit used. These costs are usually the same as variable costs but there are exceptions, for example, depreciation of machinery, which is both fixed and direct.

Indirect costs are generally fixed and are referred to as overheads. They are not directly related to the level of production or selling, and have to be paid regardless of output levels.

Other ways of classifying costs

Marginal cost is the cost of producing one extra unit. As fixed costs do not change in the short term, the cost of producing one extra unit is regarded as the increase in variable costs from producing the extra unit.

Average (unit) costs are total costs divided by the total output. This classification is useful for setting prices.

Opportunity cost is the cost of the next best alternative foregone (see Unit 1).

22.3 Profits

Having considered revenues and costs it is now appropriate to focus on a prime motive for businesses: profit. Profit is a comparison of revenues and costs. This comparison determines whether or not an enterprise makes any profit. As we saw at the beginning of this unit the key formula is:

Profit = total revenue − total costs

However, it is worth remembering that some businesses are not established with the objective of making profits. Not-for-profit businesses, also known as social enterprises, operate with other objectives. For example, Katie Alcott from Bristol received an entrepreneurship award in 2007 for her social enterprise Frank Water. Katie's business sells bottled spring water in the UK, and uses the proceeds to provide clean, safe water for villages in India and Africa. Her aim is to support others, not to make a profit.

Calculating profits

Although the profit formula is simple (revenue − costs), it is easy to make mistakes when calculating the figures. The problems rarely come from calculating revenue; the hard part is getting total costs right. The following example may help.

> Gwen and John's pasta restaurant charges £10 for three courses and has an average of 800 customers per week. The variable costs are £4 per customer and the restaurant has fixed costs of £3400 per week. To calculate profit:
>
> 1 calculate revenue: price × no. of customers
>   £10 × 800 = £8000
> 2 calculate total costs: fixed costs + total variable costs (no. of customers x variable costs per meal)
>   £3400 + (800 × £4 = £3200)
> 3 calculate profit: total revenue − total costs
>   £8000 − (£3,400 + £3200) = *£1400 per week*

See the Workbook section for exercises that will allow you to practise this very important skill.

The types of profit

Although profit is always revenue minus costs, there are different profit figures that are used. Managers frequently refer to operating profit. This is the amount remaining once all fixed and variable costs have been deducted from total revenue, but before tax has been paid.

Perhaps a more important measure is profit after tax, since this is the profit that the business can decide how to allocate. The most important uses to which these profits can be put are:

- payments to the owners of the business, to partners or to shareholders in the form of dividends

- reinvestment into the business to purchase capital items such as property and machinery.

High-grade application

Reducing costs gives business a chance of profits

A Scottish tourist attraction has been saved from closure due to increasing losses. The Hydroponicum in Wester Ross is famous for growing plants without any soil and for producing tropical plants such as bananas in the cool Scottish climate. The business has attracted up to 10,000 visitors a year, but had fallen on hard times. As a result it had been put up for sale and bought by a local company.

The new owners have agreed to lease the business back to three former Hydroponicum employees who hope to be able to make the business profitable again. The three new directors of the Hydroponicum have agreed to work without pay while putting a new business plan into action. The three directors plan to reduce costs by restricting opening hours, reducing staffing levels and limiting the menu offered by the Hydroponicum's café.

Source: adapted from BBC News, 8 May 2007
(http://news.bbc.co.uk/1/hi/scotland/highlands_and_islands/6635599.stm)

22.4 The importance of profit

Undeniably profits are important to the majority of businesses. Profits are usually assessed in relation to some yardstick – for example, the amount invested or sales revenue. We will consider how to measure profits in relation to other variables in Unit 25.

Profits are important for the following reasons:

- they provide a measure of the success of a business (important for a new business)

- they are the best source of capital for investment in the growth of the business (e.g. to finance new store openings or to pay for new product development)

- they act as a magnet to attract further funds from investors enticed by the possibility of high returns on their investment.

However, it is not uncommon for a new business to fail to make profits in the first months – or even years – of trading. The need to generate profits becomes more important as time passes. A business ultimately needs to make profits to reward its owners for putting money into the enterprise.

22.5 Contribution costing (marginal costing)

Contribution refers to the amount of money remaining after the **variable costs** (direct or unit costs) of making a product or service have been deducted from its price. This amount can then be said to *contribute* to fixed cost (overheads).

Therefore contribution is not the same as profit, which is where the **total cost** (fixed plus variable costs) of making a product or service is deducted from the price.

This is an important distinction in business, since it allows businesses to overcome the problem of allocating fixed costs to products and services.

The calculations for contribution and profit are:

Contribution per unit = price – direct or variable cost

Total contribution = contribution per unit ? total number of sales

Profit = total revenue – total cost

It is very important to learn these three calculations, as they are often part of any analysis of how businesses make decisions about their output, pricing and profit. The following example may help.

A business makes specialist garden chairs and tables for garden centres. The price of a chair is £100 and the variable cost of producing each chair is £20. The fixed costs are £3000 which includes rent of the workshop.

Contribution per unit = £100 − £20 = £80

Therefore if the business sold 500 chairs, the total contribution would be:

Total contribution = contribution per unit = £80 × 500 = £4000

This means that the chairs are making an overall contribution of £4000 to the fixed costs of the business.

Remember: this is not profit.

In order to calculate the profit made, it is necessary to deduct the fixed costs or overheads.

Profit = total contribution − fixed costs = £4000 − £3000 = £1000

22.6 Contribution and decision-making

Decisions such as ceasing production/sale of a product or service, or taking on special orders, are made much easier by using contribution costing techniques.

Contribution is a valuable tool for business. It allows the business to calculate the contribution made by each product/service in a whole portfolio. It can then decide whether it is worthwhile to continue with a product or not.

Sometimes it is the case that even if a product is making a loss, it adds so much to the whole product portfolio that the positive contributions made by the other products are able to cover it. Getting rid of the product simply because it isn't making a profit might result in a fall in demand for the rest of the products.

It is generally the case that a business is only interested in a product which covers its variable costs, so the profit per type of product is not calculated. Businesses are interested in whether the products are making an overall profit; they are not interested in which product is paying for the fixed costs. The decision whether to stop producing a product such as the medium suitcase in the example will be based on market conditions, whether the demand for the other products in the range will be affected and other production and marketing factors.

Special orders

Businesses are often asked to take on special orders. A number of factors have to be considered in order to make the decision. Remember, in business there is more to a decision than just the monetary benefits attached to it. Other factors include:

- capacity available
- the contribution made by the order
- the size of the order
- the price paid for the order
- future business from this order
- the response of the workforce
- the effect on existing customers.

Childsafe Ltd make and sell booster seats for children in cars. The demand has increased significantly since a change in the law in 2006. The business has one small factory unit and its overheads are £100,000. Sales in 2008 have now reached 6,000 seats. The seats are sold for £250 each. Table 22.3 shows the contribution and profit made from existing sales. It shows that existing sales already easily cover the overheads of the business.

Example

A business makes suitcases. Most ranges of suitcases have a large suitcase, a medium suitcase and a small suitcase for cabin luggage. Table 22.2 shows the calculations for contribution per suitcase, total contribution, profit per type of suitcase and total profit. The total fixed costs for the business are £1,800,000.

It is often easier to draw up a simple table of calculations if there is more than one product.

From the table, it can be seen that:

- All types of suitcase are making a positive contribution to fixed costs.
- Sales of the medium suitcase are significantly lower than the large or small suitcase.
- The fixed costs have been allocated equally between the three types of suitcase
- The medium suitcase makes no profit, whereas the other two make a substantial profit.
- The three suitcases in the set make a significant profit.

Should the business cease to make the medium suitcase?

Table 22.2 Contribution costings for a suitcase manufacturer

	£ Large	£ Medium	£ Small	£ Total
Price	300	200	100	
Variable (direct) costs	60	80	50	
Contribution per unit	240	120	50	
Sales (units)	15,000	5,000	25,000	
Total contribution	3,600,000	600,000	1,250,000	
Fixed costs (overheads)	600,000	600,000	600,000	
Profit for each type	3,000,000	0	650,000	
Total profit				**3,650,000**

Table 22.3 Childsafe Ltd contribution and profit

Sales (seats)	6,000
Price per seat	£250
Variable (direct) cost per seat	£100
Contribution per seat	£150
Total contribution (sales × contribution)	£900,000
Overheads	£100,000
Profit	£800,000

A minibus company who have been asked to supply booster seats with their buses has contacted Childsafe Ltd. The order is for 300 booster seats and the bus company is willing to pay £120 per seat. Table 22.4 shows the total contribution to be gained from the order.

Table 22.4 Contribution from the special order

Sales for special order	300
Price of seats to bus company	£120
Variable (direct) costs	£100
Contribution per seat	£20
Total contribution	£6,000

Since existing sales cover the overheads of the business, it is likely that the business will accept the order based on these calculations alone – they will gain an extra £6,000 contribution from the order. However, other factors, such as future demand from existing customers, effect on the workforce, available capacity and long-term increases in overheads, will also contribute towards the final decision.

Issues For Analysis

- Forecasting costs and revenues can be tricky for an entrepreneur starting a new business. It is not possible to look back at trading records for guidance and therefore the likelihood of inaccuracy is greater. At this stage of a business's history all cost and revenue figures are forecasts and therefore not necessarily correct. It is possible that entrepreneurs will underestimate fixed and variable costs and overestimate revenues, thereby suggesting higher profits (or lower losses) than proves to be the case.

- A key element with respect to the revenues earned by a business is the relationship between the price charged and the volume of sales achieved. Choosing the right price is an exercise requiring considerable judgement on the part of the entrepreneur. Simply raising price will not necessarily provide more revenue for a business. If a 10% price rise causes customer numbers to fall by 15%, the business will have lower revenues than it started with. Factors influencing consumers' decisions will include the quality of the products in question and how strong the competition is.

- You might like to consider circumstances in which firms might earn higher revenue by raising prices, and when the opposite could be true. Do you think a firm could earn more revenue by *lowering* its price?

22.7 Costing

an evaluation

One important issue for evaluation in relation to costs, revenues and profits for a new enterprise is to judge the likely accuracy of the forecast figures and the degree of reliance that can be placed upon them. This is an important judgement for a number of stakeholders who may have an interest in the new business. Investors will obviously look closely at any forecast figures before committing money to the enterprise and suppliers will want to be assured of payment before agreeing to supply any raw materials.

It is also worth thinking about whether profits are the best measure of success for a new business. A successful first year of trading may see an enterprise gain a customer base and repeat orders by supplying at competitive costs. This may result in small profits initially, while the business builds a reputation. Profits may become a more important measure of success in the longer term.

An assessment of the true worth of a business's performance as measured by its profits would also take account of the general state of the economy: are businesses in general prospering or is it a time of recession? They would also take into account any unusual circumstances such as, for example, the business being subject to the emergence of a new competitor.

Key terms

Contribution: a method of costing which ignores fixed costs and only takes account of variable costs. Defined as sales revenue minus variable costs. Allows businesses to make decisions about pricing, product life and special orders.
Fixed costs: do not vary as output (or sales) vary.
Piece-rate labour: paying workers per item they make (i.e. with no regular pay).
Profit: total revenue minus total cost. Takes account of all fixed (overhead) costs.
Total costs: all the costs of producing a specific output level (i.e. fixed costs + total variable costs).
Total variable costs: all the variable costs of producing a specific output level (i.e. variable costs per unit x the number of units sold).
Variable costs: the costs that vary as output varies (can also be known as unit variable costs).

Exercises

A. Revision questions

(50 marks; 50 minutes)

1 Why might a business initially receive relatively low revenues from a product newly introduced to the market? (3)

2 State two circumstances in which a company may be able to charge high prices for a new product. (2)

3 For what reasons might a firm seek to maximise its sales revenue? (4)

4 If a business sells 4000 units of Brand X at £4 each and 2000 units of Brand Y at £3 each, what is its total revenue? (4)

5 State two reasons why firms have to know the costs they incur in production. (2)

6 Distinguish, with the aid of examples, between fixed and variable costs. (4)

7 Explain why fixed costs can alter only in the long term. (3)

8 How is the contribution of a product calculated? (2)

9 How is the profit of a product calculated? (2)

10 Give two reasons why profits are important to businesses. (2)

11 Outline one advantage and one disadvantage that may result from a business deciding to lower the proportion of profits it distributes to its owners. (4)

12 State two purposes for which a business's profits might be used. (2)

13 Explain **two** reasons why a business might calculate contribution rather than profit in order to make a decision. (6)

14 To what extent is the calculation of contribution useful when deciding whether to take on a special order? (10)

B. Revision exercises

B1 Calculation practice questions

(30 marks; 30 minutes)

1 During the summer weeks, Devon Ice Cream has average sales of 4000 units a week. Each ice cream sells for £1 and has variable costs of 25p. Fixed costs are £800.

(a) Calculate the total costs for the business in the summer weeks. (3)

(b) Calculate Devon Ice Cream's weekly profit in the summer. (3)

2a If a firm sells 200 widgets at £3.20 and 40 squidgets at £4, what is its total revenue? (3)

2b Each widget costs £1.20 to make, while each squidget costs £1.50. What are the total variable costs? (3)

2c If fixed costs are £300, what profit is the business making? (3)

3 'Last week our sales revenue was £12,000, which was great. Our price is £2 a unit, which I think is a bit too cheap.'

(a) How many unit sales were made last week? (2)

(b) If a price rise to £2.25 cuts sales to 5600 units, calculate the change in the firm's revenue. (4)

4 BYQ Co has sales of 4000 units a month, a price of £4, fixed costs of £9000 and variable costs of £1. Calculate its profit. (4)

5 At full capacity output of 24,000 units, a firm's costs are as follows:

managers' salaries	£48,000
materials	£12,000
rent and rates	£24,000
piece-rate labour	£36,000

(a) What are the firm's total costs at 20,000 units? (4)

(b) What profit will be made at 20,000 units if the selling price is £6? (1)

B2 Case study

Cleaning up

Mary Ruffett saw the building of a large new housing estate across the road from her home as an opportunity, not an eyesore. The estate contained 500 new homes and was nearing completion with only a few houses left to sell. Most were large detached houses and Mary had noticed that there were no window cleaners offering their services on the estate. Although she had no experience as an entrepreneur or a window cleaner, Mary was interested.

Mary did some sums and researched local window cleaners in the *Yellow Pages* – there was only one listed. She could take out a loan to purchase a van, a ladder and the other equipment needed. She estimated that this would cost her £350 each month to repay. Her variable costs per house cleaned would be minimal – she estimated 50p per house. The tricky bit was the price to charge – eventually she estimated £4 per household. Limited research among the new occupants of the estate suggested that she might be able to clean the windows of 125 houses each month. At a price of £5 per household she forecast that she would have 100 customers monthly.

Questions

(25 marks; 30 minutes)

1 Which of Mary's two prices would provide her with the higher monthly revenue? (3)

2 Calculate Mary's monthly profits (or losses) in each case. (6)

3 Analyse two possible reasons why Mary's financial forecasts might not prove to be accurate. (7)

4 Analyse the case for and against Mary charging £5 per household for her window-cleaning service. (9)

B3 Case study

Chalfont Computer Services Ltd

Robert has decided to give up his job with BT and to work for himself offering computer services to local people. He has paid off his mortgage and owns his house outright, so feels this is the time to take a risk. Robert has no experience of running a business, but is skilled in repairing computers and solving software problems. In the past Robert has repaired computers belonging to friends and family, and is aware of the costs involved in providing this service. He believes that with the increase in internet usage there will be plenty of demand for his services. Robert has spoken to a few people in his local pub and this has confirmed his opinion. Robert needs to raise £10,000 to purchase equipment for his business and to pay for a new vehicle, and intends to ask his bank for a loan.

The work Robert has already done allows him to forecast that the average revenue from each customer will be £40, while the variable costs will be £15. His monthly fixed costs will be £1000. Robert estimates that he will have the following number of customers:

Month	Number of customers
January	40
February	50
March	60
April	82

Questions

(25 marks; 30 minutes)

1 What is meant by the term 'variable costs'? (2)

2 Calculate Robert's forecast profits for his first three months' trading. (5)

3 Robert estimates that if he cut his prices by 10% he would have 20% more customers each month. Calculate the outcome of these changes and whether this would benefit Robert. (8)

4 Examine the case for and against a bank lending Robert £10,000 on the basis of his forecast profits. (10)

C. Essay questions

(40 marks each)

1 Discuss whether a new ethnic restaurant, trading in a very competitive market, should aim to maximise its revenue, rather than its profits, during its first year of trading.

2 For all new enterprises it is vital to sell at the right price – this is the most important determinant of profits. Discuss whether this view is always correct.

3 The newly opened Bolton Bakery is the first upmarket baker in the town. The owners expect to make a £50,000 profit in their first year. Evaluate the factors that might stop them from achieving this.

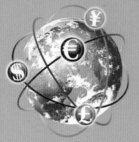

BREAK-EVEN ANALYSIS

23.1 Introduction

The starting point for financial management is to know how much goods or services cost to produce. This was covered in detail in Unit 22. Businesses also benefit from knowing how many products they have to produce and sell in order to cover all their costs. This is particularly important for new businesses with limited experience of their markets. It is also of value for established businesses that plan to produce a new product.

Look at Table 23.1, which shows the forecast revenue and cost figures for Burns & Morris Ltd – a business that is planning to start manufacturing silk ties.

You can easily identify that 400 is the number of sales Burns & Morris Ltd must achieve each week to break

even. Note what happens to its profits if sales are different from 400 units:

- below 400 units the company makes a loss because costs are higher than revenue

- above 400 units the company makes a profit.

To calculate the break-even point we need information on both costs and prices. A change in costs or in the firm's pricing will change the level of output at which the firm breaks even.

Break-even can be calculated and shown on a graph. The calculation of break-even is simpler and quicker than drawing break-even charts.

Table 23.1 Forecast revenue and cost figures for Burns & Morris Ltd

Output of ties (per week)	Sales income (£ per week)	Total costs (£ per week)
0	0	10000
100	4000	11500
200	8000	13000
300	12000	14500
400	16000	16000
500	20000	17500
600	24000	19000

23.2 Calculating break-even

Calculating the break-even point for a product requires:

- the selling price of the product
- its **fixed costs**
- its variable costs per unit.

Fixed costs are expenses that do not change in response to changing demand or output. Fixed costs have to be paid whether or not the business is trading; examples include rent, business rates and interest charges. On the other hand, variable costs will alter as demand and output adjust. An increase in output will require greater supplies of fuel and labour, for example, and the costs of these items will rise. A doubling of demand will double variable costs.

The break-even output level can be calculated by the formula:

$$\text{Break-even output} = \frac{\text{Fixed costs}}{(\text{selling price per unit} - \text{variable cost per unit})}$$

The following example shows how to use this formula to calculate break-even as part of the planning for a new enterprise.

> **Example: Sue's Guided Tours**
> Sue Pittman is planning to offer an open-top bus tour in London during the summer months to take tourists on sightseeing tours of the capital. The bus will conduct four trips each day and Sue estimates that the cost of each trip will be £400 in fuel, food and wage costs for the driver and courier. The trip will include a snack and soft drinks for all the passengers, as well as a London guidebook. She estimates that these items will cost £10 for each passenger on the bus. The maximum number of passengers Sue is allowed to take on each trip is 40. Sue intends to price the day trips at £30 per passenger.

The first thing we should note is that the fixed cost of each tour is forecast to be £400. Sue will have to pay for the fuel for the bus and the wages of her employees as well as depreciation on the vehicle, irrespective of how many passengers she has. So it is easy to fill in the top of the formula we set out above. Fixed costs per tour are £400.

Calculating the bottom half of the formula is only a little more difficult. We know that she will charge each passenger £30 per tour and that the variable costs associated with each passenger will be £10. This is to pay for the snacks and drinks and the guidebook given to each passenger. The amount left (the **contribution**) will be £20 for each customer. So the formula will look like this:

$$\text{Sue's break-even output} = \frac{\text{Fixed costs}}{(\text{selling price per unit} - \text{variable cost per unit})}$$

$$= \frac{£400}{(£30 - £10)}$$

$$= \frac{£400}{£20}$$

$$= 20 \text{ passengers}$$

In other words, Sue will need 20 passengers on each of her tours if she is to break even.

As we have seen, break-even level of output can be calculated using the simple equation above. A greater understanding of the sensitivity of the relationships between costs, sales revenue and production can be achieved through the use of break-even charts.

23.3 Break-even charts

A break-even chart is a graph showing a business's revenues and costs at all possible levels of demand or output. The break-even chart is constructed on a graph by first drawing the horizontal axis to represent the output of goods or services for the business in question. The vertical axis should represent costs and sales values in pounds. The horizontal axis shows output per time period – usually output per month or year.

> **Example: Berry & Hall Ltd**
> Berry & Hall Ltd are manufacturers of confectionery. The company is planning to launch a new line called Aromatics – a distinctive sweet with a very strong fragrance. The company intends to sell these sweets for £1 a kilogram. The variable (or marginal) cost of production per kilogram is forecast at 60 pence and the fixed costs associated with this product are estimated to be £50,000 a year. The company's maximum output of Aromatics will be 250,000 kg per year.

First, put scales on the axes. The output scale has a range from zero to the company's maximum output – this will be 250,000 kg. The vertical axis records values of costs and revenues. Since revenue is usually the higher figure we simply multiply the maximum output by the selling price and then place values on the axis up to this figure. In this case it will have a maximum value on the axis of £250,000 (£1 × 250,000).

Having drawn the axes and placed scales upon them, the first line we enter is fixed costs. Since this value does not change with output it is simply a horizontal line drawn at £50,000.

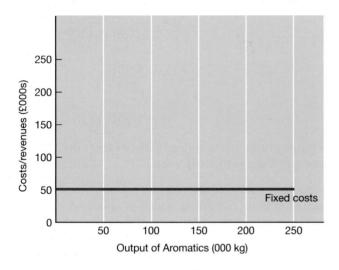

Figure 23.1 Fixed costs for Aromatics

These costs cover rent and rates for the factory that will be used to produce Aromatics and also interest paid on loans taken out by Berry & Hall Ltd to establish production of the new sweet.

Next, add on variable costs to arrive at total costs. The difference between total costs and fixed costs is variable costs. Total costs start from the left hand of the fixed costs line and rise diagonally. To see where they rise to, calculate the total cost at the maximum output level. In the case of Aromatics this is 250,000 kg per year. The

total cost is fixed costs (£50,000) plus variable costs of producing 250,000 kg (£0.60 × 250,000 = £150,000). The total cost at this level of output is £50,000 + £150,000 = £200,000.

This point can now be marked on the chart (i.e. £200,000) at an output level of 250,000 kg. This can be joined by a straight line to total costs at zero output: £50,000. This is illustrated in Figure 23.2.

Finally, sales revenue must be added. For the maximum level of output calculate the sales revenue and mark this on the chart. In the case of Aromatics the maximum output per year is 250,000 kg; multiplied by the selling price this gives £250,000 each year. If Berry & Hall do not produce and sell any Aromatics it will not have any sales revenue. Thus zero output results in zero income. A straight diagonal line from zero to £250,000 represents the sales revenue for Aromatics (see Figure 23.3).

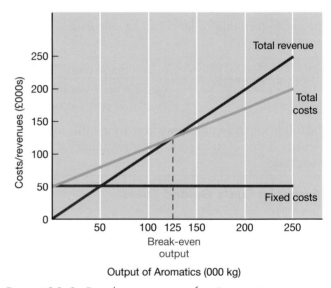

Figure 23.3 Break-even output for Aromatics

This brings together costs and revenues for Aromatics. A line drawn down from the point where total costs and sales revenue cross shows the break-even output. For Aromatics, it is 125,000 kg per year. This can be checked using the formula method explained earlier.

23.4 Using break-even charts

Various pieces of information can be taken from break-even charts, such as that shown in Figure 23.3. As well as the level of break-even output, it also shows the level of profits or losses at every possible level of output. Many conclusions can be reached, such as those noted below.

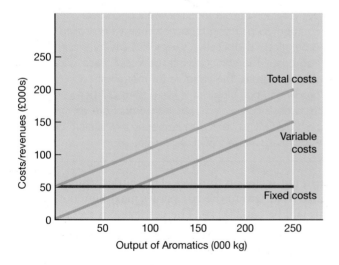

Figure 23.2 Fixed, variable and total costs for Aromatics

- Any level of output lower than 125,000 kg per year will mean the product is making a loss. The amount of the loss is indicated by the vertical distance between the total cost and the total revenue line. For example, at an output level of 90,000 units per year Aromatics would make a loss of £14,000 for Berry & Hall Ltd. This is because sales are worth £90,000 but costs are £104,000 (£54,000 + £50,000).

- Sales in excess of 125,000 kg of Aromatics per year will earn the company a profit. If the company produces and sells 150,000 kg of Aromatics annually it will earn a profit of £20,000. At this level of output total revenue is £150,000 and total costs are £130,000. This is shown on the chart by the vertical distance between the total revenue line (which is now the higher) and the total cost line.

- The **margin of safety**: one feature of a break-even chart is that it can show the margin of safety. This is the amount by which demand can fall before the firm starts making a loss. It is the difference between current sales and the break-even point. If annual sales of Aromatics were 175,000 kg, with a break-even output of 125,000 kg, then the margin of safety would be 50,000 kg:

Margin of safety = 175,000 − 125,000 = 50,000 kg

That is, output could fall by 50,000 units before Berry & Hall incurred a loss from its new product. The higher the margin of safety the less likely it is that a loss-making situation will develop. The margin of safety is illustrated in Figure 23.4.

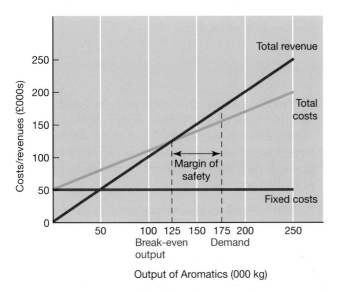

Figure 23.4 Margin of safety

23.5 Break-even analysis in a changing environment

The application of break-even analysis to the planned production of Aromatics shows how the technique operates. But it assumed a very stable (and therefore unrealistic) business environment. Competitors might have reacted to the introduction of Aromatics by producing similar products if it was a genuinely new idea or was generating high profits. This competition may have forced Berry & Hall to reduce the price of Aromatics even before they are entered onto the market. Alternatively, competitors' actions may have generated the need for more advertising, raising Berry & Hall's costs. In either case the break-even point and the break-even chart would change.

Suppose that Berry & Hall did have to carry out additional advertising for the launch of Aromatics and that this advertising cost £15,000 over the first year. What impact would this have upon the break-even point and the break-even chart? The extra costs would require a higher output (and income) to break even. The rise in marketing costs can be regarded as a fixed cost because this cost must be borne whatever the level of output. This is shown in Figure 23.5.

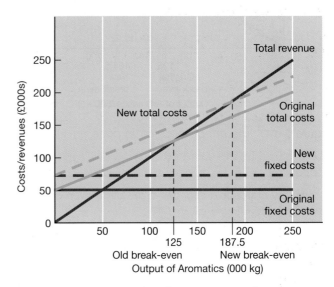

Figure 23.5 A rise in fixed costs

The break-even chart shows the increased fixed cost and total cost lines, which create a higher break-even output. This also has the effect of reducing the level of profit (or increasing the loss) made at any level of output. Any factor leading to a fall in fixed costs will have the opposite effects.

Other external factors can impact upon the break-even level of output and associated profits. If the cost of materials decline, then the variable cost and total cost will be lower. The total cost line will rise less steeply, leading to a lower break-even point of higher profits (lower losses) at any given level of output. The curve pivots (rather than making a parallel move) because at lower levels of output the saving from lower variable costs is proportionately reduced.

If costs remain unchanged and prices fall then this will result in a higher break-even level of production. Lower prices mean that more has to be produced and sold before a profit-making position can be reached. Conversely, a rise in price will result in a lower level of production necessary for break-even to be attained. Figure 23.6 illustrates the impact of a fall in the market price of a product.

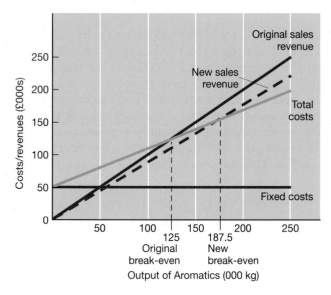

Figure 23.6 *The effects of a fall in price*

Summary of possible changes to the break-even chart that can occur in the exam

1 Prices can go up or down. If a price is increased, the revenue line starts in the same place but rises more steeply.
2 Fixed costs can rise or fall, so you might have to draw a new horizontal line. But remember that a change to fixed costs will also affect the total cost line.
3 Variable costs can rise or fall. An increase will make the variable cost line rise more steeply, though it will still start at the same point – at the fixed cost line. A change in variable costs will change the total costs line as well.

Note that each of these three changes will alter the break-even point.

Figure 23.6 shows the effects of a fall in prices. When using break-even analysis a business may draw several charts using different prices to assess the impact of various prices for a new product. This approach is particularly useful in markets where prices may be volatile.

23.6 The value of break-even analysis

Strengths

Break-even analysis is simple to understand, and useful – particularly for small and newly established businesses, where the managers may not be able to employ more sophisticated techniques. Businesses can use break-even to:

- estimate the future level of output they will need to produce and sell in order to meet given objectives in terms of profits

- assess the impact of planned price changes upon profit, and the level of output needed to break even

- assess how changes in fixed and/or **variable costs** may affect profits, and the level of output necessary to break even

- take decisions on whether to produce their own products or components, or whether to purchase from external sources

- support applications for loans from banks and other financial institutions – the use of the technique may indicate good business sense as well as provide a forecast of profitability.

Weaknesses

- The model assumes that costs increase constantly and that firms do not benefit from bulk buying. If, for example, a firm negotiates lower prices for purchasing larger quantities of raw materials then its total cost line will no longer be straight. It will in fact level out at higher outputs.

- Similarly, break-even analysis assumes the firm sells all its output at a single price. In reality firms frequently offer discounts for bulk purchases.

- A major flaw in the technique is that it assumes that all output is sold. This may well not be true and, if so, would result in an inaccurate break-even estimate. In times of low demand, a firm may have difficulty in selling all that it produces.

- Break-even analysis is only as good as the data on which it is based: poor-quality data can result in inaccurate conclusions being drawn.

High-grade application

Recently launched carbon-neutral food market closes

A £1.5 million carbon-neutral food market in Devon has gone into administration just three months after it started trading. Foodeaze was a good market with associated restaurants, operating with the objective of sustainability. The business, based in Exeter, sold locally produced products and ran its delivery vehicles on bio-diesel. The closure of the market has resulted in the loss of 60 jobs.

Foodeaze owner Nick Hess said it could not compete with the new £220 million Princesshay retail development in Exeter. Mr Hess said the development had a huge impact on Foodeaze's sales and its financial position. He said that, within five weeks of opening, they were close to their break-even point, but then the opening of the new retail development had a bigger impact than originally forecast.

'We put a percentage into our business plan for the effect we thought it was going to have but unfortunately it was far greater than we actually forecast,' he said. 'The new development is stunning and I'm not criticising it – it's just unfortunately one of those things of bad timing.'

Source: adapted from BBC News (http://news.bbc.co.uk/1/hi/england/devon/6660947.stm)

High-grade application

Newquay airport targets break-even point

Managers at Newquay airport in Cornwall have announced plans to expand its passenger capacity ahead of schedule. The airport enlarged its existing terminal in 2005, which allowed it to handle 400,000 passengers each year, well short of its break-even level of 750,000 passengers annually. However, managers recognised that further expansion was essential to make the airport profitable and had drawn up a long-term plan to increase passenger numbers and make the airport profitable.

Rising demand for air travel to Cornwall brought about by competitive prices and the rising popularity of the region as a tourist destination has forced the airport's managers to bring their expansion plans forward, however. Several airlines, including bmibaby, have increased flights to Newquay in response to increasing demand from surfers and other tourists. Cornwall County Council has approved plans to build a new terminal south of the runway, which should allow the airport to exceed its break-even figure of 750,000 passengers each year.

Table 23.2 How changes in business circumstances affect the break-even chart

	Cause	Effect
Internal factors	Extra launch advertising	Fixed costs rise, so total costs rise and break-even point rises
	Planned price increase	Revenue rises more steeply; break-even point falls
	Using more machinery (and less labour) in production	Fixed costs rise while variable costs fall; uncertain effect on break-even point
External factors	Fall in demand	Break-even point is not affected, though margin of safety is reduced
	Competitors' actions force price cut	Revenue rises less steeply; break-even point rises
	Fuel costs rise	Variable and total cost lines rise more steeply; break-even point rises

Issues For Analysis

- Analytical issues in relation to break-even centre upon the effective use of break-even charts. It is important to appreciate how changes in the business environment might affect the break-even position of a business. Any analysis of break-even should recognise that changes in revenues or costs will impact upon the level of break-even output.

- As an example, you should be able to state whether, in the following circumstances, break-even output will rise or fall:
  - wage negotiations result in a 4% pay rise
  - the business rate levied upon a firm's premises is increased
  - the market price for the business's product increases
  - a change in the price of oil means that fuel prices fall by 5%.

- A break-even chart shows the level of profit or loss at any level of output. If the business's circumstances change it is important to be able to quantify the extent to which profitability changes at any level of output.

23.7 Break-even analysis

an evaluation

There is a risk in exams of assuming that break-even charts tell you 'facts'. Break-even analysis seems simple to conduct and understand. It appears to be cheap and quick to carry out. That assumes, of course, that the business knows all its costs and can break them down into variable and fixed. Tesco certainly can, but not every business is as well managed. Football clubs such as Leeds United, Brentford and Darlington have hit financial problems partly because of ignorance of their financial circumstances. Similarly, few NHS hospitals could say with confidence how much it costs to provide a heart transplant.

Break-even analysis is of particular value when a business is first established. Having to work out the fixed and variable costs will help the managers make better decisions – for example, on pricing. It also shows profit and loss at various levels of output, particularly when presented in the form of a chart. Indeed it may be that financial institutions will require this sort of financial information before lending any money to someone aspiring to run a business.

As long as the figures are accurate, break-even becomes especially useful when changes occur, such as rising raw material costs. The technique can allow for changing revenues and costs, and gives a valuable guide to potential profitability.

Key terms

Break-even chart: a line graph showing total revenues and total costs at all possible levels of output or demand from zero to maximum capacity.
Contribution: total revenue less variable costs. The calculation of contribution is useful for businesses which are responsible for a range of products.
Fixed costs: fixed costs are any costs which do not vary directly with the level of output, for example, rent & rates.
Margin of safety: the amount by which current output exceeds the level of output necessary to break-even.
Variable costs: variable costs are those costs which vary directly with the level of output. They represent payments made for the use of inputs such as raw materials, packaging and piece-rate labour.

Key formulae

Break-even output: $$\frac{\text{fixed costs}}{\text{contribution per unit}}$$

Contribution per unit: selling price – variable costs per unit
Margin of safety: sales volume – break-even output
Total contribution: contribution per unit × unit sales

Exercises

A. Revision questions

(25 marks; 25 minutes)

1 What is meant by the term 'break-even point'? (2)

2 State three reasons why a business might conduct a break-even analysis. (3)

3 List the information necessary to construct a break-even chart. (4)

4 How would you calculate the contribution made by each unit of production that is sold? (2)

5 A business sells its products for £10 each and the variable cost of producing a single unit is £6. If its monthly fixed costs are £18,000 how many units must it sell to break even each month? (3)

6 Explain why the variable cost and total revenue lines start at the origin of a break-even chart. (3)

7 What point on a break-even chart actually illustrates break-even output? (2)

8 Explain how, using a break-even chart, you would illustrate the amount of profit or loss made at any given level of output. (2)

9 Why might a business wish to calculate its margin of safety? (2)

10 A business is currently producing 200,000 units of output annually, and its break-even output is 120,000 units. What is its margin of safety? (2)

B. Revision exercises

B1 Data response

Paul Jarvis is an entrepreneur and about to open his first hotel. He has forecast the following costs and revenues:
- maximum number of customers per month 800
- monthly fixed costs £10,000
- average revenue per customer £110
- typical variable costs per customer £90

Some secondary market research has suggested that Paul's prices may be too low. He is considering charging higher prices, though he is nervous about the impact this might have on his forecast sales. Paul has found his break-even chart useful during the planning of his new business, but is concerned that it might be misleading too.

Questions

(45 marks; 60 minutes)

1a Construct the break-even chart for Paul's planned business. (9)

1b State, and show on the graph, the profit or loss made at a monthly sales level of 600 customers. (4)

1c State, and show on the graph, the margin of safety at that level of output. (4)

2 Paul's market research shows that, in his first month of trading, he can expect 450 customers at his hotel.

(a) If Paul's research is correct, calculate the level of profit or loss he will make. (5)

(b) Illustrate this level of output on your graph and show the profit or loss. (3)

3 Paul has decided to increase his prices to give an average revenue per customer of £120.

(a) Draw the new total revenue line on your break-even chart to show the effect of this change. (3)

(b) Mark on your diagram the new break-even point. (1)

(c) Calculate Paul's new break-even number of customers to confirm the result shown on your chart. (6)

4 Paul is worried that his break-even chart may be 'misleading'. Do you agree with him? Justify your view. (10)

B2 Data response

The Successful T-Shirt Company

Shelley has recently launched the Successful T-Shirt Company. It sells a small range of fashion T-shirts. The shirts are available in a range of colours and all bear the company's logo, which is becoming increasingly desirable for young, fashion-conscious people.

The shirts are sold to retailers for £35 each. They cost £16.50 to manufacture and the salesperson receives £2.50 commission for each item sold to retailers. The distribution cost for each shirt is £1.00 and current sales are 1000 per month. The fixed costs of production are £11,250 per month.

The company is considering expanding its range of T-shirts and has approached its bank for a loan. The bank has requested the company draw up a business plan, including a cash-flow forecast and break-even chart.

Questions

(30 marks; 40 minutes)

1 What is a break-even chart? (4)

2 Calculate the following:
  (a) the variable cost of producing 1000 T-shirts
  (b) the contribution earned through the sale of one T-shirt. (6)

3 Shelley has decided to manufacture the shirts in Poland. As a result, the variable cost per T-shirt (including commission and distribution costs) will fall to £15 per T-shirt. However, fixed costs will rise to £12,000.

  (a) Calculate the new level of break-even for Shelly's T shirts.
  (b) Calculate the margin of safety if sales are 1000 T shirts per month. (10)

4 Should Shelley rely on break-even analysis when taking business decisions? Justify your view. (10)

C. Essay questions

(40 marks each)

1 'Break-even is the most vital part of a business plan for a new enterprise.' Do you agree with this statement? Justify your view.

2 'Break-even analysis is of limited value to a start-up business because it ignores the market.' To what extent do you agree with this statement?

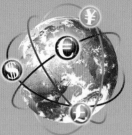

INVESTMENT DECISIONS

24.1 Investment decisions

At some stage, every business must make decisions to invest large amounts of money back into the business. These investments can range from up-to-date machinery to new premises.

All investment is made with the intention of making gains in the future. However, most investments will be a risk to the business. Whether the overall cost can be measured in hundreds or millions of pounds, the level of risk will be relative to the size of the business. A bad investment decision might result in disaster for many of the stakeholders in the business.

The size of an investment made by a business will depend upon several factors:

● The size of the organisation: for example, an investment which is large for a sole trader will not be on the same scale as one made by a multi-national.

● The amount of money available to the business.

● The economic life of the investment: this is difficult to measure because it is often dependent on external considerations such as the global economy.

● The objectives of the business and the effect of the investment on different stakeholder groups: for example, a large investment in new methods of production may reduce the amount of profit available for distribution to shareholders, wages to employees and payments to lenders.

● External constraints such as the rate of interest, environmental considerations and market changes.

24.2 Investment appraisal

As with many decisions made in business, there are quantitative methods available to reduce the level of risk.

These are known as methods of 'investment appraisal'. Before using these methods businesses must answer the following questions.

● What is the cost of the investment?

● How long will it take before the investment makes money?

● How long will it take for the business to pay back the money?

● How much money will be generated from the investment?

● Are there alternative investments that could yield more money?

Payback period

One method of appraisal is the **payback period**. This is the amount of time it takes for a project to pay back the initial cost. This can be compared with other projects to help make a final decision. The calculation is based on the firm's ability to predict the expected **cash inflows** that will be gained from each project, *not* the profits.

For example:

Cost of Project A   £20m

Cost of Project B   £24m

The projected cash flows back into the business are as follows:

Net cash inflow

	Project A	Project B
Year 1 –	£5m	£8m
Year 2 –	£5m	£8m
Year 3 –	£5m	£8m
Year 4 –	£5m	£3m
Year 5 –	£5m	£2m

In this case, Project A will pay back the initial investment of £20 million in four years and Project B will pay back in three years. At first glance it would seem that Project B would be the best option. However, payback takes no account of the costs involved and the cash flows that arise after payback; it does not answer the question about whether the business can initially afford an outlay of £24 million and takes no account of the future cash inflows or any other external factors, such as effect on the workforce and other stakeholders. It is, however, a useful first indicator and it may simply be better to choose the project with the shortest payback time in order to cover the cost as quickly as possible and to avoid unforeseen circumstances in the future.

Accounting rate of return

An alternative method that can be used is the **accounting rate of return** (ARR). This method attempts to calculate the average return from a project expressed as a percentage of the cost of the project. Therefore, unlike payback, it takes account of the profitability of the project.

Using the figures in the previous example:

Expected life of Project A and Project B is 5 years

Step 1 Add all cash inflows for each project.
Project A = £25m
Project B = £29m

Step 2 Deduct the initial capital cost. Therefore:
Project A = £5m (25 – 20)
Project B = £5m (29 – 24)

Step 3 Divide the net figure by the expected life of the project. Therefore:

Project A = £1m (5/5)
Project B = £1m (5/5)

Comparison of Investment Appraisal Methods

Method	Advantages	Disadvantages
Payback	Quick and easy to calculate	Takes no account of the overall profitability of a project.
	Can concentrate on short term targets due to emphasis on speed of cash flows	Ignores cash flows after the payback period
	Useful where liquidity is more important than profitability	Encourages short termism which may lead to projects being rejected if they take a longer time to payback
	Easy for managers to understand	Does not consider the timing of cash flows during the payback period
ARR	Uses all the cash flows over the lifetime of the project	Ignores timing of cash flows
	Takes account of profitability, the main objective of most businesses	Based on estimated cash flows which may not be accurate in later years
	Easily understood and can be assessed against the profit objectives of the business	No account is taken of the time value of money
	Can compare several different projects that are competing for limited investment funds	

Step 4 Express the average return as a percentage of the capital cost:

(A) $\dfrac{1m \times 100}{20m} = 5\%$ (B) $\dfrac{1m \times 100}{24m} = \mathbf{4.16\%}$

When there are several projects to be considered the one with the highest rate of return will usually be chosen. Using ARR, Project A would now be chosen as it has the highest ARR. However, as with the payback period, there are many factors to take into account, not least that ARR takes no account of the time value of money. It does, however, take account of the profitability of the projects and of all the cash inflows in the whole life of the project.

Investment appraisal techniques are useful tools, but they rely on predictions and are effective only if their limitations are recognised and they are used as one part of the decision-making process.

24.3 Dealing with risk

Starting a business carries huge risks, financial and emotional. The fear of failure is very off-putting; it can not only be embarrassing but also stressful. Academics at the US university Massachusetts Institute of Technology suggest that there are 14 key characteristics of successful entrepreneurs (see figure 24.1). Several relate to risk, such as 'low fear of failure' and 'tolerance of ambiguity (uncertainty)'. Quite simply, individuals who fear the unknown will not start their own business.

Real entrepreneurs, though, have to deal with risk on a day-to-day basis. Every business decision is about the future, so each carries a risk that it will be wrong, or that circumstances will change and make it wrong.

Examples of business risk include:

● Stoner Builders wins its £26,000 quote for turning a derelict garage into an office; after four weeks' work John Stoner realises that the problems of damp in the building are far more serious than expected; he ends up spending £31,000 in costs for £26,000 of revenue

● hiring a bright, lively young person with a track record of job-hopping, instead of an older, duller but safer person

● July 2007 was the wettest on record, with floods along the Severn and Thames rivers; on 21 July educational supplier Brynteg Books lost more than £200,000 of stock, in its fourth flooding in as many weeks.

To succeed, risks such as these should not cause the entrepreneur concern or sleepless nights. A builder should know that some contracts will go wrong and just make sure that enough profits are made overall to make up for the occasional dog. Every job selection decision is difficult, but it will rarely turn out right to always make the safe choice.

The general lesson is that risk is not something to be feared, it is simply part of business life. A good entrepreneur will be able to make risky decisions quickly, without dithering or getting stressed; and will have good enough judgement to usually manage to get them right.

> ### Key terms
>
> **Accounting rate of return:** the average profit from an investment expressed as a percentage of the cost of the project.
> **Cash inflow:** the flow of cash into the business as a result of the investment.
> **Payback period:** the time it takes for the initial cost of an investment to be paid back.

● Drive and energy
● Self-confidence
● High initiative and personal responsibility
● Internal locus of control
● Tolerance of ambiguity
● Low fear of failure
● Moderate risk taking

● Long-term involvement
● Money as a measure, not merely an end
● Use of feedback
● Continuous pragmatic problem solving
● Good use of resources
● Self-imposed standards
● Clear **goal-setting**

Source: Jeffrey Timmons and colleagues, MIT, quoted on the Open University website: www.open2.net

Figure 24.1 Fourteen characteristics of entrepreneurs identified by MIT

Exercises

A. Revision questions

(10 marks; 10 minutes)

1 Identify one risk from each of the following business decisions. Briefly explain what you think the risk is.
   a Doubling the advertising budget when a firm's sales haven't increased compared to last year (2)
   b A bakery switching to a new supplier of flour (2)
   c An entrepreneur borrowing £80,000 secured against his house, when interest rates are nice and low at 3.25 per cent. (3)

2 Why may a successful entrepreneur be good at 'moderate risk-taking' rather than 'high risk-taking'? (3)

B. Revision exercises

B1 Data response

A large bakery is losing valuable production time and quality due to the constant maintenance needed on the existing ovens, which are 30 years old. In order to compete it needs to invest in a new oven complex, which will cost £150,000. The expected life of the ovens is ten years. An alternative is to upgrade the worst-performing oven, which will cost £30,000 and last five years.

The cash inflows of each option are expected to be:

	New oven complex £	Oven upgrade £
Year 1	15,000	10,000
Year 2	20,000	10,000
Year 3	20,000	10,000
Year 4	20,000	8,000
Year 5	20,000	8,000
Year 6	20,000	
Year 7	20,000	
Year 8	15,000	
Year 9	4,000	
Year 10	2,000	

Question

(20 marks; 25 minutes)

1 Using payback and ARR, and any other relevant information you think would be necessary to make the decision, assess which option the bakery should choose.

B2 Data response

Organic growth

After two years of booming sales, is Dales Organic Foods Ltd ready for a second outlet? Its Harrogate supermarket is doing well, but what about opening up in Leeds? Managing director Jim Dale says that 'With five times the population, a Leeds branch should do five times the business. That will put us in a much stronger position with our suppliers.' Chairperson Kim Dale is not so sure, but she has let Jim commission a market research study of the likely sales. From this he has been able to work up some possible cash flow figures for a Leeds outlet. These are as follows:

All figs in £000s		
	Cash in	Cash out
Now		400
Year 1	300	400
Year 2	600	500
Year 3	800	600
Year 4	1000	700
Year 5	1000	700

Kim has asked Jim to work these up into final investment appraisal figures, bearing in mind that there may be a rise in the current interest rate of 5%.

Appendix A: Other financial data from Dales Organic Foods Ltd's latest annual accounts

Cash at bank: £150,000   Long-term loans: £400,000

Overdraft: £220,000   2006/07 profit: £320,000

Appendix B: Other data that might be relevant

National growth rate in organic food sales: 2005: +12%, 2006: +7%, 2007: +2.2%

24.4 Workbook

Number of organic food shops in Harrogate: 3;
Number of organic food shops in Leeds: 1

Number of Tesco outlets stocking organic foods:
2004: 35, 2007: 240

Questions

(20 marks; 25 minutes)

1 Calculate the investment appraisal for the Leeds store, using both payback and ARR. Recommend whether or not the business should open this second outlet on purely numerical grounds. (8)

2 Discuss the other issues raised in the case material, then make a justified recommendation about whether or not the firm should proceed. (12)

25 DECISION-MAKING AND FINAL ACCOUNTS

Unit

DEFINITION

The final accounts of a business consist of the trading, profit and loss account and the balance sheet. They are used to monitor the performance of the business and to aid its decision-making.

25.1 Measuring performance

The performance of organisations may be measured in many ways, such as:

- sales or sales growth

- market share

- the job satisfaction of its employees

- its track record on environmental issues

- customer satisfaction.

The most appropriate measure(s) will depend on the nature of the organisation; a hospital may look at the number of successful operations, a university may measure the number and class of the degrees of its students, and a sports club may measure the number of matches played and won. However, one of the most common measures of success for organisations is net profit.

Net profit measures the profit left after all the operating costs of the business have been deducted. These costs may include the costs of producing and marketing the products, as well as fixed costs (such as rent). Net profit is the lifeblood of the organisation, because unless the business makes a profit, it cannot finance growth. In a growing economy, with new opportunities arising all the time, a business that cannot grow is condemned to a slow death. The perfect example of this is Woolworths. In its 2007 financial year it made a net profit that was less than 1% of its sales. In other words, of every £1 taken through a Woolworths till, less than 1p was the company's net profit. Can Woolworths survive with such meagre rewards? To find out, it is useful to check Woolworth's final accounts.

25.2 Final accounts

The final accounts of a business provide information to stakeholders about its performance and give an overall view of the business's financial position at a particular time. Final accounts are usually produced once a year, and should show a true and fair view of the business at a particular date. Final accounts consist of the profit and loss account, balance sheet and cash flow statement (see Unit 21).

Profit and loss account

The profit and loss account shows the revenues, **expenses** and level of profit or loss for a given time period, usually a year, although profits for public limited companies are normally declared every six months. The complexity of the accounts will depend upon the legal status of the organisation.

Table 25.1 shows the layout of the profit and loss account of a company, and includes corporation tax, interest payments and dividends. The profit and loss account of a sole trader or partnership would not include these items and *operating profit* would be *net profit* in these cases.

Sales revenue (turnover)

This figure includes all sales, whether on credit or in cash, made in a period. Unlike the cash flow statement the figure does not depend on the money that has actually been received by the business.

Cost of sales

This figure represents the money the business must spend in order to produce or buy stock to sell. For example, a business that makes bread would expect to

Table 25.1 Profit and loss account year ending March 2009(£)

Sales revenue (turnover)		500,000
Less cost of sales	100,000	
Gross profit		**400,000**
Less expenses	80,000	
Operating profit		**320,000**
Less interest payable	20,000	
Net profit		300,000
Less tax	45,000	
Less dividends	100,000	
Retained profit		**155,000**

sell the bread for a higher price than it cost to make it and to buy the raw materials. When calculating this figure it is important *only to include* the stock of products actually sold in the period *not those* that are still in the stock room. Therefore it is important that the business makes an accurate assessment of stock at the end of the year. *The opening stock figure for a year is the closing stock figure of the previous year.*

Cost of sales is calculated in the following way:

opening stock + purchases (stock bought in the year) – closing stock

For example:

	£
opening stock	45,000
+ purchases	110,000
– closing stock	55,000
cost of sales	100,000

Therefore the actual amount of stock bought and sold cost £100,000.

The role of the profit and loss account

The profit and loss account has two columns. The latest year's figures are on the left and the previous year's on the right. This allows the business and stakeholders to make comparisons regarding the performance of the business, and helps to make decisions about future plans for the business. For example:

- setting objectives and targets for the future

- making decisions about future projects and expenditure

- provides banks with information about whether a business is able to pay back loans, shareholders with information about profit levels and dividend payments, suppliers with an indication of whether the business will be able to pay their bills

- the Inland Revenue can judge whether the correct amount of **tax** has been paid

- it is a legal requirement under the Companies Act to maintain accounts.

However, future decisions must be seen in the whole context of the business and its objectives. Levels of profit are very important to this process but must be considered in the light of factors such as the economy, the market, government legislation and the effect of decisions on all stakeholders.

The balance sheet

The balance sheet (see the example in Table 25.2) is not an account. It is a statement of the value of the business at a certain time. It balances the value of what a business *owns* – its **assets** – with what a business *owes* – its **liabilities**. The balance sheet reflects the financial health of the business, and shows whether it can meet its short- and long-term debts. Like the profit and loss account, it allows comparisons to be made with previous years.

Fixed assets are those assets that can be seen, such as premises and machinery. Other assets, such as the goodwill of the business, are also shown under fixed assets. Fixed assets are depreciated (amount taken off for wear and tear) at a certain rate in order to give a realistic value of the business.

Current assets such as debtors can be converted into cash and can be used to pay off short-term debts such as overdrafts and creditors (*current liabilities*). Some current assets, such as stock, may take longer to sell and turn into cash.

Working capital is a very important figure. It is calculated by subtracting the current liabilities from the current assets. The business calculates working capital to ensure that it has enough cash to finance the everyday running of the business. From this figure managers can make decisions about credit control and stock management, which may improve the working capital situation in the future.

Net assets shows the actual value of the business, having taken account of long-term liabilities such as loans and mortgages.

Table 25.2 Balance sheet for Lugitall Ltd, 31 March 2009

Fixed assets		100,000
Less depreciation (10%)		(10,000)
		90,000
Current assets		
Cash	6000	
Stock	60,000	
Debtors	20,000	
Total current assets		86,000
Current liabilities		
Overdraft	5000	
Creditors	5000	
Total current liabilities		10,000
Working capital		76,000
Less long-term liabilities		(20,000)
Net assets		**146,000**
Shareholders' funds		
Share capital		100,000
Retained profit		46,000
		146,000

Shareholders' funds show the total amount that the company owes to its shareholders.

Role of the balance sheet

The balance sheet can be used for:

● obtaining loans from a bank – banks can assess the value of the assets of the business, which might be used for security against borrowing

● monitoring the amount owed by customers (debtors) in order to put credit control systems in place

● monitoring stock control to ensure that the optimum level of stock is maintained

● monitoring the value of fixed assets to make decisions about future investment projects.

The balance sheet is a view at *one point in a year*. It only gives a snapshot of the business and therefore must be treated with caution. It is important that any analysis or use of the balance sheet takes account of the type of business in question, the products/services it sells and the market it serves, before coming to too many conclusions.

The risks of relying on balance sheets were shown in March 2008. Only two weeks after publishing a clean set of accounts, the Carlyle Capital Corporation was declared insolvent in America's credit crises.

25.3 Methods of improving profits

To increase profits a business must:

1 increase revenue

2 decrease costs

3 do a combination of 1 and 2.

To increase revenue a business may want to consider its marketing mix. Changes to the product may mean that it becomes more appealing to customers. Better distribution may make it more available. Changes to promotion may make customers more aware of its benefits. However, the business needs to be careful that rising costs do not swallow up the rise in sales revenues.

To reduce costs a business may examine many of the functional areas (such as marketing, operations, people and finance):

● Could the firm continue with fewer staff?

● Could money be saved by switching suppliers?

● Do the firm's sales really benefit from sponsoring the opera?

● Are there ways of reducing wastage?

Essentially, a business should look for ways of making the product more efficiently (e.g. with better technology) by using fewer inputs or paying less for the inputs being used. However, a business must be careful that when it reduces costs, the quality of service is not reduced. After all, this might lead to a fall in sales and revenue. Cutting staff in your coffee shop may cut costs but if long queues form it may also reduce the number of customers and your income. Managers must weigh up the consequences of any decision to reduce costs.

High-grade application

High-grade application
Prudential

In 2007 the Prudential insurance company announced a 15% profit increase at the same time as announcing plans to cut its costs. The company also increased its dividend at the same time by 5%.

Prudential said that the targets would be achieved through a combination of internal cost-cutting and an expansion of its offshore and outsourcing operations, with around 3000 customer service and other jobs in the UK expected to be affected by the plans. The announcement of job cuts at the same time as higher profits highlights the pressure on managers to keep increasing profit.

25.4 Methods of increasing profit margins

To increase net profits in relation to sales a business could do the following.

● *Increase its price*: this would boost the profit per sale, but the danger is that the sales overall may fall so much that the overall profits of the business are reduced. (Notice the important difference again between the net profit margin and the overall level of profits – you could make a high level of profit on one can of beans relative to its price but if you only sell one can your total profits are not that impressive!). The impact of any price increase will depend on the price elasticity of demand. Price elasticity is covered in Unit 19. It is a way of measuring how sharply demand changes when the price of a product is changed. The more price elastic demand is, the greater the fall in demand will be, and the less likely it is that a firm will want to put up its prices. On the other hand, a price-elastic demand may mean it is worth cutting price. Although less profit may be made per item (there is a lower profit margin) the overall profits may increase due to the boost in sales.

● *Cut costs*: if this can be done without damaging the quality in any significant way then this clearly makes sense. Better bargaining to get the supply prices down, or better ways of producing may lead to high profits per sale. However, as we saw above, the business needs to be careful that reducing costs does not lead to a deterioration of the service or quality of the product, as this may damage sales.

25.5 Profits and the functions of business

As we can see, the profits and the profitability of a business depend on all the different functions of the business. The operations management may determine how much can be produced and sold. Human resources management may affect how many people need to be employed and the costs of staff. Marketing decisions will affect the sales and revenue earned. To boost profits you may consider each and every one of these functions to look for ways of increasing revenue and/or cutting costs.

High-grade application
Jessops

In 2007 the photographic retailer Jessops warned that it would miss its profit targets after a shortage of digital cameras over Christmas. Production problems at Canon and Nikon (which account for around 80% of the market) created a worldwide shortage and meant Jessops could not meet demand. In this case it was not the firm's own problems but those of its suppliers that caused the profit short fall.

Issues For Analysis

Many organisations survive without profit, but largely because of government or private charity. This unit is largely about business organisations that need profit to survive and, especially, to grow. If a business is as unprofitable as Woolworths it is hard to understand how it survives.

In exams there are various questions to ask yourself about a loss-making firm:

● What has caused the losses: **internal reasons** or external ones? Internal ones would include poor decision making.

● What may be the downsides to any new approach? Will staff cutbacks cost more from damaged morale than they provide from lower wage costs?

● Finally, what is the timescale of the decision making? Is the business forced to take action immediately to boost profit, or can it wait to see if today's poor circumstances ease off.

25.6 Measuring and increasing profit
an evaluation

A difficulty with questions about poor profits is that many suggestions made in exams are too obvious. As shown in Table 25.3, Sainsbury's has only half the profit margin of Tesco. But is it worth pointing out to Sainsbury's that it could look for bulk-buying discounts on its supplies? Of course not. A good exam answer will show the maturity to see that Sainsbury's managers will already be doing all they can to tackle the problem.

> ### Key terms
>
> **Assets:** anything a business owns.
> **Expenses:** these are any fixed costs and expenses incurred by a business in a time period, apart from stock.
> **Gross profit:** sales revenue – cost of sales.
> **Internal reasons:** these come within the control of the management (e.g. the quality of the materials used in production).
> **Liabilities:** anything a business owes.
> **Net profit:** operating profit – interest paid.
> **Retained profit:** profit that the business can use in any way it likes.
> **Tax:** this refers to corporation tax levied on the profits of private and public limited companies.

Figure 25.1 Long queues may turn away customers

Table 25.3 Net profit margins from selected 2007 company accounts

	Net profit	**Sales**	**% net profit margin**
Tesco	£2653 million	£46611 million	5.7%
Sainsbury's	£477 million	£17151 million	2.8%
Woolworths	£16 million	£2740 million	0.58%
Ted Baker*	£7 million	£66 million	10.6%

* Half-year only

Exercises

A. Revision questions

(26 marks; 20 minutes)

1 What is meant by 'net profit'? (2)

2 What is meant by 'revenue'? (2)

3 Does an increase in price necessarily increase revenue? (3)

4 How can revenue increase without an increase in cash inflows? (3)

5 Explain two ways of increasing profits. (6)

6 Why might cutting costs end up reducing profits? (3)

7 In what ways do the different functions of a business affect its profits? (4)

8 A business has an opening stock of £30,000, closing stock of £10,000 and cost of sales of £60,000. Calculate the value of purchases. (3)

B. Revision exercises

B1 Data response

SOFA-SOGOOD Ltd is a retailer of sofas. It had been experiencing a very slow summer. Revenues had been falling but costs had been pushed up by pay increases, higher rent costs and higher interest payments on debts. As a result, net profits had fallen by 20% on last year. Renis, the managing director, was very disappointed that revenue had fallen because he had cut prices by 5% and had expected customer numbers to increase sharply. Once it became clear that this discounting policy was not working, he imposed a pay freeze on everyone in the company and a policy of non-recruitment. If any staff member left, s/he would not be replaced.

Questions

(30 marks; 30 minutes)

1 Distinguish between revenue, costs and net profit. (3)

2 Explain why a fall in price might not have led to an increase in revenue. (5)

3 Apart from the methods mentioned in the text, analyse two other actions SOFA-SOGOOD might take to improve its profitability. (8)

4 Discuss the advantages and disadvantages to the business of the staffing cost-saving actions taken by Renis. (14)

B2 Data response

Farmoor College

Farmoor College is a private sixth form based in London that charges students to study for their A-levels. The fees are £15,000 a year. The college is proud of its small classes (average size five students) and its excellent examination results. This year it has 200 students studying with it, which is about its present capacity in terms of the number of classrooms available. The college has a core of key staff but employs other teachers and support staff depending on the levels of demand in any year. The college's net profit margin is 12% and the capital invested in the business is £15 million.

Questions

(36 marks; 36 minutes)

1 Calculate the likely net profits for the college this year. (3)

2 Outline two costs the college is likely to have. (4)

3 Explain one factor that might cause a change in demand for the college. (4)

4 Explain how the net profit of the college might be used. (5)

5 Analyse how you might measure the performance of the college apart from looking at its financial results. (8)

6 Discuss the ways in which the college might increase its profits. (12)

B3 Data response

Questions

(22 marks; 20 minutes)

1 Discuss the usefulness of a company's final accounts to those who have a stake in the business. (12)

2 Lugitall Ltd makes and sells rucksacks to professional climbers. It markets and sells its products over the internet. Using the information presented in Table 25.2 explain why the value of working capital is £76,000 and assess whether this is good position for this company. (10)

B4 Data response

Animo Ltd

Below are the balance sheets for Animo Ltd for year ending 31 December 2007 and year ending 31 December 2008. Animo Ltd make and sell specialist foods for pedigree dogs and cats. They buy their raw ingredients from farmers in the UK and the rest of Europe.

Animo Ltd	**Balance sheet**	
	31 December 2007	**31 December 2008**
	(£000s)	(£000s)
Fixed assets	1500	1500
Current assets		
Stock	200	150
Debtors	300	200
Cash in bank	600	450
	1100	800
Current liabilities		
Trade creditors	800	750
Tax payable	150	125
Net current assets (working capital)	?	?
Less long-term liabilities	100	200
Net assets	**1550**	**1225**
Shareholders' funds		
Ordinary shares	1000	1000
Retained profit	550	225
Capital employed	**1550**	**1225**

Questions

(19 marks; 25 minutes)

1 Calculate Animo Ltd's working capital for 2007 and 2008. (3)

2 Analyse the reasons why working capital is important to a business such as Animo Ltd. (8)

3 Analyse the ways in which Animo Ltd might improve its working capital. (8)

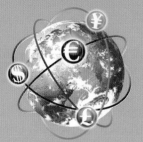

Unit 26

LABOUR TURNOVER

DEFINITION

Staff costs are usually between 25% and 50% of a firm's total costs. For this reason, firms try to measure the performance of their people objectively (i.e. in an unbiased way). Calculations such as staff productivity can be used to measure the success of initiatives such as new methods of working or payment.

26.1 The need to measure performance

Managers require an objective, unbiased way to measure the performance of personnel. The firm needs to be able to see whether:

- the workforce is fully motivated
- the workforce is as productive as it could be
- the human resources policies of the business are helping the business to meet its goals.

It is not possible to measure these things directly. How, for example, can the level of motivation of workers be measured accurately? Instead, a series of indicators are used which, when analysed, can show the firm whether its human resources policies are contributing as much to the firm as they should.

There are two main performance indicators used to measure the effectiveness of a personnel department. These are:

1 labour productivity

2 labour turnover.

26.2 Labour productivity

Calculating labour productivity

Labour productivity is often seen as the single most important measure of how well a firm's workers are doing. It compares the number of workers with the output that they are producing. It is expressed through the formula:

$$\frac{\text{output per period}}{\text{number of employees per period}}$$

For example, if a window cleaner employs ten people and in a day will normally clean the windows of 150 houses, then the productivity is:

$$\frac{150}{10} = 15 \text{ houses per worker per day}$$

At its simplest, the higher the productivity of the workforce, the better it is performing. Any increase in the productivity figure suggests an improvement in efficiency. The importance of productivity lies in its impact on labour costs per unit. For example, the productivity of AES Cleaning is 15 houses per worker per day; MS Cleaning achieves only 10. Assuming a daily rate of pay of £45, the labour cost per house is £3 for AES but £4.50 for MS Cleaning. Higher productivity leads to lower labour costs per unit – and therefore greater competitiveness, both here and against international rivals.

Remember that productivity is just one way to measure staff performance. There are others, including labour turnover.

26.3 Labour turnover

Measuring labour turnover

Labour turnover is a measure of the rate of change of a firm's workforce. It is measured by the ratio:

$$\frac{\text{number of staff leaving the firm per year}}{\text{average number of staff}} \times 100$$

So a firm that has seen 5 people leave out of its staff of 50 has a labour turnover of:

$$\frac{5}{50} \times 100 = 10\%$$

As with all these figures, it would be a mistake to take one figure in isolation. It would be better to look at how the figure has changed over a number of years, and to look for the reasons why the turnover rate is as it is.

Causes of labour turnover

If the rate of labour turnover is increasing, it may be a sign of dissatisfaction within the workforce. If so, the possible causes could be either internal to the firm or external.

Internal causes of an increasing rate of labour turnover could include the following.

● A poor recruitment and selection procedure, which may appoint the wrong person to the wrong post. If this happens, then eventually the misplaced workers will wish to leave to find a job more suited to their particular interests or talents.

● Ineffective motivation or leadership, leading to workers lacking commitment to this particular firm. They will feel no sense of loyalty to or ownership of the business, and will tend to look outside the firm

for promotions or new career opportunities, rather than looking for new ways in which they could contribute to 'their' firm.

● Wage levels that are lower than those being earned by similar workers in other local firms: if wage rates are not competitive, workers will feel dissatisfied with their position; they may look elsewhere to find a better reward for doing a similar job.

External causes of an increasing rate of labour turnover could include the following.

● More local vacancies arising, perhaps due to the setting up or expansion of other firms in the area.

● Better transport links, making a wider geographical area accessible for workers. New public transport systems such as Manchester's network of trams or Newcastle's Metro links enable workers to take employment that was previously out of their reach.

Consequences of high labour turnover

A high rate of labour turnover can have both negative and positive effects on a firm. The negative aspects would be:

● the cost of recruitment of replacements

● the cost of retraining replacements

High-grade application

Labour turnover at Red Carnation Hotels (RCH)

Liz McGivern joined the RCH luxury hotel chain just after the 2001 terrorist attack on New York. Business was soon down by 20% as American tourists disappeared. Yet she noticed a shocking detail about RCH; its labour turnover was 80%. This would be poor for any hotel, but luxury hotels have to offer good service, which would always be tricky if new, inexperienced staff were dealing with guests. Nothing could be done about nervous flyers, but the high labour turnover was inexcusable.

Liz carried out some internal research which revealed high levels of staff dissatisfaction due to poor management and strained internal relationships. Her solution was to implement a company-wide training programme focusing on improved customer service. The cost per person was in the order of £1000 so, with a staff of more than 500, this was a substantial investment by the directors. Fortunately it went well, resulting in improved repeat business from guests and a fall in labour turnover to 29%. Even more importantly for the business, the revenue received per room rose by 11% at a time when the market trend was towards falling room rates.

Source: www.people1st.co.uk

Figure 26.1 Transport links affect worker turnover

- the time taken for new recruits to settle into the business and adopt the firm's **culture**

- the loss of productivity while the new workers adjust.

On the positive side, labour turnover can benefit the business in several ways:

- new workers can bring new ideas and enthusiasm to the firm

- workers with specific skills can be employed rather than having to train up existing workers from scratch

- new ways of solving problems can be seen by workers with a different perspective, whereas existing workers may rely on tried and trusted techniques that have worked in the past.

On balance, then, there is a need for firms to achieve the *right* level of labour turnover, rather than aiming for the lowest possible level.

26.4 Evaluating the success of human resources management

Productivity and labour turnover data provide the firm with a commentary on its performance. Poor productivity and high labour turnover might be a commentary on poor management in the workplace. For the most effective comparisons, good managers analyse the figures to identify:

- changes over time (this year versus last)

- how the firm is performing compared to other similar firms

- performance against targets, such as a 20% improvement on last year.

Each of these comparisons will tell the firm how it is performing in relation to a yardstick. This will indicate to the firm where it is performing well and where it may have a problem. The firm must then investigate carefully the reasons for its performance before it can judge how well its personnel function is operating.

For example, labour productivity may have fallen over the past 12 months. Closer investigation may show that this fall is due to the time taken to train staff on new machinery installed at the start of the year. Figures may show that productivity in the last six months was actually higher than at any time in the past, and the firm can be confident that future productivity will continue to increase. In this case, an apparent problem is actually masking an improvement for the firm.

Issues For Analysis

There are several important business issues relating to personnel performance indicators.

- Business success comes from being the best and staying the best. This is always hard, but is the only way to be sure of staying at the top. Football managers might say all that counts is what happens on the pitch, but lateness or absence from training is often a good indicator of problems to come. Every manager should be alert to early warning signs, find out the reasons and tackle them straightaway.

- Human resources issues are considered 'soft' by some employers. Who cares about labour turnover or health issues, they say, as long as the job gets done and profits are high? This may be true in the short term; for firms pursuing long-term growth, however, the quality and involvement of staff is crucial. So morale matters – as do absence and lateness.

26.5 Labour turnover

an evaluation

Performance ratios such as labour turnover raise questions – they do not supply answers. Follow-up staff surveys or chats may be needed to discover the underlying problems. Figures such as these give the firm an indication of what issues need to be addressed if the firm is to improve its position in the future, but this must be taken within the context of the business as a whole. A high labour turnover figure may have been the result of a deliberate policy to bring in younger members of staff who may be more adaptable to a changing situation at the factory.

Measures of personnel effectiveness are merely indicators for a firm to see where it may be facing problems. The measures may indicate poor performance, or reflect the short-term effect of a change in business strategy.

It must be remembered that these figures are all looking to the past. They tell the firm what has happened to its workforce. Although this has a strong element of objectivity, it is not as valuable as an indication of how the indicators may look in the future.

Key terms

Culture: the accepted attitudes and behaviours of people within a workplace.
Labour productivity: output per person.
Labour turnover: the rate at which people leave their jobs and need to be replaced.

Exercises

A. Revision questions

(27 marks; 27 minutes)

1 Define the following terms:
   (a) labour productivity
   (b) labour turnover. (4)

2 Why might an increase in labour productivity help a firm to reduce its costs per unit? (3)

3 In what ways might a hotel business benefit if labour turnover rose from 2% to 15% per year? (4)

4 Some fast food outlets have labour turnover as high as 100% per year. What might be the effects of this on the firm? (4)

5 How might a firm know if its personnel strategy was working effectively? (5)

6 Briefly distinguish between labour productivity and labour turnover. (3)

7 Outline one positive and one negative effect of an increase in labour turnover on a firm's performance. (4)

B. Revision exercises

B1 Data response

A firm has the following data on its personnel function:

	Year 1	Year 2
Output	50,000	55,000
Average no. of workers	250	220
No. of staff leaving the firm	12	8
Working days per worker – possible	230	230
Average no. of staff absent	4	3

Questions

(15 marks; 15 minutes)

1 Calculate the following ratios for both years:
   (a) labour productivity
   (b) labour turnover. (5)

2 Explain what questions these figures might raise in the minds of the firm's management. (10)

B2 Data response

Monitoring personnel performance at Best Motors

James West, the new human resources officer at Best Motors, manufacturer of the world-famous handmade sports cars of the same name, sat down at his desk and considered the figures in front of him. He would need to report on the existing position of the business to Elizabeth Best, the chief executive, on Friday.

James knew the company operated for 50 weeks of the year (closing down only for the annual works holiday), and that all employees worked full-time, five days each week. He opened his briefcase and got out a calculator. 'The first thing to do is determine the key human resource indicators,' he thought to himself as he got to work.

Questions

(25 marks; 30 minutes)

1 Calculate labour turnover and labour productivity at Best Motors for all five years. (10)

2 Using your results, evaluate the effectiveness of Best Motors' human resources management. (8)

3 What additional information would you seek in order to help James gain a better understanding of how staff have been managed at Best Motors? Explain your reasoning. (7)

Personal performance at Best Motors (B2)					
	4 YEARS AGO	**3 YEARS AGO**	**2 YEARS AGO**	**LAST YEAR**	**THIS YEAR**
NUMBER OF LEAVERS	3	2	4	6	7
WORKING DAYS LOST TO ABSENCE	124	102	145	169	204
TOTAL OUTPUT	780	803	805	790	811
NUMBER OF SHOP FLOOR ACCIDENTS	5	3	7	2	4
AVERAGE NUMBER OF EMPLOYEES	23	25	25	24	26

B3 Case study

Turner's Butchers is a chain of three shops in a large town in the north of England. The shops are all supplied with prepared and packaged produce from Turner's Farm, owned by the same family.

The management is particularly concerned at present by the differing performance of the three shops. In particular, they feel there may be a problem with the human resources management in the chain. The concerns were highlighted recently in a report looking at various indicators of personnel effectiveness. The key section of the report is shown below.

Questions
(30 marks; 45 minutes)

1 Briefly outline your observations on each of the three shops in terms of their human resources management. (12)

2 Give possible reasons for the factors you described in answer to question 1. (9)

3 Taking the business as a whole, make justified recommendations as to how any problems could be tackled by the management. (9)

Workforce performance data per shop (B3)			
	Grayton Road	**St John's Precinct**	**Lark Hill**
Staff (full-time)	8	6	7
Labour turnover	25%	150%	0
Absence rate	5%	12%	1%
Sales per employee (£000s)	14	15	18

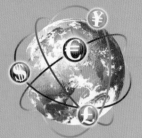

Unit 27

MOTIVATION IN THEORY

DEFINITION

One key theorist (Professor Herzberg) believes motivation occurs when people do something because they *want* to do it; others think of motivation as the desire to achieve a result. The difference between these two definitions is important and should become clear in this unit.

27.1 Introduction

A recent study by the Hay Group found that just 15% of UK workers consider themselves 'highly motivated'. As many as 25% say they're 'coasting' and 8% admit to being 'completely demotivated'. In the same survey, employees felt they could be 45% more productive if they were doing a job they loved, and 28% more productive with better training. Poor management is part of the problem, as 28% say they would be more productive with a better boss.

The Hay Group calculates that if the under-performance was tackled successfully, the value of UK output would rise by more than £350 billion a year. So motivation matters. This is why it merits a unit to itself – and why many consider motivation theory to be the most important topic within Business Studies.

27.2 F. W. Taylor and Scientific Management

Although there were earlier pioneers, the starting point for the study of motivation is F. W. Taylor (1856–1917). As with most of the other influential writers on this subject, Taylor was American. His influence over the twentieth-century world has been massive. Much business practice in America, Europe, Japan and the former Communist countries is still rooted in his writing and work.

A recent biography of Taylor is titled *The One Best Way*; this sums up neatly Taylor's approach to management. He saw it as management's task to decide exactly how every task should be completed, then to devise the tools needed to enable the worker to achieve the task as efficiently as possible. This method is evident today in every McDonald's in the world. Fries are cooked at 175 degrees for exactly three minutes, then a buzzer tells employees to take them out and salt them. Throughout every McDonald's is a series of dedicated, purpose-built machines for producing milkshakes, toasting buns, squirting chocolate sauce, and much else. Today, 100 years after his most active period working in industry, F. W. Taylor would feel very much at home ordering a Big Mac.

So, what was Taylor's view of the underlying motivations of people at work? How did he make sure that the employees worked effectively at following 'the one best way' laid down by managers?

Taylor believed that people work for only one reason: money. He saw it as the task of the manager to devise a system that would maximise efficiency. This would generate the profit to enable the worker to be paid a higher wage. Taylor's view of human nature was that of 'economic man'. In other words people were motivated only by the economic motive of self-interest. Therefore a manager could best motivate a worker by offering an incentive (a 'carrot') or a threat (the 'stick'). Taylor can be seen as a manipulator, or even a bully, but he believed his methods were in the best interests of the employees themselves.

Taylor's influence stemmed less from his theories than his activities. He was a trained engineer who acted as a very early management consultant. His methods were as follows:

- observe workers at work, recording and timing what they do, when they do it and how long they take over it (this became known as time and motion study)

- identify the most efficient workers and see how they achieve greater efficiency

- break the task down into small component parts that can be done quickly and repeatedly

- devise equipment specifically to speed up tasks

- set out exactly how the work should be done in future; 'each employee', Taylor wrote, 'should receive every day clear-cut, definite instructions as to what he is to do and how he is to do it, and these instructions should be exactly carried out, whether they are right or wrong'

- devise a pay scheme to reward those who complete or beat tough output targets, but that penalises those who cannot or will not achieve the **productivity** Taylor believed was possible; this pay scheme was called **piece rate** – no work, no pay.

As an engineer, Taylor was interested in practical outcomes, not in psychology. There is no reason to suppose he thought greatly about the issue of motivation. The effect of his ideas was profound, though. Long before the publication of his 1911 book *The Principles of Scientific Management*, Taylor had spread his managerial practices of careful measurement, monitoring and – above all else – control. Before Taylor, skilled workers chose their own ways of working and had varied, demanding jobs. After Taylor, workers were far more likely to have limited, repetitive tasks; and to be forced to work at the pace set by a manager or consultant engineer.

Among those influenced by Taylor was Henry Ford. His Model T was the world's first mass-produced motor car. By 1911 the Ford factory in Detroit, USA, was already applying Taylor's principles of high **division of labour**, purpose-built machinery and rigid management control. When Ford introduced the conveyor belt in 1913, he achieved the ultimate Taylorite idea: men's pace of work dictated by a mechanical conveyor belt, the speed of which was set by management.

Eventually workers rebelled against being treated like machines. **Trades union** membership thrived in factories run on Taylorite lines, as workers wanted to organise against the suffocating lives they were leading at work. Fortunately, in many western countries further developments in motivation theory pointed to new, more people-friendly approaches.

27.3 Elton Mayo and the Human Relations Approach

Elton Mayo (1880–1949) was a medical student who became an academic with a particular interest in people in organisations. Although an Australian, he moved to America in 1923. Early in his career, his methods were heavily influenced by F. W. Taylor. An early investigation of a spinning mill in Pennsylvania identified one department with labour turnover of 250% compared to 6% elsewhere in the factory. His Taylorite solution was to prescribe work breaks. These had the desired effect.

Mayo moved on to work at the Hawthorne plant of Western Electric Company in Chicago. His investigations there are known as the Hawthorne Experiments.

He was called in to Hawthorne to try to explain the findings of a previous test into the effects of lighting upon productivity levels. The lighting conditions for one work group had been varied, while those for another had been held constant. The surprise was that whatever was done to the lighting, production rose in *both* groups. This proved that there was more to motivation and efficiency than purely economic motives.

Between 1927 and 1932 Mayo conducted a series of experiments at Hawthorne. The first is known as the Relay Assembly Test. Six volunteer female assembly staff were separated from their workmates. A series of experiments was carried out. The results were recorded and discussed with the women. Every 12 weeks a new working method was tried. The alternatives included:

- different bonus methods, such as individual versus group bonuses

- different rest periods

- different refreshments

- different work layout.

Before every change, the researchers discussed the new method fully with the operators. Almost without exception productivity increased with every change. At the end, the group returned to the original method (48-hour, 6-day week with no breaks) and output went up to its highest level yet! Not only that, but the women claimed they felt less tired than they had at the start.

The experiments had started rather slowly, with some resistance from the operatives. Progress became much more marked when one member of the group retired. She was replaced by a younger woman who quickly became the unofficial leader of the group.

Mayo's conclusions

● The women gained satisfaction from their freedom and control over their working environment.

● 'What actually happened was that six individuals became a team and the team gave itself wholeheartedly and spontaneously to cooperation in the experiment' (Mayo, 1949).

● Group norms (expectations of one another) are crucial and may be influenced more by informal than official group leaders.

● Communication between workers and managers influences morale and output.

● Workers are affected by the degree of interest shown in them by their managers; the influence of this upon motivation is known as 'the Hawthorne effect'.

The consequences of Mayo's work were enormous. He influenced many researchers and writers, effectively opening up the fields of industrial psychology and industrial sociology. Many academics followed Mayo's approach in what became known as the Human Relations school of management.

Businesses also responded to the implications of Mayo's work for company profitability and success. If teamwork, communications and managerial involvement were that important, firms reasoned that they needed an organisational structure to cope. In Taylor's era, the key

person was the engineer. The winners from Mayo's work were personnel departments. They grew throughout America and Britain in the 1930s, 1940s and 1950s as companies tried to achieve the Hawthorne effect.

27.4 Maslow and the hierarchy of needs

Abraham Maslow (1908–70) was an American psychologist, whose great contribution to motivation theory was the 'hierarchy of needs'. Maslow believed that everyone has the same needs – all of which can be organised as a hierarchy. At the base of the hierarchy are physical needs such as food, shelter and warmth. When unsatisfied, these are the individual's primary motivations. When employees earn enough to satisfy these needs, however, their motivating power withers away. Maslow said that 'It is quite true that humans live by bread alone – when there is no bread. But what happens to their desires when there *is* bread?' Instead of physical needs, people become motivated to achieve needs such as security and stability, which Maslow called the safety needs. In full, Maslow's hierarchy consisted of the elements listed in Table 27.1.

Ever since Maslow first put his theory forward (in 1940) writers have argued about its implications. Among the key issues raised by Maslow are the following.

● Do all humans have the same set of needs? Or are there some people who need no more from a job than money?

● Do different people have different degrees of need – for example, are some highly motivated by the need for power, while others are satisfied by social factors?

Table 27.1 Maslow's hierarchy of needs: implications for business

Maslow's levels of human need	Business implications
physical needs, e.g. food, shelter and warmth	pay levels and working conditions
safety needs, e.g. security, a safe structured environment, stability, freedom from anxiety	job security, a clear job role/description, clear lines of accountability (only one boss)
social needs, e.g. belonging, friendship, contact	team working, communications, social facilities
esteem needs, e.g. strength, self-respect, confidence, status and recognition	status, recognition for achievement, power, trust
self-actualisation, e.g. self-fulfilment; 'to become everything that one is capable of becoming,' wrote Maslow	scope to develop new skills and meet new challenges, and to develop one's full potential

If so, the successful manager would be one who can understand and attempt to meet the differing needs of her/his staff.

● Can anyone's needs ever be said to be fully satisfied? The reason the hierarchy diagram (Figure 27.1) has an open top is to suggest that the human desire for achievement is limitless.

Maslow's work had a huge influence on the writers who followed him, especially McGregor and Herzberg. The hierarchy of needs is also used by academics in many subjects beyond Business Studies, notably Psychology and Sociology.

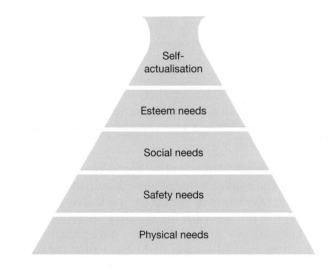

Figure 27.1 *Maslow's hierarchy of needs*

27.5 Herzberg's two factor theory

The key test of a theory is its analytic usefulness. On this criterion, the work of Professor Fred Herzberg (1923–2000) is the strongest by far.

The theory stems from research conducted in the 1950s into factors affecting workers' **job satisfaction** and dissatisfaction. It was carried out on 200 accountants and engineers in Pennsylvania, USA. Despite the limited nature of this sample, Herzberg's conclusions remain influential to this day.

Herzberg asked employees to describe recent events that had given rise to exceptionally good feelings about their jobs, then probed for the reasons why. 'Five factors stand out as strong determiners of job satisfaction,' Herzberg wrote in 1966, 'achievement, recognition for achievement, the work itself, responsibility and

advancement – the last three being of greater importance for a lasting change of attitudes.' He pointed out that each of these factors concerned the job itself, rather than issues such as pay or status. Herzberg called these five factors 'the motivators'.

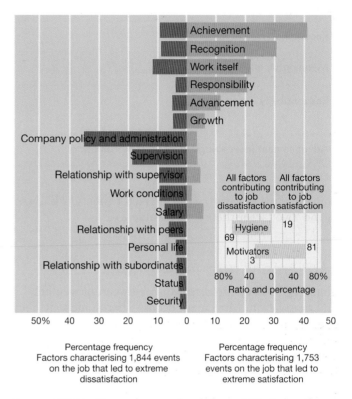

Figure 27.2 *Comparison of satisfiers and dissatisfiers*

The researchers went on to ask about events giving rise to exceptionally bad feelings about their jobs. This revealed a separate set of five causes. Herzberg stated that 'the major dissatisfiers were company policy and administration, supervision, salary, interpersonal relations and working conditions'. He concluded that the common theme was factors that 'surround the job', rather than the job itself. The name he gave these dissatisfiers was '**hygiene factors**'; this was because fulfilling them would prevent dissatisfaction, rather than causing positive motivation. Careful hygiene prevents disease; care to fulfil hygiene factors prevents job dissatisfaction.

To summarise: motivators have the power to create positive job satisfaction, but little downward potential; hygiene factors will cause job dissatisfaction unless they are provided for, but do not motivate. Importantly, Herzberg saw pay as a hygiene factor, not a motivator. So a feeling of being underpaid could lead to a grievance; but high pay would soon be taken for

Table 27.2 Herzberg's two factor theory

Motivators (can create positive satisfaction)	Hygiene factors (can create job dissatisfaction)
Achievement	Company policy and administration (the rules, paperwork and red tape)
Recognition for achievement	Supervision (especially being over-supervised)
Meaningful, interesting work	Pay
Responsibility	Interpersonal relations (with supervisor, peers, or even customers)
Advancement (psychological, not just a promotion)	Working conditions

granted. This motivator/hygiene factor theory is known as the 'two factor theory' (see Table 27.2).

Movement and motivation

Herzberg was keen to distinguish between movement and motivation. Movement occurs when somebody does something; motivation is when they *want* to do something. This distinction is essential to a full understanding of Herzberg's theory. He did not doubt that financial incentives could be used to boost productivity: 'If you bully or bribe people, they'll give you better than average performance.' His worries about 'bribes' (carrots) were that they would never stimulate people to give of their best; people would do just enough to achieve the bonus. Furthermore, bribing people to work harder at a task they found unsatisfying would build up resentments, which might backfire on the employer.

Herzberg advised against payment methods such as piece rate. They would achieve movement, but by reinforcing worker behaviour, would make them inflexible and resistant to change. The salaried, motivated employee would work hard, care about quality and think about – even welcome – improved working methods.

Job enrichment

The reason why Herzberg's work has had such an impact on businesses is because he not only analysed motivation, he also had a method for improving it. The method is job enrichment, which he defined as 'giving people the opportunity to use their ability'. He suggested that, for a job to be considered enriched, it would have to contain the following.

- A *complete unit of work:* not just a small repetitive fragment of a job, but a full challenging task; Herzberg heaped scorn upon the 'idiot jobs' that resulted from Taylor's views on the merits of high division of labour.

- *Direct feedback:* wherever possible, a job should enable the worker to judge immediately the quality of what s/he has done; direct feedback gives the painter or the actor (or the teacher) the satisfaction of knowing exactly how well they have performed. Herzberg disliked systems that pass quality inspection off onto a supervisor: 'a man must always be held responsible for his own quality'. Worst of all, he felt, was annual appraisal, in which feedback is too long delayed.

- *Direct communication:* for people to feel committed, in control and to gain direct feedback, they should communicate directly – avoiding the delays of communicating via a supervisor or a 'contact person'. In itself, it is hard to see the importance of this. For a student of Business Studies, it leads to an important conclusion: that communications and motivation are interrelated.

Conclusion

Herzberg's original research has been followed up in many different countries, including Japan, Africa and Russia. An article he wrote on the subject in the *Harvard Business Review* in 1968 (called 'Just one more time, how do you motivate employees') has sold more than one million reprinted copies. His main insight was to show that unless the job itself was interesting, there was no way to make working life satisfying. This led companies such as Volvo in Sweden and Toyota in

Table 27.3 Key quotes from Professor Herzberg

On the two factor theory	'Motivators and hygiene factors are equally important, but for different reasons'
On movement	'If you do something because you want a house or a Jaguar, that's movement. It's not motivation'
The risks of giving bonuses	'A reward once given becomes a right'
The importance of training	'The more a person can do, the more you can motivate them'
The importance of always treating staff fairly	'A remembered pain can lead to revenge psychology . . . They'll get back at you some day when you need them'
On communication	'In industry, there's too much communication. And of course it's passive . . . But if people are doing idiot jobs they really don't give a damn'
On participation	'When participation is suggested in terms of control over overall goals, it is usually a sham'

Japan to rethink their factory layouts. Instead of individual workers doing simple, repetitive tasks, the drive was to provide more complete units of work. Workers were grouped into teams, focusing on significant parts of the manufacturing process, such as assembling and fitting the gearbox, and then checking the quality of their work. Job enrichment indeed.

27.6 Drucker, Peters and Waterman

Peter Drucker wrote *The Practice of Management* in 1955 and developed the idea of 'management by objectives' (MBO). The idea of MBO is that employers and employees devise, develop and work towards a common set of objectives and targets based on the corporate objectives of the business. The objectives must be SMART and agreed by all parties, so that there is limited conflict. In theory, this type of agreed approach should provide workers with motivation and consequent reward.

Tom Peters and R Waterman prioritised some of the issues addressed by twentieth-century theorists in their 2001 book *In Search of Excellence*, simply as follows:

● people

● customers

● action.

They identified eight themes of companies that are performing well:

1 A bias for action, active decision-making: 'getting on with it'.

2 Close to the customer: learning from the people served by the business.

3 Autonomy and entrepreneurship: fostering innovation and nurturing 'champions'.

4 **Productivity through people:** treating rank and file employees as a source of quality.

5 Hands-on, value-driven: a management philosophy that guides everyday practice, with management showing its commitment.

6 'Stick to the knitting': stay with the business that you know.

7 **Simple form, lean staff:** some of the best companies have minimal headquarters staff.

8 Simultaneous loose–tight properties: autonomy in shop-floor activities, plus centralised values.

In terms of motivation, Peters and Waterman emphasised the idea of reducing bureaucracy and concentrating on the workforce who are the key source of added value to a business. The workforce should be encouraged to try out new ideas and their qualities and potential should be recognised. In this way, the workforce would feel valued by management and improvements in productivity would occur.

27.7 Motivation in theory

an evaluation

Most managers assume they understand human motivation, but they have never studied it. As a result they may underestimate the potential within their own staff, or unthinkingly cause resentments that fester.

The process of managing people takes place in every part of every organisation. By contrast, few would need to know the financial concept of 'gearing' in their working lives. So lack of knowledge of motivation theory is particularly unfortunate – and has exceptionally widespread effects. In some cases, ignorance leads managers to ignore motivation altogether; they tell themselves that control and organisation are their only concerns. Other managers may see motivation as important, but fail to understand its subtleties.

For these reasons, there is a case for saying that the concepts within this unit are the most important in the whole subject.

Issues For Analysis

● In an exam context, the starting point is to select the most appropriate theory to answer a question. If a case study context suggested poor relations between management and workforce, Elton Mayo's would be very suitable. If motivation was weak, Herzberg's theory provides a comprehensive analysis.

● When applying a theory, the analysis is strengthened by using a questioning approach. Herzberg's theory is admirable, but it is not perfect. It provides insights, but not necessarily answers – and certainly not blueprints. A job enrichment programme might be highly effective in one situation, but a disappointment in another.

● This leads on to another key factor: the success of any new policies will depend hugely on the history of trust – or lack of it – in the workplace. Successful change in the factors involved in motivation may be very difficult and slow to achieve. There are no magic solutions.

● Accordingly, when a firm faces a crisis, changes in factors relating to motivation will rarely provide an answer. A crisis must be solved in the short term, but human motivation requires long-term strategies.

Key terms

Division of labour: subdividing a task into a number of activities, enabling workers to specialise and therefore become very efficient at completing what may be a small, repetitive task.

Hygiene factors: 'everything that surrounds what you do in the job', such as pay, working conditions and social status – all potential causes of dissatisfaction, according to Herzberg.

Job satisfaction: the sense of well-being and achievement that stems from a satisfying job.

Piece rate: paying workers per piece they produce (e.g. £2 per pair of jeans made).

Productivity: output per person (i.e. a measure of efficiency).

Trades union: an organisation that represents the interests of staff at the workplace.

Further reading

Herzberg, F. (1959) *The Motivation to Work*. Wiley International.

Maslow, A. H. (1987) *Motivation and Personality*. HarperCollins (1st edn 1954).

Mayo, E. (1975) *The Social Problems of Industrial Civilisation*. Routledge (1st edn 1949).

Exercises

A. Revision questions

(44 marks; 44 minutes)

1 Which features of the organisation of a McDonald's could be described as Taylorite? (3)

2 Explain the meaning of the term 'economic man'. (3)

3 Explain how workers in a bakery might be affected by a change from salary to piece rate. (3)

4 Give a brief outline of Mayo's research methods at the Hawthorne plant. (4)

5 How may 'group norms' affect productivity at a workplace? (3)

6 Explain the meaning of the term 'the Hawthorne effect'. (2)

7 Which two levels of Maslow's hierarchy could be called 'the lower-order needs'? (2)

8 Describe in your own words why Maslow organised the needs into a hierarchy. (3)

9 State three business implications of Maslow's work on human needs. (3)

10 Herzberg believes pay does not motivate, but it is important. Why? (3)

11 How do motivators differ from hygiene factors? (3)

12 What is job enrichment? How is it achieved? (3)

13 Briefly explain what is meant by motivation. (3)

14 Suggest two reasons why employee motivation is important to a business. (2)

15 Give two examples of hygiene factors and two examples of motivators. (4)

B. Revision exercises

B1 Data response

Look back at Figure 28.2. It shows the results of Herzberg's research into the factors that cause positive job satisfaction and those that cause job dissatisfaction. The length of the bars shows the percentage of responses.

Questions

(20 marks; 25 minutes)

1 Which of the factors had the least effect on satisfaction or dissatisfaction? (1)

2 One of Herzberg's objectives was to question whether good human relations were as important in job satisfaction as claimed by Elton Mayo. Do you think he succeeded? (6)

3 Herzberg found that responsibility had the longest-lasting effects on job satisfaction. Why may this be the case? (5)

4 Discuss which of the factors is the most important motivator. (8)

B2 Case study

Tania was delighted to get the bakery job and looked forward to her first shift. It would be tiring after a day at college, but £52 for eight hours on a Friday would guarantee good Saturday nights in future.

On arrival, she was surprised to be put straight to work, with no more than a mumbled 'You'll be working packing machine B.' Fortunately, she was able to watch the previous shift worker before clocking-off time, and could get the hang of what was clearly a very simple task. As the 18.00 bell rang, the workers streamed out, but not many had yet turned up from Tania's shift. The conveyor belt started to roll again at 18.16.

As the evening wore on, machinery breakdowns provided the only, welcome, relief from the tedium and discomfort of Tania's job. Each time a breakdown occurred, a ringing alarm bell was drowned out by a huge cheer from the staff. A few joyful moments followed, with dough fights breaking out. Tania started to feel quite old as she looked at some of her workmates.

At the 22.00 meal break, Tania was made to feel welcome. She enjoyed hearing the sharp, funny comments made about the shift managers. One was dubbed 'Noman' because he was fat, wore a white coat and never agreed to anything. Another was called 'Turkey' because he strutted around, but if anything went wrong, got into a flap. It was clear that both saw themselves as bosses. They were not there to help or to encourage, only to blame.

Was the bakery always like this, Tania wondered? Or was it simply that these two managers were poor?

Questions

(25 marks; 30 minutes)

1 Analyse the working lives of the shift workers at the bakery, using Herzberg's two factor theory. (8)

2 If a managerial follower of Taylor's methods came into the factory, how might s/he try to improve the productivity level? (7)

3 Later on in this (true) story, Tania read in the local paper that the factory was closing. The reason given was 'lower labour productivity than at our other bakeries'. The newspaper grumbled about the poor attitudes of local workers. Consider the extent to which there is some justification in this view. (10)

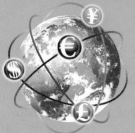

MOTIVATION IN PRACTICE

Assessing how firms try to motivate their staff and how successful these actions appear to be. In this context, companies take 'motivation' to mean enthusiastic pursuit of the objectives or tasks set out by the firm.

28.1 Introduction

There are four main variables that influence the **motivation** of staff in practice:

1 the financial reward systems

2 job design

3 empowering the employees

4 working in teams.

All four will be analysed with reference to the theories outlined in Unit 27.

Motivation: famous sayings

'The worst mistake a boss can make is not to say well done.' *John Ashcroft, British executive*

'Motivation is everything. You can do the work of two people, but you can't be two people. Instead, you have to inspire the next guy down the line and get him to inspire his people.' *Lee Iacocca, successful boss of Chrysler Motors*

'I have never found anybody yet who went to work happily on a Monday that had not been paid on a Friday.' *Tom Farmer, Kwik-Fit founder*

'Motivating people over a short period is not very difficult. A crisis will often do just that, or a carefully planned special event. Motivating people over a longer period of time, however, is far more difficult. It is also far more important in today's business environment.' *John Kotter, management thinker*

'My best friend is the one who brings out the best in me.' *Henry Ford, founder of Ford Motors*

28.2 Financial reward systems

Piecework

Piecework means working in return for a payment per unit produced. The payment itself is known as piece rate. Pieceworkers receive no basic or shift pay, so there is no sick pay, holiday pay or company pension.

Piecework is used extensively in small-scale manufacturing – for example, of jeans or jewellery. Its attraction for managers is that it makes supervision virtually unnecessary. All the manager need do is operate a quality control system that ensures the finished product is worth paying for. Day by day, the workers can be relied upon to work fast enough to earn a living (or a good) wage.

Piecework has several disadvantages to firms, however:

● scrap levels may be high, if workers are focused entirely on speed of output

● there is an incentive to provide acceptable quality, but not the best possible quality

● workers will work hardest when they want higher earnings (probably before Christmas and before their summer holiday); this may not coincide at all with seasonal patterns of customer demand

● worst of all is the problem of change; Herzberg pointed out that 'the worst way to motivate people is piece rate...it reinforces behaviour'; focusing people on maximising their earnings by repeating a task makes them very reluctant to produce something different or in a different way (they worry that they will lose out financially).

Performance-related pay

Performance-related pay (PRP) is a financial reward to staff whose work is considered above average. It is used for employees whose work achievements cannot be assessed simply through numerical measures (such as units produced or sold). PRP awards are usually made after an appraisal process has evaluated the performance of staff during the year.

On the face of it, PRP is a highly attractive system for encouraging staff to work towards the organisation's objectives. The usual method is:

1 establish targets for each member of staff/management at an appraisal interview

2 at the end of the year, discuss the individual's achievements against those targets

3 those with outstanding achievements are given a Merit 1 pay rise or bonus worth perhaps 6% of salary; others receive between 0% and 6%.

Despite the enthusiasm they have shown for it, employers have rarely been able to provide evidence of the benefits of PRP. Indeed the Institute of Personnel and Development concluded in a report that:

> It was not unusual to find that organisations which had introduced merit pay some years ago were less certain now of its continued value … it was time to move on to something more closely reflecting team achievement and how the organisation as a whole was faring.

This pointed to a fundamental problem with PRP: rewarding individuals does nothing to promote teamwork. Furthermore it might create unhealthy rivalry between managers – each going for the same Merit 1 spot.

Other problems for PRP systems include the following.

● *Perceived fairness/unfairness*: staff often suspect that those awarded the maximum are being rewarded not for performance but out of favouritism; this may damage working relations and team spirit.

● *Whether they have a sound basis in human psychology*: without question Professor Herzberg would be very critical of any attempt to influence work behaviour by financial incentives; a London School of Economics study of Inland Revenue staff found that only 12% believed that PRP had raised motivation at work, while 76% said it had not; Herzberg would approve of the researchers' conclusion that 'The current system has not succeeded in motivating staff to any significant degree, and may well have done the reverse.'

As the last point illustrates, a key assumption behind PRP is that the chance to be paid a bit more than other employees will result in a change in individual behaviour, in increased motivation to work. A survey for the government publication *Employment in Britain* found that 'pay incentives were thought important for hard work by fewer than one in five, and for quality standards by fewer than one in ten.

So why do firms continue to pursue PRP systems? There are two possible reasons:

1 to make it easier for managers to manage/control their staff (using a carrot instead of a stick)

2 to reduce the influence of collective bargaining and therefore trades unions.

High-grade application
The greatest benefit?

In early 2007, *Human Resources* magazine asked a research company to analyse the impact of different benefits on employees 'engagement level' (i.e. their level of commitment and satisfaction at work). The most successful benefit proved to be home working (i.e. allowing staff to work at home for one day a week). Profit-related pay proved to have a very small benefit. The engagement level of staff without profit-related pay was 66.9%; with profit-related pay it was 69.3%. This increase of 2.4% compares with an increase of 8.4% when employees have the benefit of home working.

Despite this evidence, a spokesperson for John Lewis pointed out that the business had just paid out £155 million to its 'partners', giving a profit share worth 18% of annual salary. He made it clear that John Lewis staff 'don't take it for granted'.

Profit sharing

A different approach to financial incentives is to provide staff with a share of the firm's annual profit. This puts staff in the same position as shareholders as, in effect, they are paid an annual dividend. This offers clear psychological benefits, as outlined below.

● Staff can come to see profit positively. Before, they may have regarded it as an unfair way of diverting pay from their own pockets to those of shareholders.

● Herzberg and other theorists warn that financial incentives distort behaviour. For example, if you pay a striker £500 per goal, wave goodbye to passing in the penalty area. Profit sharing, however, is more of a financial reward than an incentive. It may encourage

Table 28.1 The pros and cons of profit sharing

Pros	Cons
Encourages staff to think about the whole business, not just their own job	If the employee share is only a small proportion of annual profit, the payouts may be meaninglessly small
Encourages thinking about cost saving as well as revenue raising	Large payouts, though, may either hit shareholder dividends or reduce the investment capital for long-term expansion
Focus on profit may make it easier for staff to accept changes in working practices (i.e. it may lessen resistance to change)	Because no single individual can have much impact on overall profits, there may be no incentive effect

people to work harder or smarter, but should not stop them working as a team.

- If paid to staff in the form of free shares, the employees may develop a strong sense of identity with the company and its fortunes.

Profit sharing can represent a substantial bonus on top of regular earnings. For instance, the John Lewis Partnership pays an annual bonus that can be worth over 20% of an employee's earnings, typically around £2000. In other cases, such as Tesco, the profit share amounts to no more than £100 or so. At such a low level it is clearly more of a thank you than a serious incentive.

Fringe benefits

These are forms of reward other than income. Some managers have generous expense accounts; many have company cars. Usually all maintenance and running costs are paid by the company. In some cases, even petrol for private mileage can be charged to the employer. Other fringe benefits include:

- membership of clubs or leisure centres
- low-interest-rate loans or mortgages
- discounts on the company's products, such as the British Airways' staff perk of air fares at 90% off.

In all cases, fringe benefits are offered to encourage staff loyalty and to improve human relations.

28.3 Job design

Herzberg's theory (see Unit 27) emphasised the importance of job design. He wanted employers to create jobs with the maximum scope to be motivating. For example, when Jose Mourinho became Chelsea manager, he was allowed the independence and authority to buy

and sell players as he thought best. He had full power over the tactics and the budget for running the team. Two years later, club owner Abramovic had brought in a managing director and a director of football to restrict the manager's powers. Players were bought against Mourinho's wishes. The result was Mourinho's evident job dissatisfaction during the 2006/07 season. His job had been redesigned in the worst way possible. Instead of being empowered to show what he could do, Mourinho was being held back by his bosses.

Job design is the thought process of deciding what tasks each employee must do, what equipment they will have, what decision-making power they will have and whether they are working alone or in a team. F. W. Taylor believed that management should design jobs to be simple, repetitive and easily monitored. Today, the term job design usually refers to job enrichment or job enlargement.

Job enrichment

Professor Herzberg defines job enrichment as 'giving people the opportunity to use their ability'. A full explanation of his theory is outlined in Unit 24.

How can job enrichment be put into practice? The key thing is to realise the enormity of the task. It is not cheap, quick or easy to enrich the job of the production line worker or the supermarket checkout operator. The first thought might be to add more variety to the work. The supermarket operator might switch between the checkout, shelf-stacking and working in the warehouse. Known as job rotation, this approach reduces repetition but still provides the employee with little challenge. Herzberg's definition of job enrichment implies giving people 'a range of responsibilities and activities'. Job rotation only provides a range of activities. To provide job enrichment, workers must have a complete unit of work (not a repetitive fragment), responsibility for quality and for self-checking, and be given the opportunity to show their abilities.

Full job enrichment requires a radical approach. Take a conventional car assembly line, for example. As shown in Figure 28.1, workers each have a single task they carry out on their own. One fits the left-hand front door to a car shell that is slowly moving past on a conveyor belt – every 22 seconds. Another worker fits right-hand front doors, and so on. Job enrichment can be achieved only by rethinking the production line completely.

Figure 28.1 Traditional production line

Figure 28.2 shows how a car assembly line could be reorganised to provide a more enriched job. Instead of working in isolation, people work in groups on a significant part of the assembly process. An empty car shell comes along the conveyor belt and turns in to the Interior Group Area. Six workers fit carpets, glove boxes, the dashboard and much else. They check the quality of their own work, then put a rather impressive-looking vehicle back on the conveyor belt. Not only does the teamwork element help meet the social needs of the workforce, but there are also knock-on effects.

Figure 28.2 Enriched 'teamworking' line

The workers can be given a time slot to discuss their work and how to improve it. When new equipment is needed, they can be given a budget and told to get out to meet potential suppliers. In other words, they can become managers of their own work area.

Such a major step would be expensive. Rebuilding a production line might cost millions of pounds and be highly disruptive in the short term. There would also be the worry that team working might make the job more satisfying, yet still be less productive than the boring but practical system of high **division of labour**.

Job enlargement

Job enlargement is a general term for anything that increases the scope of a job. There are three ways in which it comes about.

1 *Job rotation:* increasing a worker's activities by switching between tasks of a similar level of difficulty. This does not increase the challenge, but may reduce the boredom of a job.

2 *Job loading:* increasing workload, often as a result of redundancies. It may mean having to do more of the same, but often entails one or two extra activities that have to be taken on.

3 *Job enrichment:* this enlargement of the scope of the job involves extra responsibilities and challenges, as well as extra activities/workload.

Of these, only job enrichment is likely to provide long-term job satisfaction. Employers may like to use the term job enrichment, but often they are really carrying out job rotation or job loading.

28.4 Empowerment

Empowerment is a modern term for delegation. There is only one difference between the two. The empowered worker not only has the authority to manage a task, but also some scope to decide what that task should be. An IKEA store manager has power delegated to him/her, but head office rules may be so rigid that the manager has little scope for individual judgement. An empowered store manager would be one who could choose a range of stock suited to local customers, or a staffing policy that differs from the national store policy.

Empowerment means having more power and control over your working life, having the scope to make significant decisions about how to allocate your time and how to move forward. It is a practical application of the theories of Mayo and Herzberg. It may lead to greater risks being taken, but can also lead to opportunities being identified and exploited. Above all else, it should aid motivation.

The only major worry about empowerment in recent years has come from the financial services industry. A trader called Nick Leeson carried out a series of reckless trades that lost hundreds of millions of pounds and brought about the collapse of Barings Bank. In the credit squeeze of 2007, a series of other speculative failures emerged. In most cases, a fundamental problem was that the company bosses did not understand fully the risks that were being taken. Empowerment is highly dangerous in a situation of ignorance.

28.5 Team working

Team working is the attempt to maximise staff satisfaction and involvement by organising employees into relatively small teams. These teams may be functional (the 'drive-thru crew' at a McDonald's) or geographic. The key features of such teams are that they should be:

- multi-skilled, so that everyone can do everyone else's job

- working together to meet shared objectives, such as to serve every customer within a minute or produce a gearbox with **zero defects**

- encouraged to think of the future as well as the present, in a spirit of **kaizen (continuous improvement)**.

From a theoretical point of view, team working fits in well with Mayo's findings on the importance of group working and **group norms**. It can also be traced back to Maslow's emphasis on social needs. In practical terms, modern managers like team working because of the flexibility it implies. If worker A is absent, there are plenty of others used to dealing with the job. Therefore there is no disruption. Team working also gives scope for motivating influences such as job enrichment and quality circles.

Professor Charles Handy suggests in his book *Inside Organisations* (BBC Books, 1990) that 'a good team is a great place to be, exciting, stimulating, supportive, successful. A bad team is horrible, a sort of human prison.' It is true that the business will not benefit if the group norms within the team discourage effort. Nevertheless, team working has proved successful in many companies in recent years. Companies such as Rolls-Royce, Trebor, Rover and Komatsu have reported major improvements in absenteeism and labour turnover, and significant shifts in workforce attitudes.

High-grade application
Motivation at the RNLI

How do you motivate 4500 unpaid staff? Especially when you require them to put you before everything else, including family? This is the task of Ali Peck, human resources director for the RNLI, the Royal National Lifeboat Institution. If a boat capsizes in stormy weather, the lifeboatmen must stop whatever they are doing, put out to sea, and risk their own lives to save someone else's; 2006 saw a record number of rescues.

Peck's task is made more difficult because the 230 lifeboat stations are, of course, dotted around the coast. So the only way to bring people together is through training. Every lifeboatman has to go through a retraining programme every three to five years. This takes place at a purpose-built college. This is also where new volunteers are trained. Peck explains that the RNLI spends 50% more per head on training than any comparable organisation. It is crucial, because if the volunteers drifted away from the job, the organisation would fold. In the case of the RNLI, the staff motivations come from the teamwork and from a real sense of personal achievement and pride. The lifeboatmen certainly aren't in it for the money.

Issues For Analysis

The key ways to analyse motivation in practice are as follows.

- To select and apply the relevant motivation theory to the method being considered: good analysis of methods such as Performance Related Pay or job rotation require a critical eye.

- To question the publicly stated motives of the organisation or manager concerned: businesses can be very loose in their use of words such as motivation or empowerment. They can be euphemisms for tougher targets and greater pressure. If the recent history of a firm makes employees sceptical of the goodwill of managers, students should be equally questioning.

- As John Kotter has said, 'Motivating people over a short period is not very difficult.' The key test of a new approach to motivation is over a two- to five-year period, not the early months of a new initiative. So always consider the timescale.

28.6 Motivation in practice

an evaluation

There are many aspects of business studies that point solely towards money. How profitable is this price or that? What is the forecast net cash flow for April? And so on. In such circumstances it is understandable that human implications may be forgotten. Setting a high price for an AIDS cure may be profitable, but life-threatening to those who cannot afford the medicine. April's positive cash flow might be achieved only by sacking temporary staff.

When covering motivation in practice, there is little excuse for ignoring the implications for people. Exaggerated commissions or performance-related pay can lead sales staff to oversell goods or services, which may cause customers huge difficulties later on, such as cosmetic surgery or questionable investments. Also, within the workplace, serious problems can arise: bullying to 'motivate' staff into working harder, or creating a culture of overwork which leads to stress.

Fortunately, there are many businesses in which the management of motivation is treated with respect – companies which know that quick fixes are not the answer. Successful motivation in the long term is a result of careful job design, employee training and development, honesty and trust. It may be possible to supplement this with an attractive financial reward scheme, but money will never be a substitute for motivation.

Key terms

Division of labour: subdividing a job into small, repetitive fragments of work.
Group norms: the types of behaviour and attitude seen as normal within a group.
Kaizen **(continuous improvement):** moving productivity and product quality forward in regular, small steps.
Motivation: to professor Herzberg, it means doing something because you want to do it; most business leaders think of it as prompting people to work hard.
Zero defects: production that is right first time, therefore requiring no reworking; this saves time and money.

Exercises

A. Revision questions

(49 marks; 49 minutes)

1 'Job design is the key to motivation.' Outline one reason why this might be true, and one reason why it might not. (4)

2 Look at the famous saying by Lee Iacocca earlier in this Unit. Explain in your own words what he meant by this. (3)

3 How *should* a manager deal with a mistake made by a junior employee? (4)

4 State three reasons why job enrichment should improve staff motivation. (3)

5 Distinguish between job rotation and job enrichment. (4)

6 How does 'empowerment' differ from 'delegation'? (4)

7 Identify three advantages to an employee of working in a team. (3)

8 State two advantages and two disadvantages of offering staff performance-related pay. (4)

9 What might be the implications of providing a profit share to senior managers but not to the workforce generally? (5)

10 What problems might result from a manager bullying staff to 'motivate' them? (6)

11 Identify three key characteristics of a meaningful and well-designed job. (3)

12 State three ways in which employers can reward staff financially. (3)

13 Briefly explain the difference between job enlargement and job enrichment. (3)

B. Revision exercises

B1 Data response

Gambling on people

Procter & Gamble is the world's biggest advertiser and one of America's most respected companies. It is the company behind such brands as Fairy Liquid, Ariel, Crest, Max Factor, Head & Shoulders, Vidal Sassoon, Pringles, Sunny Delight and hundreds more. Behind its marketing success lies an exceptionally strong company culture and an advanced approach to the management of its people.

Procter & Gamble (P&G) was an early advocate of motivating staff by empowerment and job enrichment. Dave Swanson was the principal architect of the organisational design of the system. Swanson joined P&G in the early 1950s after studying at the Manchester Institute of Technology (MIT). While at MIT he had been inspired by the lectures of Professor Douglas McGregor. McGregor attacked the theory of command-and-control management, advocating empowerment. When Swanson had the opportunity to design a new detergent plant in Augusta, Georgia, he enlisted McGregor's help.

Processes were put in place to make communications and control flow up, down and sideways in a very easy, uninhibited way. They emphasised knowledge of the business and learning new skills for all employees of the plant. The objective was to push the Augusta plant to be as unstructured as possible: 'We were trying to take away the rule book and substitute principle for mandate . . . We wanted people to reach for responsibility,' Swanson said. They did. Factory productivity went up 30% and the system was expanded to other P&G plants.

In his book *What America Does Right*, Robert Waterman describes P&G as a pioneer in pushing leadership, responsibility and decision making down to the plant floor.

Source: C. Decker *P&G99*. HarperCollins

Questions

(30 marks; 35 minutes)

1 How might motivation be affected by 'taking away the rule book'? (6)

2 Explain the importance to staff motivation of freely flowing, accurate communication. (6)

3 Explain how the views of McGregor were put into practice by P&G's Dave Swanson (8)

4 In this case, high motivation boosted productivity by 30%. Discuss whether increased motivation need always result in increased productivity. (10)

B2 Activity

Write a questionnaire for self-completion by full-time employees. Your research objectives are to discover:

- whether there are any policies in place for encouraging workplace involvement/ consultation

- whether job enrichment or job rotation measures exist (and what their effect is)

- how your respondents would describe the workplace culture

- whether there are any financial bonuses available, such as piece rate or performance-related pay, and what is their effect on motivation

- how highly motivated they feel themselves to be

- how highly motivated they believe their colleagues are.

This questionnaire should be conducted with at least ten respondents. It is preferable for the questionnaire to be conducted face-to-face, but if that is not possible, self-completion is acceptable.

When the research is completed, analyse the results carefully and write a summary of them in report form.

B3 Data response

Training is the key choice for graduates

Training and development are rated more highly by graduates than the size of their salaries, according to a recent survey. The findings came from a web poll conducted for accountants Ernst & Young in 2007. The research found that 44% of the 1051 graduates who responded rated training opportunities most highly among potential first employers, with only 18% identifying salaries and benefits as their top concern. According to Stephen Isherwood, Ernst & Young's head of graduate recruitment, 'Despite the many concerns students have when thinking about their future employer, it is still critically important for many of them that their new job offers them opportunities to learn, and to develop their own careers.' Other aspects of work rated in the survey included work/life balance (16%), business reputation (12%), and people and culture (8%). Despite the recent interest by businesses in promoting their social credentials, ethical and environmental reputation received only 3% of the vote.

Source: Adapted from bbc.co.uk

Questions

(25 marks; 25 minutes)

1 Describe two costs associated with training employees. (3)

2 Using a suitable theory, examine the link between training and worker motivation. (8)

3 To what extent do you believe that the research carried out for Ernst & Young confirms the view that money does not motivate? Explain your answer. (14)

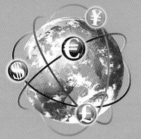

LEADERSHIP

DEFINITION

Management involves getting things done through other people. Leadership, at its best, means inspiring staff to achieve demanding goals. According to Peter Drucker, a manager does things right; a leader does the right thing.

29.1 Introduction to leadership styles

The way in which a manager deals with their employees is known as their management style. For example, some managers are quite strict with workers: they always expect deadlines to be met and targets to be hit. Others are more relaxed and understanding: if there is a good reason why a particular task has not been completed by the deadline, they will be willing to accept this and give the employee more time. Although the way in which everyone manages will vary slightly from individual to individual, their styles can be categorised under three headings: **autocratic**, **democratic** and **paternalistic** (see Table 29.1).

Autocratic managers are authoritarian: they tell employees what to do, and do not listen much to what workers themselves have to say. Autocratic managers know what they want doing and how they want it done. They tend to use one-way, top-down communication. They give orders to workers and do not want much feedback.

Democratic managers, by comparison, like to involve their workers in decisions. They tend to listen to employees' ideas and ensure that people contribute to discussion. Communication by a democratic manager tends to be two-way. The manager puts forward an idea and employees give their opinions. A democratic manager would regularly delegate decision-making power to junior staff.

The delegation of authority which is at the heart of democratic leadership can be approached in one of two main ways:

- Management by objectives, in which the leader agrees clear goals with staff, provides the necessary resources, and allows day-to-day decisions to be made by the staff in question; this approach was advocated by management guru Peter Drucker and by Douglas McGregor (see below) in his support for what he called the Theory Y approach to management.

- Laissez-faire ('let it be') management; this occurs when managers are so busy or so lazy that they do not take the time to ensure that staff know what to do or how to do it. Some people respond very well to the freedom to decide how to work; others may become frustrated.

It is said that, in the early days of Microsoft, Bill Gates hired brilliant students and told them no more than to create brilliant software. Was this a laissez-faire style or management by objectives? Clearly the dividing line can be narrow.

A paternalistic manager thinks and acts like a father. He or she tries to do what is best for the staff/children. There may be consultation to find out the views of the employees, but decisions are made by the head of the 'family'. This type of manager believes employees need direction, but thinks it is important that they are supported and cared for properly. Paternalistic managers are interested in the security and social needs of the staff. They are interested in how workers feel and whether they are happy in their work. Nevertheless it is quite an autocratic approach.

Table 29.1 Assumptions and approaches of the three types of leader

	Democratic	Paternalistic	Autocratic
Style derived from:	Belief in Maslow's higher order needs or in Herzberg's motivators	Mayo's work on human relations and Maslow's lower and middle order needs	A Taylorite view of staff
Approach to staff	Delegation of authority	Consultation with staff	Orders must be obeyed
Approach to staff remuneration	Salary, perhaps plus employee shareholdings	Salary plus extensive fringe benefits	Payment by results, e.g. piecerate
Approach to human resource management	Recruitment and training based on attitudes and teamwork	Emphasis on training and appraisal for personal development	Recruitment and training based on skills; appraisal linked to pay

29.2 McGregor's Theory X and Theory Y

In the 1950s, Douglas McGregor undertook a survey of managers in America and identified two styles of management, which he labelled Theory X and Theory Y (see Table 29.2).

Theory X managers tend to distrust their subordinates; they believe employees do not really enjoy their work and that they need to be controlled. In McGregor's own words, many of these managers believe that 'the average human being has an inherent dislike of work and will avoid it if he can'. Note that McGregor is not putting it forward as a theory about workers, but about managers. In other words, Theory X is about the view that managers have of their workforce.

Theory Y managers, by comparison, believe that employees do enjoy work and that they want to contribute ideas and effort . A Theory Y manager is, therefore, more likely to involve employees in decisions and give them greater responsibility. The managerial assumptions identified by McGregor as Theory Y included:

● 'Commitment to objectives is a function of the rewards associated with their achievement.'

● 'The average human being learns, under proper conditions, not only to accept but to seek responsibility.'

● 'The capacity to exercise a relatively high degree of imagination, ingenuity and creativity in the solution of organizational problems is widely, not narrowly, distributed in the population.'

(Source: *The Human Side of Enterprise*, D. McGregor, Penguin Books, 1987, first published in 1960)

It is clear that Theory Y managers would be inclined to adopt a democratic leadership style. Their natural approach would be to delegate authority to meet specific objectives.

Table 29.2 Beliefs of Theory X and Theory Y managers

Beliefs of Theory X managers	Beliefs of Theory Y managers
Employees dislike work and will avoid it if they can	Putting some effort into work is as natural as play or rest; employees want to work
Employees prefer to be directed, want to avoid responsibility and have little ambition	Employees want responsibility, provided there are appropriate rewards
Employees need to be controlled and coerced	Employees are generally quite creative

The Theory X approach is likely to be self-fulfilling. If you believe people are lazy, they will probably stop trying. Similarly if you believe workers dislike responsibility, and fail to give them a chance to develop, they will probably stop showing interest in their work. They end up focusing purely on their wage packet because of the way you treat them.

In his book *The Human Side of Enterprise*, McGregor drew upon the work of Maslow and Herzberg. It need be no surprise that there are common features to the theories of these three writers. McGregor's unique contribution was to set issues of industrial psychology firmly in the context of the management of organisations. So whereas Herzberg's was a theory of motivation, McGregor's concerned styles of management (and therefore leadership).

So, which is the 'right' approach? Clearly a Theory Y manager would be more pleasant and probably more interesting to work for. However, a Theory X approach can work. It is especially likely to succeed in a business employing many part-time, perhaps student, workers, or in a situation where a business faces crisis.

High-grade application

On 19 February 2008, the Liverpool FC manager Rafa Benitez was under intense pressure. A bright start to the season had descended into patchy league form and an embarrassing FA cup defeat to Barnsley. Now it was make or break, with a Champions League game against the mighty Inter Milan. A defeat would surely lead to a Benitez resignation; a victory would give a small amount of breathing space (until the second leg, at least). Among Liverpool supporters, there had always been faith in Benitez, and criticism of the club's American owners. But this match would be a huge test of leadership. Could he inspire the players to give everything for him and for the club?

Unlike the Premier League's best managers, Arsène Wenger and Alex Ferguson, Benitez had always seemed rather distant. Wenger and Ferguson practise a management style that is simultaneously paternalistic and autocratic. Benitez seemed only autocratic, making decisions on team selection that baffled everyone, yet never feeling the need to explain.

90 minutes after writing this, Liverpool had won 2-0 and Benitez was the hero.

29.3 Charismatic leadership

Gordon Brown is a highly intelligent man whose leadership of the British economy between 1997 and 2006 was brilliant. Yet he has no charisma, which is to say that people are not inspired by him; they do not even warm to him. He therefore has an enormous difficulty in communicating his ideas in a way that makes people want to follow his lead. There is a strong case for saying, therefore, that personal charisma is an important quality in a leader.

Yet it is important to remember that some charismatic historical leaders, such as Napoleon and Hitler, have led people to disaster. Perhaps some charisma is good, but too much is dangerous. In recent times in business, the most charismatic leader was BP's Lord Browne. On 25 July 2006, *The Guardian* ran a leader article that began 'Lord Browne, the chief executive of the BP group, is the nearest thing British business has to a rock star'. The paper went on to describe Richard Branson as a 'mere pygmy' compared with the leader of 'one of the world's largest companies'. The article also said that 'the 96,000 people employed by BP around the world all have cause to admire Lord Browne's achievements'. Within six months, Lord Browne had resigned from BP in a personal scandal. Those looking back today at Lord Browne's leadership are largely critical, especially of his company's approach to safety and the environment.

Figure 29.1 Richard Branson: enough charisma, but not too much?

29.4 Which is the best style of leadership?

Each style of management can work well in different situations. If there is a crisis, for example, people often look for a strong leader to tell them what to do. Imagine that sales have unexpectedly fallen by 50 per cent, causing uncertainty, even panic, within the organisation. The management needs to take control quickly and put a plan into action. An autocratic style might work well at this moment. In a stable situation where employees are trained and able to do their work successfully, a more democratic leadership style might be more appropriate. It is often said that countries elect very different types of leaders when there is a threat of

Figure 29.2 Factors affecting leadership style

war or economic instability than when the country is doing well. Similarly, think about how people react when they are learning to drive. For the first few lessons they are uncertain what to do and are grateful to be told. Once they have passed their test and have driven for several years they will no doubt resent anyone telling them how to drive better!

The best style of management at any moment will depend on an enormous range of factors, such as the personalities and abilities of the manager and the workers, and the nature of the task (see Figure 29.2). Imagine a confident manager who knows her job well but is faced with an unusually difficult problem. If the staff are well trained and capable, the manager would probably ask for ideas on what to do next. If, however, the manager was faced with a fairly routine problem, she would probably just tell the employees what to do because there would be no need for discussion.

A manager's style should, therefore, change according to the particular situation and the people involved. It will also vary with the time and degree of risk involved. If a decision has to be made urgently and involves a high degree of risk, the manager is likely to be quite autocratic. If there is plenty of time to discuss matters and only a low chance of it going wrong, the style may well be more democratic.

29.5 Does the style of management matter?

The way in which a manager deals with his or her colleagues can have a real impact on their motivation and how effectively they work. An experienced

workforce which is used to being involved in decisions may resent a manager who always tries to tell them what to do. This might lead to a reduction in the quality of their work, a fall in productivity and an increase in labour turnover. If, however, these employees were involved in decision-making, the firm could gain from better ideas and a more highly motivated workforce. This does not mean that everyone wants to be involved or indeed that it is appropriate. Employees may lack the necessary training or experience, and so a democratic approach might simply mean taking longer for management to reach the decision it was going to make anyway.

What is the most common style of management?

The style of management which people adopt depends on many factors such as their personality, the particular circumstances at the time and the culture of the organisation. Although we have discussed three main styles, the actual approach of most managers is usually a combination of all of them, depending on the task or the nature of the situation. If an order has to be completed by tomorrow and time is short, for example, most managers are likely to be autocratic to make sure it gets done. If, however, there is plenty of time available, the manager may be more democratic. No-one is completely autocratic or completely democratic, it is simply a question of degree. However, some managers do tend to be more autocratic than others. This often depends on their own experiences (What was their boss like? What worked well when they were being trained?) and their personality (Do they like to be in control of everything? Are they willing to delegate? Do they value the opinions of others?).

In recent years there has been a move towards a more democratic style of management in the UK. This is probably because employees expect more from work than they did in the past. They are better educated, have a higher basic standard of living and want more than just money in return for their efforts. Having satisfied their lower level needs, they are now looking to satisfy their higher level needs. The growth of democratic management and greater participation has also coincided with the move towards lean production and the emphasis on techniques such as total quality management. These methods of production require much more involvement by the employees than in the past. Employees are given control over the quality of their own work, given the authority to make decisions over the scheduling of work and expected to contribute ideas on how to improve the way they are working. This approach requires much more trust in employees than was common many years ago. It has to be matched with a more democratic leadership style.

29.6 How leaders increase productivity

Increase investment in modern equipment

With modern, sophisticated machines and better production processes, output per worker should improve. Many modern factories have very few production workers; mechanisation and automation are everywhere. However, firms face financial constraints and should be cautious about assuming that mechanisation guarantees higher profits.

Many managers call for new technology when in fact more output can be squeezed out of the existing equipment. It may prove more efficient to run the machines for longer, spend more on careful maintenance to prevent breakdowns and discuss how to improve working practices. Firms can often achieve significant productivity gains without new equipment. This is the reason for the success of the *kaizen* approach taken by many firms. Important benefits can be achieved from what seem like relatively small changes to the way the firm operates rather than large-scale investment in technology.

Improve the ability level of those at work

To increase productivity a firm may need to introduce more training for its employees. A skilled and well-trained workforce is likely to produce more and make fewer mistakes. Employees should be able to complete the task more quickly and will not need as much supervision or advice. They will be able to solve their own work-related problems and may be in a better position to contribute ideas on how to increase productivity further.

However, firms are often reluctant to invest in training because employees may leave and work for another firm once they have gained more skills. Training also involves higher costs in the short run, which the business may not be able to afford, and the actual training period may cause disruptions to the normal flow of work. There is also a danger that the training will not provide sufficient gains to justify the initial investment, so any spending in this area needs to be properly costed and researched. Simply training people for the sake of it is obviously of limited value. However, in general UK firms do not have a particularly good record in training and more investment here could probably have a significant effect on the UK's productivity levels.

It should also be remembered that elaborate training may not be necessary for a firm that recruits the right people. Great care must be taken in the selection process to find staff with the right skills and attitudes. A firm with a good reputation locally will find it much easier to pick the best people. This is why many firms take great care over their relations with the local community.

Improve employee motivation

Professor Herzberg once said that most people's idea of a fair day's work was less than half of what they could give if they wanted to. The key to success, he felt, was to create the circumstances in which people wanted to give all they could to the job. His suggestions on how to provide job enrichment are detailed in Unit 24.

There is no doubt that motivation matters. A motivated salesforce may achieve twice the sales level of an unmotivated one. A motivated computer technician may correct twice the computer faults of an unmotivated one. And, in both cases, overall business performance will be affected.

The role of management

The management's style and ability can have a significant impact on motivation and on how effectively resources are used. Good managers can bring about substantial productivity gains through well-organised work, the effective management of people and the coordination of resources. Bad managers can lead to wastage, inefficiency and low productivity.

High-grade application
Motivation on the pitch

When Fulham Football Club appointed a new groundsman, few people even noticed. The fans had always been proud of the pitch, but newly appointed Frank Boahene was not impressed. He thought the pitch needed a dramatic improvement before the August start to the new season. With no time to re-seed the pitch, he decided the best way to strengthen the grass was to cut it three times a day! First thing in the morning and last thing in the afternoon was not a problem, but he also chose to 'pop back' from his home in Reading (an hour's drive) to do the third cut at 11 o'clock at night. That's motivation!

Perhaps the key management role is to identify increasing productivity as a permanent objective. For example, Japanese bulldozer company Komatsu set a target of a 10% productivity increase every year, until the world-leading American producer Caterpillar had been overtaken. In many firms, productivity is not a direct target – the focus, day by day, is on production, not productivity. After all, it is production that ensures customer orders are fulfilled. An operations manager, faced with a 10% increase in orders, may simply ask the workforce to do overtime. The work gets done; the workforce is happy to earn extra money; and it's all rather easy to do. It's harder by far to reorganise the workplace to make production more effective. Managers whose main focus is on the short term, therefore, think of production not productivity.

Key terms

Autocratic managers: managers who keep most of the authority to themselves; they do not delegate much or share information with employees. They tend to tell employees what to do.

Democratic managers: managers who take the views of their subordinates into account when making decisions. They discuss what needs to be done and employees are involved in the decision.

Paternalistic managers: managers who believe that they know what is best for the employees. They tend to tell employees what to do but will often explain their decisions. They are also concerned about the social needs of employees.

Issues For Analysis

Management style can have a significant impact on the way people work. Managed with the right approach, employees are likely to be more motivated and show greater commitment. Therefore, effective analysis of leadership should be rooted in the theories of writers such as Mayo and Herzberg.

● The 'correct' management style will depend on factors such as the task, the people involved and the amount of risk. There is no one style which is always appropriate. Therefore the context of the business case is always relevant.

● It may not be easy for managers to change their style. There may be situations in which managers should be more democratic; this does not necessarily mean they will be. Effective management training could be a useful way to persuade managers to be flexible.

● There is some debate about the extent to which you can train people to become effective managers or leaders. One extreme view is that good managers and leaders are born that way: if this is true, companies have to put their resources into finding the right sort of people. It is more likely that a good leader is made by a combination of training and personal characteristics.

29.7 Leadership
an evaluation

All firms seek effective managers. Good managers make effective use of the firm's resources and motivate the staff; they provide vision and direction and are therefore a key element of business success. Look at any successful company and you will usually find a strong management team. The problem is knowing what it is that makes a good manager and what is the 'best' management style. Even if we thought we knew the best style, can we train anyone to adopt this approach or does it depend on their personality? There are, of course, no easy answers to these questions. The 'right' style of management will depend on the particular circumstances and the nature of the task. While it is possible to help someone develop a particular style, it will also depend on the individual's personality. As employees have benefited from a higher standard of living in the UK and have higher expectations of their work, managers have generally had to adopt a more democratic style in order to motivate people. However, there are plenty of autocratic managers who also succeed.

Exercises

A. Revision questions

(40 marks; 45 minutes)

1 Distinguish between autocratic and paternalistic management. (4)

2 Identify two features of democratic management. (2)

3 Outline one advantage and one disadvantage of an autocratic management approach. (4)

4 Distinguish between McGregor's Theory X and Theory Y. (4)

5 Why is it 'clear that Theory Y managers would be inclined to adopt a democratic leadership style'. (4)

6 Is there one correct leadership style for running a football team or a supermarket chain? (4)

7 Explain why autocratic managers may be more use in a crisis than democratic ones. (4)

8 Explain a circumstance in which an autocratic approach to leadership may be desirable. (4)

9 Many managers claim to have a democratic style of leadership. Often their subordinates disagree. Outline two ways of checking the actual leadership style of a particular manager. (4)

10 Analyse the leadership style adopted by your teacher/tutor. (6)

B. Revision exercises

B1 Data response

Leadership and management styles

Some business writers like to suggest that management is getting progressively better. Modern approaches, such as Human Resource Management and Investors In People, are presented as forces for good. Many seem to believe that autocratic management is a thing of the past, whereas modern managers are democratic and forward-thinking.

This optimism has recently been confounded by the Chartered Management Institute's 2007 *Quality of Working Life* report, which polled 1500 middle managers about the management styles they experience in the workplace; 40% (the highest response) experience a bureaucratic management style, 30% say it is autocratic, and just 17% describe it as innovative and 13% as entrepreneurial (see Figure 29.2).

Junior managers had an even worse impression of the prevailing approach, with 50% seeing it as bureaucratic and 40% as autocratic. Compared with a similar report three years before, there were increases for all three of the negative rankings.

What makes it all the more extraordinary is that there is clear evidence that firms would be better off with a more open, involving management approach. In the organisations with an autocratic style, only 44% enjoy their work, compared with 71% for those in other firms. The same report mentions rising absenteeism and labour turnover. No wonder people are leaving for new jobs if they think they can find greater job satisfaction elsewhere.

Perhaps the saddest finding is that the situation is even worse in the public sector than in the private. Teachers, nurses and civil servants work under the most bureaucratic and autocratic bosses around. So the problem does not really lie with the profit motive. As business journalist Simon Caulkin puts it: 'Most employees work in command-and-control organisations – in effect, centrally planned dictatorships that are set up to take orders from the chief executive rather than the customer.'

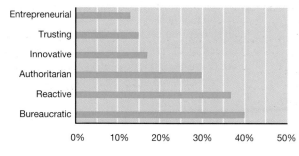

Figure 29.3 Management style where I work

Questions

Questions

(26 marks; 25 minutes)

1 Identify and explain the sections of the text that fit in with the ideas of Theory X and Theory Y. (5)

2a What types of leader would be suggested by a 'bureaucratic' style of management? (2)

2b Outline two possible effects on a large business of this type of management style. (4)

3 Discuss the implications for a company such as Apple of operating as a 'centrally planned dictatorship set up to take orders from the chief executive rather than the customer'. (15)

B2 Data response

Leading Tesco's rise

Terry Leahy became Tesco's Chief Executive in 1997. Since then he has hardly put a foot wrong. An article in *Management Today* (February 2004) probed him on his approach to leadership:

When you meet Leahy, you're not confronted with some huge presence … Blink and you would miss him.

What's his leadership style? 'I spend a lot of my time working on how I manage…' He meets with his executive committee every Monday and Wednesday morning for two hours, but what makes Leahy different is the extraordinary degree to which he chats with junior staff and absorbs their views, and the attention he pays to customers.

In Leahy's Tesco, the two – staff and customer – have become blurred. Tesco, he says, has always prided itself on being an 'egalitarian organisation'. It's a philosophy he's scrupulously followed. 'There are only six levels between me and a check-out assistant.' Every member of staff has the opportunity to train and rise up the ladder. This year, 10,000 Tesco staff will undergo training to move upwards.

'There's no officer class at Tesco, we don't have a graduate elite intake, there's no fast-track.' So speaks the chief who followed a girlfriend to London, got a casual job stacking

shelves in the local Tesco and never left. There can't be a store he hasn't visited, a job he doesn't know.

The people he started out with back then in 1979 are still his friends today, many of them at senior levels in the business. 'I must have spoken to thousands of staff – I've grown up with many of them,' he says.

In June, he went to a store in Royston and mucked in as a general assistant. Come on, this sort of thing – it's all for show, isn't it? 'Not at all, I enjoy it, I find it very satisfying. I'm learning as well. I want a better understanding of how these jobs are done.' Leahy makes all his senior staff do it. Last year, 1,000 store managers worked in other stores and 1,000 staff from head office did the same.

Questions

(25 marks; 30 minutes)

1 Analyse how Terry Leahy's approach compares with that of a charismatic leader. (6)

2 Explain which leadership style is closest to (Sir) Terry Leahy's leadership of Tesco. (8)

3 Discuss whether it is a good use of senior managers' time to spend a day working on the shopfloor. (11)

B3 Assignment

An investigation into a leader

1 Arrange to interview an employee. Preferably this person should be a full-timer who has worked for at least a year. The employee could be a manager but should not be a director.

2 Your objective is to gain a full understanding of the leadership style prevailing at the employee's workplace, and the style employed by the individual's own manager.

3 Devise your own series of questions in advance, but make sure to include the following themes:

a) How open are communications within the business?

b) Are staff encouraged to apply a questioning or critical approach?

29.4 Workbook

c) Are there any forums for discussion or debate on important policy issues affecting staff?

d) What does the organisational hierarchy look like? Where is your employee on that diagram? How powerful or powerless does he or she feel?

e) How exactly does the employee's boss treat him or her? Is there delegation? Consultation? How effective is communication between the two of them?

Write at least 600 words summarising your findings and drawing conclusions about how well the experience conforms to the leadership theory dealt with in this Unit.

C. Essay questions

1 'A good leader can always turn an ineffective business into a successful one.' To what extent can good management make a difference to the success of a firm?

2 'Management is no longer about leading others; it is about working with them.' Critically assess this view.

3 Consider the view that autocratic management has no place in today's business world.

4 'Good managers are born and not made.' Discuss this view.

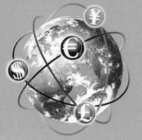

Unit 30

ORGANISATION STRUCTURE

DEFINITION

Organisational structure is the formal and systematic way the management of a business is organised. When presented as a diagram, it shows the departmental functions and who is answerable to whom.

30.1 Introduction

As organisations became larger and more complex, early management thinkers such as F. W. Taylor and H. Fayol considered how to structure an organisation. Both saw the function of organisations as converting inputs – such as money, materials, machines and people – into output(s). Therefore, designing an organisation was like designing a machine, the objective being to maximise efficiency. Early managers wanted to be told the best way to manage and the organisational structure that would work best.

Taylor and Fayol based their thoughts largely on the way an army is organised. The key features of the hierarchy would be:

● to break the organisation up into divisions with a common purpose – in business, this was usually the business functions (marketing, finance, and so on)

● every individual would answer to one person – their **line manager**

● no manager would be overloaded with too many subordinates, so the **span of control** was kept low

● to achieve low spans of control, it was necessary to have many management layers (see Table 30.1).

Table 30.1 Management layers

Military	Business
Captain	Senior manager
Lieutenant	Manager
Sergeant	Team leader
Corporal	Supervisor
Foot-soldier	Shop-floor worker

30.2 The growing business

In the early stages of a new business, there are often only one or two people involved. When the business is so small the day-to-day tasks are carried out by the owner(s). It is not necessary to have a formal organisation structure, as communication and coordination will be carried out on an informal, face-to-face basis. However, as the business grows and more people become involved, the firm will need to develop a more formal organisational structure. This will show the roles, responsibilities and relationships of each member of the firm. This is often illustrated through an organisational chart; this is a diagram that shows the links between people and departments within the firm. It also shows communication flows/channels, lines of authority and layers of hierarchy. Each of these terms will be explained later in the unit.

Consider the example in the box.

Case study: Crazy Beetles

Sara developed a small, but successful, business refurbishing old camper vans. The firm, called Crazy Beetles, started out on a very small scale but Sara soon discovered that there was a growing market for her services. The increasing demand led to her employing James as he had in-depth knowledge of the second-hand camper van market. Between them they did the buying, restoring, advertising and selling of the revamped vans. However, as the business grew, they needed to expand the workforce and this called for a more formal organisational structure. They decided to divide their business into three areas, as follows.

1 The *operations department* was involved in sourcing and buying old vans that needed revamping and then carrying out the necessary repairs and improvements.

Continued . . .

This was headed by Luke, who was a trained mechanic. Luke was responsible for five workers in his department; one of the workers, Pete, had two people in his section: Jon and Will.

2 The second department focused on *marketing* the finished product. This department advertised the vans and organised events to promote the company's name and services. Martha was in charge of this department as her business degree and additional experience equipped her with the skills and knowledge required. She had three subordinates (people she managed) in her department.

3 The final department was run by Steve, an accountant, who was responsible for managing the firm's *finances*. He had two financial assistants. The three department heads – Luke, Martha and Steve – were answerable to James, who dealt with the day-to-day issues; he, in turn, was answerable to Sara, who focused on the long-term plans for the business.

When reading this short case study, it is easy to become confused about the different roles and responsibilities adopted by those involved in the business. An organisational chart illustrates these more clearly and enables those within the firm and outside the firm to identify, more easily, who does what and who answers to whom. Figure 30.1 is a representation of the roles and responsibilities at Crazy Beetles.

30.3 The roles and relationships

This section describes the different roles and relationships within organisations and illustrates these with reference to Figure 30.1.

Roles

This describes the different tasks that the individuals are responsible for. At this point it is important to define responsibility, authority and accountability. Responsibility means carrying the burden of blame, even if an error is made by a subordinate. After all, if Alex Ferguson plays his reserve goalkeeper in a football match, it is Ferguson who will be blamed if the keeper lets in a soft goal. Authority means having the power to make a decision or carry out a task. However, if Martha delegated authority to Cathy to carry out a particular task, Martha would still retain the overall responsibility for that task. This shows how important it is for a manager to consider carefully to whom they delegate tasks. Accountability is the extent to which an individual is held responsible for her/his decisions and actions.

Directors

Members of 'the board' (i.e. the board of directors), who handle the most senior appointments and set out the main aims and objectives of the business. There are two types of director.

1 Executive directors are appointed to the board

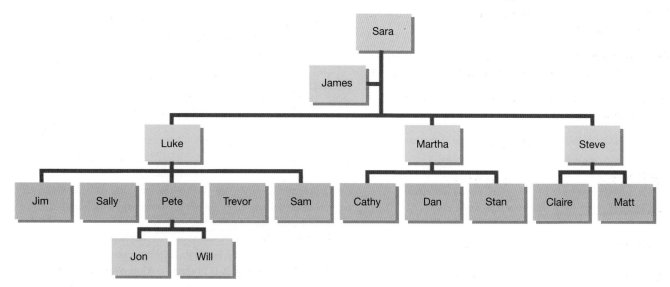

Figure 30.1 Crazy Beetles: roles and responsibilities

because they head up important divisions or departments (e.g. the marketing director).

2 Non-executive directors are part-time directors from outside the business; their job is to take an independent view of the shareholders' best interests.

Manager

Person responsible for organising others to carry out tasks. A line manager is the person immediately above someone in the organisational chart. For example, Stan's line manager is Martha.

Team leader

This role will usually arise in firms that organise themselves in a **matrix management** structure. This is where the firm allocates its workers to project teams rather than departments, and a team leader will manage the workers involved in a particular project. Project teams will be made up of people with different skills – for example, in a typical team there will be financial, marketing and operations specialists. This will enable them to make integrated decisions for the project. Building and engineering firms usually adopt this matrix approach in which the team leader is responsible for the management of the tasks and people involved.

30.4 Other key terms

Levels of hierarchy

These show the number of different supervisory and management levels between the bottom of the chart and the top of the hierarchy. In Crazy Beetles there are four levels of hierarchy.

Span of control

This describes the number of people directly under the supervision of a manager. Luke has the biggest span of control as he has four workers directly under him. If managers have very wide spans of control, they are directly responsible for many staff, in which case they may find that there are communication problems or the workers may feel that they are not being given enough guidance. The ideal span of control will depend upon the nature of the tasks, and the skills and attitude of the workforce and manager. (Table 30.2 lists the advantages and disadvantages of a narrow span of control.)

Chain of command

This shows the reporting system from the top of the hierarchy to the bottom (i.e. the route through which information travels throughout the organisation). In an organisation with several levels of hierarchy the chain of command will be longer; this could create a gap between workers at the bottom of the organisation and managers at the top. If information has to travel via several people there is also a chance that it may become distorted.

Centralisation and decentralisation

This describes the extent to which decision-making power and authority is delegated within an organisation. A centralised structure is one in which decision-making power and control remains in the hands of the top management levels. A decentralised structure delegates decision-making power to workers lower down the organisation. Many organisations will use a combination of these approaches depending upon the nature of the decision involved. For example, in many schools and

Table 30.2 Advantages and disadvantages of a narrow span of control

Advantages	**Disadvantages**
Allows close management supervision – vital if staff are inexperienced, labour turnover is high or if the task is critical (e.g. manufacturing aircraft engines)	Workers may feel over-supervised and therefore not trusted; this may cause better staff to leave, in search of more personal responsibility
Communications may be excellent within the small, immediate team (e.g. the boss and three staff)	Communications may suffer within the business as a whole, as a narrow span means more layers of hierarchy, which makes vertical communications harder
Many layers of hierarchy mean many rungs on the career ladder (i.e. promotion chances arise regularly – though each promotion may mean only a slightly different job)	The narrow span usually leads to restricted scope for initiative and experiment; the boss is always looking over your shoulder; this will alienate enterprising staff

colleges, the decisions concerning which resources to use will be decentralised (i.e. taken by teachers as opposed to the senior management team). Other decisions, concerning future changes in subjects being offered, may be centralised – that is, taken by senior managers.

Case study: Sugar Treat plc

Sugar Treat plc makes high quality cakes for large functions all over the country. As more and more people and businesses demand higher standards for the catering which they lay on at these functions, the business has grown in strength and now has six small factories operating in different parts of the country. The factories are run as separate profit centres and have their own production and training facilities. Marketing and all other functions are organised and run by the Board of Directors at their Head Office which is based in London.

Last year the HR Director received letters from the managers of two of the factories explaining that they did not feel qualified to train the workforce and that they had received complaints about the quality of some of the food served, and the attitude of some of the staff, at the functions.

The HRM Director decided to propose that they organise all training at Head Office so that a consistent standard of quality can be maintained.

Can you think of what advantages there are to Sugar Treat plc of giving each factory control over the production of cakes?

Do you think it is a good idea for the company to centralise all their training at their Head Office?

Communication flows

As firms grow, their organisational structure becomes more complex. Spans of control increase as more staff are hired, then get reduced when the business introduces a new layer of management. Staff love the extra promotion opportunities, but hate the disruption to their job role and, perhaps, status.

When these changes happen there can be severe effects on communication flows. A small team may be used to informal communication at every morning's coffee break and every Friday evening's drink after work. As more staff get taken on it may be necessary to have formal department meetings with notes ('minutes') taken. This may make the team weaker and the communication less effective.

The introduction of more layers of hierarchy is also problematic. Vertical communication becomes slower and less effective, especially if messages are conveyed verbally. Worst of all is that messages may possibly make it from the bottom to the top of the organisation, but rarely does the feedback follow on. So a policeman who wants to complain about racism in his/her station may never hear the outcome of the complaint.

A recent CIPD survey showed that just 55% of employees believed they were being kept informed about what the company was doing. 65% felt they were being given enough information to do their jobs effectively, implying that 35% were not! The survey went on to discover the three most effective communication channels:

1 Team briefings, 64%

2 Email, 59%

3 Intranet 38%

It is striking that none of these involves any real discussion between people. There is no way of telling whether that's how people like it, or perhaps they just don't see the opportunity for discussion.

Delegation

Delegation means passing authority down the hierarchy of a business, thereby spreading power down towards shop-floor staff. Effective delegation can be hugely motivating, turning time-clock-watching staff into enthusiasts who come in early on Mondays. The key is to make sure that staff take pride in the responsibility they are able to show and the trust that is shown in them. The key is for a manager to delegate meaningful tasks, rather than simply offloading the difficult or dull jobs. Among the many business benefits from delegation are:

● can motivate staff

● makes it easier in future to identify staff with the qualities needed for promotion

● allows the boss the opportunity to spend time planning and thinking, rather than doing.

High-grade application

Duncan Green is the managing director of a property-management company, Green Locations Ltd. He says: "I started my business from scratch and was used to being the main decision maker ... The company had reached a critical stage and I realised I needed to offload some work. Now, with my good managers, everything runs smoothly and I'm happy to give some of them full autonomy."

"Communication with employees about tasks they're taking on is important. But this means explaining what you need, rather than telling them how to do it. My employees might do something differently to the way I would, but providing they carry out tasks ethically and get the same or a better result, that's fine."

"I've had a very positive response. My working day tends to be less stressful now, because there's less on my plate. I have a bit more thinking time, while my employees enjoy having more responsibility and with it a greater sense of achievement ... Have trust in your employees and make the most of the skills that they have. Your delegating will improve their skills and they will become more motivated and productive."

Source: www.hie.co.uk

30.5 Organisation and management

A business is dynamic and evolves all the time. Its success is a function of the people who are involved in it and the way they are organised and managed. A structure is set at one point, with certain managers and employees in certain departments performing particular functions. As a business grows and develops, the organisation must be flexible enough to adapt to changes such as the introduction of new technology, changes in population structure, changes in legislation, changes in distribution methods etc.

But the organisation itself is not the only thing that must change. Managers cannot use the same methods of managing people as they did years ago. Employees are well educated and used to taking responsibility, and managers must react positively to this. When change takes place managers should, in many cases, respond by involving the workforce in planning and decision-making. Of course this is more important when managing strategic change.

Different organisational structures suit different types of manager:

- a wide flat structure with large spans of control suits a manager who is more democratic and uses delegation as part of their managerial style.

- a very tall structure with many layers and narrow spans of control better suits a less democratic manager who wants a greater degree of control over the workforce.

- a centralised structure means that all decisions go through the manager who has complete control of the business. This suits an autocratic manager.

- a decentralised structure takes decision-making away from the centre and delegates more responsibility to the employees. Decentralisation can take place by product or by geographical area.

30.6 Recent changes in organisation structures

In the past, some firms had very tall hierarchical structures, which meant many layers of management, often with quite narrow spans of control. This made them expensive to run because of the management salaries that had to be paid. Tall structures also resulted in longer chains of command, which could have a negative impact on communication. More recently, companies have liked to announce that they are becoming flatter – meaning fewer layers of management, with each manager having a wider span of control. Although some managers dislike this increased responsibility, their workers may thrive under the increased independence that is gained. Furthermore, the firm will have reduced overhead costs, which should mean greater efficiency.

Case study: Sugar Treat plc

Chuck Nuts plc has been making engineering parts for production machinery since the early 20th Century. Until 15 years ago their market was reasonably stable and profit levels had been maintained. However the outlook for engineering in this country has worsened with the introduction of new technology, and the closure, or relocation abroad, of many manufacturing businesses. The Board of Directors have decided that CN plc needs to invest in new products and expand into developing countries such as India and China. This will cost a significant amount of money and will include a major restructuring of the business.

Continued ...

At the moment the factory is divided into eight production areas with a Foreman, Supervisor and eight workers in each section. The Production Director has decided to combine the areas and create four sections with six multi-skilled workers in each and only one Supervisor for each section.

Why might the proposed restructure benefit Chuck Nuts plc?

How do you think these changes will effect the employees of Chuck Nuts plc?

Why is organisational structure so important?

As a firm grows, more people become involved. To ensure that the different tasks are fulfilled it is vital that every person is clear about what their role involves and who they are answerable to. Poor organisational structures will lack coordination and the following problems could result:

- poor communication leading to mistakes
- duplication of tasks
- tasks being overlooked
- different departments failing to work together effectively.

In the longer term, these problems will create a sub-standard service, and this will have an impact on the firm's sales, revenue and profit. As a firm expands, it must ensure that its organisation structure accommodates the growth.

Issues For Analysis

- When discussing the topic of organisation structure, it is important to recognise that the structures are not static and they should adapt to the environment in which they operate. If more people enter the firm, then changes should take place, and this may have an impact on the roles and relationships of the existing workers.

- The key to a top exam answer is to think about the match between the structure and the type of organisation. When Google started up, it had virtually no structure – brilliant people were hired and told to do brilliant things; the structure was deliberately loose. Today Google is a vast business, needing a tighter structure, but probably not so tight as to strangle innovation.

Key terms

Line manager: a manager responsible for meeting specific business targets, and responsible for specific staff.
Matrix management: where staff work in project teams in addition to their responsibilities within their own department; therefore staff can be answerable to more than one boss.
Span of control: the number of staff who are answerable directly to a manager.

30.7 Organisation structure
an evaluation

There is no 'ideal' organisational structure or span of control. What works for one business may fail in another, even if both are the same size. In exams there will usually be hints about whether the structure is working. A flat hierarchy may be at the heart of an innovative business, or there may be signs that staff lack direction and morale. A tall hierarchy may be at the centre of a focused, career-oriented workforce, or it may be bureaucratic and incapable of a quick decision. The judgement is yours.

Exercises

A. Revision questions

(47 marks; 47 minutes)

1 What is meant by the chain of command? (2)

2 Define span of control. (2)

3 Some theorists believe that the ideal span of control is between three and six. To what extent do you agree with this? (5)

4 Explain two implications of a firm having too wide a span of control. (4)

5 Explain what an organisational chart shows. (4)

6 Why is it important for a growing firm to think carefully about its organisational structure? (4)

7 State three possible problems for a business with many levels of hierarchy. (3)

8 What is meant by the term 'accountable'? (2)

9 What do you think would be the right organisational structure for a hospital? Explain your answer. (4)

10 Identify two reasons why a business might use an organisational chart. (2)

11 Explain what is meant by a narrow span of control. (3)

12 Describe one benefit and one drawback for a business of reducing the levels within its hierarchy. (4)

13 Outline two elements required for successful delegation. (4)

14 Outline two potential barriers to communication within a firm. (4)

15 Draw up a table showing the advantages and disadvantages to the **business** and to the **workforce** of:
   ● a centralised business
   ● a decentralised business by product
   ● a decentralised business by geographical area.

B. Revision exercises

B1 Data response

These following questions are based on the organisation structure of Crazy Beetles, featured in this unit.

Questions

(25 marks; 30 minutes)

1 Describe the chain of command that Sara would use if she needed to discuss overtime with Pete. (3)

2 What symptoms would indicate that James' span of control was too wide? (5)

3 Explain the usefulness of this chart for a new member of staff. (2)

4 How might Crazy Beetles use a matrix management approach? (5)

5 To what extent would Sara benefit if she introduced a more decentralised approach? (10)

B2 Data response

Chicken Little

Peter (known as 'Paxo') Little set up his free range chicken farm in the early 1990s. At the time it was an unusual move, especially on the grand scale envisaged by 'Paxo'. His farm had the capacity to produce 250,000 chickens every 45 days, making 4 million birds a year. Since then the business has grown enormously, to a turnover of £25 million today.

But Paxo is getting concerned that his business is not as efficient as it used to be. As Managing Director, he finds that he rarely hears from junior staff; not even the quality manager's 5 staff, who used to see him regularly. As he said recently to the Operations Director, 'the communication flows seem like treacle today, whereas they used to be like wildfire'.

Fortunately, the boom in demand for free range and organic produce has helped the business. So even though the team spirit seems to have slipped away, profits have never been higher. Unfortunately the Marketing Director keeps talking about rumours that a huge Dutch farming business is about to set up poultry farms in Britain. That might set the cat among the chickens.

Questions

(25 marks; 30 minutes)

1 a) What is the Managing Director's span of control? (1)

1 b) Comment on the strength and weaknesses of this organisational structure. (6)

1 c) How important does Human Resources seem within this business? (3)

2 Explain why vertical communications may not be as effective today as they used to be in the past at Chicken Little. (5)

3 Discuss the ways in which the Factory Manager might benefit or suffer from the organisational structure shown in the diagram. (10)

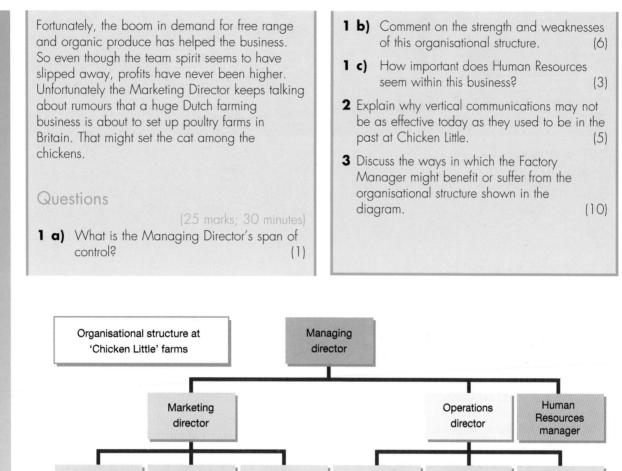

Figure 30.2 *Organisational structure at 'Chicken Little' Farms*

B3 Data response

Activities4U plc runs activity centres in four areas of the country. The centres offer courses for schools, colleges and large companies.

The head office of the company is in Manchester. The directors are based at the head office and oversee the marketing, finance and administration of the business. All other functions such as training and human resource management are decentralised and carried out within each activity centre. The training for company employees involves communication techniques, health and safety, team building, motivation and management.

There have been several complaints made by customers, especially about the attitude of some of the course leaders, and recently there was a

serious accident at one of the centres. The directors are aware that they are ultimately responsible for any compensation payments and that a poor safety record may affect the image of the business. They propose to centralise all training at head office.

Questions

(18 marks; 20 minutes)

1 Explain two reasons why marketing is centralised at the head office of Activities4U. (6)

2 Argue the case for centralising training at head office rather than within each activity centre. (12)

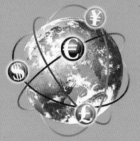

Unit 31

OPERATIONAL EFFICIENCY

DEFINITION

Capacity utilisation is the proportion of maximum possible output that is currently being used. A football stadium is at full capacity when all the seats are filled. A company producing 1500 units a week when the factory is capable of 2000 units has a capacity utilisation of 75%.

31.1 Operational targets

To run a successful operation such as Primark requires brilliant organisation and clear targets. The role of the targets is to help all staff aim at the same goal. The target at a hotdog stand outside a concert venue is to serve as many people as possible as quickly as possible, before and after the show. To achieve this the stallholder will plan ahead, cooking the sausages in advance and getting the onions ready. The most efficient stallholder will almost always make more money than the best cook. It is all down to clear targets and clear objectives.

There are three main targets focused on by operations managers:

1   quality targets (e.g. to have no more than 1 in 100 customers demand a refund)

2   capacity utilisation targets (e.g. that the factory should be working at 85–95% of its maximum possible capacity)

3   unit costs (e.g. keeping the average cost per unit at below £1.99, in order to keep the selling price below £2.99).

31.2 How is capacity utilisation measured?

Capacity utilisation is measured using the formula:

$$\frac{\text{current output}}{\text{maximum possible output}} \times 100$$

What does capacity depend upon? The amount a firm can make is determined by the quantity of buildings, machinery and labour it has available. Maximum capacity is achieved when the firm is making full use of all the buildings, machinery and labour available. The firm is said to be working at full capacity, or 100% capacity utilisation.

For a service business the same logic applies, though it is much harder to identify a precise figure. This is because it may take a different time to serve each customer. In a shop or a bank branch, demand may exceed capacity at certain times of the day, in which case queues will form. At other times the staff may have little to do. A service business wishing to stay cost-competitive will measure demand at different times of the day and then schedule the staffing level to match the capacity utilisation.

Many service businesses cope with fluctuating demand by employing temporary or part-time staff. These employees provide a far greater degree of flexibility to employers. Part-time hours can be increased, or extra temporary staff can be employed to increase capacity easily. If demand falls, temporary staff can be laid off without redundancy payments, or part-time staff can have their hours reduced, thus reducing capacity easily and cheaply. Many businesses like this flexibility as it limits wastage on staff costs. However, the situation may not be as appealing for employees, who have fewer rights than their full-time salaried predecessors. Figure 31.1 shows how flexible staffing (C) can reduce the wastage implied by having under-used full-time staff (A).

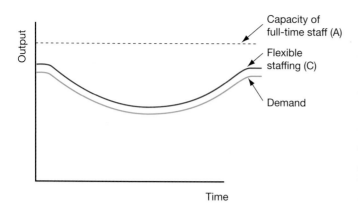

Figure 31.1 How flexible staffing (C) can reduce the wastage implied by having under-used full-time staff (A)

31.3 Fixed costs and capacity

It is vital to understand clearly the relationship between fixed costs and capacity utilisation. Fixed costs are fixed in relation to output. This means that whether capacity utilisation is 50% or 100%, fixed costs will not change. The implication of this is clear. If a football club invests in a huge, expensive playing staff (whose salaries are a fixed cost), but matches are played to a half-empty stadium, the fixed costs will become a huge burden. This is because the very fact that fixed costs do not change *in total* as output changes means that they do change *per unit* of output/demand. A half-empty stadium means that the fixed costs per unit are double the level at maximum capacity (see Table 31.1).

When the stadium capacity utilisation is at 50%, then, £10 of the ticket price is needed for the players' wages alone. The many other fixed and variable costs of running a football club would be on top of this, of course.

The reason why capacity utilisation is so important is that it has an inverse (opposite) effect upon fixed costs

per unit. In other words, when utilisation is high, fixed costs are spread over many units. This cuts the cost per unit, which enables the producer either to cut prices to boost demand further, or to enjoy large profit margins. If utilisation is low, fixed costs per unit become punishingly high. This problem was faced in 2007 by airline start-up Silverjet, which found its £12.8 million of revenue swamped by £31 million of costs.

The ideal level of capacity utilisation, therefore, is at or near 100%. This spreads fixed costs as thinly as possible, boosting profit margins. There are two key concerns about operating at maximum capacity for long, however. These are:

High-grade application

Gordon Ramsay: footballer, chef, TV personality. . .and business guru?

In his TV series *Ramsay's Kitchen Nightmares*, the renowned chef spent a lot of time swearing and criticising chefs for the way they cooked. The series placed Gordon at a failing restaurant for a week. His task was to wave a magic wand and turn it into a profitable business. In almost every episode of the series, Ramsay identified each restaurant's failure to use anything near its full capacity. Commonly, he suggested the introduction of a simple lunchtime menu to boost trade during the day, in addition to speeding up service in the evenings to ensure that every table would see at least two sittings in the main evening session. Ramsay's advice, delivered in his own inimitable way, was simply a call to push capacity utilisation higher in order to spread each restaurant's fixed costs over more units of output (customers). The advice usually worked.

Table 31.1 Fixed costs and capacity

	Full stadium	**Half-empty stadium**
	50,000 fans	25,000 fans
Weekly salary bill (fixed costs)	£250,000	£250,000
Salary fixed cost per fan	£5	£10
	(£250,000/50,000)	(£250,000/25,000)

1 the risk that if demand rises further, you will have to turn it away, enabling your competitors to benefit

2 the risk that you will struggle to service the machinery and train/retrain staff; this may prove costly in the long term, and will increase the chances of production breakdowns in the short term.

The production ideal, therefore, is a capacity utilisation of around 90%.

31.4 How to get towards full capacity

If a firm's capacity utilisation is an unsatisfactory 45%, how could it be increased to a more acceptable level of around 90%? There are two possible approaches, as discussed below.

Increase demand (in this case, double it!)

Demand for existing products could be boosted by extra promotional spending, price cutting or – more

High-grade application

Odeon: filling seats with anyone it can

Odeon is acutely aware of the dangers of having capacity empty during quiet times. In an attempt to increase capacity utilisation during the day and on quieter evenings, Odeon has introduced a number of specialised film showings, catering for groups who are more likely to visit the cinema during 'quiet periods':

● Odeon kids – Saturday and Sunday mornings and every day during school holidays
● Senior screen – mid-morning showings of traditional and modern classics for 'mature guests', with free tea and coffee
● Odeon Newbies – for parents with babies, mid-morning showings with volume quieter than usual and lights higher than usual, to try to create a calming environment for babies and parents
● Director's Chair – showing foreign-language, independent and art-house films for serious film buffs, one quiet evening per week.

Even with reduced ticket prices for some of these options, each seat sold is still making a contribution to covering fixed costs as capacity utilisation edges higher for the cinema chain.

fundamentally – devising a new strategy to reposition the products into growth sectors. If supermarket own-label products are flourishing, perhaps offer to produce under the Tesco or Sainsbury's banner. If doubling of sales is needed, it is unlikely that existing products will provide the whole answer. The other approach is to launch new products. This could be highly effective, but implies long-term planning and investment.

Cut capacity

If your current factory and labour force is capable of producing 10,000 units a week, but there is demand for only 4500, there will be a great temptation to cut capacity to 5000. This might be done by cutting out the night shift (i.e. making those workers redundant). This would avoid the disruption and inflexibility caused by the alternative, which is to move to smaller premises. Moving will enable all fixed costs to be cut (rent, rates, salaries, and so on), but may look silly if, six months later, demand has recovered to 6000 units when your new factory capacity is only 5000.

How to select the best option

A key factor in deciding whether to cut capacity or boost demand is the underlying cause of the low utilisation. It may be the result of a known temporary demand shortfall, such as a seasonal low point in the toy business. Or it may be due to an economic recession, which (on past experience) may hit demand for around 18–24 months. Either way, it might prove a mistake in the long run to cut capacity. Nevertheless, if a firm faces huge short-term losses from its excess fixed costs, it may have to forget the future and concentrate on short-term survival.

31.5 Why and how to change capacity

Firms may find themselves with **excess capacity** if demand for their products slows down. Unless the reduction in demand is just a short-term glitch, a firm will seek to find ways to reduce its maximum capacity. This process is commonly called **rationalisation** – it means reorganising in order to boost efficiency. The three main elements of rationalising are as follows.

1 Closing down and selling off a factory or part of a factory if the space will not be needed in the foreseeable future. Alternatively, the firm may decide to lease out factory space to other companies on a short-term basis. This will enable it to get the extra space back if demand improves.

2 Machinery can be sold off second-hand or for scrap. A more flexible solution is to rent machinery rather than buy it outright in the first place. This would enable the firm to return machinery in times when capacity needs to be reduced.

3 Redundancy is the obvious answer for a firm with too large a workforce. As this can prove expensive, firms may redeploy their employees to other jobs. This may be difficult for the employee, who feels pushed towards a job s/he had never wanted. Many firms with excess labour will cut down the length of time worked by employees, perhaps by shortening shifts.

31.6 Dealing with non-standard orders

Firms organise their operations around the amount they expect to sell in coming months. For a brand such as Marmite, which has sold quite steadily for more than 100 years, the factory can be set up to mass produce Marmite around the clock. Sales of the brand are not especially seasonal, and change little year on year. So an automated production line can be set up, requiring a minimum of labour and therefore minimal costs.

Figure 31.2 A brand such as Marmite may use subcontracting to deal with non-standard orders

A problem arises, though, when a non-standard order arrives. Perhaps China, not known for its Marmite eating, is influenced by a TV programme into deciding that it loves, rather than hates, the taste. So Chinese shops suddenly put through a series of huge orders to the UK Marmite factory. How can it cope if it is already being run at a high capacity utilisation?

The answer may lie in subcontracting. In other words, the main Marmite factory may have a permanent arrangement with a food-processing factory that it will supply Marmite, when ordered, within an agreed lead time. So, the extra order can be accepted, the product delivered within, perhaps, two weeks and the customer will be happy. The subcontracted production will have to be checked extra carefully for quality, but that is not difficult. Marmite itself will probably make less profit from subcontracted production than when using its own factory, yet it will still work out far better than permanently running an under-utilised factory just in case an extra order comes along.

Issues For Analysis

When developing an argument in answer to a case study or essay question, the following lines of analysis should be considered.

● The time frame of the question: is spare capacity caused by a short-term fall in demand or is there a longer-term downward trend? Only if the demand decline is a long-term trend should capacity be cut. It must be remembered, though, that it is always hard to be sure of these things. In the early 1990s, falling attendance at football matches meant that when clubs such as Manchester United and Newcastle rebuilt their stadiums, they cut the crowd capacity. Looking back, with Arsenal playing in the new Emirates stadium and Liverpool's new, bigger Anfield being built, it is easy to say they were wrong. At the time they made what seemed the right decision. So consider the timescale, but be careful of sounding too definite about the 'right' solution.

● The link between capacity utilisation, fixed costs per unit and profitability: if dealing with a question about how to improve profitability, increasing capacity utilisation could well be a valid solution. If profits are poor, be sure to ask what capacity utilisation is at present.

● Modern production theory praises systems such as just-in-time, **flexible specialisation** and lean production: successful management of all three of these approaches is likely to mean capacity utilisation that is well below 100%. This is because all these approaches require flexible responses to customer requirements/orders. In turn, this requires spare capacity. Can lean production yield enough other benefits to compensate for the poor capacity utilisation?

31.7 Operational efficiency
an evaluation

Most firms will aim to operate close to full capacity, but probably not at 100%. A small amount of spare capacity is accepted as necessary, bringing a certain degree of flexibility in case of need. In this way, sudden surges of demand can be coped with in the short run by increasing output, or **downtime** can be used for maintenance. Spare capacity can be a good thing, particularly in small doses.

Firms operating close to full capacity are those that may be considering investing in new premises or machinery. Building new factories takes time, as well as huge quantities of money. Can the firm afford to wait 18 months for its capacity to be expanded? Perhaps the firm would be better served subcontracting certain areas of its work to other companies, thus freeing capacity.

Capacity utilisation also raises the difficult issue of cutting capacity by rationalisation and, often, redundancy. This incorporates many issues of human resource management, motivation and social responsibility. There are fewer more important tests of the skills and far-sightedness of senior managers.

When tackling case studies, it is important that you take a step back from any that deal with such a situation, to consider the cause and the effect. Is excess capacity the problem or an indicator of another problem, such as declining market share? By showing the broader picture in this way you can also show the skill of evaluation.

Key terms

Downtime: any period when machinery is not being used in production; some downtime is necessary for maintenance, but too much may suggest incompetence.

Excess capacity: when there is more capacity than justified by current demand (i.e. utilisation is low).

Flexible specialisation: a production system based upon batches of goods aimed at many market niches, instead of mass production/mass market.

Rationalisation: reorganising in order to increase efficiency. This often implies cutting capacity to increase the percentage utilisation.

Exercises

A. Revision questions

(30 marks; 30 minutes)

1 What is meant by the phrase '100% capacity utilisation'? (3)

2 At what level of capacity utilisation will fixed costs per unit be lowest for any firm? Briefly explain your answer. (4)

3 What formula is used to calculate the capacity utilisation of a firm? (2)

4 How can a firm increase its capacity utilisation without increasing output? (3)

5 If a firm is currently selling 11,000 units per month and this represents a capacity utilisation of 55%, what is its maximum capacity? (4)

6 Use the following information to calculate profit per week at 50%, 75% and 100% capacity utilisation.

Maximum capacity	800 units per week	
Variable cost per unit	£1800	
Total fixed cost per week	£1.5 million	
Selling price	£4300	(9)

7 Briefly explain the dangers of operating at 100% capacity utilisation for any extended period of time. (5)

B. Revision exercises

B1 Data response

R. Sivyer & Co was founded 50 years ago. It has a successful history of manufacturing high-quality bicycle chains, which are supplied direct to retailers. In recent years, orders from retail customers have fallen, meaning that the firm is now manufacturing and selling only 12,000 chains per month.

The following cost information has been made available:

Materials cost per unit	80p
Shop floor worker's salary	£10,000 p.a.
Salary paid to other staff	£12,000 p.a.
Manager's salary	£32,000 p.a.
Maximum capacity	20,000 units per month
General overheads	£40,000 per month
Current selling price	£5.80
Number of managers currently employed	3
Number of shop floor staff currently employed	10
Number of other staff currently employed	4

The finance manager has called the other two managers to a meeting to discuss the firm's future. She puts forward two alternative courses of action:

1 make four shop floor and two other staff redundant, thus cutting the firm's fixed costs, and reducing maximum capacity to 12,000 units per month

2 sign a contract to supply a large bicycle manufacturer with a fixed quantity of 8000 chains per month at £5.80 each for the next four years; breaking the contract will lead to heavy financial penalties.

Questions

(30 marks; 35 minutes)

1 What is the firm's current monthly profit? (5)

2 Calculate the monthly profit that would result from each of the two options. (10)

3 Explain the advantages and disadvantages of each option. (10)

4 State which of the two options you would choose, and list any other information you would need before making the final decision. (5)

B2 Data response

Out of the red and into success

Steven Carragher had decided to set up a specialist sports goods store shortly after injury cut short his football career. With limited business experience, but plenty of local contacts, he bought a ten-year lease on a large high-street shop with plenty of floor space, along with storage on the two floors above the shop. He felt confident that business would be brisk as there were few specialised sports stores in Cheshire at the time. He blew most of his budget in preparing for the start-up, paying for the lease, a refit, staff training and plenty of stock to fill his stock rooms. With a little left over for a launch marketing campaign, he was optimistic on opening day. The first week was busy, with plenty of people coming in but few actually buying. By the end of the first month's trading, the picture had turned decidedly negative, with revenues failing to cover running costs and the store far from break-even.

Steven's old colleague Robbie knew a little about business and he pointed out that Steven was trying to run a small business in the sort of premises that a major chain store would expect to use. Robbie's solution had two main features:

1 turn the top floor of the building into a three-bedroom flat that could be rented out to cover 50% of the rent that Steven was paying

2 divide the shop in two, renting half the shop space to another retailer to help Steven cover the rent and bills.

When the two met again in 12 months, Steven paid for lunch. With both the flat and smaller shop unit rented out, he was now covering the costs of his shop comfortably. Meanwhile, Steven had set up an online ordering service that was proving to be highly successful.

Questions

(25 marks; 30 minutes)

1 Using the concept of capacity utilisation, analyse why Steven's business had initially failed to cover its costs. (6)

2a Explain why Robbie's ideas were always likely to improve Steven's profit. (4)

2b What crucial assumptions did Robbie make when offering his advice. (3)

3 Steven had few other options as a result of the length of his lease on the property. Use this case as a starting point to discuss why flexibility is vital in a small business start-up. (12)

32 Unit

APPROACHES TO ORGANISING PRODUCTION

32.1 Operational targets

The starting point for every operations manager is to obtain a plausible forecast of demand (i.e. how many products will be needed and when). This enables

High-grade application

Getting the sums right

Before the iPhone was launched in 2007, many financial analysts made forecasts of the likely level of sales. As can be seen from Table 32.1, the variations were extraordinarily wide, from 0.25 million to 1.7 million. This shows that getting operational targets correct is especially difficult when a new product is being launched.

In fact, Apple later reported that the actual sales volume was 1,120,000 in the period up to the end of September 2007, so Piper Jaffray & Co produced a brilliant forecast.

operational targets to be set. When the iPhone was launched in America in 2007, Apple ensured that it had stockpiled enough units to meet sales of 300,000 phones in the first day and a half. Often the launch of new products such as this gets bogged down with inadequate supplies and frustrated customers. A well-run organisation will do all it can to avoid this.

Setting targets can be helpful in any business context. They give staff something to work towards and give the firm something against which to check its actual performance. Achieving these targets is the fundamental indicator of successful operations management. Targets are the key to most operational decisions.

Different firms will have different operational targets, including:

● unit costs

● quality

● capacity utilisation.

Table 32.1 Apple iPhone: sales forecasts

	Sales to Sept 2007	Sales in year to Sept 2008
American Technology Research	250,000	–
Bear Stearns Ltd	650,000	–
Credit Suisse	1,700,000	12,300,000
Pacific Crest Securities	800,000	4,800,000
Piper Jaffray & Co	1,200,000	8,000,000
UBS AG	950,000	8,100,000
Apple Innovation Blog	1,500,000	10,500,000

Source: analysts' research reports, reported at Bloomberg.com

Unit costs

The cost of one unit of output is a raw measure of the efficiency of a firm's operations. Unit cost is calculated by dividing the total cost of production for a period by the number of units produced, as shown below:

$$\frac{\text{Total cost}}{\text{Total output}} = \text{unit cost}$$

For example:

$$\frac{\text{Total cost for March}}{\text{Total output for March}} = \frac{£64,000}{32,000 \text{ units}} = £2 \text{ per unit}$$

Unit costs can be reduced in one of three ways: by cutting variable costs, perhaps by running the business with lower wastage levels; by cutting fixed costs; or by increasing sales volumes so that the firm's existing fixed costs are spread over more units of sale.

If a firm can lower its unit costs it can make a decision between two attractive alternatives:

1 cut the selling price to boost customer demand; if the product is **highly price elastic**, this would probably be the most attractive choice

2 keep the selling price constant, but make a **higher profit margin** on each unit sold; that would be the sensible approach if the product's price elasticity was low.

Such a desirable choice explains why so much management energy is focused on trying to reduce unit costs through increases in efficiency. However, unit costs themselves are not the only operational target that a business will set itself.

Capacity utilisation

Since a high level of capacity utilisation means that fixed costs are spread across more units of output, ensuring that a firm's capacity is nearly fully used all the time is an excellent way of keeping unit costs low. Therefore many firms will set themselves targets for capacity utilisation. Though operating at 100% capacity utilisation will bring the lowest unit costs, most capacity utilisation targets will be set just below that level. This is to allow for time to carry out routine maintenance, space to accept special orders, or just a slight margin for error in case of breakdowns.

Quality

The race to produce output as quickly as possible and reduce labour costs per unit can lead to mistakes.

Setting targets for unit costs and capacity utilisation is risky unless targets for quality levels are also taken seriously. As will be discussed in Unit 33, poor-quality output has a number of negative consequences. Errors in products will lead to higher unit costs as a result of wasted materials or correcting the faults. This will slow production rates as a result of needing to correct the mistakes.

32.2 Matching production to demand

Many factors can cause sales levels to fluctuate, including:

● fashion

● temperature and weather

● marketing activity

● competitors' actions.

Some of these are predictable and others are unpredictable. Sales forecasting can help in production planning, especially for predictable changes in demand. However, the fundamental issue is the same for most businesses: how to organise their operations to cope with varying levels of demand for their products or services.

The issue of matching production to demand considers a firm's ability to make sure that whenever customers want to buy, there is something to supply them with. A factory manufacturing lawnmowers may be an ideal illustration. Sales are likely to follow a monthly pattern, as shown in Figure 32.1. Every springtime there will be a sales peak as people decide to replace their old lawnmowers – unused all winter.

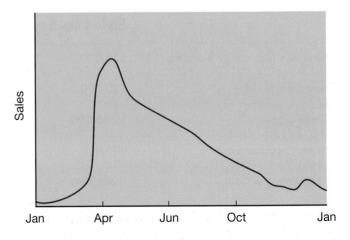

Figure 32.1 Lawnmower sales

The question facing the firm is, how should production be spread through the year. Figure 32.2 offers two alternative extremes: option A is where the firm maintains a constant production level throughout the year; option B shows a scenario where the firm exactly matches monthly production with monthly demand.

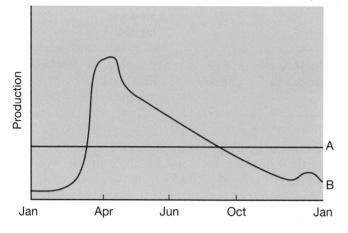

Figure 32.2 Possible production

There are a number of issues raised by each option.

Key issues (and some possible solutions)

Option A is to hold production constant. Surprisingly, this is how Cadbury's produces its Creme Eggs, even though sales only really take place in the lead-up to Easter. This approach offers the easiest solution in terms of planning, since it largely ignores demand fluctuations, and keeps production at a stable level. This has clear benefits: high capacity utilisation and maintaining a skilled and loyal workforce. Yet it implies that production in May will have to be stockpiled for more than six months before being sold in the run-up to the following Easter.

The cost involved in keeping stock will be huge. It is not just the physical costs of keeping stock, such as space for storage and the people whose job it is to organise the storage facilities – many businesses will find that stock becomes worthless over time. Food manufacturers may be forced to throw out stock that has passed its sell-by date, while fashion-related manufacturers and retailers do not want to find themselves heavily discounting last season's stock in a desperate attempt to empty their stock rooms. Service providers such as hairdressers face an even greater problem in that they cannot keep stock. If the salon is capable of dealing with 50 customers every day, but this demand level occurs only on Friday and Saturday, costs per customer will be unnecessarily high. Stylists are at

work, being paid, but cannot generate revenue when there are no customers.

The result is that many firms look towards option B: tailoring staffing and capacity levels to cope with expected demand. To achieve this, firms need to find ways to operate more flexibly; in particular, they need staff to be more flexible. The main ways to achieve this are through:

- overtime
- hiring temporary and part-time staff
- subcontracting.

Overtime

Paying staff extra to work longer hours than their contracts state may be a way of coping with busy periods. Of course, this requires staff who are willing to work overtime. Furthermore, staff generally expect a higher rate of pay if they are working overtime – pushing up labour costs.

High-grade application

Bovine overtime

The hot summer of 2006 saw Scottish ice cream maker Mackie's struggling to cope with a huge surge in demand for its ice cream. Staff at the company worked overtime, some up to an extra six hours per day, in order to maintain the increased production levels required to meet demand. This was only possible as a result of overtime being worked by the company's own cows. They were milked more often – up to four times a day during their busy period – something that the cows rather enjoy. The cows also illustrate how a company can cope with excess capacity: in quieter ice cream periods, Mackie's sells the cows' milk to other firms for other uses.

Hiring temporary and part-time staff

Temporary and part-time staff give extra flexibility to an employer. Temporary staff can be hired on fixed-term contracts designed to last only as long as the expected busy period. Most tourist attractions keep very few full-time staff, relying instead on an army of summer temps to run their attractions. Part-time staff can be hired with contracts that include flexible working hours, offering employers the chance to call them in during busy periods to work longer shifts. This is a phenomenon common among students working in retail over the Christmas period. Through the use of temporary or part-time staff, a company can reduce its fixed salary costs, thus reducing the break-even point to a level that is sustainable during quiet periods.

However, there are drawbacks. Motivating and communicating with temporary staff and part-timers can be much harder than with a stable workforce of full-timers. Quality and customer service issues may arise that have a damaging effect on a firm's reputation.

Subcontracting

Subcontracting is the term used to describe a situation where one firm is doing the work of another. A company struggling to cope with a rush of demand may subcontract its excess work to another. This depends on a good relationship with another company, and is also reliant on the other company having the capacity to cope with the order. On the other hand, a firm that finds its capacity is under-used may try to win work from other businesses looking to subcontract some of their work. This practice can be found not just in the manufacturing sector but in the service sector too. An insurance company whose call centres are overwhelmed with work may look to subcontract some of its claims to other call centres. Similarly, busy builders often subcontract some of their work to other building companies.

32.3	Efficiency and production methods

Efficiency requires that inputs be combined in the best way to achieve the objectives of the business and the customer. This requires planning and may change as the business grows. In order to achieve efficiency a business must:

- use an appropriate method of production

- organise resources to meet the needs of customers

- produce a good or service at a lower cost than the market price of the product

- monitor the production process

- achieve economies of scale through production at as near full capacity as possible.

Traditionally, there have been three methods used to produce goods, as illustrated in Figure 32.3. **Job production** is appropriate for designer dresses and custom-made furniture. **Batch production** is used for products such as tyres and screwdrivers, and for bread. **Flow production** can be used for any standardised product, from cars to baked beans.

These methods are still used by many businesses, but in a much more flexible way than previously. The use of CAD (computer-aided design) and CAM (computer-

Table 32.2 Producing goods: the traditional methods

Production method	JOB	BATCH	FLOW
Quantity of products	One-off item	Group of products produced together	Large quantities
Variety of products	Very flexible	Can vary from batch to batch	Not flexible

aided manufacturing) has meant that consumers can have their products both custom-made and delivered quickly. The type of production that is chosen will depend upon the type and uniqueness of the product, the number required and the life cycle of the product.

Not only have the systems that produce products changed, but also other factors have become increasingly important. Some of these are:

- waste

- minimum wage

- health and safety, including COSHH (Control of Substances Hazardous to Health).

Traditional methods of manufacture have resulted in problems of efficiency that can no longer be ignored. For example, batch production processes often lead to high stock levels as items wait to move between process stages. This might result in deterioration and waste – an increased cost for the firm and society.

In order to overcome these new issues, which could be seen as a threat to the more dominant objectives of the firm such as profitability, expansion and shareholder satisfaction, businesses have had to consider different approaches to the style of their production processes.

The Japanese adopted a total approach to eliminating waste known as **lean production**. This approach slims down mass production into flexible, or 'lean', production systems.

Waste is any activity that increases costs without adding any value to the product. It is caused by poor control of operations within a firm. Examples include:

- time wasted by staff waiting for materials to arrive, or moving about to get resources or tools

- overstocking of raw materials that deteriorate and become unusable

- factory smoke, noise levels and emissions, which increase costs to business through fines and compensation payments

- defective products.

Lean production attempts to overcome some of these problems (see Table 32.2).

Lean production techniques have had a real impact on the car industry in particular, as noted in the accompanying box.

Globalising the car industry

The car industry is going through a profound revolution in its method of production. Lean production techniques are lowering the cost of making small cars, and making it more efficient for car companies to change models quickly, in response to changing consumer taste. The lean production system – based on a 'just-in-time' manufacturing system – is encouraging car companies to locate their assembly plants in or near their major markets, bypassing trade barriers.

That allows them to keep closer to the different consumer tastes in the three key world regions – Asia, Europe and North America.

Source: www. news.bbc.co.ik/1/hi/business

One aspect of lean production is the use of cell working, or **cell production**, which involves dividing the workplace into cells, or areas, where similar types of work take place. Each cell deals with a product family – for example, kitchen cabinets – that requires a sequence of similar operations. The idea is that the appropriate machines are grouped together and a team of workers work within the cell and see the production through from start to finish. All problems are identified within the team and solutions put in place.

Table 32.3 How the aims of lean production are achieved

Aims of lean production	How they are achieved
Eliminate waste/use less/reduction in unit costs of production	JIT, frequent deliveries, minimise use of resources, preventative maintenance, lower buffer stocks and flexible equipment.
Maintain quality/produce more/better-trained workforce	TQM, flexible workforce/CAD/CAM, team working and quality circles

The advantages of this approach include:

- less space required than traditional production line

- movement and handling time reduced

- teams are encouraged

- lead times are cut

- may improve health and safety and maintenance issues.

32.4 Other types of operational decision

Rationalisation

Longer-term reductions in demand may require long-term solutions to matching production with demand. Firms which find that sales have fallen due to changes in technology may choose **rationalisation** (i.e. to increase efficiency by permanently reducing overall capacity). This may be done by closing entire branches or factories, or simply shedding staff across the whole firm. At the time of writing, the BBC faces staff unrest, having announced that the workforce will be cut by some 3000 over the coming years. Rationalisation programmes must be handled carefully to minimise damage to the morale of the remaining staff and to minimise bad external publicity. Redundancies are never popular, but voluntary redundancy is a more attractive proposition than compulsory redundancy; however, neither is as pain-free as using **natural wastage** to rationalise.

Stock management

The issues already covered show the importance of managing stocks effectively. Stocks of finished goods waiting to be sold may be seen as a buffer against sudden surges in demand. However, keeping too much stock is a dangerously expensive habit. The balancing of stock levels is one of the major issues facing operations managers. Meanwhile, stock of raw materials and components presents similar problems. A lack of production inputs may force production to grind to a halt, while too much stock may lead to wasted materials or space.

Non-standard orders

Sometimes firms will be approached by customers with special orders at a different price to their regular selling price. A customer with special requirements, such as a different design or a very short delivery date, may offer a price above the norm. In other cases customers may try to buy special orders at specially low prices. Retailers such as Lidl and Tchibo sell cheaply to the public because of their skill at buying cheaply.

High-price special orders

Example: an Airbus super-jumbo bought and kitted out for Prince bin Tolal of Saudi Arabia.

In these cases, the order is likely to look profitable at first glance. However, the special nature of the order is such that it will be more expensive to produce. This will mean that unit costs are going to be higher. Perhaps overtime or subcontracting will be necessary to meet a tight order deadline or to adjust the standard design to meet the customer's needs. In these cases, extra costs must be factored into any calculation of the possible profit from the order.

Low-price special orders

Example: TK Maxx offers to buy 10,000 of last season's Ted Baker t-shirts for £5 each.

There are several reasons why a firm may consider accepting an order at lower than the usual selling price. The key is whether a firm has enough under-used capacity to meet the order and if the order will generate a positive contribution per unit. If the firm is already breaking even, a low-price order that generates a positive contribution per unit will generate extra profit. A further reason to accept the order is the possibility that it could lead to a new customer becoming a regular if they are happy with the quality and delivery of the order.

Issues For Analysis

● Whenever operational targets are missed, managers will want to know why. In these cases it is vital that you show a clear understanding of cause and effect. There will clearly be links between the three major target variables of unit cost, quality and capacity utilisation. Good analytic arguments will show a clear understanding of which events have caused which consequences. For example, an answer could suggest that unit costs have risen as a result of operating at a lower than anticipated level of capacity. This may have been the result of a fall in demand caused by a poor reputation, caused by poor quality levels last month.

● It is useful to experiment by taking each of the three target variables as a starting point, then thinking through the impact on the other two. For example, if capacity utilisation falls, what is the impact on unit costs and what might be the effect on quality? Or, what if quality performance falls?

● Another major analytical theme is likely to be an awareness of the arguments for and against keeping a stable production level month by month, as opposed to attempting to exactly match production with demand. Logically constructed arguments on both sides of this question are likely to lead to effective judgements when asked to evaluate.

32.5 Organising production
an evaluation

Operations decisions are at the very heart of any business. Efficiency is king – without it, no firm will last long. Few customers are willing to wait for an unavailable product, while few firms have the financial resources to indefinitely fund inefficient stock-holding. The magical formula for matching production to demand does not exist. Instead, it is important to show an awareness that the forecasting skills and experience of operations managers will need to go hand in hand to ensure that a business is operationally efficient.

Key terms

Batch production: a method of production that completes one operation at a time on all units before performing the next.

Cell production: where the workplace is divided into 'cells' that focus on the production of a 'product family'.

Flow production: a method of production where each operation on a product is performed continuously one after the other.

Higher profit margin: a wider gap between price and unit cost; if sales volumes stay the same, this must increase total profit.

Highly price elastic: when customers are so focused on price that a small price change can cause a big switch in customer demand (e.g. price up 5%, sales down 20%).

Job production: involves the production of one-off or custom-made products one at a time.

Lean production: a system of continuous improvement that aims to produce more by using less.

Natural wastage: the 'natural' annual fall in staff levels caused by employees retiring, moving away or finding better jobs elsewhere.

Operational targets: the numerical goals set by management at the start of the year (e.g. output of 220,000 units with a quality wastage rate of no more than 1%).

Rationalisation: reorganising in order to increase efficiency; this usually leads to redundancies.

Exercises

A. Revision questions

(50 marks; 50 minutes)

1 Briefly explain what is meant by capacity utilisation. (2)

2 Explain why a high level of capacity usage makes cost per unit fall. (2)

3 Calculate the unit cost for a firm that manufactured 23,000 units with total costs of £11,500. (3)

4 Explain why quality targets may suffer if management is concerned only with meeting unit cost targets. (4)

5 Explain what is meant by the term rationalisation. (2)

6 Explain two methods that could be used to improve the level of capacity utilisation in a clothing factory. (4)

7 Explain two possible drawbacks to a farmer of relying on temporary staff when picking strawberries. (4)

8 Explain two benefits to a farmer of using temporary staff to pick strawberries. (4)

9 Explain two reasons why a company might agree to provide a customer with a special order at a selling price lower than its average unit cost. (4)

10 Outline three possible reasons why a cake manufacturer may try to closely match production with demand in order to reduce stock levels to a minimum. (6)

11 Each of the following is an industry that carries out production:
- a bakery
- a construction company
- an electronic component manufacturer
- a coffee shop.

Think about what type of production method may traditionally have been used in each business. How might they have improved their production methods using modern techniques? Would the cost of the change outweigh the benefits? (15)

B. Revision exercises

B1 Data response

Hotel Torres is a part of the Hoteles Benitez group of hotels in Spain. For hotels, the main operational target is occupancy rates: the percentage of rooms that are occupied at any time. The chain's head office is assessing last year's performance at each branch and is particularly interested in the data shown below relating to the Hotel Torres in Barcelona.

Hotel Torres data (B1)

	Quarter 1	Quarter 2	Quarter 3	Quarter 4
Average occupancy rate (%)	53	66	84	62
Target occupancy rate (%)	55	70	90	75
Group average occupancy rate (%)	58	72	90	75
Cost per guest (euros)	64	58	50	60
Target cost per guest (euros)	62	55	40	55

Questions

(20 marks; 20 minutes)

1 Explain what the table reveals about Hotel Torres's operational efficiency during the year. (4)

2 Use the data in the table to explain the possible link between room occupancy performance and cost per guest. (6)

3 Analyse the benefits that the hotel might gain by setting targets for occupancy rates and cost per guest. (6)

4 Briefly explain two possible reasons why Hotel Torres failed to meet its targets. (4)

DWS Ltd is a toy manufacturer, operating in the UK from a factory in the north-east. Having been running for 20 years, DWS is used to the particular problems posed by operating in such a seasonal industry. With 70% of sales being made in November and December, the managers have experience of battling to match production to demand. Their problem is intensified by the short product life cycles involved in manufacturing toys designed to tie in with the latest television and films. The table below shows units sold, output and maximum capacity month by month for last year.

The firm uses a range of methods to boost its maximum capacity during busy periods. These include overtime, temporary staff and subcontracting work to another trusted local manufacturer.

DWS has been approached by a major UK greetings card retailer, which is looking for a manufacturer of stuffed toys themed around various holidays, including Valentine's Day, Easter and Halloween. The initial contract would cover a 12-month period and would mean that sales levels would treble in January, March and October. The firm would pay a price equivalent to 5% above the variable cost of each unit of output.

Questions

(35 marks; 45 minutes)

1a Draw a graph to show units sold, output and maximum capacity. (6)

1b Shade the areas on the graph that represent under-use of capacity. (2)

2 Analyse the problems that DWS might experience by maintaining a consistent level of production all year round in order to avoid using overtime, temporary staff and subcontracting. (9)

3 Describe the pros and cons of two possible methods of increasing maximum capacity in the three affected months. (6)

4 Discuss whether DWS should accept this special order. (12)

	Sales (units)	Output (units)	Maximum capacity (units)
January	10,000	5,000	20,000
February	10,000	10,000	20,000
March	15,000	15,000	20,000
April	15,000	15,000	20,000
May	20,000	20,000	20,000
June	20,000	20,000	20,000
July	20,000	20,000	40,000
August	30,000	30,000	40,000
September	60,000	100,000	120,000
October	100,000	280,000	300,000
November	380,000	300,000	300,000
December	320,000	300,000	300,000

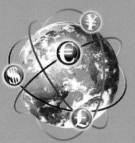
QUALITY

DEFINITION

Quality management means providing what the customer wants at the right time, with the right level of quality and consistency, and therefore yielding high customer satisfaction.

33.1 What is quality?

W. Edwards Deming, the American quality guru, said that 'quality is defined by the customer'. The customer may insist on certain specifications, or demand exceptional levels of customer comfort. Another definition of quality is 'fit for use'. Although hard to define, there is no doubt that customers are very aware of quality. Their perception of quality is a key part of the buying decision.

Customers will accept some **trade-off** between price and quality. There is, however, a minimum level of quality that is acceptable. The customer wants the product to work (be fit for use), regardless of the price. If the customers think that the quality is below a minimum level they will not buy the product. Above the minimum level of acceptable quality, customers will expect to get more as they pay more.

The importance of quality is related to the level of **competitiveness** in the market. When competition is fierce, the quality of the product can tip the balance in the customer's decision making. Dell is a hugely successful computer manufacturer, which sells directly to customers through the internet or newspaper advertising. Its mission statement is: 'Customers must have a quality experience and be pleased not just satisfied.'

For all customers, quality is about satisfying their expectations. The customer will take into account the total buying experience. Customer service and after-sales service may be as important as the product itself. The way the product is sold, even *where* it is sold, all contribute to the customer's feelings about the quality of the product.

Quality is a moving target. A quality standard that is acceptable today may not be in the future. Customer expectations of quality are constantly changing. As quality improves, customer demands also increase.

Quality:

- is satisfying (preferably beating) customer expectations
- applies to services as well as products
- involves the whole business process, not just the manufacturing of the product
- is an ever-rising target.

High-grade application

Mattel

Mattel, the world's largest toy maker, had a quality disaster in 2007. It was forced to withdraw millions of toys from the market at an eventual cost of £20 million.

Mattel first said that the problem was that toys made in China had unacceptable levels of lead in the paint. Then they said loose parts could be a danger to children. The world's media used the story to condemn China for poor quality standards. The American press went to town on this. Business media said it highlighted the difficulty of controlling quality when large businesses outsource manufacturing. At first Mattel said it would implement plans for additional checking and shift production away from subcontractors, i.e. back to its own factories. The company said it hoped that these moves would restore public confidence in its products.

Some weeks later Mattel faced the further embarrassment of admitting that "The vast majority of these products that we recalled were the result of a flaw in Mattel's design, not through a manufacturing flaw in Chinese manufacturers" (Thomas Debrowski, Mattel's Vice President for Worldwide Operations). Mattel had managed to make themselves look foolish twice over.

33.2 Quality defined by customer specifications

Where the customer is in a powerful position, quality is directly defined by the customer. Many firms lay down minimum standards for their suppliers. Large businesses, such as supermarkets and chain stores, are able to insist on quality standards. They have the buying power to force their suppliers to conform. For many years, Marks & Spencer has worked with suppliers to ensure that standards are met. Other large purchasers, such as government departments and local authorities, are also able to insist on high standards for supplies. As new roads and motorways are built, their surface is checked to ensure its quality. If the surface does not conform to the required standards the contractor will have to re-lay the area.

Other firms, and in particular local and central government agencies, will insist that their suppliers have obtained ISO 9000 (see box). This ensures that suppliers are operating within a quality framework.

High-grade application

ISO 9000

ISO 9000 is an international standard for quality systems. It is a British standard that is recognised worldwide. Companies that are registered can display the BSI symbol. In order to register, companies have to document their business procedures, prepare a quality manual and assess their quality management systems. They are assessed by an independent assessor. After obtaining the award, businesses are visited at regular intervals to ensure compliance. It is necessary that everyone in the organisation follows the processes outlined in the quality manual. Firms who have registered say that this has provided a range of benefits to the business. These include:

● less waste
● cost savings
● fewer mistakes
● increased efficiency
● improved competitiveness
● increased customer satisfaction
● increased profits.

Quality

Firms looking to ensure the quality of anything that they do, face a choice between quality control and quality assurance.

Quality control methods for customer service involve spotting defective service. The problem here is that poor customer service can be spotted only once it has been delivered, and this means at least one unhappy customer. Anyone who has rung a call centre is likely to have heard an announcement that 'Your call may be recorded for quality control purposes.' Those working in the retail sector are at the mercy of '**mystery shoppers**', who are paid to visit stores and report back on the customer service provided. Other methods of quality control involve planned or unannounced management checks.

Quality assurance is the attempt to introduce systems to ensure that quality errors cannot occur. Therefore quality assuring customer service systems must involve staff training. Given the key role of staff in meeting customer expectations, they will need to be 100% clear on how to deal with any situation they may face. The problem is that staff can start to see themselves, not the customers, as the focal point of the business. Management may keep saying 'the customer is king' or 'the customer is always right', but the staff don't really believe it.

Quality standards

Companies can apply for quality standards certification to show the rest of the world that they are serious about the quality of what they do. The basic **ISO 9000** certification series covers customer service in organisations for which the skill is relevant. However, for customer service specialists, there are customer service-specific standards:

● ISO 10002 – a customer complaint handling standard

● the BSI runs the CCA Standard – a special quality standard for call centres

● Charter Mark – administered by the government, this is a customer service standard for public- and voluntary-sector organisations, along with firms that provide a public service in the passenger train and bus, water, gas and electricity supply industries.

33.3 Why is quality management important?

Quality is an important competitive issue. Where the consumer has choice, quality is vital. For a new business, effective quality management may mean the difference between success and failure. If the product or service cannot get a good reputation the business will not last long.

Table 33.1 Quality control vs quality assurance

Quality control	Quality assurance
'Your call may be recorded for quality purposes'	Thorough, ongoing training in customer service
Mystery shoppers	Customer service is a key feature of company culture
Management checks	Clear systems, set out in writing, about how to deal with each type of customer complaint

A reputation for good quality brings marketing advantages. A good-quality product will:

● generate a high level of repeat purchase, and therefore a longer product life cycle

● allow brand building and cross-marketing

● allow a price premium (this is often greater than any added costs of quality improvements; in other words, quality adds value – it generates additional profit)

● make products easier to place (retailers are more likely to stock products with a good reputation).

High-grade application

Cadbury fined £1 million over chocolate that made people ill

In spring 2006, 42 people became ill with salmonella food poisoning after eating Cadbury's chocolate. In June 2006 the company withdrew a million bars of its chocolate from sale. Later, the company was prosecuted for breaking food safety regulations. In 2007 it was fined £500,000 for putting unsafe chocolate on sale, and a further £500,000 for offences related to poor hygiene conditions at its Marlbrook factory.

The court case revealed that, in 2003, the company had decided to change its quality control standards. Before that, it would destroy any chocolate that tested positive for any level of salmonella cells – there was a **zero defects** policy. This led to a lot of wastage.

The change in policy allowed for a very low level of salmonella cells, assuming there would be no health risk. But the court was told that there is no such thing as a safe level for salmonella and that it could survive in chocolate for years.

The company apologised for what had happened and said 'We have spent over £20 million in changing our procedures to prevent this ever happening again.'

Source: Adapted from bbc.co.uk material which appeared on and in *Scotsman*, 14 July 2007

33.4 How can firms detect quality problems?

The ideal is to detect quality problems before they reach the customer. This can be done by:

● inspection of finished goods before sale – this has been the traditional method; it may be all goods or only a sample

● self-inspection of work by operatives – this is being used more as businesses recognise that quality needs to be 'everyone's business'

● statistical analysis within the production process – this can be used to ensure that specifications stay within certain limits; for example, Mars might set a target weight for 100 g bags of Maltesers of between 96 and 104 g (see Figure 29.1); only if the weight slips outside this range will an alarm indicator be triggered to warn that the specifications are not being met; staff could then stop the production line and readjust the machine to ensure that the correct weight is being given.

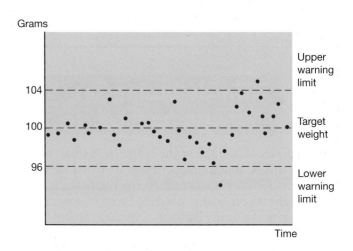

Figure 33.1 Actual weight of 100 g bags of Maltesers coming off the production line

Table 33.2 Implications of poor product or service quality

Marketing costs	Business costs
Loss of sales	Scrapping of unsuitable goods
Loss of reputation	Reworking of unsatisfactory goods – costs of labour and materials
May have to price-discount	Lower prices for 'seconds'
May impact on other products in range	Handling complaints/warranty claims
Retailers may be unwilling to stock goods	Loss of consumer goodwill and repeat purchase

Quality quotes

'Reducing the cost of quality is in fact an opportunity to increase profits without raising sales, buying new equipment, or hiring new people.' *Philip Crosby, American quality guru*

'Quality is remembered long after the price is forgotten.' *Gucci slogan*

'The only job security anybody has in this company comes from quality, productivity and satisfied customers.' *Lee Iacocca, successful boss of Chrysler Motors*

'Good management techniques are enduring. Quality control, for instance, was treated as a fad here, but it's been part of the Japanese business philosophy for decades. That's why they laugh at us.' *Peter Senge, US business author*

'Quality has to be caused, not controlled.' *Philip Crosby*

'Quality is our best assurance of customer allegiance, our strongest defence against foreign competition, and the only path to sustained growth and earnings.' *Jack Welch, General Electric chief*

33.5 How do businesses manage quality?

This depends on the size of the business. A small new business will be able to inspect every item and ensure that each customer is satisfied. As the business grows, keeping checks on quality needs to be more systematic. In large manufacturing businesses, quality control has traditionally been the responsibility of the production department. Most quality control processes were concentrated in the factory. These were intended to prevent faults leaving the factory. Today, firms are more likely to see quality as having product and service aspects.

There are four stages to quality management that apply to all businesses. These are prevention, detection, correction and improvement.

Prevention

This tries to avoid problems occurring. It requires thought and care at every stage:

- in the initial product design, to 'build in' quality

- in purchasing raw materials and components (i.e. not just trying to buy the cheapest supplies, but caring about quality)

- designing the factory layout to minimise production errors

- ensuring that all staff feel empowered to care about quality; at Toyota car plants, any factory worker with a quality concern can pull an alarm (*jidoka*) chord that stops the whole assembly line; this shows how seriously management takes quality.

Detection

This ensures that quality problems are spotted before they reach the customer. This has been the traditional emphasis of quality control. The use of electronic scanning has given firms better tools to detect faults.

Correction

This is not just about correcting faults. It is also about discovering why there is a problem. Once the problem is identified steps can be taken to ensure it does not recur.

Improvement

Customer expectations of quality are always changing. It is important that businesses seek to improve quality. Therefore staff need to be encouraged to put forward ways in which their jobs can be done better; the Japanese term *kaizen* (meaning continuous improvement) has become common in British manufacturing.

33.6 Programmes for managing quality

As the importance of quality for both marketing and cost control has been recognised, there has been a growth in initiatives to control and improve quality. Techniques for quality control, such as inspection and statistical control, continue. They have been supplemented by other policies aimed at controlling and improving quality. These include total quality management, quality control and quality assurance.

Total quality management

Total quality management (TQM) was introduced by American business guru W. Edwards Deming in the early 1980s. He worked with Japanese firms, and his techniques are said to be one of the reasons for the success of Japanese businesses. TQM is not a management tool: it is a philosophy. It is a way of looking at quality issues. It requires commitment from the whole organisation, not just the quality control department. The business considers quality in every part of the business process – from design right through to sales. TQM is about building-in rather than inspecting-out. It should draw closely on the Japanese experience with *kaizen*, set out on the next page.

Quality control

Quality control (QC) is the traditional way to manage quality, and is based on inspection. Workers get on with the task of producing as many units as possible, and quality control inspectors check that the output meets minimum acceptable standards. This might be done by checking every product – for example, starting up a newly built car and driving it from the production line to a storage area. Or it might be done by checking every 200th KitKat coming off the end of the factory's production line. If one KitKat is faulty, inspectors will check others from the same batch and – if concerned – may scrap the whole batch. The problem with this system is that faulty products can slip through, and it stops staff from producing the best quality: all they need focus on is 'good enough' to pass the checks. TQM is therefore a superior approach.

Table 33.3 Pros and cons of TQM, QC and QA

	TQM	QC	QA
Pros	Should become deeply rooted into the company culture (e.g. product safety at a producer of baby car seats) Once all staff think about quality, it should show through from design to manufacture and after-sales service (e.g. at Lexus or BMW)	Can be used to guarantee that no defective item will leave the factory Requires little staff training, therefore suits a business with unskilled or temporary staff (as ordinary workers needn't worry about quality)	Makes sure the company has a quality system for every stage in the production process Customers like the reassurance provided by a badge such as 'ISO 9000'; they believe they will get a higher-quality service and may therefore be willing to pay more
Cons	Especially at first, staff sceptical of management initiatives may treat TQM as 'hot air'; it lacks the clear, concrete programme of QC or QA To get TQM into the culture of a business may be expensive, as it would require extensive training among all staff (e.g. all British Airways staff flying economy from Heathrow to New York)	Leaving quality for the inspectors to sort out may mean poor quality is built in to the product (e.g. clothes with seams that soon unpick) QC can be trusted when 100% of output is tested, but not when it is based on sampling; Ford used to test just 1 in 7 of its new cars; that led to quality problems	QA does not promise a high-quality product, only a high-quality, reliable process; this process may churn out OK products reliably QA may encourage complacency; it suggests quality has been sorted, whereas rising customer requirements mean quality should keep moving ahead

Quality assurance

Quality assurance (QA) is a system that assures customers that detailed systems are in place to govern quality at every stage in production. It would start with the quality-checking process for newly arrived raw materials and components. This includes schemes such as ISO 9000. Companies have to have in place a documented quality assurance system. This should be an effective quality system that operates throughout the company, and involves suppliers and subcontractors. The main criticism of QA is that it is a paper-based system and therefore encourages staff to tick boxes rather than care about quality.

33.7 Other quality initiatives

Continuous improvement (kaizen)

This is a system where the whole organisation is committed to making changes on a continual basis. The Japanese call it kaizen. It is an approach to doing business that looks for continual improvement in the quality of products, services, people and processes. In 1991 a book was published in Japan about Toyota, called 40 Years; 20 Million Ideas. This alerted western business to the amazing ability of the Japanese car companies to get suggestions for improvement from their factory employees.

Six Sigma

A programme developed by America's General Electric Company, which aims to have fewer defective products than 1 per 300,000. To achieve this, staff are trained to become 'Green Belt' or 'Black Belt' quality experts. Although gimmicky, this has been followed widely by other companies.

Quality circles

A quality circle is a group of employees who meet together regularly for the purpose of identifying problems and recommending adjustments to the working processes. This is done to improve the product or process. It is used to address known quality issues such as defective products. It can also be useful for identifying better practices that may improve quality. In addition, it has the advantage of improving staff morale through employee involvement. It takes advantage of the knowledge of operators.

Zero defects

The aim is to produce goods and services with no faults or problems. This is vital in industries such as passenger aircraft production or the manufacture of surgical equipment.

Benchmarking

Benchmarking is a process of comparing a business with other businesses. Having identified the best, businesses attempt to bring their performance up to the level of the best, by adopting its practices.

Most of these initiatives rely on employee involvement. In addition to quality improvements and cost reductions, most businesses find that the initiatives in themselves deliver benefits. These include better working practices, improved employee motivation, increased focus on tasks and the development of team working.

33.8 Is quality expensive or free?

The traditional belief was that high quality was costly: in terms of materials, labour, training and checking systems. Therefore managements should beware of building too much quality into a product (the term given to this was 'over-engineered'). The alternative approach, put forward by the American writer Philip Crosby, is that 'quality is free'. The latter view suggests that getting things **right first time** can save a huge amount of time and money.

- The time required to make it work – quality initiatives take time. Workers may be away from their jobs while attending training or quality groups.

- Short-term versus long-term viewpoints – there may be a conflict between short-term costs and longer-term results. Shareholders may want returns today, but often quality initiatives require a long-term view. The investment will be a current cost. The benefits, however, may take some time to show. They may also be difficult to measure.

If quality control is to be effective it must balance the costs against the advantages; 100% quality is possible but it may make the product so expensive that it cannot be sold.

Issues For Analysis

When looking at quality issues in an exam question, the following are issues that need to be considered.

- The importance of quality to the business: this will depend on the type of business, the type of product or the service. It will also depend on the market in which the business is operating.

- Whether the firm has adopted the right approach to quality management: perhaps a firm using quality assurance should switch to TQM.

- Quality issues are often closely interwoven with other parts of the business. The role of the employee in quality control is an important issue. Interlinked with this are the changes in management styles and philosophies that come with many of the quality initiatives.

Remember that quality is not just about manufacturing, it is about the whole experience of contact with the business. A poor call centre could just as easily lose a sale as a faulty product.

This change in emphasis has not been without problems. The shift to a focus on the customer and the role of the employee could result in additional costs. Unless this results in increased profits, shareholders may feel that they are losing out. Some businesses have found that changing cultures is not easy. Resistance from workers and management has often caused problems.

Key terms

Benchmarking: comparing a firm's performance with best practice in the industry.

Competitiveness: the ability of a firm to beat its competitors (e.g. Galaxy is a highly competitive brand in the chocolate market).

ISO 9000: the International Standards Organisation (ISO) has a quality assurance certification system called ISO 9000.

Mystery shoppers: employed to test customer service by visiting a shop or sales outlet unannounced, and therefore have the same experience as customers.

Right first time: avoiding mistakes and therefore achieving high quality with no wastage of time or materials.

Trade-off: accepting less of one thing to achieve more of another (e.g. slightly lower quality in exchange for cheapness).

Zero defects: eliminating quality defects by getting things right first time.

33.9 Quality

an evaluation

In recent years there has been a change in the emphasis on quality. The quality business has itself grown. The management section of any book shop will reveal several titles dedicated to quality management. The growth of initiatives such as TQM and continuous improvement goes on. The number of worldwide registrations for ISO 9000 increases by more than 25% a year. Not all of these are from British businesses – there has been a rapid rise in overseas registrations. With an increase in the international awareness of quality, British businesses will have to ensure that they continue to be competitive.

This growth in emphasis on quality has undoubtedly brought benefits to business. Increased quality brings rewards in the marketplace. Companies have also found that the initiatives, especially where they are people-based, have brought other advantages: changes in working practices have improved motivation and efficiency, and have reduced waste and costs.

Exercises

A. Revision questions

(35 marks; 35 minutes)

1 State two reasons why quality management is important. (2)

2 How important is quality to the consumer? (3)

3 Suggest two criteria customers might use to judge quality at:
   (a) a budget-priced hotel chain (2)
   (b) a Tesco supermarket (2)
   (c) a McDonald's. (2)

4 Why has there been an increase in awareness of the importance of improving the quality of products? (3)

5 Give two marketing advantages that come from a quality reputation. (2)

6 What costs are involved if the firm has quality problems? (3)

7 Explain what is meant by the Gucci slogan shown among the Quality quotes earlier in this Unit (4)

8 What is total quality management? (4)

9 Outline two benefits of adopting quality circles to a clothing chain such as Topshop. (4)

10 Outline two additional costs that might be incurred in order to improve quality. (4)

B. Revision exercises

B1 Data response

Trac Parts

Trac Parts is a major manufacturer of parts for farm and construction machinery. It has been operating from a new centralised warehouse for four years. This year the company applied for ISO 9000. It gained accreditation. The main reason for applying was that several large customers had indicated that they would only deal with ISO 9000 companies when negotiating new contracts. The warehouse manager has been pleasantly surprised by the operational performance figures since accreditation:

- orders completed on time up from 75% to 84%
- errors in completing orders reduced by 40%
- average time from order receipt to dispatch reduced by two days.

Questions

(25 marks; 30 minutes)

1 What is ISO 9000? (3)

2 Why might a business want to become ISO 9000 approved? (4)

3 Examine the benefits to Trac Parts of the performance improvements identified in the text. (6)

4 In order to be accepted by ISO 9000, the firm will have had to introduce procedures to ensure that levels of quality are maintained. Using the four stages of quality control (prevention, detection, correction and improvement) examine the actions it might have taken. (12)

B2 Case study

Manufacturing defects – producer comparisons: PcNow

PcNow is a small computer manufacturer based in the East Midlands. It tailor-makes computers and accessories based on customers' own specifications. Although business grew steadily initially, it is now worried about falling sales. It believes it is losing sales to Japanese and American companies that have set up manufacturing facilities in Europe, as well as to other European and UK-based firms. An industry survey has produced data on industry levels of production defects. It has added its own figures and produced the chart shown below.

The firm realises that survival depends upon addressing the quality problems. It has decided to employ a quality manager, Cara Davenport, to address the issues. Her first suggestion is to get together workers from each department to discuss the problems and issues. Following a survey of the factory she has also suggested that the layout of the production facilities should be changed. This will be an expensive exercise, and management is reluctant to make the changes as they will require production to stop for a week and there will need to be investment in new equipment. The firm's weak cash flow position makes it hard for the owners to accept new capital spending. The other area that Cara has identified is a problem with one particular component. She has suggested that a new supplier should be found, or that she should work with the existing supplier to improve the quality of the component.

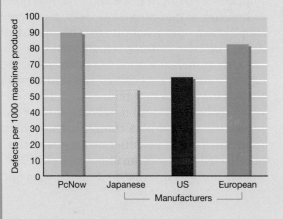

Figure 33.2 Manufacturing defects – producer comparisons

Questions

(40 marks; 50 minutes)

1a What does the chart show? (2)

1b What further data would help to make the bar chart more useful? (4)

2 From the case study, identify two reasons for the quality problems experienced by PcNow. (2)

3 What are the marketing implications for PcNow of the data in the bar chart? (8)

4 Outline the advantages PcNow might get from the discussion group formed to discuss the quality problems. (8)

5 How might Cara convince the firm's management to change the layout of the production facilities? (6)

6 Once these changes have been made, the firm needs to ensure that quality is maintained and improved. Discuss the implications for the firm of implementing a total quality management initiative. (10)

C. Essay questions

(40 marks each)

1 'Quality control is about building quality in, not inspecting it out.' Discuss.

2 Consider whether quality management is solely a matter for the production department.

3 To what extent is quality a major competitive issue in service businesses?

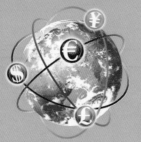

34 Unit

STOCK CONTROL

DEFINITION

Suppliers are other businesses that provide products or services to a firm. The relationship with suppliers is likely to have a critical impact on a firm. Operational success demands high-quality supplies delivered on time in the right quantities.

34.1 Key factors to consider when choosing suppliers

Cost

Cheaper supplies mean higher profit margins. The incentive to find a cheap supplier is huge for any firm; therefore, the price charged by a supplier will be a key factor in the relationship between a firm and its suppliers. Large businesses may be able to almost dictate prices to their suppliers. This is because the quantities they purchase may account for the whole output of the supplier, giving a huge amount of power to the buyer. However, for small businesses with limited purchasing power, the supplier may have the upper hand.

As a result of this, small businesses may be advised to shop around, looking for the cheapest supplier they can find. However, this may not always be the most sensible course of action – there are other important factors to consider when choosing suppliers.

Quality

There is frequently a trade-off between the price charged by suppliers and the quality of their offering. The cheapest supplier may be one with a poor reputation for the quality of its products or service. Choosing to use a supplier with quality problems is likely to lead to operational problems. Poor-quality supplies can lead to machinery breakdowns, along with poor-quality output. This can lead to problems with customer complaints, guarantee claims or reputation. Choosing the cheapest supplier may sow the seeds of long-term problems for a business.

Reliability

Supplies at the right price and of a high quality may be of little use if they arrive late. It is important that a supplier can offer reliability to a business. Failure to deliver on time can stop a manufacturing process or leave shop shelves empty. Suppliers' reliability will be easy to assess once a business has started working with them. However, a new business or a business sourcing new supplies may need to rely on word-of-mouth reputation to inform its choice. Larger firms may be able to impose certain penalties on suppliers who prove unreliable but, again, small businesses will be in a weaker position if trying to threaten a supplier.

Frequency

Depending on the type of business and the production system it uses, frequent deliveries may be needed from suppliers. Firms selling fresh produce will need to ensure that they are using suppliers that can supply and deliver frequently – probably a new batch each day. Similarly, a firm that uses a **just-in-time (JIT)** production system will need very frequent deliveries to feed its production system without it having to hold stock (Honda, for example, requires hourly deliveries of parts to its Japanese car factories). For firms such as these, it makes sense to look for a local supplier – they are far more likely to be willing to deliver with a greater level of frequency.

JIT is a production method used to minimise stock levels at all stages of production. Stocks should be as low as possible and supplies should be delivered when they are needed.

Flexibility

In a similar way to ensuring the right frequency of supplies, many firms will need to find a supplier with the capacity to cope with widely varying orders. Businesses selling products with erratic demand patterns, caused by changes in the weather or fashion, will need to find themselves suppliers that can meet their ever-changing needs. Probably the most common scenario is to ensure that suppliers have the spare capacity available to cope with sudden rush orders. In addition, some firms will need to find suppliers that can supply at the right time – perhaps night-time deliveries are needed for firms in congested town centres, or in areas where lorries are banned during the day. A key to supplier flexibility is a short **lead time** (i.e. there should not be too long a period between placing an order and receiving a delivery).

Payment terms

Most business transactions are on credit, not for cash. If Tesco wants to order 2000 cases of Heinz Beans, the bill is unlikely to be paid until 30 or more days after the goods have been delivered. This gives time for the goods to be sold, providing the cash to make it easy to pay the bill. Small business start-ups will struggle to get the same terms. A newly opened corner shop will not be given credit by Heinz. The supplier will want to be paid in cash until the new business has shown that it can survive and pay its bills. So a new small firm has to pay up front, placing extra strain on its cash flow. This should not be a problem as long as it has been anticipated (i.e. built in to its start-up cash flow forecast).

High-grade application

Going the extra mile(s) for quality

The Flying Fortress play centre in Sussex chose a supplier based on quality of product. The main feature of this indoor play centre for children is a huge aircraft-shaped climbing frame, supplied by a Canadian firm. Since the centre opened in 2005 it has proved hugely popular. This success was thanks to a supplier willing to provide a quality service as well as a quality product. The frame was constructed in Canada and transported to Britain. It proved a struggle to construct, threatening the big launch day for the play centre. The problem was solved when the supplier flew in more staff, who worked through the night to ensure the centrepiece was ready on time.

Source: http://www.flying-fortress.co.uk/home.htm

34.2 The role of suppliers in improving performance

Some businesses enjoy telling their shareholders how tough they are with their suppliers – after all, the lower the supply cost, the higher the profit. Many firms encourage competition between rival suppliers by threatening to go elsewhere if the terms are not what they want. This approach has been important in building the hugely profitable business of many high-street stores, which find cheap goods by negotiating toughly in Cambodia, China or the Philippines.

An alternative approach was followed in the past by Marks & Spencer, and today by car firms such as Toyota and Honda. These companies build long-term relationships with their suppliers, with the aim of working with, rather than against, them. There are many potential benefits from this approach, as discussed below.

Working together on new product development

Developing new products involves many considerations. One of these will be how the product is to be manufactured, what materials will be used and what properties will be needed. Meanwhile, launching a new product will require careful production planning to ensure that consumers can get hold of the new product that the marketing department has told them about. The result is that suppliers have a major part to play in developing and launching new products. Many firms have recognised the importance of this and work hand in hand with their suppliers from the very earliest stages of developing a new product.

Flexibility

A strong relationship with a supplier should mean it is willing to make special deliveries if a business is running low on stock. A strong relationship may also allow some flexibility on payment. A toy shop may be struggling for cash in the months leading up to Christmas, so a trusting supplier may accept a delay in payment. This could be the lifeline required for the small firm. However, no supplier is likely to be able to sustain this generosity for a long period.

Sharing information to improve the efficiency of the supply chain

Large businesses with sophisticated IT systems have direct links between their cash tills and their suppliers. Cadbury knows at any hour of the day how many Creme

Eggs are selling at Tesco. This enables Cadbury to plan its production levels (e.g. pushing up output if sales are proving brighter than expected). The supermarket can even allow Cadbury to make the decisions on how much stock to produce and deliver on the basis of the information it is receiving.

Small grocers use the same laser scanning software at their tills, but it would be rare for a small business to have a direct electronic link with a supplier. This means the shopkeeper has to make the purchasing decisions, or go to a wholesaler to buy the goods, which is much less efficient than the electronic systems of the big companies.

34.3 Stock control

A simple way to reduce **waste** is to select the correct method of stock control.

There are three types of stock:

1 raw materials

2 work in progress

3 finished goods.

As with many control techniques the stock control method chosen will depend upon various criteria. These include:

● type of product (e.g. consumable or durable)

● reliability of supplier/lead times

● storage conditions

● demand.

Figure 34.1 shows a traditional stock control chart. In order to construct a chart like this, a business will need the following information:

● production figures and targets, in order to assess the stock required

● lead times – the time between ordering and receipt of stock

● reliability of suppliers

● minimum stock levels in order to maintain production.

Sometimes the chart will change as suppliers are unable to meet delivery requirements. In this case it is important that the business shows the increased lead time on the chart, and perhaps adjusts the minimum stock level accordingly. It may be that a supplier

continually delivers poor quality or the wrong stock. In this case further action may have to be taken to change suppliers, since the priority in all businesses is that production targets be met and demand fulfilled.

For example, a computer hardware retailer sells hard drives, monitors and keyboards. The demand for monitors is constant, the supplier is reliable and the shop has limited storage space. The demand for keyboards and hard drives is also constant but the suppliers are unreliable.

In this case it would be best for the shop to operate different types of stock control system for the monitors and for hard drives and keyboards. JIT might be better for the monitors as regular deliveries would use less storage space and demand would be met. On the other hand, perhaps a more traditional approach, such as that illustrated in Figure 34.1, would be more appropriate for keyboards and hard drives as demand is constant and therefore needs to be met, but suppliers are unreliable and therefore some level of **buffer stock** needs to be kept to compensate for this.

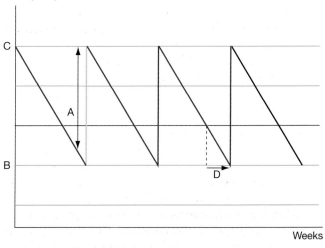

Key

A – this line represents the desired order quantity required to bring stocks up to the maximum stock level

B – this line represents the *buffer*, or minimum stock level, below which demand may not be met, which will result in lost revenues (*cost of not holding stock*)

C – represents the maximum stock level required before *costs of holding stock* increase (e.g. deterioration, insurance)

D – this arrow represents *lead time* or the time between the order being made, when the stock reaches B and delivery taking place

Figure 34.1 A traditional approach to stock control

Many businesses have now computerised their stock systems.

High-grade application
Computerised stock control

Stock management is important to McDonald's because it has to meet a constant demand for a wide range of products. McDonald's now runs a sophisticated computerised stock control system that stock takes each night and organises deliveries three times a week from a network of areas. Therefore, it is important that there is a strong relationship between McDonald's and the supplier. Due to this, McDonald's does not have to have large storage areas and has to keep only about 5% of stock to avoid running out.

Source: www.Times100

Issues For Analysis

- Although firms are likely to try to build a long-term relationship with their suppliers, there will be times when a business will consider changing supplier. This is an issue that has a number of aspects that need consideration, in addition to the standard factors covered earlier. There will be an existing relationship with the current supplier and this may bring advantages that would not be available with a brand new supplier. Meanwhile, the cliché that 'the grass is always greener on the other side' may be a factor in the motive for changing.

- When analysing any choice between suppliers, be sure to consider the consequences of the differences between them. Failure to consider consequences will lose analysis marks. Think through the consequences in your answers with lines of argument such as 'poor-quality materials may lead to poor-quality output, which could lead to customer disappointment, which will hit reputation, probably damaging future sales'.

Key terms

Buffer stock: stock level at which any unforeseen increase in demand or problems with supply can be covered.
Just-in-time (JIT): ordering supplies so that they arrive 'just in time' (i.e. just when they are needed); this means operating without reserves of materials or components held 'just in case' they are needed.
Lead time: the time the supplier takes between receiving an order and delivering the goods.
Waste: any activity that increases costs without adding value to the product/service.

High-grade application
Why do it yourself if suppliers can help?

Wickes is a DIY retailer that has worked hard to develop closer relations with its suppliers. The company invested in improved IT systems to enable better transfer of information between retail outlets and suppliers. Store-level sales and stock data are sent daily to suppliers to allow them to improve their production planning, ensuring the right amount is available to be delivered to each Wickes store. The system has also enhanced the role played by suppliers in the planning and development of new own-brand products for the stores. In the future, the group is hoping to move towards a system where store stock levels are actually monitored and managed by the suppliers themselves.

34.4 Working with suppliers
an evaluation

Evaluative themes relating to suppliers will centre on judgements that firms make as to which supplier to choose. This unit has covered a range of factors that need to be considered, but effective evaluation will, as always, come from a willingness to appreciate which factors are most important for the particular business being considered. A retailer that sells high volumes of cheap products at low prices may be right to compromise on quality to use the cheapest suppliers. The reverse would be the case for a firm with a luxury image or targeting socially conscious consumers. Take some time before putting pen to paper to work out which factors will be most important for the firm mentioned in the question.

Another judgement that should improve your answers is who has the most power in the relationship between company and supplier. Larger firms tend to have more power – indeed there are concerns over the way Britain's huge supermarket chains treat small farmers. However, size may not be the only factor to consider. A supplier with a patent on a particular component will need to be dealt with even if it fails to prove 100% reliable. Evaluation will shine through if a candidate judges effectively where power lies in the specific business relationship featured in an exam question.

Exercises

A. Revision questions

(40 marks; 40 minutes)

1 Explain why the cheapest supplier may not be the best choice. (4)

2 Identify two businesses for which daily deliveries may be absolutely crucial. (2)

3 Briefly explain two problems that may arise when a firm uses a supplier with poor levels of quality. (4)

4 Describe why attractive credit terms from a supplier will be particularly useful for a new business. (4)

5 Outline two reasons why a firm might choose to change its supplier of an existing component. (4)

6 Examine one benefit a mobile phone shop might receive from encouraging several suppliers to compete with each other for every month's order of components. (4)

7 What benefits might the mobile phone shop miss out on by not building a long-term relationship with its suppliers? (4)

8 Describe how a car manufacturer such as Ford might benefit from including its component suppliers in the development process when designing a new car. (4)

9 Select one of the following and investigate how a business you have studied has approached the management of waste. You need to look at its costs and benefits for the business.
- Recycling
- Creation of by-products
- Landfill
- TQM (10)

B. Revision exercises

B1 Data response

Doll's Choice

KMH Ltd is a small manufacturer of children's toys. Having developed a brand new child's doll, it is considering which supplier to use for the plastic used in moulding the doll (see table). Having started up only 12 months ago, the firm has done well and is eagerly anticipating the Christmas rush that will begin soon. The management hopes that the new doll will be a best-seller this Christmas.

Supplier	A	B	C
Price per unit (£s)	3.20	3.50	3.65
Reject rate (per 000 products delivered)	28	18	5
Credit terms (days)	0	60	30
Lead time (days)	7	1	4

Questions

(20 marks; 25 minutes)

1 Which supplier offers the best:
  (a) quality
  (b) lead time
  (c) credit terms (3)

2 Explain why lead time is important. (5)

3 Which supplier should the firm choose, and why? (12)

B2 Data response

Crepe Heaven

Carla Turner set up Crepe Heaven in early 2007. As the only creperie in her local area, she attracted some attention with the launch of her small café specialising in French pancakes. Business was more brisk than she had expected and she often found herself popping out to the local supermarket to buy extra ingredients halfway through the day. The supermarket was more expensive than her catering suppliers, but Carla found it hard to predict sales in the early months of the business. Her stock of eggs, milk and fruit for fillings had a very limited life and the last thing she wanted to do was buy ingredients she would have to throw away.

Having been trading successfully for six months, Carla had an encouraging letter from the catering supplier she had been using, telling her that it was now willing to make an afternoon delivery if she needed extra supplies. This lowered her running costs – just what was needed as the interest payments on her bank loan were now biting hard into her cash flow. She also realised that she would need a second crepe-making machine if she was to make sure that waiting times during busy periods were kept to a minimum. She contacted the French supplier of her first machine, to be told that it would be two months before they could deliver and install the model she wanted. Furthermore she would have to pay cash on delivery – something she could ill afford.

Shopping around on the internet, she found a supplier in America who could deliver in a week. This was great news as she knew that some customers took one look at her peak-period queues and headed off to other cafés in the area. She was also grateful that the supplier was willing to accept a small deposit on order followed by 60 days' interest-free credit. This seemed perfect and she placed her order immediately.

The delivery went smoothly, though she had some trouble installing the new machine as it was rather different to her existing one. Worse was to come some months later, as the new machine started smoking when in use for more than a couple of hours. The American supplier was unhelpful, insisting that the fault must have been due to Carla failing to install the machine properly. The next few months were tough for Carla, as she struggled to get her money back from the US supplier. Fortunately, the shop remained popular and within six months she replaced the second machine with one from her original supplier.

Questions

(30 marks; 35 minutes)

1 Explain why Carla tended to under-order ingredient supplies in the early days of the business. (5)

2 Explain which two factors may have been most important to Carla when originally choosing her ingredient supplier. (6)

3 Analyse the benefits to Carla of choosing the American supplier for her second crepe machine. (8)

4 To what extent does the case study support the view that building a long-term relationship with a supplier is a better approach than shopping around for 'the best deal'? (11)

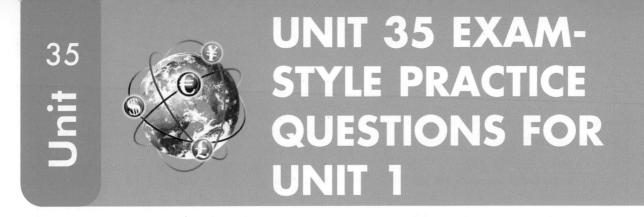
These five questions should take you one hour. To practise an exam situation, time yourself. Do not read the questions, or the case study text, before the hour begins.

You face a mixture of short and long questions, with 60 marks' worth of questions to be tackled in 60 minutes. You will need five minutes to read the text, so you have less than a minute per mark to write the answers.

The key to success is to keep your answers very brief when there are only two or three marks on offer. For example, on question 1 (below), it is fine to write one-word answers. If you are really quick with the short questions, you should have a minute per mark on the questions that are worth 12 or 16 marks.

To prepare for these questions:

1   Download the specification for AS Unit F291 from www.ocr.org.uk and go through each line, checking the meaning of every word and phrase.

2   Make sure that you know the difference between **analysis** and **evaluation**. Evaluative questions (starting with 'Discuss' or 'To what extent') ask you to make and justify judgements. Analytic questions only require you to develop an answer, not to draw conclusions from it.

When answering the practice questions, and in the exam, concentrate on the precise wording of the questions. The key answers will be the ones you give to the questions that carry between 10 and 16 marks. It is vital to practise the skill of writing longer answers.

Some questions have an asterisk (*) beside them. In the exam, an asterisk means that the examiner will check additionally to mark the quality of your written English.

Answers to the following questions are provided in Unit 37 of this book.

35.1 Exam-style practice questions for Unit 1

Read this material, and then answer the questions that follow

In 2007, Innocent Drinks Ltd achieved sales of £130 million. Not bad for a business less than ten years old. It has enjoyed growth rates as high as 100 per cent a year for several years, buoyed by its quirky advertising and the terrific fit between the trend for healthier lifestyles and the Innocent message of 'Nothing, but nothing but fruit'. Over the past ten years Innocent has moved 'smoothies' into the mass market. Ten years ago you found a smoothie in a posh deli; today it's in Tesco.

Adapted from *The Grocer*, 15th March 2008

Figure 1

According to Andrew Richards, sales director at Britvic, 'More than 80 per cent of households believe that eating five portions of fruit and vegetables a day is the most important consideration when buying food and drink... Two out of three people now agree that they have changed their drinks buying behaviour to reflect this trend.' So although sales of fizzy drinks are now falling, sales of juices and smoothies rose by 16.7% in 2006 and 7.9% in 2007. They now stand at £1,400 million a year.

Adapted from *The Grocer*, 15th March 2008

Figure 2

The company most embarrassed by Innocent's rise is the giant PepsiCo. Pepsi owns Britain's two leading fruit juice brands, Tropicana and Copella. It also, in February 2005, bought PJ Smoothies, the brand that started the smoothie market a couple of years before Innocent. Yet despite its strong brands and huge financial resources, PepsiCo has just watched open-mouthed at the rise of Innocent.

Until now. In late 2007, PepsiCo announced a new strategy. It would launch a new range of Tropicana Smoothies at high pricing points, alongside Innocent; and, in a pincer movement, would cut prices on PJ Smoothies, to try to win market share. Tropicana Smoothies were launched in February 2008, and may make the summer of 2008 quite hot for Innocent.

Adapted from *The Grocer*, 15th March 2008

Figure 3

Answer **all** questions.

1 Identify three ways the size of 'the giant PepsiCo' could be measured. (3)

2 There have been times when Innocent has struggled to keep supply levels high enough to match the demand for its smoothies. Analyse two possible reasons why a business might suffer supply shortages. (6)

3a) State three features of a private limited company such as Innocent. (3)

3b) *To what extent would you expect Innocent's business objectives to be different today compared with when the business first started? (12)

	Value 2007	Share % 2007	% change (since 2006)
Total juices and smoothies	£1,407m	100	+7.9%
From concentrate	£499m	35.5	+2.2%
Juice drinks	£449m	31.9	0
Not-from-concentrate	£305m	21.7	+19.8%
Smoothies	£130m	9.3	+37.6%
Freshly squeezed	£24m	1.7	+30.7%

Source: TNS Worldpanel 2007, quoted in The Grocer, 15th March 2008

Figure 4

4a) Outline the importance of human resource planning when a firm is growing as rapidly as Innocent. (4)

4b) *In the future, Innocent might decide to go public, floating its shares on the stock market. Discuss whether that would be of benefit to its key stakeholders. (14)

5 *Discuss whether the changes in Innocent's market in 2007 and 2008 point to a successful or unsuccessful future for the business in the years to come. (18)

Total marks: (60)

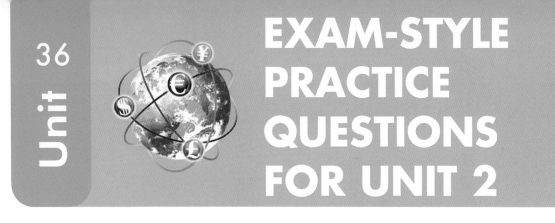

These questions are presented in two parts, A and B. It should take you two hours to answer them all. To practise an exam situation, time yourself. There are 90 marks available in total.

Part A presents six short questions that range across the Unit 2 subject content. Typically the questions are marked out of 2 or 4 marks, and the mark total is 18. You should spend no more than 20 minutes on these questions, i.e. pace yourself at about a mark a minute.

Part B is based on a long passage of text and data, which appears on page 263. Read this **before** the time when you take the practice questions. Your job is to think about the case fully enough, in advance, to make it possible to answer the questions on the day with barely a glance at the case itself.

Preparing in advance, using pre-seen material, is an important skill for the OCR Unit 2 exam. The Unit 2 exam will include questions about a pre-seen case study, including a diagram: the case itself is sent to teachers in advance and will be available for you to download from two or three months before the exam. To download the material, go to www.ocr.org.uk and follow the trail to Business Studies AS/A Level. You will not be allowed to bring your prepared case into the exam: a fresh copy is given out in the exam room.

To prepare for these questions, and for the exam itself:

1 Go through the pre-seen material, looking up every business term or phrase that is used. A useful reference book is the *Complete A-Z Business Studies Handbook* (published by Hodder Education).

2 Re-read the material, summarising each section of the story. You will have to decide how to break the case up into sections, perhaps by time or by the key events. Within this process, ask yourself:

 ● What are the goals/objectives of the business?

 ● What are the main internal constraints it faces: that is, factors within the business that may be holding it back, such as poor leadership. What are its internal strengths?

 ● What are the main external constraints the business faces: that is, factors outside the business that may either be holding it back at the moment, or may threaten it in future, for example increased competition. What opportunities are presented by the external conditions faced by the business?

3 Go through each table of data with great care; consider some possible questions on the data and try out your answers.

4 As you get closer to the exam, try to explain the case to others (parents are helpful here, as are fellow students); this helps you see how well you have the key storylines fixed in your brain. For the same reason, try to write out summaries without looking at the material.

5 On the day, concentrate on the precise wording of the questions set. With pre-issued cases, many students write general answers, whereas examiners want precise ones. The key answers will be the ones you give to the 16 and 20 mark questions.

Having taken no more than 20 minutes on Section A, you will have 100 minutes for the 72 marks of questions on section B. That means that you should allow a minute and a quarter per mark, so allow 20 minutes for answering the 16-mark questions and 25 minutes for a 20-mark one. That will give you a few spare minutes at the end for checking your answers.

Answers to the following questions are provided in Unit 37 of this book.

36.1 Exam-style practice questions for Unit 2

Section A

Answer **all** questions.

1a) 'Batch' is one type of production. Identify two others. (2)

1b) State two factors that can reduce a firm's break-even point. (2)

1c) What is meant by the term 'Theory X'? (2)

1d) Last year, Barton Bakery sold 800 hot cross buns at 50p each on the Friday before Easter. This year Mr Barton put the price up to 60p and sales fell to 680 buns. Calculate the price elasticity of hot cross buns at Barton's. (4)

1e) Outline two possible advantages that a business may gain from adopting a system of budgeting. (4)

1f) Explain two possible benefits for a firm such as Cadbury's from using the Boston Matrix. (4)

Section A total marks: (18)

Section B Case study: the bingo club

Ida often moaned about work. She saw her three A Levels as a passport to university and the fulfilment of a dream. Working 18 hours a week in a bingo club just got in the way. The pay was £6 an hour flat rate, with no overtime, weekend or performance-related supplements. It wasn't much, but she needed the money.

The bingo club in South London was huge, taking a possible 1,100 players at a time and with an annual turnover of £3 million. Twelve full-time and fifteen part-time staff looked after the customers, some of whom would stay from eleven in the morning until eleven at night. Ida was always scheduled to work at the canteen, providing customers with drinks and light snacks throughout the day. The club treated the canteen as a profit centre in its own right, so although prices were kept low, the staff had to keep costs down. Yet certain things seemed absurd to Ida, such as the regular customer complaint that the menu was too dull. She pressed the canteen manager for a 'dish of the day' or even a 'dish of the week', but was told that 'customers just like moaning; specials would increase our wastage levels and I'd get flak from Head Office'.

One thing she quite liked about the club was the overall club manager, Kamal. He was large, loud and friendly. He spent at least half an hour a day on the floor of the bingo hall, talking to customers and staff, and every month he called each staff member into his office for a chat. Ida found this awkward at first, but came to like his ability to get her thinking and talking about the business and her own hopes for the future. A frustration remained, however. She often suggested ways to make the business run better, such as job rotation, but even if Kamal sounded positive, nothing seemed to change. The club was one of the most profitable in the country and 'why rock the boat?'

Kamal's most unusual characteristic was his attitude to absence. In everything else he was relaxed, even laissez-faire. Yet if you called in sick he would phone you personally and give you a very hard time. When she phoned in sick for the first time (it was on her fourth Sunday working there) he demanded to speak to her and told her never to return unless she was in within 45 minutes. She was there in 30, and soon felt much better than she did when she was lying in bed.

Ida sometimes thought it would be easier if she wasn't studying Business Studies A level. It was so frustrating to see the canteen staff take customers for granted, serving them with lukewarm food and often leaving pies in the hot display counter for longer than was allowed. They preferred that customers should have a dried-out

pie rather than add to the wastage levels. Yet behind the scenes, the two women in the small sandwich-making area seemed happy to waste ingredients. They carelessly cut too much cheese, then threw it away when it was not needed. As for stock control, the ordering system was such a mess that excess ham might be going past its sell-by date while beef had run out.

Just two months before her final A2 exams, things started to catch up with the club. A new, multi-million pound refurbishment was completed at a nearby bingo rival. Ida's club saw its customers drain away. Some turned up again after a couple of weeks, saying the other club had great food and super prizes, but was 'a bit pricey'. Nevertheless, takings were down sharply.

At the end of that summer, Ida achieved the grades she wanted and set off to Derby University. It was goodbye to her old workmates, but hello to a new set as she joined the Derby branch of the same chain of bingo clubs. With the excitement of Freshers' Week and meeting new people, it took a while for Ida to realise that the Derby branch was dramatically different from London. Above all else, the manager set the tone for an unforgiving, distant management style. Ida had been there six weeks, never seeing the manager once, when she was summoned to 'go to the manager's office immediately'. A customer had complained that Ida spilt tea on her 'and I think she meant to'. The manager gave Ida a sharp lecture about customer care, then sent her away without even asking how she was settling in to a new town and a new job.

As the weeks went by, it became clear that labour turnover was very high. No-one seemed to stay in the job for more than 3 months. The pay was not bad for the area, but the staff were worn down by the dull jobs and the resentment they felt towards management. In the kitchen, staff enjoyed wasting time, comfortable in the knowledge that the manager rarely left her office. When she did come round, the staff were quiet, but clearly resentful; they did not want her to feel welcome. So some bad practices were never noticed, such as the absurdly high buffer stock levels of fresh food. As in London, the Head Office focus on wastage levels meant that staff were not doing things the best way; they were simply trying to prevent being criticised on the measure Head Office seemed most concerned about.

Another strange thing about the Derby club was the management structure. According to the organisational chart, the personnel officer was quite junior. Yet she seemed to wield an extraordinary amount of power: staff who looked bored or complained about management were moved to worse jobs, or found themselves on worse shifts. One day Ida came in to find that she had been scheduled for a Thursday afternoon, which was a day of

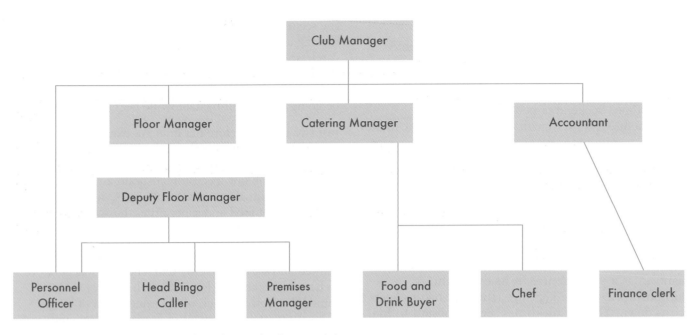

Figure 36.1 Organisational chart for Derby bingo club

lectures at uni. She went to object, but was told sharply that 'work sometimes has to be the priority'. When Ida complained to the floor manager, she was told that the personnel officer 'is in charge of everything to do with staff'.

Half-way into her first year at Derby, Ida found a new job and left the bingo club. No-one in management asked her why she was leaving, so nothing was learnt.

When Ida popped in to see her old South London boss that Easter, he said that the Derby personnel officer had been promoted, but the Derby branch was closing down. South London, he was glad to say, had recovered from the new competition and was thriving. He had the grace to say, 'You were right about the canteen food. We've improved it a lot, and it's helped bring customers back.'

Appendix A: Analysis of competition faced by the South London bingo club

Within a one-mile radius:
Direct competition: 2 bingo clubs, both with major refurbishment in past 18 months
Indirect competition: 2 bowling alleys, 1 greyhound racing track, 52 pubs and 12 clubs

Wider competition:
Internet Bingo: 8 major websites offering prizes of up to £125,000
National newspaper bingo: 3 major newspapers offering large prizes

Key factors:	Kamal's club	Competitor 1	Competitor 2
Entrance fee	£2	£5	Free
Price per game	£1	£1	£1
Top prize per game	£20	£100	£20
Advertising spending	£20,000 a year	£50,000 a year	£30,000 a year

Section B questions

Answer **all** questions.

2a) Outline one weakness in the management structure in Derby, as shown on the organisational chart. (4)

2b) Discuss the leadership style of Kamal, the club manager in London. To what extent do you think it proved effective? (16)

2c) Discuss how the bingo club chain might have improved its stock control. (16)

2d) Evaluate the bingo club chain's quality of service. Recommend what you believe to be the best way to improve it. Explain your reasoning. (16)

2e) Kamal wants to increase his club's sales revenue by 10–15% in the coming year. Discuss a suitable marketing strategy for his club. (20)

Section B total marks: (72)

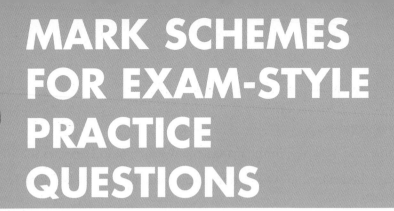
37.1 Mark schemes for questions in Unit 35

1 Identify three ways the size of 'the giant PepsiCo' could be measured. (3)

Three of the following:
- By turnover
- By profit
- By number of employees
- By market share

One mark for each reasonable point.

2 There have been times when Innocent has struggled to keep supply levels high enough to match the demand for its smoothies. Analyse two possible reasons why a business might suffer supply shortages. (6)

Level	Features of answer	Marks
3	Some analysis of reasons for supply shortages, using some element of theory in the answer.	5–6
2	Some understanding of reasons for supply shortages, perhaps without using theory to back up the argument.	3–4
1	Some knowledge about supply.	1–2

3a State three features of a private limited company such as Innocent. (3)

Some possible answers:
- Limited liability
- Shares owned; shareholders have the right to vote and receive dividends
- Allows access to capital from outside investors.

One mark for each reasonable point.

3b To what extent would you expect Innocent's business objectives to be different today compared with when the business first started? (12)

At the start, the objective may simply have been survival, or perhaps to break even within a year. The objectives were probably only focused on shareholders and customers. Now, with so many staff, the objectives may have widened out to consider more stakeholders, such as the staff.

Level	Features of answer	Marks
4	Some evaluation shown by supporting a judgement about the differences between starting up and running a big business. Complex ideas expressed clearly and fluently using a style of writing appropriate to the subject. Consistently relevant argument. Well-structured sentences and, especially, paragraphs.	10–12
3	Some analysis of Innocent's business objectives, backed by theory. Relatively straightforward ideas expressed with some clarity and fluency. Arguments are generally relevant.	7–9
2	Some understanding of Innocent's business objectives, but perhaps little theory. Some straightforward ideas expressed in the context of this case material.	4–6
1	Some knowledge shown of objectives. Some simple ideas expressed, probably not in the context of this case.	1–3

4a Outline the importance of human resource planning when a firm is growing as rapidly as Innocent. (4)

HR planning means comparing the staff you have with the needs you're expecting in future. This is especially important when growth is rapid, as it's very hard to pick up the recruitment and training needs without planning.

Level	Features of answer	Marks
2	Some understanding of reasons for supply shortages, perhaps without using theory to back up the argument.	3–4
1	Some knowledge about supply.	1–2

4b In the future, Innocent might decide to go public, floating its shares on the stock market. Discuss whether that would be of benefit to its key stakeholders. (14)
- Staff may feel it gives them more prominence and therefore boosts their CV.
- Shareholders would love it as it gives them the chance to make a great deal of profit quickly.
- Suppliers may like it because it gives prospects of faster growth.

Level	Features of answer	Marks
4	Some evaluation shown by supporting a judgement about which stakeholders might benefit and which might not. Complex ideas expressed clearly and fluently using a style of writing appropriate to the subject. Consistently relevant argument. Well-structured sentences and, especially, paragraphs.	11–14
3	Some analysis of the benefits and drawbacks of floating, backed by theory. Relatively straightforward ideas expressed with some clarity and fluency. Arguments are generally relevant.	7–10
2	Some understanding of floating, but perhaps little theory. Some straightforward ideas expressed in the context of this case material.	3–6
1	Some knowledge shown of floating. Some simple ideas expressed, probably not in the context of this case.	1–2

5 Discuss whether the changes in Innocent's market in 2007 and 2008 point to a successful or unsuccessful future for the business in the years to come. (18)

Success factors:
- Figure 4 shows the rapid growth in smoothies, plus the clear evidence that there's plenty of opportunity for further growth (smoothies are not even 10% of the market).
- The message in Figure 1 ('Nothing, but nothing but fruit') fits in perfectly with the message in Figure 2 that more than 80% of us believe in the need to consume five items of fruit or vegetables per day.

Fail factors:
- PepsiCo's clever pincer movement, perhaps squeezing Innocent at the top and bottom ends of its market.
- Perhaps Innocent will start to suffer from diseconomies of scale now that it is a big business.

Level	Features of answer	Marks
4	Some evaluation shown by supporting a judgement about the likelihood of success. Complex ideas expressed clearly and fluently using a style of writing appropriate to the subject. Consistently relevant argument. Well-structured sentences and, especially, paragraphs.	13–18
3	Some analysis of the likelihood of success, backed by theory. Relatively straightforward ideas expressed with some clarity and fluency. Arguments are generally relevant.	8–12
2	Some understanding of the likelihood of success, but perhaps little theory. Some straightforward ideas expressed in the context of this case material.	4–7
1	Some knowledge shown of Innocent's market. Some simple ideas expressed, probably not in the context of this case.	1–3

Total marks for questions in Unit 35: 60

37.2 Mark schemes for questions in Unit 36

1a 'Batch' is one type of production. Identify two others. (2)

Two of the following:
- Job
- Mass
- Flow
- Lean

1b State two factors that can reduce a firm's break-even point. (2)

Two of the following:
- Increased price
- Reduced fixed costs
- Reduced variable costs per unit

1c What is meant by the term 'Theory X'? (2)

McGregor's theory about managers' attitudes to staff: that Theory X managers believe staff are inherently reluctant to work hard or contribute.

One mark for naming McGregor; one mark for identifying what the theory is about; one mark for stating the theory (up to a maximum of two marks).

1d Last year, Barton Bakery sold 800 hot cross buns at 50p each on the Friday before Easter. This year Mr Barton put the price up to 60p and sales fell to 680 buns. Calculate the price elasticity of hot cross buns at Barton's. (4)

Marks are allocated for the steps in the working, as follows:

$$\text{Price elasticity} = \frac{\text{percentage change in quantity}}{\text{percentage change in price}} \quad (1)$$

Price increases by 20% (10p/50p x 100) (1)

Quantity reduces by 15% (120/800 x 100) (1)

$$\text{Price elasticity} = \frac{-15\%}{+20\%} = -0.75 \quad (1)$$

1e Outline two possible advantages that a business may gain from adopting a system of budgeting. (4)

It will make the business more careful to think through its expected future revenues and costs. By using variances it is easy to monitor performance, and then to make changes if policies (e.g. cost cutting) are not working.

Level	Features of answer	Marks
2	Suitable advantages outlined or explained.	3–4
1	Suitable advantages identified, or weakly outlined/explained.	1–2

1f Explain two possible benefits for a firm such as Cadbury's from using the Boston Matrix. (4)

Helps make decisions about marketing priorities, e.g. increase spending on Creme Eggs, as they're a rising star; cut spending on Double Decker (a bit of a dog).

Helps in pricing decisions, i.e. you might keep prices quite low on a problem child which you think could grow into a rising star.

Level	Features of answer	Marks
2	Suitable advantages outlined or explained.	3–4
1	Suitable advantages identified, or weakly outlined/explained.	1–2

2a Outline one weakness in the management structure in Derby, as shown on the organisational chart. (4)

The Personnel Officer appears to be accountable both to the Club Manager and the relatively junior Deputy Floor Manager. Usually, each employee has one boss, their 'line manager'.

The Floor Manager appears to be responsible for only one person (the Deputy); this seems a poor use of a senior manager.

Level	Features of answer	Marks
2	Suitable weakness outlined or explained.	3–4
1	Suitable weakness identified, or weakly outlined/explained.	1–2

2b Discuss the leadership style of Kamal, the club manager in London. To what extent do you think it proved effective? (16)

- Analyse Kamal's leadership in relation to textbook categories: democratic, autocratic or paternalistic (broadly, he is paternalistic, but with slight elements of other styles).

Make good use of the case material, especially noting the one-to-ones (with the implied time-commitment); the tough-love approach to absences; and the fact that Kamal continued to be interested in Ida, even after she'd left.

Show an appreciation that although Kamal's people-management skills were quite sound, his leadership qualities were undermined by his failure to listen effectively and to think ahead (surely he knew the local rival was refurbishing). He was a better manager than leader.

Level	Features of answer	Marks
4	Some evaluation shown by supporting a judgement about the effectiveness of Kamal's leadership style. Complex ideas expressed clearly and fluently using a style of writing appropriate to the subject. Consistently relevant argument. Well-structured sentences and, especially, paragraphs.	12–16
3	Some analysis of Kamal's leadership style, probably using either McGregor's theory or the standard styles: paternalistic, democratic, etc. Relatively straightforward ideas expressed with some clarity and fluency. Arguments are generally relevant.	7–11
2	Some understanding of Kamal's leadership style, but perhaps little theory. Some straightforward ideas expressed in the context of this case material.	3–6
1	Some knowledge shown of leadership. Some simple ideas expressed, probably not in the context of this case.	1–2

2c Discuss how the bingo club chain might have improved its stock control. (16)

Head Office could stop interfering; it imposes pressure to minimise 'wastage', but in such arbitrary ways that staff seem to be pushed to act in illogical ways. By leaving things to the individual clubs, it would allow freedom to balance the desire to cut costs against the need to provide customers with attractive, varied and fresh food; using profit centres should provide a sufficient form of management control.

It could have imposed a system from head office (e.g. stock management software) which sets out target buffer stock levels for each item.

The Catering Manager should help staff be a lot clearer on keeping the right balance between large order sizes (with possible bulk-buying benefits) and low average stock levels.

Level	Features of answer	Marks
4	Some evaluation shown by supporting a judgement about a suitable approach to improving stock control. Complex ideas expressed clearly and fluently using a style of writing appropriate to the subject. Consistently relevant argument. Well-structured sentences and, especially, paragraphs.	12–16
3	Some analysis of the strengths and weaknesses of the club's current approach to stock management, incorporating some knowledge of issues such as buffer stocks or JIT. Relatively straightforward ideas expressed with some clarity and fluency. Arguments are generally relevant.	7–11
2	Some understanding of the club's current approach to stock management, perhaps without using theory to back it up. Some straightforward ideas expressed in the context of this case material.	3–6
1	Some knowledge shown of stock control. Some simple ideas expressed, probably not in the context of this case.	1–2

2d Evaluate the bingo club chain's quality of service. Recommend what you believe to be the best way to improve it. Explain your reasoning. (16)

Quality is weak in relation to food, which must be important to those there from 'eleven in the morning until eleven at night'.

Weak quality was exposed in London by the quick acceptance of the more expensive rival (though Kamal showed his qualities by recovering from a difficult position); there was clear evidence in London of underlying customer loyalty.

Quality was undermined in Derby by the high labour turnover, which was in turn a consequence of an alienated workforce.

To improve, the management should listen to staff, who are in direct contact with customers, and act on staff suggestions, which in turn will help staff motivation and a sense of teamwork (no 'them and us').

Level	Features of answer	Marks
4	Some evaluation shown by supporting recommendation about how to improve the chain's quality of service. Complex ideas expressed clearly and fluently using a style of writing appropriate to the subject. Consistently relevant argument. Well-structured sentences and, especially, paragraphs.	12–16
3	Some analysis of the quality of service at the bingo clubs, probably using some theory, e.g. TQM (culture) versus quality control checking. Relatively straightforward ideas expressed with some clarity and fluency. Arguments are generally relevant.	7–11
2	Some understanding of the problems of quality at the clubs, perhaps without using theory to back it up. Some straightforward ideas expressed in the context of this case material.	3–6
1	Some knowledge shown of quality issues. Some simple ideas expressed, probably not in the context of this case.	1–2

2e Kamal wants to increase his club's sales revenue by 10–15% in the coming year. Discuss a suitable marketing strategy for his club. (20)

Kamal needs to start with some primary research among his regulars, to find out what they like about the club, and among irregular customers, to find out why they don't come more often; this research should also be designed to find out what image customers have of Kamal's club and the competitors (is the one with the £5 entrance fee regarded as 'the classy one'?).

He needs to consider what marketing budget he can afford; he will surely need to spend more than he is at the moment, perhaps outspending Competitor 2.

He must integrate the strategy: he has improved the catering part of the 'Product' (but is the prize money too low?), he has a moderate 'Price', apparently weak 'Promotion' and a 'Place' that is perhaps undermined by such close competition.

To boost sales revenue by 10–15% it would clearly be risky to push his prices up: perhaps a combination of higher prize money promoted by heavier advertising is the right approach, but he must check that he won't simply achieve higher sales at high cost, leaving profit unchanged or even falling.

Level	Features of answer	Marks
4	Some evaluation shown by putting forward and justifying a suitable marketing strategy based on the evidence. Complex ideas expressed clearly and fluently using a style of writing appropriate to the subject. Consistently relevant argument. Well-structured sentences and, especially, paragraphs.	14–20
3	Some analysis of the marketing strategy used by the three competitors, probably using some theory, such as the marketing mix. Relatively straightforward ideas expressed with some clarity and fluency. Arguments are generally relevant.	8–13
2	Some understanding of marketing strategy, perhaps without using theory to back it up. Some straightforward ideas expressed in the context of this case material.	4–7
1	Some knowledge shown of strategy. Some simple ideas expressed, probably not in the context of this case.	1–3

Total marks for questions in Unit 36: 90

Index